Guidance:
A Behavioral Approach

Guidance: A Behavioral Approach

RICHARD HILL BYRNE
University of Maryland

Prentice-Hall, Inc., Englewood Cliffs, New Jersey 07632

Library of Congress Cataloging in Publication Data

BYRNE, RICHARD HILL.
　Guidance.

　Includes bibliographies and index.
　1. Personnel service in secondary education.
2. Behavior modification.　I. Title.
LB1620.5.B94　　　373.1'4　　　76–40126
ISBN 0–13–368001–0

**PRENTICE-HALL SERIES
IN COUNSELING AND HUMAN DEVELOPMENT**
Norman R. Stewart, *editor*

© 1977 by Prentice-Hall, Inc., Englewood Cliffs, New Jersey　07632

All rights reserved.
No part of this book may be reproduced
in any form or by any means without
permission in writing from the publisher.

10　9　8　7　6　5　4　3　2　1

Printed in the United States of America

PRENTICE-HALL INTERNATIONAL, INC., London
PRENTICE-HALL OF AUSTRALIA PTY. LTD., Sydney
PRENTICE-HALL OF CANADA, LTD., Toronto
PRENTICE-HALL OF INDIA PRIVATE LIMITED, New Delhi
PRENTICE-HALL OF JAPAN, INC., Tokyo
PRENTICE-HALL OF SOUTHEAST ASIA PTE. LTD., Singapore
WHITEHALL BOOKS LIMITED, Wellington, New Zealand

Contents

PREFACE   xi

1   THE GUIDANCE MOVEMENT   1

    Introduction   1   The Political Roots of the Guidance Movement   2
    The Beginnings of the Guidance Movement   7
    Other Forces Shaping Guidance Growth   17
    Current Characteristics and Needs for Change   18
    Summary   23   References   24

2   GUIDANCE GOALS AND OBJECTIVES   26

    Introduction   26   Highlights of Systems Theory   26
    Difference between Goals and Objectives   28
    Establishing Guidance Goals and Objectives   28
    Specifying Guidance Objectives   33
    Two Other Pervasive Guidance Objectives   40
    Nurturing and Restorative Objectives of Guidance Programs   43
    Summary   44   References   44

3 SPECIALISTS IN THE GUIDANCE PROGRAM 45

Introduction 45 The Problem in Fantasy City and its Solution 46
The Problem in Real City and its Solution 47
Members of the Basic Guidance Team and Their Functions 53
Youth Development—
a Basis for Determining Guidance Specialists' Functions 53
The Title Question—Again 57
Nurturing Functions of the Behavior Specialist 59
Youth's Guidance Needs 59
The Nurturing Functions of the Counselor 63
Additional Guidance Team Members 65
Three Other Guidance Occupations 67
The Complete Guidance Team 71
Considerations for Training 73
Competency and Training Summary 77 Summary 77
References 80

4 SCIENTIFIC BASE OF GUIDANCE TECHNOLOGY 83

Introduction 83 The Need for Theory 84
Theory and Technology 85 Characteristics of Scientific Theories 88
First Summary 105 Characteristics of Scientists and of Science 105
Taking the Measure of Behavior Theories 110 Third Summary 113
References 114

5 PRINCIPLES OF BEHAVIOR 116

Introduction 116
Stimulation, Activity, and Behavior Development 117
Respondent Conditioning 123
Instrumental or Operant Conditioning 127
The Cognitive or Symbol System 136 The Penultimate Word 141
Evaluating Behavior Principles by Chapter 4's Criteria 142
References 143

**6 CONCERNS ABOUT
APPLYING BEHAVIORAL SCIENCE**   *144*

    Introduction *144*
    The Pleasure-Seeking, Pain-Avoiding Principle *146*
    Operant Conditioning: New and Trendy? *149*   References *157*

7 PRINCIPLES OF DEVELOPMENT   *158*

    Introduction *158*   Social Systems and Human Development *159*
    The School's Goals, Program Regularities, and Behavior
    Regularities *166*   The Course of Development *173*
    The High School *185*   References *185*

8 MEDIATING BEHAVIOR   *187*

    Introduction *187*   Characteristics of Guidance Practitioners *189*
    Behavior Mediation—Complexity *191*
    Two Modes of Mediating Behavior *193*
    Direct Verbal Mediation Procedures *193*
    Contingency Management *209*
    Illustrations of Contingency Management *210*
    Consultation in Behavior Mediation *216*
    Principles Applied to Groups *217*   Summary *218*
    References *219*

9 CAREER DEVELOPMENT   *221*

    Introduction *221*   Definitions *221*
    Career Development in Schools *224*
    Occupational Decision Making *229*   References *237*

10 GUIDANCE OCCUPATIONS AND PROGRAMS IN CAREER DEVELOPMENT   239

Introduction 239   Special Career Development Conditions 264
Summary 266   References 268

11 SELF-MANAGEMENT SKILLS AND SOCIAL COMPETENCY BEHAVIORS   270

Introduction 270   Self-Management 270
The Procedures of Self-Management 273
Principles of Behavior as the Base 277
Teaching Principles of Behavior in High School 278
Social Competency Behaviors 281
The Guidance Objectives in this Domain 282
A Homogenous Society? 285   References 286

12 THE COUNSELOR'S ROLE IN THE SEVERAL DOMAINS   288

The Counselor and Career Development 288
Outcome of Other Readying Activities 302
Are Tenth-Grade Objectives Reached? 302
Is This a Counselor's Function? 302
The Counselor and Other Domains 304
The Complete Group Program 306   References 306

13 APPRAISAL PRINCIPLES AND PROCEDURES   307

Purposes 307   Appraisal Based on Behavior Principles 309
Principles of Appraisal 310
Parametric and Nonparametric Data 313

Issues in Administering an Appraisal Program 325
Appraisal and Members of the Guidance Team 328
The Case of Francine 331   Further Appraisal Activities 335
Epilogue 336   Summary 337   References 338

14 PROFESSIONAL ISSUES 339

Introduction 339   Are Guidance Occupations Professions? 340
Shifting Sands: a Poor Base for Guidance Practices 344
Professional Issues Regarding Guidance Occupations 346
Preparation of Team Members 349
Federal Government Recognition of the Guidance Movement 351
Professional Associations 353
Guidance Programs in Other Settings 355   The Future 358
The Last Word 360   References 360

Appendix A   JOB DESCRIPTION: The Career Development Technician in Secondary Schools   361

Appendix B   ETHICAL STANDARDS OF THE AMERICAN PERSONNEL AND GUIDANCE ASSOCIATION   363

INDEX   375

Preface

This volume is an introductory text for the study of guidance. It also is intended for high school educators who wish to upgrade their guidance programs, particularly for those who aim to make guidance programs and personnel accountable for their productivity.

The guidance movement, if it has ever been accountable, has not been accountable enough in the past decades. Consequently, it has been less productive than it can or should be in assisting students with their concerns. That situation, I propose, results largely from the emergence some years ago—and from the continuation—of the belief that the sum total of school guidance is *what counselors do*. This false equation, Guidance = Counselors, is, in itself, a sufficient impediment to productivity. Its ill effects on guidance are compounded by the equally potent belief of the past quarter century that what counselors do is done primarily—if not exclusively—with individual students in private conferences. The effect of these two interacting deficiencies has been magnified by the lack of scientific procedures available for use in those private conferences.

The result has been not only less productivity than possible but less productivity than the guidance movement's several publics have been promised. Those publics—students, educators, parents—are asking for delivery-as-promised *now*.

The guidance movement is also less healthy than it can be. What is needed—for health, productivity, and accountability—is for guidance practitioners to root their practices in a research-based discipline and to operate according to systems principles.

The necessary scientific discipline and systems principles, then, are the meat of this book. It lays out the disciplinary base as thoroughly as an overview text can and demonstrates the guidance practices that rest on that base. The book also outlines how to structure guidance programs on systems. The disciplinary base is the science of behavior, which has produced the body of documented precepts known as the principles of behavior.

Many of my positions about guidance, or various aspects of them, have been with me for a long time, but often they have been less developed, more isolated, concepts than the integrated array found herein. Those positions acquired more clarity and integration during my directorship of the eastern regional center of the Interprofessional Research Center on Pupil Personnel Services—(IRCOPPS), from 1963 to 1968. They have been continuously tested, clarified, and integrated through an IRCOPPS-type research project I have been directing in a Montgomery County, Maryland, high school since 1973. I am indebted to the county school system for providing this arena and to James A. Crabtree, assistant principal, who heads the research project's steering committee. I am particularly indebted to Adam Zetts, counselor, who has performed the arduous in-school tasks as research coordinator of this project since its inception. This research effort originated in the inventive mind of my able department chairman, Dr. George L. Marx. It was supported continuously by him as well as by Dr. John S. Jeffreys, head of the Pupil Services section of the Maryland Department of Education, the other unit that sponsors this inquiry. These colleagues and others unmentioned have contributed in some manner to the content.

The give-and-take I have had with my other colleagues has helped me to better organize my thinking about secondary school guidance programs. One person must be singled out as having contributed the most when I sought to test ideas and bring about a better integration of concepts—Dr. David J. Rhoads. He generously donated a sizable share of that scarce resource of the professional person—time—in his most valuable critique of my ideas during frequent discussions and in the review of several chapters.

I acknowledge with thanks the help of Dr. Norman R. Stewart of Michigan State University, the editor of Prentice-Hall's Counseling and Human Development Series. He has nurtured this venture and has been instrumental in sharpening my ideas and improving the way I present them here. There would have been no manuscript upon which to make improvements had it not been typed by my wife, Joy, who also provided cheery support and editorial acumen, for all of which I am grateful.

The people mentioned above are but a few of those to whom I am indebted for ideas and encouragement. I can but hope that the unnamed many, some of whom may see their own thoughts mirrored here, will assume my gratitude, even if it is unspoken.

College Park   RICHARD HILL BYRNE

Guidance:
A Behavioral Approach

1 The Guidance Movement

INTRODUCTION

The guidance movement in education has grown impressively in the past 60-odd years—until recently. Now skepticism and demands for reform prevail.

The movement gained popular support because it encouraged the schools to attend to the good development of pupils as individuals, a parent-pleasing condition, instead of treating them en masse. Equally valued were the movement's concern, and programs implementing that concern, for carrying a student's good development forward to result in a successful future in a career after school.

All aspects of a person's future, not just the occupational aspect, are caught up in that word "career," and the guidance movement has always carried a career emphasis, either narrowly or broadly conceived. Interestingly enough, it is around that same topic—a career focus—that most of the recent criticism against guidance has been offered. The argument is that the guidance movement, increasingly over the years, has abrogated its historical career emphasis.

The movement's present weakened state among its several constituencies is due to a quality and rate of delivery below implied promise. An alert, educated public, accountability-conscious, is no longer satisfied merely with guidance rhetoric. It asks for guidance program accomplishments.

The gap between rhetoric and promise is closing, however. The change in rhetoric is occurring through substituting specific guidance objectives for fuzzy general goals such as good development. Attainment of specific guidance objectives can be demonstrated; attainment of vague global goals rarely can. In addition, improvement in guidance program accomplishments is more and more noticeable, resulting from the application to guidance program activities of the recently emerged technologies based on a behavioral approach to human affairs, the approach around which this text is written.

As a result of these emerging changes, guidance, which was casual and nondirectioned in its recent history, can now be systematic. Guidance *must* be systematic to fulfill its potential commitment to youths. This chapter offers a selected and interpreted history of guidance through which its current nature can be understood. The substance of that history constitutes the case for systematic guidance, the details of which are examined in the chapters that follow.

THE POLITICAL ROOTS OF THE GUIDANCE MOVEMENT

I find the origins of the guidance movement to be rooted in the Declaration of Independence. Although our nation's first state paper spoke about government, about political separation from England, it was primarily a heroic and revolutionary statement about a society based on certain human values. These were not new values, not new ideas about mankind. What was new was the commitment of a society to those ideas, a new political system to effectuate them, and a dedication of "our Lives, our Fortunes, and our Sacred Honor" to their furtherance. It is within those ideas about mankind, those values about humanity, that is found the root of developments that eventually produced the guidance movement in education. That movement did not take form and substance until the beginning of the twentieth century. Given the view of humans stated in the Declaration, and the slow but steady implementation of those values in other sectors of society, the emergence of the guidance movement in education was inevitable.

The guidance idea could not have emerged in any other country, at least until recently, and to so observe is merely to state the historical elements in reverse. It is posited here that the guidance movement is rooted in the values about humans set down in the Declaration of Independence, and that this country is, or until recently was, the single society where such principles were fundamental to governmental structure and the management of political affairs. It follows, then, that not only was it inevitable that the guidance movement would emerge here, but also that it could not have emerged in other countries, except in rudimentary form. Even today the guidance movement would fit poorly in many societies.

The movement is a school system's commitment to the principles of "life, liberty, and the pursuit of happiness" for its students. The movement can now provide a technology for enhancing personal liberty and pursuing maximum happiness. And these are rights owed to each student: each student is to be given an equal opportunity, and each is to be held in equal value.

In Belkin's (1975) view, the guidance movement "arose as a natural consequence of the movement of individual Americans as they fulfilled their national and personal destinies" (p. 10). It was the Declaration of Independence that "set the tone for what was to become the great American theme . . . namely, that the individual's right to freedom has priority over everything else, and that this right includes the freedom to find happiness in this life" (p. 10). Freedom was to be matched by opportunity. In the new society envisioned by the Declaration there was to be no formalized upper class whose happiness was attained by standing on the shoulders of a lower class, a European and British tradition against which the Declaration revolted. If the guidance movement is the school's enactment of the essential principles of our society, why did it take so long—almost 150 years—for that movement to appear in education?

The Declaration was and is a statement of ideal values about humans. We can guess safely that most citizens today have some familiarity with its statements and that most would agree with its principles. Not so in 1776. The colonists were not marching arm-in-arm down the mall of the future, but were in fact bitterly divided on many large and small issues.

Most of the colonists were poorly schooled and lettered, there was a pronounced gap between the manor-dwelling, often slave-owning, gentry and wealthy city merchants committed to a class system on the one hand, and the horny-handed sons of toil on the other. However, it would be unfair to criticize the population of that day for their ignorance when today polls show a fearsome ignorance on the part of the general citizenry about public issues. In the mid-1700s the majority of citizens was concerned only with maintaining adequate subsistence, which required arduous work, while those on the frontier were occupied primarily with maintaining life itself. This stance, necessitated by the newness of the environment and society, was magnified by the Calvinism that imbued the values of so many colonists, a view of man's relationship with a harsh-judging God as necessitating hard work with little play, behaviors strongly reinforced by society at large.

Those engaged in political leadership were generally classifiable into two groups, but these, like our two chief political parties today, had their subgroups and permutations of subgroups. Thus, leaders as well as the general populace were rarely of like mind.

In sum, the Declaration of Independence had a difficult birth. Tom Paine's *Common Sense,* described in today's schoolbook histories as the catalyst that precipitated ideas that later appeared in the Declaration, was roundly condemned back then by the friends of empire and foes of democracy, those "People of Sense & Property, who before would not believe that there were any Persons of Consequence, either in or out of the Continental Congress, who harboured such intentions" (Inglis, 1776, quoted in Miller, 1943). Vexations were vigorously aired in the press and on the stump. Whig and Tory leaped into the same anti-independence bed (after having not spoken for a long time) and begat pamphlets attacking Paine's republicanism. After all, some Whigs had supported the revolutionary cause hoping for the restoration of traditional liberties of Englishmen, not for radical ideas of the ilk being peddled by that rascal Tom Paine. Even in 1776, a half-year before the Declaration was signed, officials in Maryland, Pennsylvania, New Jersey, and Delaware were committed to oppose independence. Two months before the signing of the Declaration, Pennsylvania's delegation to the Continental Congress was opposed to independence.

The point behind this recital? It gives us the first part of the answer to the question posed earlier—why there was 150 years between the Declaration, given as part of the root stock of the guidance movement, and the appearance of that movement. This brief retelling of our early history reminds us that issuance of our idealistic founding document was doubtful right up to mid-1776. Once promulgated, rather than becoming a vital basis on which our institutions immediately began to operate, its ideals remained rhetoric for a long time.

The sociological accounting for this is relatively obvious. The principles of the document were a moral stance about humanity, and simply declaring human values does not create moral behavior. History, in the form of preservation of culture, was too much against the prompt effectuation of those principles. We see this again in the instance of the United Nations Charter. The culture of the American colonies—the history of behaviors commonly practiced—was far short of the ideals set out in the Declaration and was bound to change slowly.

For example, "all men are created equal." The statement is idealistic. In practice "all men" meant only white males. Thus there could be slavery, stealing of land from those who had lived there for centuries, and the denial to women of a say in their government ("Governments . . . derive . . . their just powers from the consent of the governed . . .") and their pursuit of happiness (no careers, no higher education for women).

In 1776 the design of a full-grown tree was put on paper, but in fact only a seedling existed. We can speak of the Declaration as being not a map of the country in which we lived, but a map of the Promised Land far away. In 1776 we started the long march toward that land. Typically we have inched along the route; occasionally we took big leaps (for example, the 13th, 14th, 15th, and 19th Amendments to the Constitution, recent

Supreme Court decisions, federal legislation of the 1960s). In the beginning of the twentieth century our society needed the guidance movement to help in that long march. Thus that movement was almost foreordained to start then, just as other conditions of the prior decades had made it impossible for that movement to emerge earlier.

From the Declaration of Independence to the emergence of the guidance movement is a long leap in time, and the relationship between the document and the movement has been only tenuously established so far. Their relationship is firmed by first attending to one of the value statements of the Declaration.

Pursuit of Happiness

Happiness receives a limited operational definition here by use of two concepts that have some relationship to happiness: education and occupation. Historical developments prior to 1900 in each of those two enterprises are important and can be sufficiently reviewed in a few paragraphs.

EDUCATION. A case can be made that education and happiness are positively correlated, although far from perfectly. In other words, the more education a person has (as long as that means inclusion of career-related study), the increased probability that he[1] will be happy. For purposes of the latter sentence the word "happy" will be defined by relative degree of control over one's life, amount of income, the capacity to acquire creature comforts and to engage in recreational activities, and the opportunity to acquire prestige. If we were asked to designate public policies and actions that would be expected to result in happiness for a country's citizens, we would name education as one of the more important. And indeed the public policy in this country, public support of education, testifies to this belief.

But this was not the view at the start of our history. At the beginning of the nineteenth century few persons were formally educated at any level. There were few tax-supported schools. By the end of the nineteenth century, grammar school education was common for most white children, and public high schools could be found in large communities, although few youths were expected to attend. Public higher education was widely available too, but again with the expectancy that only a very small proportion of

---

[1] This is a bite-the-bullet moment—the first place where a singular, third-person pronoun is used this way, necessitating facing the gender issue. In speech and in less formal writing, I use either male/female pronouns, or write them that way, such as s/he. Publishing convention and ease of reading find me, most reluctantly, using throughout this text the historical male pronoun for both genders when the referent sex is not specified.

the small number of high school graduates would enter public colleges. The huge proportion of those in high school and colleges by 1900 were white males. Thus, the long march toward the attainment of the Declaration's ideals was well under way by 1900, although the distance yet to be traveled was great.

OCCUPATION. The word "happiness," as used in the phrase "pursuit of happiness," was given a simple operational definition by two words, education and occupation. Happiness was further defined in the prior section by three phrases from among many that could be used: increasing control over one's life, acquiring a reasonable amount of income, and acquiring prestige, which can be rephrased as self-respect. It is apparent that those phrases can also be applied to occupations. To be employed provides income that potentially can contribute to happiness, yet an occupation contributes to happiness in another important way, in that it can be a source of psychic income—the intrinsic satisfaction that comes from creative activity, from a sense of accomplishment, from providing services that are needed and for which gratitude is shown by those who use the services. In general, the more the education, the better the occupation, the higher the income, the more complex the service to be carried out in the occupation, and thus the higher the psychic income. Even if the correlation between education and occupation is not perfect, thus making invalid the use of a metaphor that views education and occupation as the two sides of a coin, their relationship is inextricably bound. To have much education while having little occasion to make it pay off in an occupation is a source of discontent, not happiness, as is demonstrated by reports from societies where this condition exists. To have only a little education accompanied by little demand for educated persons in occupations is a description of what we call primitive societies, even though that is a less than accurate description. To be well educated and occupationally trained and to be employed in a "good"[2] occupation is no guarantee of happiness. To be so educated, however, greatly increases the *probability* of happiness. Rephrased in the terms of the Declaration, for most persons in this society the pursuit of happiness requires the pursuit of education and of a good occupation.

In 1900 most persons were not in good occupations. But that observation can be made only in retrospect. That is, most persons today would not like to be employed in occupations in which large numbers were then employed. But we also know that, even then, many did not like the conditions associated with the occupations in which they were employed,

[2] Because this modifier must be given meaning, which is not done at this point, it is placed in quotation marks for this first use. This acknowledges that the word can have a variety of meanings as used in these paragraphs and acknowledges that each reader will impute his own meanings to it.

as evidenced by the ever-increasing strength of the labor union movement at the start of this century.

THE BEGINNINGS OF THE GUIDANCE MOVEMENT

Our story has brought us to the beginning of the twentieth century. We find then an ever-increasing number of youths going on to high school. We find a continuing demand for persons to fill both old jobs and the new ones that were the product of burgeoning technological changes. The lot of workers had begun to improve, and the ideals of the Declaration continued their slow spread through the society, like an underground root system, popping up here, emerging there. Not unopposed, of course. The Tories of the day would still say "The Public be damned," would still keep black citizens and Indians (noncitizens in their native land) "in their place," would still fight against child labor laws and other legislation and social actions that would implement those ideals. Of course, one line of Tory defense still held—women were kept out of polling booths. But, all in all, the long march continued, and for every instance of a recalcitrant economic or political baron fighting to increase his fiefdom, exploiting whomever he could, there were numerous instances of countermovements, actions, and organizations of selfless concern for the improvement of the lot of all citizens, old and new, female as well as male, white and nonwhite.

There is need to look at one other force that played a role in the emergence of the guidance movement in the early 1900s. This is the scholarly rather than political or institutional element. Psychology by then was emerging as a science and despite only a few years of growth was already casting long shadows. Psychology gave the political and institutional areas a substantive base for expressing a concern for individuals. The first psychological clinic in this country was barely a decade old when the guidance movement emerged in an identifiable form.

The Guidance Movement Starts

Given:

1. Care for and interest in the welfare of youth, particularly noting the development liabilities of the poor and undereducated;
2. An increasing multiplicity of occupations that differ in the occupational behaviors expected; and
3. An awareness that individuals differ in the way they are put together or, in more formal terms, differ in personality,

it was inevitable that actions would be taken *to help youth to choose, prepare for, enter, and be successful in an occupation.*[3] Those actions began in community institutions and in a few high schools at about the same time around 1910. Because the emphasis was limited to that period of youths' lives just prior to and after entry into the job market, the form of guidance begun then was called *vocational guidance.*

For a concept to become a social movement, there is need for two of the capital investments of social movements: personnel and time. To become a movement, vocational guidance required the investment by institutions of personnel to be vocational guides and time for those persons to do their guiding. The ripeness of the country for this embryonic movement is documented by the fact that in 1913 there were so many vocational guidance practitioners that their recognition of their need to band together into an interest group resulted in the formation of the National Vocational Guidance Association. That group adopted as the definition of vocational guidance the description in italics given earlier and began a history marked continuously by vitality and initiative. By 1916, a mere half-decade after the guidance movement was underway, 1,000 counselors were reported to be employed in schools (Armor, 1969). The purpose and functions of the early vocational guides, titled vocational guidance counselors, were readily understandable because they were narrowly conceived and marked by a simple technology. This simplicity was soon to be altered by technological forces and changes of a magnitude that would have been inconceivable to the first vocational guidance counselors and that are awesome to think of even from the perspective of the present day.

It is not just the development of things and technological processes in themselves that are so staggering to contemplate, but the complicating effects these products of technology have had on society. Recall the century of change in education from 1800 to 1900. By democratic values that change was ever onward and upward, but by contrast to changes in education in the past few decades, the changes of that century were snail-paced. In 1900 a minority of youths entered high school. The present is marked by great concern for the minority who do not finish high school. College entrance was a rarity in 1900. Today about one-third of college-aged youths are in some form of postsecondary education or training. The entitlement to as full an education as wished is now the accepted state for females, and all know the current efforts to ascertain that quality education will be provided for all youths, thus amending our shameful history in the

---

[3] Even though the Soviets have been claiming for years that all social and technological innovations were discovered or invented by them, some readers may assume that helping youths with job selection and entry is an American invention. The facts are otherwise and the historical balance is most readably established by Zytowski (1972) in an article aptly titled "Four Hundred Years before Parsons."

education of racial and ethnic minorities. When we examine almost any demographic topic, we find that change, revolutionary change, is the predominant characteristic of that area between the late 1800s and the recent past, let alone the present.

Stern (1967) has pointed out many of these changes. For example, in the late 1800s we were a nation of farmers and dwelled mainly in rural areas; now less than 10 percent of the population lives in what the U.S. Census Bureau classifies as farm areas. No longer do most adolescent children of second- and later-generation immigrants grow up in the locality where both or at least one parent was raised, with that growing up occurring in an extended family (several adult family members in addition to parents). Now one is astonished if an adult's reply to the query "Where are you from?" is "Here." Whether from "here" or elsewhere, the youth will likely have been reared in a nuclear family (parents and their children only), with physical independence from even this small unit made easy by automobiles, two or more of which in every carport now being the goal that has replaced the chicken every Sunday of a half-century past.

The unit for measuring time was once days or even weeks or months. Hours may now be too imprecise for accounting for most of our time, which has to be accounted for by minutes, or even seconds. Traveling from Chicago to St. Louis took a day or more for some of our grandparents; soon it will be possible to leave New York and arrive in Los Angeles before we left New York, by clock time.

Our progenitors generally ate what they grew, and maybe provided food for a small number of other persons if they were farmers. Knowledge of world affairs was almost nil for many of them, or, if they had such knowledge, it was attained weeks behind events. When they did learn of something happening in other countries, those places were so remote in distance and significance that the typical response was "So what?" Now we eat what a few grow and eat worldwide foods at that. Many now not only know what is happening worldwide, watching events on television as they are occurring, but have grave reason to care about societies everywhere. Young people, formerly provincial, are now world travelers, many on their own resources (or ingeniously on others' resources) or through the worldwide tours arranged by the Department of Defense. Crime was wrong and sports were played back then. Crime and sports now are commercial enterprises, properties to be bought and sold, fought over, the one accepted with bored tolerance, the other excitedly received over the electronic marvel, giving some zest to an existence found otherwise unexciting for many.

The effects of most of these transformations and of any not included will be assessed by any one person as good, bad, or both. Humans in our society can expect to live at least 15 years longer than their grandparents or great-grandparents. Is that good? It depends on the quality of living, of course. At least we can reach that greater age with less pain as a result of the incredible increase in medical knowledge. But can most economically afford to use that advanced knowledge? At one time the few hours of leisure available to a family were used either for recuperation for the next work week or for simple recreation. Now most people have ample leisure time, and more and more leisure time will come with such practices as the 4-day work week.

Pursuit of happiness? Year by year we can conduct a better chase, but for each new tool for such pursuit there is a potential frustration. These conflicting characteristics of life accentuate the need for the guidance movement in education, for guidance programs that put that movement into effect, and for guidance practitioners who are specialized in preparation and function.

The Problem of Titles

One way to attend to changes that have occurred in the guidance movement is to examine the history of the occupational title of the dominant guidance practitioner, the occupation mostly referred to today as counselor. Numerous texts use that title without a modifying term, and that unmodified word "counselor" will be used in this text for one of the guidance practitioners discussed here. The guidance history examined up to this point may suggest that the full title ought still to be as it once was, vocational guidance counselor. Not so, and to find out why not, another sweep is made through the past 65 years.

In those 65 years high schools became increasingly complicated, with increasingly more persons enrolling and far more complex programs of study organized into several curricula. If we jump from 1910 to 1930 we see that finding one's way through a now-complex high school had become a problem for youth, a here-and-now need of priority, and thus also a priority for the vocational guidance counselor. In addition there was an expanding number of young people going into postsecondary education and training. This was coupled with a spread among the population of the awareness that going to college involved more than just choosing a nearby institution or the prestige one from which a parent (likely only the father) had been graduated. For more and more youths their going to college was the first such event in their family. Thus it came to be that the vocational guidance counselor now also became a vocational and educational guidance counselor.

One more factor needs recording in this sweep through the history of labels, because this factor added yet another modifier to the counselor's already cumbersome title.

As noted earlier, the impulses generated by the human values set out in the Declaration of Independence were relentlessly if slowly working their way through the social fabric. American high schools in 1900, partly modeled on German secondary education, were scarcely representative of democratic ideals. "Fit in or Get out" might have served as a motto for many schools then. By 1930 there was increased concern on the part of school leaders and teachers about the *quality* of "fitting in" shown by youth, with that concern resulting in actions to help those young people who had trouble fitting in. School systems began to employ psychologists and social workers, albeit few in number and serving only a small minority of schools. Even these few were a further reflection of the increasing interest in helping nonadapting youths adjust to high school.

If principals, teachers, psychologists, and social workers were now showing this concern, it is natural to expect that the vocational and educational guidance counselor should also become an agent for aiding youths in concerns that were focused less immediately on education and occupation. This third order of concerns, although having a significance for education, was more complex than choosing high school courses or making postsecondary educational choices. These concerns naturally acquired the label "personal." The difficulty a youth was having with parents, for example, although it likely had some effect on his attainments in school and might have deleterious effects in his later occupational life, would be thought of as a personal problem rather than an educational (school-generated) or vocational (occupational-choice-generated) one.

Now we have a practitioner who can be called an educational, vocational, and personal guidance counselor. But, of course, no one would call him that, so all the adjectives atrophied, and today we have either guidance counselors, school counselors, or just counselors, although guidance teacher and guidance consultant appear occasionally.

By whatever title these practitioners are known, one mission of this book will be to clarify what counselors and other guidance specialists do and might do. For some readers this might seem a sufficient task without taking time and space to discuss titles and adjectives. Yet nomenclature is important for those starting a systematic study of a field, so two last comments will be appended. One about the word "guidance" and the other again about the title "counselor."

The comment about guidance is brief: some find it a distracting word, while others find it useless but harmless. On the other hand, some find it an imperative component of the construct we are examining, because its semantic history has given it important meaning. The arguments for abandoning the use of that word have had a longish history (Pierson & Grant, 1959; Wrenn, 1962) but not a numerous body of pleaders, one of whom I was at one time (Byrne, 1963). Some opt to not use the word "guidance," but to catch up the program components under the terms "pupil services," "pupil personnel services" (a gaucherie, if ever there was one!), or "student services." Most writers, however, have not been persuaded to forego use of the word "guidance," but have argued for its retention (Hoyt, 1962)[4] Recent reconceptualizations now cause me to see the usefulness of the word, despite its ambiguities.

The unmodified word "counselor" is a somewhat different sack of grain. The word is ages old and has been applied to countless humans. Any human is a counselor—that is, one person might seek another's counsel if the first person thinks the other person knows something about a topic that the first person does not know but needs to, or if the first person thinks that the second person can propose a course of action or resolve a dilemma for him. The essential component is that phrase, "thinks the other person knows something about." Knowing about a topic in today's technological, advanced-education world will usually mean being specifically educated and trained in that topic, as well as having a credential in it.

Assume that you have $100,000 to invest, but have no investment knowledge or history. You wish financial counsel, so you seek out someone whose discipline (his education, training, and experience) is finance. A very sore throat and fever cause you to seek counseling about your health, so you look for a person whose discipline is medicine. You need to sue your neighbor, so you seek legal counsel from a person disciplined in law. In each case, it is readily noted, the word "counsel" or "counseling" had a modifier, and the expert giving counsel had a discipline.

What can we say of the terms "guidance" or "school counselor"? Guidance counselor is a redundant term, because a counselor guides. Someone might refer to himself as a financial guidance counselor, if he wishes to identify the substance of his area of counseling, but the latter two words still comprise a redundancy. School counselor describes only the setting. A nurse is a school counselor in that she or he gives health counseling in a school setting. If by the title school counselor there is conveyed the idea that the practitioner counsels *about* schooling, then an erroneous communication has been made because counseling as it occurs in schools is about concerns in addition to schooling. What to do? What

---

[4] This question was reviewed by Byrne (1963) with a more recent examination made by David C. Cook (1971, pp. 518–520), which includes the arguments for continued use of the word offered by Kenneth B. Hoyt and C. Harold McCully. Hoyt (1969) reexamines this history, and concludes that "as we approach the 1970s, the term 'guidance' is far from dead and, as a matter of fact, appears healthier than ever." In my conceptualization the term "pupil services" is too broad. It includes a number of central-office programs and practitioners. This text focuses on the assistance to youths carried out by single schools, for which the term "guidance" has long been used. For me the word "personnel" in the alternate term is offensive. It is an unnecessary borrowing from the commercial world.

modifier to use? From what discipline does the counselor in schools come, meaning the counselor who started out being called a vocational guidance counselor?

Because psychology is one discipline that undergirds the professional behaviors of the counselor, if it is not *the* discipline, the title psychological counselor was proposed as long ago as 1950.[5] This title is palatable for my tastes; I use the term to describe one practitioner in whose preparation I participate. As accurate as the title is, however, its adoption by school officials was precluded because the modifier "psychological" is just not commonly acceptable in schools, and persons working under that title could be confused with school psychologists.

The unmodified title counselor is now part of the culture and likely will persist. If any modifying term has to be used, an appropriate one is "development" or "developmental" (e.g., Blocher, 1966), for those terms summarize the counselor's concern: the behaviors that for youths in general and for any one youth in particular can be identified as best development. Were this the understood modifier, then the title counselor also is appropriate for that specialist serving in elementary schools.

Another term is more recent, yet perhaps the most appropriate of all: life style counselor. The connotations are correct; they convey the interest of the counselor in the integrity of the individual, and they acknowledge differences among individuals. Moreover, that term accurately connotes the counselor's interest in assisting an individual to plan a future, not around isolated components of that future, but in all the ramifications needed to permit the person to practice the life style to which he is committed. For ease of communication, however, the underbrush of terminology is cut away, and, as noted earlier, the unmodified title counselor will be used here.

Another Look at the Growth of the Guidance Movement

The number of vocational guidance practitioners steadily increased, and there appeared the social phenomena that show up whenever there are large numbers of persons with similar interests. One phenomenon, which we have already seen, was the setting up of the interest association, the National Vocational Guidance Association (NVGA) in 1913. There followed the development of university courses, then programs of courses to prepare counselors, which in turn permitted setting up certification require-

---

[5] For example by Bordin (1950), by a special conference convened by C. Gilbert Wrenn, then President of the American Psychological Association (APA) unit known at the time as the Division of Counseling and Guidance (now the Division of Counseling Psychology), and later by a Committee on Definition of that division.

ments by state education departments. These latter two developments were enormously amplified through the U.S. Office of Education's entry into the guidance arena in 1938. The natural effect, typical of all kinds of movements, was to create an ever-widening spiral of status improvement, lengthening preparation, and increased certification requirements.

Counselor Training Starts and Expands

Counselor preparation merits separate inspection because programs to prepare counselors have had influence on professional behaviors, on certification, and on the central orientation of the guidance movement. This topic is picked up by noting that by the 1930s when courses in guidance began to spread, high school teacher certification was at the bachelor-degree level. Counselors for schools were taken from teacher ranks (as they still commonly are). Thus, guidance courses were fixed at the graduate level in many institutions and were bound to be affected by a graduate school wariness about nonintellectual, nonresearch-oriented study, both of which seemed to be characteristics of guidance courses. If guidance courses were to remain in graduate schools, they were going to have to gain respectability by acquiring a research orientation and greater sophistication.

GUIDANCE AS PSYCHOTHERAPY. A new thrust burst in on counselor preparation about three decades ago: psychotherapy-made-easy and for everyone. Psychotherapy is a higher status function than vocational and educational guidance, abetted by the mysteriousness and indefinability of that term among the general populace. Whatever psychotherapy is, however, it became the ritual for helping youths with personal problems. A Gresham's law that related to youth development caused the "bad money" of counselors doing what they wanted to do to drive out of circulation the "good money" of counselors helping youths do what was necessary to construct an effective future.

Two attributes of the psychotherapy movement that submerged and redirected the guidance movement are of importance to fix in this history. First, the procedures proposed and commonly taught were not merely ascientific, they were antiscience. The guidance movement was taken along the only theoretical path available to it then, and in consequence the guidance movement did not gain scientific theoretical substance for the quarter-century during which it was characterized by psychotherapy. In fact, the quasi-religious fervor marking the psychotherapy movement militated for years against guidance's rooting itself in scientific theoretical substance when it became available 10 or more years ago. The science-antiscience conflict still persists, though in diminishing degree.

The other attribute of the psychotherapy movement was its redirecting guidance from programs, which might or might not have been run by counselors, to the false equation of guidance = counselors = counseling. What counselors did became important; guidance became counselor-centered, not program-centered.

COLLEGE COUNSELORS PARAMOUNT. Another variable affecting the preparation of counselors for high schools was operating in some universities. The oldest and highest status counselor education programs were oriented to preparing counselors for university counseling centers, at the doctor's degree level. Persons with less lofty goals were accepted in the counselor preparation programs of those institutions, but often their scholarly fare was made up of the intellectual crumbs that dropped from the high table of the doctoral candidates. Such universities were fully justified in their concern with readying counselors for their own centers, but the consequence of the higher education focus on research in such institutions for prospective high school counselors was a need to do much translating of what they learned to fit the school setting.

CONCERNS ABOUT INTELLECTUAL SUBSTANCE. In the 1950s and 1960s the concern about avoiding nonintellectual substance, along with the increasing status of psychotherapeutic practices, brought many counselor training programs in universities to the view that the core of counselor preparation was training in psychotherapeutic relationship skills, and, if counselors engaged in this kind of relationship, it was held that youth could solve problems in consequence. That is, the counselor would not need to work on the problem directly. It became outmoded in some university training programs to propose that counselors would give direct and directive assistance by way of helping youths attain specific, real goals in the real world. Activism, youth advocacy, and ombudsmanship were defined out of the counseling concept. Those who have come to acquire this view (relationship is necessary and sufficient, and detailed assistance, such as in occupational decisions, is not important) are likely to disagree with the assertion made here that study of the psychosociology of man at work is the study of the meaning of life and is highly intellectual. They might also disagree with another position of this text, that the approach to helping a person is to mediate his behaviors in the directions he desires through the same learning channels through which he acquired all his behaviors—procedures in which a brief relationship with another will contribute only a relatively minor influence of change. Their focus on psychotherapy will give them no reason to hold that one's occupation is the watershed down which the rest of his life flows.

Wherever the culture of counseling has come to be marked by the view that study of humans at work is skimpy intellectual fare, that counselors serve only individuals individually, and that the chief characteristic of counseling is the quality of interpersonal relationship between counselor and counselee, we can expect that condition that youth surveys report: that counselors are either not even mentioned or are low on a list of persons seen by students as ones to help them with any kind of concern, particularly with career decisions.

It can be said with reasonable assurance that in the past two decades counselors have been less and less oriented and prepared for the function of providing assistance to students in career decision making. Data supplied by Armor (1969) document this. These date are from two surveys within the past 10 years that analyze counselor functions, one that he carried out, and the other conducted by the U.S. Office of Education. Armor's data showed that only 11 percent of counselor time was given to vocational counseling, and the USOE study showed 17 percent. Historical tides appear to have changed again, however. Attention increasingly is being given to the original guidance focus, but now with far more sophisticated knowledge about the psychosocial dynamics of individuals and of occupations. Now, too, there is an array of newly developed strategies for readying youths to cope with decisions about their futures.

More and more persons appear to be finding that there is indeed intellectual substance to be found in a consideration of the sweep of humans as they develop and then move to bring some of society's variables under their command. To be prepared to help a human do this requires psychological and sociological understanding and skill in applying these understandings. It is held here that the study of man at work and the study of how to assist an individual in the occupational decision process are the hub activity of the preparation of counselors of youth, the activity to which study of all other topics, such as interview procedures, are subordinate. Indeed, if only certain concerns of youth can be encompassed by the guidance movement, instead of the many currently within the movement's compass, concern about occupational and career development must remain no matter what other concerns and functions are dropped.

This is stated not as a function of historical conservatism. This stand is taken for a reason presented earlier, but restated now in a different manner: a maximum way for a person to attain purposefulness and full expression of his being is through his occupational career. Pursuit of happiness requires pursuit of a career, with rare exceptions. In addition the ever-increasing complexity of development in our manifold society requires assistance to youth. Thus, as said earlier, career decision assistance is an increasingly important focus of the guidance movement in high schools. It is not the concern of high school counselors alone. The guidance movement is not a counselors' movement; it is an educational movement. Thus it can be written here again, as it has been written and said for decades, that, unless a school system is guidance-oriented, the career development of youths will be far less than it can be.

OTHER FORCES SHAPING GUIDANCE GROWTH

The face of guidance was realigned by the counselor-as-psychotherapist movement recently ended. Two major movements that preceded the psychotherapy movement had left their marks on guidance practices, both appearing rather early in guidance's history. These are the mental health and mental measurement (testing) movements.

Younger readers who take society's concern with mental health to be as much of a given as public education may be surprised to know that knowledge and social concern about mental health are scarcely 50 years old. Because the guidance movement was oriented toward individual development, whatever impinged on development and provided indices of good development was wind for guidance's sails. The mental health movement clearly qualified.

At about the same time, with particular impetus during World War I, mental measurement acquired a technology and empirical support and thus quickly acquired its place in the sun. A psychologically naïve, pragmatic, give-us-quick-answers society accepted mental measurement technology as but another example of American genius. A country that devised a technology for letting one person speak to another over great distances, or to move through the air to reach the other person, had now come up with a device for charting the interior lands of the mind that for so long had been *terra incognita*. The voice of the test administrator was heard throughout the land—that administrator often being the all-purpose school counselor. The citizenry is acquiring more sophistication about what testing can do as well as what it cannot. As another sign of change it can be noted that in many instances counselors have been able to shuck off testing duties, which they never should have had. In many school settings, however, testing is still seen as a guidance function, and therefore as a duty of counselors.

The effects of the mental health movement on guidance programs were subtle and not uniformly apparent, although guidance rhetoric maintained allegiance to the idea. The psychotherapy movement, however, found a ground made fertile by the mental health movement for its own burgeoning growth. Even while one gave support to the other, the testing and psychotherapy movements were in conflict, at least the latter with the former in that the dictates of psychotherapy included no need for testing, or even had a bias against measurement. Testing persisted and expanded, however, if for no reason other than school administrators leaned heavily on it. School guidance, in consequence, appeared to engage in the schizophrenic condition of much testing and counselor use of test results on the one hand and, on the other hand practices based on the psychotherapy movement that eschewed testing. The forces running large in those days were sufficient to deny the guidance movement an adequate theoretical base and to bring guidance practices to their present state of public skepticism because of nonproductivity.

Without having examined these two influencing movements in detail (and some others not at all), we leave this summation of guidance's history. The purpose of this review has been met: to provide a context for the next several sections of this chapter. Those seeking a fuller treatment of this history can refer to the record provided by Hoyt (1974) or by Miller (1961).

CURRENT CHARACTERISTICS AND NEEDS FOR CHANGE

In the view of many—school administrators, school theorists, guidance leaders, and parent groups, among others—guidance is in a less than healthy state today. It can be saved, however, and should be. One prevalent characteristic that can be changed for the benefit of the guidance movement is the replacement of the erroneous equation of guidance = counselors = counseling by the view that guidance is an educational movement, with personal development centering on vocational decisions as the primary thrust of that movement.

A few paragraphs earlier there was used the phrasing, "it can be written here again as it has been written and said for decades" that guidance must be an orientation of a school system if the career development of youth is to be adequately realized. "Said for decades" means at least 50 years. In 1910 the National Education Association (1918, quoted by Miller, 1961) proposed that

> Vocational guidance should be a continuous process designed to help the individual choose, to plan his preparation for, to enter upon, and to make progress in an occupation (p. 9).

The NEA statement went on to give eight elements of what it described as the *"school's program* to attain those goals" (emphasis added).

In 1971 the Chairman of the General Subcommittee on Education in the U.S. House of Representatives observed (Pucinski & Hirsch, 1971) that "the most glaring deficiency in American education can be stated quite simply: its content for the most part is empty, dull, and meaningless to students; too often, it has no immediate relationship to the adult world they will face" (p. 6). The report goes on to posit that one final opportunity is available to schools to prove their worth to the nation by preparing students for the world of work, not through a single curriculum area but *through the total program.* "To be sure, every board of education has paid lip service" to this idea of readying all youths for adulthood and employment, "but translations into action have been sketchy and weak" (p. 8). At the same time surveys administered continuously over the years show that students are concerned about their futures, at least from the ninth grade on. Yet results of a national study conducted by the American College Testing Program (1974) shows that more than 75 percent of the nation's high school juniors are not getting the assistance in this area that they seek. This is the finding despite the fact that such help was "by far the major need indicated by eleventh graders."

Rhodes (1970), the governor of Ohio, describes the substance of a volume he wrote as being

> curriculum centered, not guidance-counselor centered. I would suggest, however, that the guidance counselor has both a leadership role and a supporting role in the programs which will be outlined [in this book], if he is willing to give up the concept that he is the guidance program (p. 51).

It is Rhodes's view, based on the findings of task forces, that "the vocational guidance program in the public schools has been a failure" (p. 11), with blame to be shared by counselors, counselor education programs, and to a large degree by schools that have not incorporated school programs of vocational education. "The program has become counselor-centered, rather than curriculum-centered" (p. 15). He finds counselor education programs culpable, noting that such programs are conceptually limited. They stress the areas of counseling functions that give greater status in the educational hierarchy. Rhodes notes that emphasis is placed upon personal counseling, social counseling, educational counseling, "with many counselors identifying themselves as quasi-psychologists or psychotherapists" (p. 17).

Rhodes further observes that federal programs in support of counseling have not alleviated the problem. The National Defense Education Act (NDEA), our nation's 1958 panic reaction to the USSR's Sputnik, included Title V relating to guidance, which included the objective of increasing the number of counselors. He finds that the NDEA indeed resulted in an increase in the number of guidance counselors, but no evidence that there was significant increase in attention to vocational guidance "in any number of high schools served by those counselors" (p. 18).

He documents this last point partly with the observation that in Ohio "there are perhaps even fewer group guidance programs in the ninth-grade level than there were several years ago" (p. 18), a statement to be matched, incidentally, by the recent elimination in another state of a 6-week occupations unit offered for many years to all ninth-grade students.

Recall that this section is dealing with the need for schools to have programs of career education and guidance, in which counselors will have a part. Rhodes's comments on that topic, although dealing harshly with counselor preparation and functions, place the focus of blame where it belongs: on the absence of school system commitment to the guidance movement.

The one document that vigorously and tersely sums up the troublesome state into which present guidance practices have moved is the sixth report of the National Advisory Council on Vocational Education (1972), issuing therein "A call for change." The negative picture it reports is labeled "intolerable" (p. 4) and points the finger unflinchingly to twelve types of persons of institutional sources and closes with sixteen urgent recommendations. Much of the current great changes occurring in the guidance movement can be traced to the issuance of that report.

Counselor preparation and practices and schooling in general have been faulted for producing current inadequacies, but the faults lie only partially with them. It is easy to make public education accountable for all social ills and conversely to expect all social ills to be ameliorated by public education. Public education consumes a large portion of our Gross National Product, is everywhere, and is highly visible. It can become the convenient whipping boy whenever there is ill-focused public discontent.

Yet faults are to be found in public education, including the policies demanded by communities and implemented for them by school boards. One of these is that schooling (education) is an end in itself, extending for at least 12 years, 12 years that inform children and youth that learning is important and work is not, except for that 20 percent of youths enrolled in vocational programs. Hoyt et al. (1972) contend that our educational system has contributed to the "false and dangerous worship of the baccalaureate degree as the best and surest route to occupational success" (p. 69), a false value that has been transmitted to and is now part of the personal value system of both parents and children throughout the United States. "Our public education system has been the prime transmitter of this false value. It must become dedicated to helping all individuals acquire a personal meaning of work that holds value for them" (p. 69).[6]

---

[6] David C. MacMichael (1974) has addressed the work ethic topic in synthesis fashion in a brief article that is recommended for further reading. MacMichael masterfully examines the work ethic in relationship to class and social status of immigrants from different parts of the world, changes in black society, and changes in the occupational structure.

CAREER EDUCATION: ONE RESPONSE TO THE CHALLENGE. Career education, elaborated in detail by those writers, is seen as public education's effort to establish work values appropriate for a society in which the classical work value has atrophied, and career education is a school program, or said better, the total school program is career education.[7]

The U.S. Congress is committed to this change, and therefore so is the U.S. Office of Education. First the case is stated by the USOE (DHEW Pubn. No. [OE] 72-39, 1971):

> In typical high schools . . . young people complain that curriculums are dull and irrelevant, that their education is not opening pathways to a fulfilling adulthood.
> It is a rare high school that equips all its students to make the choice upon graduation of entering the job market with a saleable skill or of continuing their education (p. 1).

Quoting the (then) Commissioner of Education, S. P. Marland, Jr., the document observes that "conventional economic success is not necessarily compatible with every student's goal."

> Some young people . . . march to a drumbeat different from the economic rhythm of their father [have a different life style, and] often possess a deep commitment to the service of their fellowman. They too are the concern of career education, for the essential message of this program is a *useful and fulfilling life* (p. 2).

Commissioner Marland's charge to educators is that they must organize and manage schools to prepare all students to either become properly and usefully employed immediately upon graduation from high school or to go on to further formal education. Every student, in his view, should be equipped occupationally, academically, and emotionally to "spin off from the system at whatever point he chooses—whether at age 16 as a

---

[7] Some schools and school systems have had a long commitment to the vocationalization (Crites's term, 1958) of all children and youths such as the schools of Franklin, New Hampshire. Other schools and systems that have become noticeable recently for advanced programs in this area are those of Seattle; Ann Arundel County, Maryland; The T. K. Young Laboratory School of the University of Florida; schools in Ohio, such as Firestone Park Elementary, Akron, and the Lincoln School, Dayton.

The U.S. Office of Education pamphlet, listed in the references, gives tribute to some states "with outstanding examples of local efforts to install career education programs." They are Arizona, Delaware, Georgia, Mississippi, New Jersey, North Dakota, and Wyoming. Two large cities (in addition to Seattle noted above) that are "turning to career education as their basic design include those of Dallas and San Diego" (p. 10).

The Ann Arundel County program, K-through-12, has several unique characteristics. A notable one of these is the general behavioral objectives stated, cutting through all school years, and the performances that students carry out to show attainment of those objectives.

craftsman apprentice, or at age 30 as a surgeon, or age 60 as a newly trained practical nurse" (p. 3).

Career education, a new emphasis on an old idea, seeks to attain this goal. The concept holds that "all educational experiences, curriculum, instruction, and counseling should be geared to preparation for economic independence and an *appreciation for the dignity of work*" (p. 2). Career education makes schooling revelant by focusing on the learner's career choices. At the same time, the career focus in education does not require of youths a "permanent bondage to a career goal. Rather, it reveals to students their great range of occupational options and helps them to develop positive attitudes toward work" (p. 3).

The implementation of a career focus in education means changes in the purposes and ways in which many schools now provide instruction. Categorizing a school curriculum into components as "college preparatory, general, and vocational not only reflects earlier inadequate concepts, but works against students pursuing individualized year-round programs. Students should leave or enter school at almost any time to further their education or sharpen their job training" (p. 6).

In years past there were far fewer ways to implement a systemwide concern for career development, but now there is considerable know-how. In past years, the elitists and purveyors of the genteel tradition sneered at any occupational or career emphasis in education. Theirs were the voices of power, and thus career development was reduced to trade and industrial courses for the "nonacademic" youth. First just for males, of course, then in more recent years also for females. Simple logic is against those who try to keep schools intellectually "pure." If such persons cannot be persuaded by human values, by the ideals of the Declaration of Independence, they at least cannot fight logic.

Accepting 70 years as a life span, one observes that childhood takes up about one-sixth of life, and schooling takes up approximately one-fourth of life. Three-quarters of life is lived as an adult, and the two major intertwined investments of a human life as an adult are in an occupational career and in a marriage-family career. A human may measure the success of his life by the success of his occupational and marriage-family careers. The significance of this fact for schooling can be tested this way. First imagine that schooling has been completely abolished, but that new schools will be established after 2 years. Each of us serves on the committee to determine the substance and process of the new schooling. We think about the human lot and note the fact just stated: that three-quarters of life is concerned with occupational and marriage-family careers. This fact, then, is the starting point for our new schooling: our new schools' prime responsibility will be to ascertain that kind of development that will result in the "best" occupational and marriage-family careers possible for any person. All other substance in the schools is subordinate to that central purpose.

It is the quality of life in all the years it is lived that the guidance movement in education is about. That is why the guidance movement is a *school* movement, not just an array of practices performed by counselors and other guidance practitioners. Systematic guidance is the agent through which the guidance-oriented school system can meet its long-run developmental objectives for youth.

SUMMARY

The guidance movement is a uniquely American phenomenon in education. Its existence is due to the thrusts and counterthrusts of numerous societal and intellectual forces of the past eight decades. At its root,- however, what gives the movement its distinctive American identity are the views of humankind and its governance set out in the Declaration of Independence. At first more honored in the breach than in the practice, this statement of values has been slowly permeating our culture and its institutions, and at its moment in time reached public education. When it did there appeared those values about students and practices associated with those values onto which the term "guidance" fell.

The guidance movement was first expressed in form of assistance to students in occupational planning and in associated education planning. Over the passing of time, as educators and other leaders aver, concern with students' futures, except for college choice, diminished markedly. This diminution of interest in students' occupational decision making likely was accelerated by the quarter-century thrust on counselors-as-psychotherapists. This was accompanied by an emphasis on relationship between counselor and student. One-to-one interviews became the chief characterizing format in the guidance culture, accompanied by the change from the view that guidance programs are school programs to the view that guidance is a service given by counselors in individual conferences.

An active society like ours is never short of major thrusts and counterthrusts. Changes are occurring in the guidance aspect of education that reflect the further refinements in the human values on which our country started, the larger social thrust of career education, the discontent of education's numerous publics about the effect of guidance, new concepts (or revitalization of older concepts), and most significantly, new knowledge about behavior. Functions and practitioners that fall under the label "guidance" are being vigorously reexamined, and changes in functions and guidance staffing are occurring with almost indigestible rapidity.

This text moves on the stance that it will not merely record what is, but will seek to present what might be best in guidance. To that end it reaffirms the older position that guidance programs are school programs and are therefore the concern and practices of the full school faculty, not just of guidance specialists. It posits that guidance outcomes are designed to contribute to reaching school goals on the part of *all* students.

Stressing first the goals and performance objectives that let us know that goals have been reached, there follow the procedures that can be used or need to be invented so as to attain those goals. This perspective thus puts the focus on guidance specialists in a third position of concern. In schools we need to consider the kinds and numbers of specialists only after we have determined outcomes and procedures for attaining those outcomes. When the topic of specialists is to be taken up, it is not to be assumed that there are any givens. This approach, which first asks about the job to be done and the way of doing that job, will result in proposals for considerable changes in staffing a school's guidance program.

REFERENCES

American College Testing Program. *Nationwide Study of Student Career Development: Summary of Results,* Report No. 61. Iowa City: American College Testing Program, 1974.

ARMOR, D. J. *The American School Counselor.* New York: The Russell Sage Foundation, 1969.

BELKIN, G. S. *Practical Counseling in the Schools.* Dubuque, Ia.: William C. Brown, 1975.

BINGHAM, W. V. *Aptitudes and Aptitude Testing.* New York: Harper, 1937.

BLOCHER, D. H. *Developmental Counseling.* New York: Ronald Press, 1966.

BORDIN, E. S. (Ed.). *Training of Psychological Counselors.* Ann Arbor: University of Michigan Press, 1950.

BYRNE, R. H. *The School Counselor.* Boston: Houghton Mifflin, 1963.

Career Education, U.S. Office of Education (DHEW Publication No. [OE] 72-39) Washington, D.C.: Superintendent of Documents, U.S. Government Printing Office, 1971. (Catalogue No. HE 5280:80075).

Committee on Definition, Division of Counseling Psychology, American Psychological Association, Counseling Psychology as a Specialty. *American Psychologist,* 1956, *11,* 282–285.

COOK, D. C. *Guidance for Education in Revolution.* Boston: Allyn and Bacon, 1971.

Counseling and Guidance: A Call for Change. Washington, D.C.: National Advisory Council on Vocational Education, Sixth Report, 1972.

CRITES, J. O. Address to Annual Convention, American Personnel and Guidance Association, St. Louis, Mo. March 1958.

HERR, E. L., & CRAMER, S. H. *Vocational Guidance and Career Develop-*

ment in the Schools: Toward a Systems Approach. Boston: Houghton Mifflin, 1972.

HOYT, K. B., "Guidance: A Constellation of Services." *The Personnel and Guidance Journal,* 1962, *40,* 690–697.

HOYT, K. B., "Professional Preparation for Vocational Guidance." In E. L. Herr (Ed.), *Vocational Guidance and Human Development.* Boston: Houghton Mifflin, 1972.

HOYT, K. B. *A Tribute to Edward C. Roeber.* Terre Haute: School of Education, Indiana State University, Nov. 1969, Supplement to Contemporary Education.

HOYT, K. B., EVANS, R. N., MACKIN, E. F., & MANGUN, G. L. *Career Education, What It Is and How to Do It.* Salt Lake City: Olympus, 1972.

INGLIS, C. *The True Interest of American Partiality Stated.* Philadelphia, 1776. Quoted by J. C. Miller in *Origins of the American Revolution.* Boston: Little, Brown, 1943.

IVEY, A. E., & ALSCHULER, A. S. (Eds.). "Psychological Education: A Prime Function." *The Personnel and Guidance Journal,* 1973, *51,* 9.

MACMICHAEL, D. C. "Work Ethics: Collision in the Classrooms." *Manpower.* Washington, D.C.: Manpower Administration, U.S. Department of Labor, January, 1974, 15–20.

MILLER, C. H. *Foundations of Guidance.* New York: Harper & Bros., 1961.

National Education Association, Commission on the Reorganization of Secondary Education, *Vocational Guidance in Secondary Education.* Bull., 1918, N.19. Washington, D.C.: Government Printing Office, 1918, quoted in C. H. Miller, *Foundations of Guidance.* New York: Harper & Bros., 1961.

PIERSON, G. A., & GRANT C. W. "The Road Ahead for the School Counselor." *The Personnel and Guidance Journal,* 1959, *38,* 207–210.

PUCINSKI, R. C., & HIRSCH, S. P. *The Courage to Change: New Directions for Career Education.* Englewood Cliffs, N.J.: Prentice-Hall, 1971.

RHODES, J. A., *Vocational Education and Guidance: A System for the Seventies.* Columbus, Ohio: Charles E. Merrill, 1970.

STANFORD, G. "Psychological Education in the Classroom." *The Personnel and Guidance Journal,* 1972, *50* (7), 585–592.

STERN, H. J. "Social Currents of the 60's—Implications for Counselors." In A. Stiller (Ed.), *School Counseling 1967—A View from Within.* Washington, D.C.: The American Personnel and Guidance Association, 1967.

WHITLEY, J. M. (Ed.). "Deliberate Psychological Education." *The Counseling Psychologist,* 1971, *2,* 4.

WRENN, C. G. *The Counselor in a Changing World.* Washington, D.C.: The American Personnel and Guidance Association, 1962.

ZYTOWSKI, D. G. "Four Hundred Years before Parsons." *The Personnel and Guidance Journal,* 1972, *50,* 443–450.

2 Guidance Goals and Objectives

INTRODUCTION

In this chapter procedures for setting up guidance objectives and examples of objectives are presented. The absence of guidance objectives was proposed in Chapter 1 as a major reason for the guidance movement's not having delivered on some of its promises and thus having earned some public disfavor. To establish such objectives is an important element in a systems approach to guidance; and because this text seeks to edge the guidance movement closer to being fully systems-based, the first part of this chapter is given over to stating highlights of systems concepts.

That is followed in the second and major portion of this chapter by the exploration of the nature of and process for setting up guidance objectives. In later chapters systems concepts will occasionally be reexamined for the underpinning on which all elements of a guidance program will rest. However, only approximations of a systems approach can be made here.

HIGHLIGHTS OF SYSTEMS THEORY

The increasing attention in the past decade to systems concepts and systems-based procedures may lead the hurried thinker to the conclusion that systems are another of man's recent intellectual and technological discoveries. Systems, of course, have always existed. They are as natural as day and night, which, we know, are the results of the lawful procedures of the solar system. What man *has* done, rather recently, is identify the nature of systems first in the more observable and measurable material world of nature, and now more recently in the less observable, less measurable psychosocial world of human behavior and institutions. These laws constitute systems theory. To have uncovered them permits humans to have greater control over both material nature and, of greater importance, over human institutions. To know the lawful nature of systems permits humans to increase the likelihood that institutions and movements will bring about the outcomes for which they have been established.

One entry point into knowing the implications of systems theory for the future of guidance is the likelihood that a human institution, a system, is subject to one of the laws of material nature, the second law of thermodynamics. In the physical world it is known that a variety of substances interacting with each other (a system) will move toward a breakdown state, a state of chaos, *if the system is a closed system.* Closedness, in the case, means simply that no other materials are added to the original substances. A thesis of this writing, not adequately defended here for lack of space and other reasons and thus offered as an assertion, is that the guidance movement has become a relatively closed system in recent decades. It has become cut off from the larger system of education, shrunk into itself in guidance departments in high schools staffed by counselors who have come to interact less and less with teachers and others in the educational system over the years, and often not with each other. Some chaos, some degree of *entropy,* to use the technical term, was inevitable.

A picture of an effective guidance program, therefore, has to be one that is an open, metabolic system that views guidance as a *school* program, not in terms of the injurious equation, guidance = counselors = individual counseling interviews. The effectiveness of a guidance system will be partly determined by the amount and nature of input into the guidance system from larger systems (suprasystems) and the amount and nature of output into the larger systems.

Guidance: A Compact Infrasystem

Balancing the flow of energy to and from the smaller system of guidance (an infrasystem) and the suprasystems with which it should interact will be the flow of energy within the guidance program that permits it to be effective. These energies will be used in clarifying goals and objectives, determining the minute steps needed to reach objectives, establishing and revising differentiations in the system, and monitoring it. The overall term is *communication,* which includes information flow and feedback. Guidance in the past has not only been a relatively closed system; it has lacked objectives and has not been characterized by a differentiated structure. Lacking objectives, the communication system has not included feedback because correction of a system depends on the purpose of the system, which, of course, is expressed in its objectives.

Systematic guidance, a phrase to be used here often, is not a new kind of guidance. It means, instead, that study has been applied to the several components of the system that every guidance program is, and that modifications of guidance programs are put into effect when the study of the system shows up inadequacies.[1] The usefulness of a guidance system, once established in a way that lets it be useful, is maintained by the feedback element of that system. To be useful, of course, means that purpose has been defined by the specific outcomes in which the system is to result—its objectives.

DIFFERENCE BETWEEN GOALS AND OBJECTIVES

As used here, a goal statement precedes a statement of an objective in tense and development. A goal is a statement about hoped-for outcomes, and it either explicitly includes the verb "will" or implies it. An objective, short for performance objective, is tensed in the about-to-happen present, typically using the verb of command, "shall." The word "shall" does not imply an action in a future of some distant time, as the word "will" connotes in a goal statement, but connotes the immediate moment as a student is undertaking a demonstration of goal attainment.

It is necessary to work broader goals down into more specific goals prior to setting up the nature of the demonstration or performance objective that the student carries out to show that he has attained the broader goal. Once performance objectives have been set up, the specific goal to which each relates loses some importance and might not even be listed any longer. It is the performance objective that is central. It is that type of objective that determines program, that is, activities that ready students to perform the objective, and that thus also determine guidance staffing.

ESTABLISHING GUIDANCE GOALS AND OBJECTIVES

Guidance goal statements are of two kinds. One kind comprises those goals that contribute to the attainment of the school system's educational goals for all students. The other, overlapping kind of goal is comprised of

---

[1] A generator of and oft-quoted authority on general systems theory (GST), von Bertalanffy (1968) identifies the principles of GST around which such assessments would be made as wholeness, sum, centralization, differentiation, leading part, closed and open system, finality, equifinality, growth in time, relative growth, and competition.

outcomes that are unique to the guidance function in education. These latter goals may contribute to general educational goals, of course.

Career development is an illustration of the first kind of goal. It is an implicit or explicit historical educational goal of most, if not all, school systems. Guidance programs have been charged with contributing, and indeed can contribute significantly, to the attainment of this educational goal on the part of all students, although they have not made that contribution in general in past decades. An example of the other kind of goal, that is, one unique to the guidance aspect of education, is reducing the excesses of any student's coping behaviors, which indicate an inadequacy in development and can impair learning, or conversely establishing an adequate level of coping behaviors in any student deficient in them.

Incidentally, the establishment of guidance objectives for all to attain does not lead to assembly-line persons or homogenized robots. Guidance objectives do not state the quality or characteristics of persons who attain them, nor do they prescribe an equality of personality. They do prescribe another kind of equality, however: equality of opportunity, insofar as schools provide opportunities. Attainment of guidance objectives brings each student up to the starting line with equal capacity to run the race, again insofar as capacities provided by schools are concerned. How far and in what style and toward which ends each student will run will be influenced by factors other than those caught up in guidance objectives—factors that will give to each person the distinguishing characteristics that a free society prizes and cherishes.

The alternative to guidance objectives for all is guidance objectives for some. That means directing guidance program assets either to an elite or to a deficient subpopulation. If the latter were the group to which the objectives were addressed, the intention must surely be to eliminate the deficiencies so that that group moves up to the starting line on an equal basis with the nondeficient. A focus on an elite group, on the other hand, is out of the question; a focus on a deficient subpopulation is unnecessary when objectives are established for all.

The assumption has been that there are educational goals that are translated into specific guidance goals, then into performance objectives. If there are such educational goals stated by a school system, where do they come from? What are their origins?

Origins of Goals and Objectives

Educational goals are social value statements reflecting those publics that have a say in school affairs. In the history of public education in the early part of this century there are reports of communities largely populated by unschooled working-class citizens who had little interest in their communities' schools. School goals, such histories tell us, were set by a clique of educated, business-oriented citizens. The school policy set by such oligarchies called for the maintenance of an elementary school system designed to prepare employees for the community's factories and other business organizations. Secondary education often was not provided; workers did not need that much education, and "unneeded" education became a source of worker discontent. The male children of the oligarchs were schooled in private institutions.

Contrasted to that sorry period in American educational history is the situation in many suburban communities today. Such suburbs are populated by well-educated citizens who are concerned with the quality of public education. Schools are closely scrutinized, school board elections are major contests, and the setting of the school system's educational goals is not left to educators.

As true as it is to say that responsible, caring adults join with school leaders to set educational goals in that kind of community, it is equally true to state that to set goals that do not take into account the characteristics and needs of children is a relatively empty exercise. In my experience, the setting of educational goals in this decade has, more often than not, included knowledge about and from adolescents.

Career development has been given as an example of an educational goal. From what origins could it come? Surely from concerned educators and representatives of an equally concerned public, but also from youths. Time and again surveys of youths have led to the statement that among the uppermost concerns junior and senior high school students have, even when it is not the most pressing one, is a concern about *the need to make an occupational decision, to determine an appropriate occupational career.*

This concern can be stated as an end-of-schooling educational goal for a school system. It is made a more operational goal when it is analyzed into subgoals appropriate for each year of junior and senior high school. But goals, being value statements, are not blueprints. They provide no clues about how to go about achieving them. Such social value statements have to be translated into technical statements, that is, into objectives. Goals, as noted earlier, are tensed in future terms (. . . will . . .). Upon examining a goal we can ask, By what means can it be known that students have attained this goal? We find the answer in the statement, By observing what they do. Goal statements are made operational, then, by rewording the goal into performance objectives. In a fey and competent treatment of the topic, Mager (1972) includes a test: "Hey, Dad, let me show you_____." If Dad cannot be shown, objectives have not been established in performance terms. Byrne's test (others have also originated the same test) is expressed as, "How will I know one when I see one?" Implied is, "What will the person be doing so that I will know that he has attained the goal?"

The differences and relationships between goals and objectives can be clarified by returning to the main theme, in which we address the first kind of goal, the educational one.

Educational Goals and Guidance Objectives

To establish or improve a school's guidance effort, it is recommended that at first separate guidance goals be established for each educational goal, a one-to-one operation. Other guidance goals can be identified that cut across several educational goals because they are of so general a nature.

The logic that underlies this section and subsequent chapters is this:

1. The school's educational goals are either established, if this has not as yet been done, or reexamined and revised for clarity and currency. These educational goals are for *all* students.
2. School program areas that are to contribute to the reaching of these educational goals are identified. Instruction is a program area; guidance is a program area. A school's activities program may be yet another program area that contributes to one or more educational goals.
3. For each program area goals are established. These are more specific than the educational goal, of course. They are developed in answer to the question, What is the contribution of this program area to this educational goal?
4. For each program area goal one or more student competencies or performances are established as the objectives flowing out of that goal. When a student demonstrates these competency or performance objectives (the words are synonymous in their use here), it is known that the student has attained that specific goal. As with educational goals, program area competencies are to be attained by *all* students.
5. When competencies have been established, then specific program strategies can be set up to cause students to acquire that competency, to cause students to be able to perform. In the guidance area, these strategies comprise the guidance program.
6. With program strategies established, then appropriate staff to conduct those strategies can be acquired.
7. When each student has attained each objective for each program area, the school's educational goal will have been reached.

That logic is charted in Table 1, which will be laid out in parts. The first part sets out only the headings of the columns. Their numbering shows their sequence. That is, in the matter of the relationship of guidance goals and objectives to educational goals, the start has to be, naturally, with the

Table 1. Relationship of guidance elements to school goals.

1. Educational Goal	2. Program Areas That Contribute to Goal	3. Special Goals for Each Program Area	4. Competencies or Performances That Show That Program Goal Is Attained	5. Strategies to Reach Objective	6. Personnel to Conduct Strategies	7. Performance Outcome for the Educational Goal

educational goal; then one asks about the school program that bears on reaching the goal, and so on.

Before filling in this table with some specifics, two points require emphasis.

1. ALL STUDENTS. Traditional guidance activities carried out through counselors' having only individual conferences with students perforce have been ineffective in fulfilling the intended outcome of having all students acquire competencies. Different strategies are required to assure that all students attain school goals.
2. PERSONNEL. Traditionally schools have had one type of guidance practitioner, the counselor, and the question related to counselors has been, in effect, We have counselors; what work can we find for them to do? The sequence just outlined states that there are no practitioners until the sixth step, and then the assumption to be applied is not that there are counselors, but is what kinds of practitioners in what mix are required to get the job done. Whichever kinds of guidance practitioners are employed, it must be recalled that a guidance program is a *school* program. Thus the school's chief guidance official is the principal, who can delegate technical leadership duties to one of the guidance team's practitioners.

To test this logic in more specific fashion we can look at one set of educational goals established for a school system. This statement identifies seven goals, each of which has elaborating statements, although only the goal titles will be reproduced here.[2]

1. Academic skills
2. Physical development
3. Intellectual development

[2] These goal statements were established in 1973 by the Board of Education of Montgomery County, Maryland.

4. The individual and society
5. Scientific understanding
6. Aesthetic expression
7. Career development

The seven steps of the logic in Table 1 would be applied relative to each goal. Carried out for the seventh educational goal, career development, Table 1 is partially reproduced and completed this way, using only the first three and the seventh portions of the table.

1. Educational Goal	2. Program Areas That Contribute to the Goal	3. Specific Goals for Each Program Area	7. Performance Outcome for the Educational Goal
Career development (of all students)	A. Instructional program B. Guidance program C. Etc.	A1. Development of desired attitudes toward work A2. Knowledge and skills needed in a career, and some career information acquired B1. Decision-making behaviors acquired by all students	The student enters a career or into post–high school education/training determined by application of decision-making skills

SPECIFYING GUIDANCE OBJECTIVES

One guidance goal from among several is given in this partial table. It illustrates the general point, but it is not sufficient to show the full contribution of the school's guidance program toward reaching that goal. In addition, this single objective does not permit us to develop an adequate array of performances (step 4 in the logic), of strategies (step 5), and therefore of the practitioners needed (step 6).

Decision-making behaviors, the single guidance goal illustrated in the table is comprised of subsets of behaviors. Three such subsets are (1) accumulation and analysis by each student of data about himself, (2) acquisition and use of information-seeking behaviors about careers and further education/training, and (3) behaviors of integration and analysis of the data acquired through the behaviors of 1 and 2 and of testing alternatives (decision-making skills). Each of these subsets of the single goal in turn yields several subparts, and each of these subparts, then, is a more specific guidance goal, of a specificity that later will permit its translation into a performance objective.

We look closely at the second subset just named, information-seeking behaviors, for an illustration of the further identification of specific guidance goals by seeking out the subparts of that subset.

Information-seeking behaviors are of several discrete kinds. One is the consultation of printed and audiovisual materials. Another is occupation try-outs through work samples and other ways. Discussions and visits with persons employed in occupations of tenable choice are a still different kind of information-seeking behavior, as is a conference with a guidance specialist to get help in integrating and analyzing information gleaned from these several different kinds of activities.

Those specific guidance goals are now placed into the third column of the emerging table.

1. Educational Goal	2. Program Areas Contributing to This Goal	3. Specific Goals of Each Program Area
Career development	Instruction Guidance	(Instructional goals would be here) Decision-making behaviors acquired 1. Self-knowledge–seeking behaviors 2. Information-seeking behaviors a. Consultation of printed and A/V materials b. Occupational try-outs c. On-site experiences 3. Skilled behaviors in analysis of all data, in developing alternative actions, and in testing outcomes

These are guidance goals contributing to reaching the educational goal of career development. Setting them out permits and requires the next step in the logic: establishing the competency or performance objectives through which students and guidance practitioners can know that they have been attained. When a student can do the performances called for in column 4 of Table 1, he can pass Mager's test, "Hey Dad, let me show you_____," or Byrne's test, "How will I know one when I see one?" For example, how will anyone know that a student has acquired self-knowledge–seeking behaviors? Through behaviors in which he engages. How can those behaviors be observed? By creating strategies through which all students engage in those behaviors in an observable setting. These strategies comprise the guidance program. But program strategies take us into step 5, and our current task is to consider step 4, the stating of performances or competencies. Program comes later.

PERFORMANCES. As noted earlier a guidance goal is comprised of subsets and subparts of subsets. This was illustrated by subsets 1, 2, and 3 of objective A, and in subparts a, b, and c of subset 2. Subset 1 also has a least one subpart, not shown in the table. The specific guidance goal concerning self-knowledge–seeking behaviors can be stated this way: (The student will) have knowledge of and be able to analyze data related to values, interests, and aptitudes.

How will we know one when we see one—"one" meaning a student who has this knowledge and who engages in analysis? Our answer is found in those statements we generate for step 4 in our logic. Again a portion of the developing table is completed for illustration.

3. Specific Goals for Each Program Area	4. Competencies or Performances That Show That Program Goal Has Been Attained
1. ———————————— A. Self-knowledge–seeking behaviors	A1. Student lists values A2. Student inventories his career/occupational interests A3. Student summarizes in writing the information on school records related to aptitudes (tests, marks) A4. Student lists careers and entry occupations appropriate to analysis of data about self in A1 through A3

Mager's test can be passed. "Hey Dad, let me show you my list of values," or ". . . my record of career/occupational interests," and so on.

Relative to these self-knowledge performances, you may have wondered when in a student's school life these will be demonstrated. The reply is "in several succeeding years." The behaviors generated through guidance goals and objectives cannot be a one-time event for two reasons. One reason relates to student development. Here we note in relation to performance A1, to examine a specific, that the values of youth change; thus an inventory of values in the tenth school year may produce different results from one in the twelfth. Another question might follow that statement. "Then why not cause this behavior to happen only when the student is as mature as he is going to be in school, that is, in the twelfth school year?" Reply to this question serves also to give the second reason why guidance goals and objectives are not a one-time event in a student's life: in order to be as sure as one can be that any desirable behavior will be carried out whenever it should be, there should be a history of practice of that behavior. For this additional reason, therefore, examination of values, the strategy that causes the performance A1, should occur in each school year, perhaps beginning in middle or junior high school years, but at least in high school. If done but one time only in the twelfth school year, that performance could serve a useful purpose in a student's life by resulting in an appropriate career decision, but what about subsequent years? Surely it must be a tenable guidance outcome that a student acquire behaviors to be used in all career decision concerns for the rest of his life. Those behaviors, therefore, need to be established by practice, acknowledging that practice in earlier school years is just that—building a behavior repertoire—engaging in what is known as a dry run. At some point in most individuals' school life, the behaviors repeated from earlier years will no longer be for practice, but will be "for keeps."

The significance of these comments for step 4, that is, stating performances or competencies through which it can be known that guidance goals have been attained, is that there might have to be differences among the performances stated for different school years. Even if not, the strategies developed for step 5 will need to reflect these school year differences. In some cases there will be the same strategy, with the difference being in the increase of the breadth and depth of the coverage of the topic, reflecting developmental differences—a spiraling effect. In other cases, however, one year might have a strategy around one objective that is not repeated in other years.

Illustration from One High School

Although there may be numerous high schools that have explicated their school system's educational goal of career development into specific guidance objectives, I use for illustration here one school's product because it is but one portion of that school's efforts to establish a true guidance system, that is, one that is systems-based. Gaithersburg High School (Montgomery County, Maryland) has developed the guidance goals and objectives in Table 2 as those that specify the guidance program's contribution to the school system's educational goal for all students in the career development domain.

As with any objectives, school personnel responsible for these will

Table 2. Guidance goals and performance objectives—career development domain.

10th Grade	11th Grade	12th Grade
A. Students will begin to acquire occupational information-seeking behaviors	A. Students will increase occupational information-seeking behavior in both quantity and variety and engage those behaviors spontaneously when faced with a career stimulus	A. Students will spontaneously seek occupational information, other career information, and personal information in that quantity and variety needed to make a tentative or firm occupational choice
1. Given a continuing rate of occupational stimulus, the student shall increase his rate of seeking occupational information	1. Given a career stimulus, the student shall seek information from the school's Career Information Center and from other sources without stimulus from other persons to do so	1. Given a request to make a tentative or firm occupational choice, the student shall seek that quantity and variety of personal and other information needed to make that choice
2. Given the need for a type of occupational information, the student shall retrieve that information from the school's Career Information Center with sureness and accuracy		
B. Students will know the elements of the decision-making process, and how those elements are processed in making occupational decisions	B. Students will know the details of the elements of the decision-making process, will collect some of the information needed by that process, and be able to apply it to make a tentative occupational decision, and, when appropriate, to make a choice of an advanced educational institution	B. The students will know and be able to practice all components of the decision-making process, will arrive at a firm occupational choice using that process, or if he is continuing education or training beyond high school full time, shall choose an institution by application of the decision-making process
1. a. Given a hypothetical case, the student shall describe orally or in writing what information the decider needs, where the information can be found, and will name the elements of the process to be used in making an occupational decision	1. Given a request to state a tentative occupational decision, the student shall systematically follow all decision-making steps resulting in	1. In the next-to-last month of the school year, the student shall present evidence of either

37

Table 2. (Continued)

10th Grade	11th Grade	12th Grade
b. Given the need to choose a program of courses for the 11th grade, the student shall demonstrate decision-making skills by (1) Choosing the 11th-grade courses that accord best with his values and occupational objectives, and by (2) Listing alternative courses if first-choice courses are not available c. Identify one hypothetical optimal occupation d. Identify five other occupations justified by decision-making processes C. Students will know such specific information about themselves as is required by the decision-making process 1. Given a request for a written or oral report, the student shall a. Identify in terms of stanines his level of (1) Learning ability	the statement of no less than three and no more than ten rank-ordered occupations appropriate for the student. Each stated occupation shall be defended as representing an appropriate choice around decision-making variables, including knowledge acquired about self during the 11th grade 2. Given a request to name examples of advanced education/training institutions appropriate for the student's expected career, the student shall present a rank-ordered list of institutions and justify each as representing an appropriate choice around decision-making variables, including knowledge of self acquired in the 11th grade	a. Application for or acceptance into employment in an occupation chosen through application of all variables of the decision-making process, and b. Application for or acceptance into a postsecondary education or training institution chosen through application of decision-making variables, or c. In the case of homemaking, travel, or other post-high school plans not directed to paid employment or formal education, the student shall submit a plan for the alternative course

Table 2. (Continued)

10th Grade	11th Grade	12th Grade

(2) Achievement in
    (a) Vocabulary
    (b) Reading
    (c) Language use
    (d) Arithmetic concept use
(3) Achievement in class work as represented by his grade point average and his non-verbal IQ
b. Identify his aptitude code level in the vocational aptitudes measured by the GATB
c. Identify career-related personal characteristics other than those in b
d. Identify, through the GATB, occupations for which he has an aptitude
e. Identify the findings of a vocational interest inventory		

(The goals are designated by capital letters, performance objectives by arabic numerals. The goals and objectives for each topic are carried across the three high school grades.)

systematically evaluate and polish them, seeking an ever more explicit statement of outcomes as more precise behaviors are identified as being necessary. These objectives will change for other reasons too. For example, as guidance objectives in career development are made more explicit in the junior high school years, and attained by junior high school students because of a systems-based operation, the objectives in Table 2 will need to change. Major changes in the economy would be yet another source for revision of objectives, natural to an open system.

Although the following is a bit anticipatory, it is included here as a minor digression to show the role of objectives in a guidance system.

Once objectives in the career development domain were established at GHS, the next step was to ascertain whether or not those objectives were being reached. If they were, the existing guidance program would be called effective. If not, and depending by how much not, the guidance program operating in the school would have to be termed not effective for the educational goal, and modifications would then need to be made in the program. This is an illustration of the feedback activity in a system and the system-correcting function of feedback.

Seniors were asked to perform their objectives. They were unable to do so, as would be the case in just about every high school in the country, and therefore corrective steps were introduced into the system. More detail related to this process will be given in Chapter 9, but as much detail as given here provides a picture of the function of objectives in a guidance system.

TWO OTHER PERVASIVE GUIDANCE OBJECTIVES

Further detailing around Table 1 is foregone now. The principles have been established, and completing further details is inappropriate to this chapter. Educational goals are ideographic; thus each reader pursuing the matter has to start with the goals for his school or school system, acknowledging, however, that there is likely to be much agreement in goals among school systems.

The observation was made earlier in this section that beyond setting specific guidance objectives toward students' reaching of specific educational goals, there can be other guidance objectives in other domains that cut across several specific school goals. Two are tenable: social or interpersonal competency and self-management.

SOCIAL COMPETENCY. Competency in interacting with other people has long been valued by educators and other speakers for and leaders of society. Adolescents state that relationships with peers is a major concern.

The quality of such interaction has been identified as bearing on the manner in which the persons of a democracy can conduct affairs running from the broad areas of government to the daily social interactions in families, schools, and in careers. For as important as these skills have been in the past, their importance has become magnified because of increasing densities of populations, increasingly abrasive social interactions marking new social patterns in a society redressing former racial wrongs, and increased concern about the quality of living. If schools could have been one arena where social competency behaviors could have been established, but were not, the stand taken here is that now they must address this problem. There is now the technology needed to do so, and guidance goals and objectives can be established to contribute to the attainment of the educational goal of social competency behaviors. In reference to the list of seven school goals, it is apparent that social competency behaviors as outcomes relate to the goals labeled "the individual and society" and "career development." Although none of the goal labels refers directly to the quality of social interactions while a student is in school, it is equally apparent that competencies in social interactions are vital to adolescents, to the tone of the school, and thus to enjoyment of learning and to educational attainments.

SELF-MANAGEMENT. Self-control has long been another prized value of our citizenry, according to social and mental health criteria. Up to now, however, outcomes in this area have been chance outcomes, and hortatory procedures have been the prime method employed to cause children and youth to acquire self-control. The term "self-management" is used here in preference to "self-control," however, because the older term often carries a tone of moral judgment. Self-management as a term seeks to place the objectives in an educational development context rather than a moral one.

There is now a new methodology for self-management based on behavior principles. Objectives in the area of self-management are systematically attainable because the strategy for causing such objectives to be reached is now known. For students to more surely attain self-management skills also accords with the philosophical underpinnings of the guidance movement, because such skills permit each person to manage his own affairs with greater precision and thus be more self-directive and independent. Attainment of guidance objectives in this area will contribute to the attainment of all kinds of school goals and thus is particularly crucial to a school's guidance program.

Within these two comprehensive goal areas will fall a variety of objectives and associated strategies, which have been subsumed in current literature under the title "psychological education" (*The Counseling Psychologist*, 1971, 4; Stanford, 1972; *The Personnel and Guidance Journal*,

May 1973). These and other references provide conditions for stating objectives related to social competency and self-management and for developing the strategies needed to attain the objectives. These objectives and strategies will be a feature of the new look in guidance in the coming years.

Objectives for Unique Guidance Goals

Two kinds of goals have been indentified above. For each there can be guidance objectives. One kind of goal incorporates the school system's educational goals. The other refers to goals unique to guidance. This distinction is open to challenge, of course, and in the long run it matters not whether guidance objectives are related to both or only to one kind of goal. In the long run all that matters is provision of effective assistance to youth in the developmental struggle, in the fight for self-expression in a personalized, one-of-a-kind life style. The distinction of two kinds of goals is made here more for the rational exercise and the establishment of flexibility than for any major purpose bearing on youth benefit.

The weakness of the two-goal classification scheme is noticeable in the previous sections dealing with social competency and self-management goals when for comparison those are cast beside the one "unique" pair of guidance goals stated earlier. These unique guidance goals are the two converse outcomes of reducing excesses of coping behaviors on the one hand, or the establishment or increment of a deficient supply of coping behaviors on the other, as the needs of individual students require. Most such excesses are associated with interpersonal conditions and represent a lack of self-management in those areas. Providing group experiences through which all youths can acquire knowledge in those areas, but mostly behavior skills, is incumbent on schools, but easily can be attributed to the guidance aspect of education and thus to guidance programs. Yet these two have been offered as domains of guidance objectives relating pervasively to educational goals. We readily see, then, the rather fabricated nature of designating some guidance goals and objectives as related to educational goals, and others as being unique to the guidance movement. This is a distinction that will not be pursued further in the discussion of objectives because whatever value accrues to that discussion has been achieved.

REEMPHASIS: OUTCOMES FOR ALL STUDENTS. Here, perhaps, lies the difference in outcomes between present and emerging guidance practices. In theory, guidance outcomes today are for all students; the practice falls far short, as witnessed by countless student surveys. The reasons have not been pinned down as to why guidance objectives are not currently available to all students, but one reason is rather understandable when we put two facts into juxtaposition. These are the now-axiomatic equation, guidance = counseling, joined with the equally prevalent axiom that counseling is given only to those students who seek a counselor's assistance. Numerous studies show only a minority of high school students ask for and receive more than elementary assistance from counselors, and only a minute minority has counseling assistance of the length needed to acquire decision-making behaviors. Thus in some surveys less than half of high school youth reports having received guidance assistance, which, to them, of course, means conferring with a counselor.

Guidance outcomes are those that are designed for attainment by all students, with the expectancy that all students will reach them. To that end the school establishes program regularities that are experienced by all students so that all of them acquire the desired behavior regularities (Sarason, 1971). The general term "behavior regularities" refers in this case to the guidance program's specific outcomes for all students. The guidance program regularities to result in those guidance behavior regularities are in the form of group activities that are scheduled for all students, in the same way that English is scheduled for all. Professionally qualified teachers are responsible for learning in English. In like manner, professionally qualified guidance specialists "teach" student groups working toward guidance objectives. (The word "teach" is enclosed in quotation marks because that word has different connotations implied in this instance from the customary subject and class teaching.)

In the foreseeable future, then, counselors, the numerically predominant guidance team members, will be meeting students across the corner of a desk, one-to-one, for only a minority of their time, because that is a poor way to attain guidance outcomes for all. The major portion of counselor time will be dedicated to students in group sessions set up in the school's master schedule to produce guidance objectives and thus contribute to the achievement of school goals by all students.

NURTURING AND RESTORATIVE OBJECTIVES OF GUIDANCE PROGRAMS

Examination of full lists of guidance objectives will show that most are oriented toward facilitating development, which puts them in accord with a fuller occupational title considered earlier, developmental counselor. If only nurturing or developmental outcomes were given, an unreal assumption might be implied: that all high school students are healthy, ongoing, present-coping, future-oriented, motivated persons who thus need only to have these characteristics enhanced and refined. Against that unreal assumption is set the countering reality—the fact that numerous students have been forced out of the channel of good development, or at least delayed in development. This reality requires a guidance program outcome of a different class, an outcome that identifies restoration to good development as an appropriate expectancy of a guidance program. What has just been said is but another way of conveying a thought already given several times: some persons are operating with reduced effectiveness as humans because of excesses or deficiencies in coping behaviors.

The differences between nurturing and restorative guidance outcomes call in turn for differing practices and for quantitatively different preparation among types of guidance practitioners. These differences in turn have significance for staffing a school's guidance team.

SUMMARY

The guidance movement must be systems-based in order to be effective. Thus, there must be precise goals stated for it, and those goals must then be translated into performance objectives. Any institution is a system, but many institutions are not effective systems. For the guidance aspect of education to be effective, its several systems components must be attended to and perfected, and the correct starting point is the statement of demonstrations that all students are to carry out. It is through these demonstrations that we can "know one when we see one," the "one" being each student, and that which is to be known about each student is whether or not he has attained guidance goals. Although only career development goals and performance objectives were treated in this chapter, the process and outcomes are similar no matter what the domain of goals addressed.

It is possible to identify two kinds of goals, those very broad ones established by a school system as educational goals, and more tightly drawn goals distinctive to the guidance movement. This form of distinction, however, has more value as a reasoning exercise than as a basis for setting up goals. In the long run it does not matter how goals are classified; what does matter is finding out the needs and concerns of youth, incorporating those into the body of concerns identified by adults, and then setting up not only general goals, but very specific ones so that specific performance objectives can be identified.

REFERENCES

MAGER, R. F. *Goal Analysis.* Belmont, Calif.: Fearon Publications/Lear Siegler, 1972.

SARASON, S. B. *The Culture of Schools and the Problem of Change.* Boston: Allyn and Bacon, 1971.

VON BERTALANFFY, L. *General System Theory.* New York: George Braziller, 1968.

3 Specialists in the Guidance Program

INTRODUCTION

Taking the establishment of guidance objectives as a given, two questions logically follow: what are the activities and procedures that comprise the guidance program used to attain those objectives, and what kind of guidance specialists, if any, are needed? This logic was laid out in Table 1.

Logic also suggests that the program questions be answered first. The option is exercised here, however, to take up the staffing topic first. The reason for this reversal is a teaching one. A person's prior knowledge is a starting point for new learning. Most new students, my experience tells me, begin formal study from the starting point of the equation that they learned from experience, guidance = only counselors. If the staffing matter were not addressed now, many readers might be faced with cognitive dissonance as they examined program abstractions. They might consciously or unconsciously be translating those abstractions around that no longer (if ever) valid equation.

The choice is exercised, then, to prevent that confusion from occurring by eliminating that erroneous equation as the starting point or, in another metaphor, as the filter through which other substance will pass. This chapter offers a different starting point or filter that, if represented by an equation, would be partially expressed this way: guidance = that variety of guidance occupations needed to attain guidance objectives (the guidance program element is missing from this equation, so as to render the undesired equation and this one analogous). Setting out the rationale for that variety of occupations is the task of this chapter.

This chapter's topic is, in fact, much wider than just staffing. Consideration of the kinds of guidance occupations cannot be offered in a vacuum; thought about each occupation discussed requires thought about guidance programming. Each guidance occupation addressed in this chapter, therefore, is a peg on which a variety of programmatic ideas is hung, all such pegs constituting benchmarks for charting out the substance of a guidance program.

Before moving to specifics, the reminder is again offered that a school's guidance objectives can be attained through a guidance program that does not employ any guidance specialists. Their employment, however, results in a greater achievement of those objectives, so this chapter assumes the employment of a variety of specialists. In a small school, only one type of specialist might be employed, the conventional counselor, and perhaps only one of those, and perhaps only part-time. Most larger schools today employ a larger number of specialists, but, again, typically of only one kind, the counselor. Where multiple persons can be employed for guidance purposes, this chapter's theme is that instead of only counselors, other occupations should be represented, all constituting a guidance team.

To present this concept, I present a brief allegory set in imaginary Fantasy City.

THE PROBLEM IN FANTASY CITY AND ITS SOLUTION

Fantasy is a small city with a population about 7,000. This city has had no health services; its population has been poor and has not been civic-minded. Happy events, however, bring wealth to the community, and new leadership emerges. In combination, these phenomena produce a revitalization of the city, including a mounting concern for community programs for the public good. The first effort that the citizens apply their energies and wealth to is that of health.

A community health center is planned. It will function as a hospital, but, as its name implies, it will be more than that. It will be devoted to all matters and approaches to community health. The community elders somehow arrive at the figure of seven as the number of staff for the center, and, wishing to have only the best, the elders assume that the best will be provided by seven physicians. They seek these out, and in due time the center opens.

By the end of a half-year the health center is troubled by citizen and staff discontent. The physicians complain about the inappropriateness of many of the duties they are required to carry out and grumble about how those inappropriate duties prevent them from performing other functions for which they have been trained. They dislike such functions as admitting patients, nursing them, and carrying out laboratory tests, for which they see themselves as being unprepared. Moreover, they see the time spent in teaching good diet and other health practices to the citizens as a great waste of talent and as an activity that prevents their giving services according to their expertise.

The citizens who have been hospitalized complain about inadequate nursing. Out-patients complain about delay in treatment of and then complicated medical approaches to such relatively simple health problems as splinters, bruises, and very minor burns. Citizens in the hospital component of the center are disturbed by inadequate laboratory results, and nonhospitalized citizens see no attention being given to the health problems that pervade the community, such as poor diet, atmosphere and water pollution, and rodent-borne disease. A lot of good is being done, the citizens agree, but present practices are far short of the health movement the citizens had visualized and were eager to implement.

A consultant is hired to clear up the difficulties. He is able to do that after a 10-minute inspection by recommending that the staffing of the health center be changed from seven physicians to a seven-person health team. The new staffing he recommends calls for only two physicians and replacement of the other five by nurses, technical specialists, and other practitioners.

The new health team starts functioning and the complaints disappear. Only one minor, status-type behavior needs change, the consultant notes. It has been the practice of the two physicians to refer to the other health team members as "paraprofessionals." The consultant causes the physicians to see that the other team members are specialists who are adequately prepared to carry out essential functions. He causes the physicians to see that "paraprofessional" is an invidious, pejorative term that reflects an unhealthy attitude by the physicians and that its use will militate against the success of the team. The physicians are in accord and stop using the term. With that remaining obstacle cleared up, his consulting duties are completed.

THE PROBLEM IN REAL CITY
AND ITS SOLUTION

The imaginary problem in Fantasy City was handled with dispatch and wisdom. The hypothetical consultant, having earned a deserved reputation, is now asked by the Real City school district to help clear up similar community and staff dissatisfactions about the guidance services offered in its high school of 2,000 students. The school is committed to the goals of the guidance movement, but many problems that the community had hoped would be tackled when they committed the school to the guidance movement appear to not have been touched. The principal, seeking the best services, staffed the school with seven counselors, and, although there is some satisfaction among the counselors, faculty, and citizens about outcomes of their services, there is also considerable cause for complaint. Counselors dislike the time-consuming clerical and administrative duties they are required to engage in, duties that they claim prevent them from functioning at their level of trained expertise. Some students complain that their concerns are either not attended to or are treated with overelaborate procedures. Surveys show that by graduation many students have no idea about the direction of their future and that, by choice, they have never conferred with a counselor about anything. Citizens also complain that for many youths no assistance has been given in developing occupational direction and competence, that only those going on to postsecondary education, particularly to degree-granting institutions, receive attention.

The consultant, prior to his visit to the school, engages in appropriate study. He examines written materials about the school, including a statement of the educational goals and guidance objectives it seeks to attain, and what program regularities have been established by the school, particularly guidance program regularities, so as to have all students reach those goals and objectives. He studies research and newer practices, and into his analysis he incorporates the experience he had in resolving Fantasy City's health center problem.

He is led to conclude that staffing a school's guidance program with only counselors is as indefensible as staffing a community health program with only physicians. He finds the logic to be simple: students' common and unique development needs, orientations, and problems scatter along a number of dimensions, just as individuals' health needs and problems scatter; some needs are common to all, some are unique to portions of the population, or just to individuals. In a health center the medical needs of individuals run from the simple to the complex. Individual guidance needs vary similarly.

The consultant also recognizes the fact that the social systems into which individuals are locked will vary greatly in their nature. In consequence there will be great variations in the quality of development among individual students. These premises cause him to conclude that guidance programs designed to serve a wide array of behavior needs of individual students *must be staffed by a mix of guidance occupations, not just by the single occupation of counselor.*

Our consultant's study has apprised him of the fact that common outcomes of the guidance aspect of education can be identified (as in Chapter 2), but certain variables affect the attainment of those objectives.

Community cultural variables, for example. The program specifics and the kinds of guidance practitioners needed in a high school serving a predominantly poor population, or one mostly composed of Indians or Chicanos, for example, will need to be different from those of a school serving middle-income or predominantly white populations.

Our consultant concludes that, with rare exception, attainment of guidance program objectives will call for a guidance team that will have a standard or fixed component of old and new guidance occupations. He also concludes that unique community and youth characteristics will require that that standard or fixed component be complemented by other guidance occupations for as long as the need for them exists.

When he finishes his study of Real City High School, our consultant's report will not only describe the occupations of the standard guidance team, the one found in all schools, but also will suggest the mix of such occupations needed. He also will state the additional guidance occupations needed to complement the fixed guidance team, occupations based on the unique characteristics of Real City and of its high school population.

1. His study of and experience in guidance had caused him to see certain goals as appropriate for any secondary school in the country. Because he was to help one school, however, his first step was examination of the goals set for Real City High School. We shall hypothesize that he found that the goals established for RCHS were like those of high schools anywhere. Many of the guidance objectives his professional experience had led him to hold as tenable for any high school therefore also were appropriate for RCHS.

2. He surveyed the RCHS students, faculty, and a sample of Real City citizens to determine whether those educational goals were being reached by almost all students (he was able to accept 85 percent as a defensible and realistic "almost"). Data from this survey turned up a number of the variables that affect whether or not individual students achieve guidance objectives and the school's educational goals. Other data that related to individual student achievement of school goals was acquired from teachers. He also carried out a survey of graduates of the prior 3 years to obtain a time-tested measure of school goal attainment by students.

3. He conducted a survey of the community around certain economic, sociological, and mental health variables and analyzed them as to the demands these variables placed on the school as an institution and on all students or on subsets of students.

4. He studied the school as a social system and studied the program regularities (curricular and extracurricular) set up to produce the behavior regularities called for by the school goal statements.

5. Last, he analyzed all the data from these several sources and was able to make his specific recommendation about the school's guidance program and the team of guidance specialists required by that program.

50 Specialists in the Guidance Program

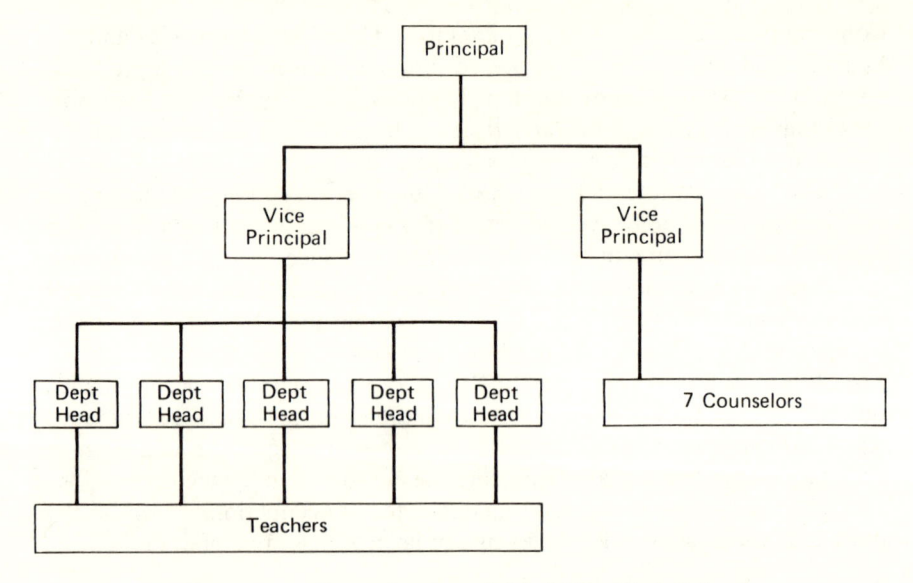

```
                          Principal
                             |
              +--------------+--------------+
              |                             |
          Vice                           Vice
        Principal                     Principal
              |                             |
  +-----+-----+-----+-----+                 |
  |     |     |     |     |                 |
 Dept  Dept  Dept  Dept  Dept          7 Counselors
 Head  Head  Head  Head  Head
  |     |     |     |     |
  +-----+-----+-----+-----+
              |
           Teachers
```

Figure 1. *Organization of Real City High School.*

On arrival the consultant found RCHS organizationally pictured as in Figure 1, a typical high school plan that varies among schools chiefly in the number of positions in each occupation except that of principal.

Likely this figure presents a picture familiar to most, although those whose experience is with smaller high schools might not find the departmental structure familiar and would remember fewer counselors. For purposes of this chapter, the focus will be put on the counselor component of Figure 1, the sole component of the present guidance team. At the same time, having served his purpose, our hypothetical consultant retires, turning the inquiry over to us.

We undertake that inquiry with a question. Anyone trying to guess what that question might be could come up with: Given these seven counselors, how can it be made certain that students receive the most and best counseling possible? But that question would head in the wrong direction. It is that kind of question, I posit, that has brought trouble to guidance programs. The correct question, one that reflects a systems approach, is: Given the school's goals and objectives of the guidance program, what guidance program functions are needed in the school to attain those outcomes and goals? We ask first about the goals and objectives to be reached; we do not ask what jobs we can find for seven counselors.

We are reminded that a guidance program is implemented by a school's adults in general, not only by counselors or other guidance specialists. Because guidance specialists are the most familiar expression of the

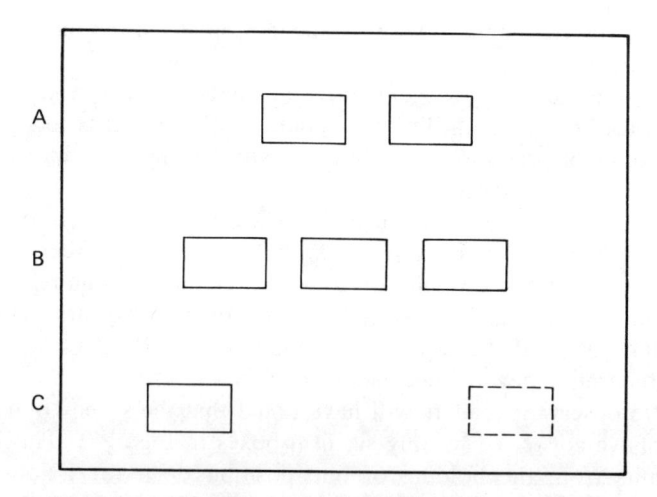

Figure 2. *The basic or standard guidance team.*

guidance movement, however, thinking about the kinds of functions to be carried out by specialists provides a good entry point for answering our question about attaining guidance objectives.

The answer begins with a simple action. We take the array of seven counseling positions as found in Figure 1 and declare them vacant. In anticipation of the kind of guidance team to be demonstrated we can in our imaginations invert those seven positions, then, figuratively speaking, push in on the ends of that column, resulting in several guidance occupations as shown in Figure 2, one of which is the occupation of counselor.

Several characteristics of Figure 2 require pointing up. Although three occupations are shown at A, B, and C,[1] the particular number of positions at each occupation—the *number* of boxes at A, B, and C in Figure 2—has been arbitrarily assigned for this moment. The actual number of positions in each job for any high school is determined by an assessment of students and their success in achieving guidance outcomes.[2]

It is also noted that the boxes are not connected by the customary lines of an organizational chart. This is an intentional omission. The usual organizational chart shows a hierarchy by means of the level at which each

---

[1] The lettering in Figure 2—A, B, and C—is a temporary device to eliminate a need to use titles for these occupations until other characteristics of the team concept have been established. Title setting right now would be distracting.

[2] The word "occupation" is used to refer to an array of functions commonly carried out in a number of places or settings. "Teacher" is the name of an occupation. The word "job" refers to an occupation carried out in a particular setting. In Real City High School there is a job called English Teacher. There are eight persons in the job of English Teacher at RCHS; each of these holds a "position" in that job.

job appears on the diagram, with job boxes connected by lines to emphasize that some jobs are superior to others, as shown in Figure 1. There might be a hierarchical arrangement of jobs in a guidance team, including the position of chairperson, but the intention of Figure 2 is to show three different kinds of practitioners on a team without implying that some jobs are perforce superior to others.

One characteristic is conveyed by showing three levels of occupations, however. This characteristic is the difference between the three occupations as to the amount of formal preparation required for each occupation. The job at A is seen here as requiring 2 years of graduate preparation, that at B, 1 graduate year, and at C only brief workshop or in-service preparation beyond a bachelor's degree.

More observant readers will have noted that the seven counselors of Figure 1 have converted to only six firm boxes in Figure 2. This discrepancy results from the holding of one position open for a job not yet determined, shown by the dotted box in the lower right corner of Figure 2. Figure 2 shows the three basic, standard, or fixed occupations on every high school guidance team (recall, however, that the mix of positions among those occupations varies among schools). The assessment of youth needs, it is predicted, will turn up the need for at least one other specialist for this hypothetical school, and eventual addition of one of those occupations would then account for the original seven positions.

The statement above that the three occupations or jobs shown in Figure 2 are the standard ones on every high school guidance team may result in challenge from some readers. "Our high school does not have seven counselors from which to make a guidance team, only two." Or, "We have only one counselor, so what you are saying does not apply to our school." I do not hold that such understandable demurrers express contravening or disallowing notions. The thrust of this volume is on the guidance objectives to be attained by all students and on the activities programmed so as to result in the achievement of those objectives. If there is but one guidance specialist, he carries out all the functions that would fall on a team of specialists, remembering that not all guidance functions are the responsibility of guidance specialists. Because a guidance program is a school program, all or most teachers have guidance functions to perform, and the principal is the chief guidance officer.

If there are two guidance specialists, the guidance functions requiring a specialist are parceled out to each in packages approximating the individuals' specialized capacities and interests. In any case first comes the identification of school goals and the guidance outcomes and procedures contributing to them. Then comes consideration of the variety of specialized guidance occupations and the number of positions within each occupation as the need demonstrates and the budget permits.

MEMBERS OF THE BASIC GUIDANCE TEAM AND THEIR FUNCTIONS

It may deserve repeating the observation that the letters A, B, and C are not to connote that occupation A is better than B, and C inferior to B. There is a training difference, but this does not make one occupation better than another. A practitioner in any one job or occupation on the guidance team has distinct functions for which the incumbent is fully qualified. In Fantasy City's health center, physicians are not better than nurses. The physicians are good at their functions, and the nurses are good at theirs. Our hypothetical consultant's duties were not completed, we noted, until he persuaded the physicians to stop referring to the nonphysician members of the health team as paraprofessionals. The physicians found that they were far less effective without the full health team, whose members' functions were not just services to physicians, but who carried out health functions independent of the physicians, with all team members coordinating their functions so as to provide the best health services possible for the city.

YOUTH DEVELOPMENT—A BASIS FOR DETERMINING GUIDANCE SPECIALISTS' FUNCTIONS

The as-yet-unlabeled occupations in Figure 2 have been posited as the basic or standard component of the guidance team. I will label them to permit easier reading of this section, but important questions around the troublesome question of these occupational labels will be examined in a later section. Postponing the rationale for use of terms, I will use "behavior specialist" for the occupation at A, a title that actually could not be used in schools, "counselor" for B, and the C occupation will be named "career development technician (CDT)." Differentiating among the functions of these specialists is the next need, and a start is made on that by relating the three occupations to the imperatives of adolescent development and to guidance outcomes.

Each adult in schools has a general interest in adequate human development, and each assesses the adequacy of development against his own model of a human functioning at his best. If an assessment sweep related to the adequacy of development were made through an entire student population, the adults would find the expected spread of results to be marked, at one extreme, by students who are on top of the pile, who are "with it," who closely approximate the model of best human functioning as held by most adults. In actuality, adults will not be in agreement about the characteristics of the model human, but for the moment let us assume their agreement.

On the other hand, there will be those youths who have undesirable developmental histories, and their behaviors reflect this poor history, causing them to fall far short of the adults' model of the human at his best. These youths are deficient because they have excesses or deficiencies in coping behaviors. They are the ones whose development is remediated by the behavior specialist.

Development Remediation Functions of Specialists at A on Figure 2: Behavior Specialists

The past 10 years have seen the development of a fantastic array of procedures for mediating an almost limitless array of behaviors. Although many of the procedures appear to be disarmingly simple, they function out of a relatively recent and ever expanding body of knowledge about how behaviors develop and are maintained. The behavior specialist will know a large portion of that body of knowledge, as well as procedures for mediating behavior. Because teachers, counselors, and career development technicians have less knowledge about behavior than behavior specialists they are not in a position to determine the best behavior mediation procedures for any student, but they can carry out the procedures determined by the more knowledgeable behavior specialist.

The behavior specialist has nurturing functions as well as the restoring or remedial one now being examined. Both functions may be better understood by considering the developmental problems of youth as a continuum. At one end of that continuum we place those problems described as short-lasting (of recent origin), contained (having little if any "spill-over" to other behaviors), and of external origin (caused by someone else or by social contingencies). At the other end of the continuum we find those problems that can be described as long-lasting, pervasive (many behaviors affected), and intrapsychic;[3] that is, although originally external in origin, they are now imbedded in the warp and woof of the individual's behaviors. Said in different words, youths at this end of the developmental continuum are marked by long histories of self-defeating behaviors. A youth at this end may have both too little and too much of otherwise normal behaviors. Behavior specialists are those who serve students with

---

[3] "Intrapsychic" is a bridging term used temporarily in this chapter on the assumption that it has meaning for readers. Within the theoretical basis of this book, "stimulus-response generalization" is the correct term.

developmental problems at this severe end of the development problem continuum. To so say requires a reminder: serving students with severe developmental problems is not the only function of behavior specialists, nor indeed their first-order purpose. As with all members of the guidance team, these practitioners carry out professional behaviors comparable to the health behaviors of the public health officer (PHO). Improvement of conditions relating to good development, a nurturing function, is a concern of all team members, just as the PHO works to improve a community's health. These nurturing functions of the behavior specialist will be examined following the presentation of his restorative (remedial) functions because then they will be better understood.

Thinking about the restoration-to-good-development function of this specialist, we look at one youth, Henry, currently served by one of them. Henry's history has caused the early acquisition of noncoping, self-defeating behaviors related to most aspects of daily life (they are pervasive) such that he has been continuously far from matching a model of a human functioning at his best. His academic attainments are well below his capacity, he is not oriented to a personally or socially productive future, and his behaviors have been marked by a history of psychological imbalance. Scorned by all but equally deficient peers, annoying to teachers, rejected by parents, one can predict for him only an accelerating rate of motion away from ideal humanness unless his behaviors are modified so as to be self-enhancing, not self-defeating. The behavior specialist could not have prevented these behaviors, but he at least knows how they can be turned around.

Although more needs to be said about behavior specialists, and much more can be said, we move on to think about other team members so as to get a full picture with minimal divergence into topics that, even though important, are peripheral to our immediate purposes. *The Considerations for Training* section near the end of this chapter will reconsider the Behavior Specialist around research-supported practices of specialists in behavior mediation.

Development Functions of Counselors, the Specialists at B on Figure 2

We can use this consideration of counselors to state one characteristic of guidance teams: Counselors, CDTs, and other occupations not yet incorporated into our guidance team can be rungs in a career ladder to "higher" guidance occupations, higher in the sense that they require greater preparation and a wider, more responsible array of functions. Counselors can continue their training to qualify as behavior specialists, for example. Of course, a counselor or career development technician might choose to remain in either occupation.[4] With the additional reminder that, as with behavior specialists, counselors first have "public health" functions and then secondarily have functions in helping individuals with problems, we inspect in more detail their problem-helping function.

Like persons of any age group, youths have to cope with those problems of that end of the problem continuum identified earlier as relatively brief, contained, and of external origin. It is for this majority of youth that counselors provide their functions. One quickly notes that the requirements for knowledge and competency among counselors differ in quantity, if not quality, from those of behavior specialists. At the same time the attention given here to the extreme ends of the developmental problem continuum might erroneously suggest a greater distinction between populations served by these two practitioners than is actually the case. To make counselor functions more operationally clear we take a brief look at a high school student named Linda.

Linda has recently acquired a wish for postsecondary training because she has recently acquired an occupational goal, but she does not know how to find out about and select an appropriate post–high school training institution, however. Her problem is exacerbated because her parents do not favor her occupational decision. She is experiencing frustration, puzzlement, and concern. She has a developmental imbalance that is relatively short-lasting, contained (it does not "spill over" into most other daily activities), and lies "outside" of herself, being caused by the normal social pressures for employment, by not unusual family frustrations, and by the impending termination of her schooling. This student has some needs beyond the information ones. If information were her only need, another practitioner instead of the counselor might have been her only contact with the team. In fact, she did go first to a CDT who found that she had concerns beyond obtaining information and thus took her across the corridor to confer with a counselor.

We again compare the behavior specialist and the counselor in general terms. Youths whose development is blocked require the mediation of their behaviors by persons who understand how behaviors originate, and who can therefore initiate appropriate behavior mediation activities—behavior specialists. Other students' development has been marked by appropriate progress. They face normal and typical problems in continuing that

[4] An investigation by Katzell, Korman, and Levine, (1970) addressed the dynamics of job mobility of practitioners in the similar field of social and rehabilitation services. One of their conclusions was that the high turnover of workers in the area of service might be reduced if persons could move laterally and vertically to more desirable jobs in an agency. The guidance team, as shown in Figure 2, numbers this possibility among its assets.

progress. They profit from strategies in decision making, information acquisition, problem identification, problem solving, social system mediation, the reinforcement (strengthening) of existing coping behaviors and the establishment of missing behaviors. The counselor provides reinforcing, problem solving, system mediation, information-supplying help, mostly to individuals in group settings.

THE TITLE QUESTION—AGAIN

The use of A and B for identifying the practitioners for a few paragraphs following Figure 2 was as clumsy to write as it was to read. What is the issue? Why not have given them titles from the outset?

If behavior specialist had been used instead of the disguise of "A," some readers might have reacted by saying, "We don't have them; we have only counselors." That rejection might have impeded learning. Likewise, if the "B" practitioner had been identified as counselor at once, readers' past histories with counselors would have mediated their understanding of the ideas presented. One can imagine, had counselor been used, the reader saying, "Counselors don't do that in *my* school!" Although it is realistic to expect that even if the newer concepts and working relationships set out here become common, the title "counselor" will stick for one type of practitioner. There is advantage to changing titles when altered functions or relationships are to be used, as history has shown, but titles are viewed here as an issue relatively subordinate to outcomes and functions, thus the effort to keep the title matter in a subordinate position.

Looking again at the A practitioner, it can also tenably be imagined that some readers have said, after hearing his functions described here, "Why, that's a psychologist." Yes and no. No, not a typical school psychologist of the recent past. As with the title "counselor," to use the title "psychologist" would be to use a word that calls up an array of preconceptions that might distract more than help. If a title like "behavior psychologist" were used, or some other modifier were employed, then this modified title of psychologist might be tenable for describing functions. But what of public acceptance? Who goes to psychologists? Which students are sent to school psychologists? "Nuts, deviates, addicts, retards, kooks, queers" regretfully are answers students often give. The negative semantic loadings are just too great to suggest that "psychologist" would be a useful title for the A practitioner.

The question of titles is raised from time to time elsewhere under a variety of auspices. In 1971 major change in titles was proposed by a group convened by the U.S. Office of Education for the purpose of examining and evaluating guidance purposes and functions and proposing changes if they concluded any were needed. The title changes proposed by that body covered all school functions, and the title suggested as a replacement for counselor was learning development specialist. The commission was not proposing only the title change, of course, but also a new array of guidance functions for the newly titled occupation.[5]

This writing goes beyond that report by its proposal for a multiple occupations team. The title "learning development consultant" might be appropriate for one of the occupations on the team and for practitioners in elementary schools wherein typically there is but one guidance occupation, one now typically but inaptly titled "counselor."

Again, if the A practitioner was called counselor, then what about the type B practitioner? Counselor aide? Emphatically no. The B specialist is a relatively distinct occupation, with functions noticeably different from the A occupation. Counselor intern? Again a not-quite-baked counselor is suggested.

One last thought. If the group of guidance occupations is called a guidance team, consideration might be given to such titles as guidance specialist for the A practitioner, and guidance technician for the B occupation. The words "specialist" and "technician" convey some of the differences in the occupations, but for these two titles and for that of learning development consultant, there is a simple deterrent: a formal title can appear in writing and be put on a sign on a door, but most communication about specialists is oral. Vocational guidance counselor became shortened to just counselor. What would persons call a practitioner who would use one of the three latter titles? They are too clumsy to use in full.

The term "behavior specialist," used throughout this text, serves an expository purpose and is a brief, accurate title for the guidance functions

---

[5] In the 1950s Dr. Raymond Patouillet, then at Teachers College, Columbia University, was speaking and writing about child development consultants for elementary schools, rather than counselors. In 1960 the Palo Alto (California) Unified School District began investigating the functions of a child development specialist who would provide "psychological and counseling services" in elementary schools (Levine et al., 1965). From 1965–1968 the Eastern Regional Research Center of the Interprofessional Research Commission on Pupil Personnel Services (IRCOPPS) conducted a field study related to elementary school pupil services, with an interdisciplinary practitioner titled child development consultant (see Byrne et al., 1968; Seidman, 1970). These child development positions are in elementary schools, of course. The concept underlying an interdisciplinary prepared person for cross-professional practice, when applied to secondary schools, also suggests need for a different title, such as the proposal to substitute the title "learning development specialist" for a number of present titles, including counselor.

The USOE report has been summarized and reacted to in "The PPS Model: A Prototype for Change?" *Impact*, 1972, 1, 21–30. *Impact* is one of the excellent publications formerly issued by the ERIC Counseling and Personnel Services Information Center, University of Michigan.

performed. As acknowledged earlier, it is not a title that would be acceptable in most schools and is not used here as a serious proposal to that end.

NURTURING FUNCTIONS OF THE BEHAVIOR SPECIALIST

In examining the secondary function of the behavior specialist, the behavior replacement function, we described the type of knowledge and skill he has and gave a valid reason why this practitioner needs 2 years of graduate training for his functions. Attention now is given to his primary function, which makes him similar to a PHO because it finds him applying his professional behaviors to pervasive school conditions. He attends to these general school characteristics so as to increase the value of the school as a social system in the maintenance of desired behaviors and the prevention of the learning of undesired behaviors. To do so acknowledges that the essential guidance needs of students are affected by the school's characteristics.

YOUTHS' GUIDANCE NEEDS

The phrase "guidance needs" is open to undesirable inference, as is the comparable phrase, "health needs." Both phrases permit the defining of needs around a concept of deficit—that is, a need of a youth, or a common need of youths, is some problem or difficulty that must be alleviated. Youths' needs are defined here in two modes, the first being the need for the stimulation of adequate psychological growth, the general and continuing nurturance of behaviors that define the good life. This requires the establishment of useful, appropriate behaviors where they are needed but often are not yet existing such as decision-making and information-seeking behaviors. The other defining element of youths' needs lies in the presence of those behaviors that work against the best interests of a youth and/or his society. Most often this second-in-importance element is assumed to be either the sole or at least the most important defining element of need. Where this secondary need is viewed as paramount, school counselors serve youths-in-crisis, youths with deficits, in the way that the physician in private practice serves those with health deficits.

This issue deserves a bit further thought, with our thinking aided by continuance of the health analogy. We examine the purposes of the physician in private practice with the contrasting purposes of the public health officer (PHO). Unlike the physician in private practice, the PHO defines health needs not only by a deficit component, but also as in the two defining components for the youth needs just defined. That is, the PHO is first concerned with abetting the health of all citizens through the continuance and magnification of present good health practices and by instituting good health procedures or conditions that are not yet present in the community. His secondary functions call for his interest in the restoration to model health of those who have a health deficit. The private practitioner in health treats the citizen who has typhoid fever, for example, trying to restore him to health and has thus carried out his sole functions. The PHO, in contrast, is first concerned about community conditions so that typhoid fever cannot occur. The physician in private practice is like a gardener whose attention to the flora around his house is to try to restore to health those individual plants that appear sick. The PHO is similar to a different gardener, one who improves the quality of the soil, fertilizes, destroys insects and other sources of harm, maintains the best moisture condition in the soil. One who, in short, first takes such steps as will likely produce the best flora possible, and then attends to the individual plant that has not responded to his nurturing efforts.

Based on the definition of youth needs given earlier, it is apparent that the professional behaviors of the behavior specialist and other practitioners on the guidance team will first be directed to the nurturing function, and secondarily to the needs of eliminating or substituting undesired behaviors with desired ones. Said another way, evolution of guidance concepts has brought to the guidance movement a concern for such contributions as the school can make to the effective behaviors of all students. The paramount need among these behaviors, incidentally, is for those that will enable each individual to ready for and enter into the best of all possible occupations for him as determined by him.

To those ends, the behavior specialist serves as the educational psychologist as that practitioner was originally developed. As the school's expert on the psychosociology of learning, he consults with teachers individually and collectively on the learning process, on identification of the learning behaviors of individuals, and on the mediation of such behaviors, both for increment in behaviors and for changing their direction.

This is described as consultation because it treats specific concerns of the teachers. Sometimes there might be formal teaching of teachers, that is, a didactic approach around behavior because one of the goals of the behavior specialist is to help teachers learn as much as they can and wish to about behavior and about behavior mediation. Formal teaching has a use, but this specialist knows enough about learning to know the correctness of Dewey's position that learning is by doing, and that a teacher seeking to solve a problem of student behavior is a good example of "doing." Thus the behavior specialist gives much time to individual teachers as they cope with concerns they face about individual students.

The Behavior Specialist as Remediator

To illustrate the behavior-replacement function of the behavior specialist, we were introduced to Henry. The behavior specialist in Henry's school is now mediating his behaviors, and that requires application of the specialist's skills directly and privately with Henry. Henry, of course, is locked into several social systems and his behaviors are those learned in those social systems. He is "held together" by the reward and punishment contingencies of such past and present systems. His present behaviors are now also partly controlled by the ways he learned to cope with those social systems and his own earlier behaviors through use of symbols, that is, through words and sentences.

The behavior specialist will engage Henry's symbol systems in his private interviews with him, but he knows that change in the youth's behaviors probably also will require changes in contingencies in the social systems in which he lives day by day. The behavior specialist, therefore, engages the youth's teachers and parents in such contingency changes. That is, by working with teachers he causes to be set up quite precise conditions under which undesired behaviors are extinguished by not being reinforced, and through which there are established and reinforced those new behaviors that Henry, along with teachers, parents, and peers, will find desirable.

We do not attend here to the specifics of the behavior specialist's professional behaviors, but we need to fix one type of outcome that falls within the topic now being considered—the pervasive, nurturing functions that are the primary duty of guidance team members. This outcome is relatively patent and thus calls for only a brief note. In helping Henry's teachers and parents work for his benefit, the teachers and parents learn about the "cause and cure" of behavior, a learning that will generalize to the behaviors of all students and generalize in Henry's family to his brother and sister. In consequence his teachers and parents can be more objective when another youth presents unwanted behaviors. They are thus able to make a more useful assessment of procedures to be used to mediate this other youth's behaviors, even though their knowledge is not sufficient to determine the specific processes to be used.

In addition to demonstrating an activity that enables the behavior specialist to carry out this PHO-type of function, this is an illustration about how other persons, not as generally knowledgeable of behavior origins and change as the behavior specialist, can successfully mediate Henry's behavior under the direction of the specialist. It also demonstrates a point made previously: that other practitioners with less training, including teachers, can carry out behavior mediation practices under the direction of the fully trained practitioner.

The procedures used by the behavior specialist for pervasively improving the behavior contingencies in the school are not exhausted by these illustrations. There are other procedures in his armamentarium, to be used with students and adults, individually and in groups, that he can employ when appropriate. The illustrations used here are sufficient for present purposes, that is, to demonstrate with samples how a behavior specialist, like other members of the guidance team, contributes to improvements in social systems to pervasively and positively affect the behaviors of all students.[6]

THE NURTURING FUNCTIONS OF THE COUNSELOR

The counselors in Figure 2 theoretically know less about how behavior is acquired and how to mediate it than to behavior specialists, and counselors also serve different functions. A counselor's contribution to the nurturance of youth development, in consequence, is of a different nature, perhaps more a by-product than a plan. From counselors' knowledge of a wide range of students, their feedback function is an important source of information for school leaders as to what is right and wrong with the school as a social system, including its curriculum. Rightness and wrongness are assessed by applying criteria about development, and specifically about the reaching of school goals and guidance objectives by all students. Counselors have more access to these data about all students than any other school functionary.

Functions of the Career Development Technician (CDT)

Goldman (1967) has proposed a guidance information technician to work under the direction of a counselor. A different functionary is proposed under the title of career development technician. He indeed is an

---

[6] The recent literature contains instance after intance of the guidance practitioner's serving this kind of consultation function with teachers. For information relating to the elementary school level, see Whitley and Sulzer (1970), who also provide a bibliography that will lead to other illustrations. Research carried out at two other IRCOPPS Research Centers demonstrates the effectiveness of the consultative function. At the University of Texas guidance team members consulted with elementary school teachers about child behavior, directed to mental health intervention (Pierce-Jones, Iscoe, & Cunningham, 1968). At Chico State College (California) the research dealt with the consultation role of counselors with parents of children in elementary and junior high schools (Shaw & Rector, 1968). Not only do the results of these researches warrant their study, but the extensive rationale provided in the final reports constitutes a complete documentation of the respective topics.

information specialist and manages the information center of the guidance area, but he is more a career specialist who works with teachers to increase the level of career development awareness throughout the school. The CDT assists teachers in relating their subject matter to occupations appropriate to students who have interest and competency in that subject. Additionally the CDT works in the community, carrying out a variety of functions, which could include some or all of these: (1) job surveys, (2) liaison with employment services, (3) job development, (4) part-time placement for students, (5) maintaining communication with business and industrial personnel officers, (6) conducting follow-up studies, (7) obtaining local job descriptions, and (8) similar functions that bear on the career development of youths. This view of the variety of in-school and out-of-school functions of this specialist accounts for holding that the word "information" in Goldman's proposed occupational title would be too restrictive. There might well be a guidance information technician serving under a career development technician, particularly because the out-of-school functions of the CDT require him to be absent from the school's career development or resource center wherein occupational information is stored. In addition, we are reminded, the CDT will be working with teachers on career-related activities. Who tends the store? Someone who will remain there, who might be titled as Goldman suggests, or, as opted for here, career development aide. Yet, when the activities of a career development center are examined, we find that such centers provide services that may be inaccurately labeled if caught up under a title that focuses on information.

The specialist remaining in the center, working under the CDT's supervision, assists students in use of the computer terminal in the center that is an extension of some program as the interactive learning system (ILS). Group discussion about occupations and careers goes on in the center, as well as part-time placement and other youth-assisting services.

An assistant to the CDT has been glibly spoken of as if he is a given on a school's guidance team, and, if that is so, some might wonder why that position is not shown in Figure 2. In response to this query it could first be observed that if only one position were available at the occupation lettered C, the CDT would carry out all functions, and this might necessitate that the career development center be closed for a few hours from time to time while the CDT was carrying out community-based activities. But then again it could be kept open all the time by using interested students or parent or teacher volunteers. Indeed in some schools the career development center may be so vital a service and the size of the student population may be such that there might well be a sizable team associated with the center itself. In the interest of parsimony, however, Figure 2 shows only one position at C.

No matter the number of assistants who stay in the center, the CDT is an information expert and is responsible for ascertaining that his assistants evaluate all information the center receives. He is often in the center, of course, and during these times he gives information-seeking help and decision-making assistance to students who ask for them.

The CDT is not a "paraprofessional" or "support person" to either the behavior specialist or the counselor. He does indeed help them, but they also help him; he fills a distinct occupation, a member of a team who acknowledges the specialized functions of the other team members, who in turn acknowledge his high level of expertise.[7]

The career development technician is still a high school rarity, and thus most readers will be unfamiliar with this relatively new occupation. Although the use of career specialists described in this chapter has been placed in association with a high school career development center, they might be more "free-floating," such as the career specialists used K through 12 in the Sonoma County (California) schools. Hoppock and Novick (1971) identified one high school in a survey they conducted in which a career specialist was used, although they found 25 other career specialist positions, under a variety of titles, serving schools in a variety of organizational structures. A number of high schools in Maryland have opted to use this functionary, and some Maryland county school systems have adopted use of this practitioner in all high schools.[8]

Perhaps the most significant datum that this is the direction of the future is to be found in a 1970 act of the Florida legislature, which has created the title of "occupational specialist" and authorizes their number to be up to 50 percent of a school's guidance team. Such specialists would not

---

[7] This stand does not accord with the policy of the American Personnel and Guidance Association. That association's policy, adopted in 1966, refers to counselors as the central, professional functionary, with other persons in the guidance area identified as support personnel. Their relationship is explained by this opening statement: "The roles and duties of support personnel must be understood in relation to the counselor, in as much as he is the professional person who provides both counseling and the leadership essential for effective service." The full policy statement and an extensive examination of this issue is found in Zimpher et al. (1970). Insofar as a journal speaks for a professional association, further exposition of issues and practices is set out in the special issue of *The Personnel and Guidance Journal* titled Paras, Peers, and Pros (1974, 53, 4). This issue includes student counselors (peers) among the paraprofessionals.

[8] More than 10 years ago I was asked to prepare a chapter (Byrne, 1966) predicting the nature of high school counseling in the foreseeable future. A number of my predictions have not materialized, but the foreseeing of an emergence of multiple occupations guidance teams was reasonably accurate. A position paper adopted in 1973 by the National Vocational Guidance Association and the American Vocational Association entitled *Career Development and Career Guidance*, identified 10 specialists in career guidance, 6 of which are appropriate for high schools. The title proposed there for the functionary who is somewhat similar to the CDT mentioned here is Occupational and Educational Information Specialist. The position taken here, however, is that the CDT would serve several functions, only one of which is information specialist.

be required to have earned even a bachelor's degree. The length and substance of preparation needed by a CDT has not received empirical test because it is a new occupation with few people. The Counselor Education Department of Florida State University is studying the preparation of the specialist by the Florida legislature at a nondegree level. One source of this specialist may be early retirees from industry who had diverse careers and held responsible positions. It can be seen that the source and preparation of this specialist will need considerable study, but in the interim this position has been filled in some cases from among the counselor ranks.

ADDITIONAL GUIDANCE TEAM MEMBERS

The guidance team occupations previously examined have been the three that comprise the standard or basic guidance team for any high school. A youth-need assessment determines which other occupations shall be added to the team, if any. In this section some of these complementing team occupations are examined.

Continuing Education Technician

In a school from which only a small proportion goes on to education /training (E/T) after leaving or being graduated from high school, this type of specialist may not be appropriate, and the needed services can be provided by the CDT. The continuing education technician (CET) is justified for a large number of high schools, however; and the number of high schools needing this specialist likely will continue to increase because the number of youths who continue E/T after high school has been increasing for 150 years. Moreover, the proportion of such youth related to all youths has been increasing for at least 50 years, although recent data show a leveling off. In addition, the nature of higher education has increased in complexity as has our technology. Decisions about postsecondary E/T require that variables be engaged, the significance of which was not understood even 10 years ago. In Figure 2 the CET could be one of the occupations appearing in the dotted box. This is not a new guidance occupation. For many years this practitioner has been found in a small proportion of high schools, most often functioning under the title "college counselor."

Even if there have not been CETs commonly in high schools, college counseling has been common. In survey after survey students document that fact when they have stated, in effect, "in my school the only persons about whom the counselors care and give attention to are those going on to college." In past practices, then, there can be found this double error: focus on degree-granting institutions and on students planning to attend them by persons who never acquired expertise related even to degree-granting institution selection.

Implicit in this text is the view that "educolatry," the worshipful pursuit of a bachelor's degree, is a societal fallacy to which the guidance movement has regularly contributed energy. That degree is an educational goal to which all should aspire, the myth goes, if career competence and contentment are to be attained. The stand taken in this text is consonant with that held by Commissioner Marland as reported in Chapter 1: schooling might have a clear starting point, but it never has an ending point—education is continuous, and after high school most youths and adults should have access to a variety of programs that do not yield a degree, with the exception of the 2-year Associate of Arts degree for some. The CET, therefore, attends to a noticeably different population of students and has information about a noticeably different array of E/T opportunities from those of the traditional college counselor, but, of course, is also expert in data related to bachelor's degree–granting institutions.

Out-Reach Counselor

Assume the existence of a high school that has recently converted from a statist stance about students to a stance consonant with the principles of the Declaration of Independence. In a school where such mass conversion has occurred, it must be assumed that the school's adults are now eager to make amends for and take actions to counter prior statist practices, which would have resulted in a large drop-out rate. Or assume a high school in a community whose subcultures cause schools to be viewed aversively, or a school where, for whatever cultural reasons, a large number of youths withdraws before completing high school, or perhaps attends with great irregularity. Each school will profit from an out-reach or field counselor, a person hired by the school who has office space in it, but who is mostly out on the streets where unemployed or irregularly attending school-aged youths are to be found.

The word "counselor" in this title is used for expediency; it is commonly known and understood. The person employed might actually be certifiable as a counselor, but likely not because the position might best be filled by a person who himself was a drop-out, perhaps even holds a police record, but is now vigorously committed to youth development. Such a person is street-wise from his past experiences, he can look and speak like the youth he seeks to serve, and he knows community resources. His intention is not primarily to return youth to school, although that will be an important option. His intention is to serve each youth in the best way possible, which for some youths may be occupational placement and for others actions such as encouragement to and assistance with enrollment in a Manpower Development and Training Act–supported program.

It may be that you find little similarity between this practitioner and the traditional case worker employed by schools under such titles as "visiting teacher," "school case worker," or "pupil personnel worker." One important difference between the proposed position and the traditional one is in the matter of preparation and in consequence the kind of person who fills the position. The other important difference is in the particular clientele served, the traditional school case worker more often serving the full spectrum of a school system's children and adolescents in a number of elementary and secondary schools.

The occupation of field counselor was used for illustration and contrasted with the more typical school case worker. In actuality more schools may profit from employment of a more traditional school case worker, thus this class of practitioner should earn our first consideration as the one to be added to the school's guidance team. On the other hand, assessment of youth needs may make the employment of both the traditional case worker and an out-reach counselor imperative.

THREE OTHER GUIDANCE OCCUPATIONS

Three other possible occupations for the guidance team remain to be described. The first of these, teacher-advisor, has origins in educational antiquity. Registrar, the second of the remaining occupations, is relatively recent, and apparently the number of registrars is increasing. The last and very new practitioner on some guidance teams, although not proposed here for the guidance team, is the peer counselor.

Teacher-Advisor

The historic high school practice of the home room included the idea of home room teacher as teacher-advisor. We speak here, however, of a level of interaction between teacher and student that goes beyond the historic practice.

One difference is found in the older practice of requiring every teacher to serve as a home room teacher in contrast to the idea here of volunteers as teacher-advisors. A second and more important difference, which grows out of the first, is that the teacher-advisor (T-A) receives some preparation from the trained members of the guidance team, has assigned time available for conferences, and engages students in more extensive consultation of educational programs and attainments than typical home room teacher–advising provided.

The needs of youth must underlie any guidance occupation. What is the need here? Why T-As? The answer begins with the plea of students to be known in the high school, to be cared about. Traditional counseling gives this knowing and caring to a small minority of students. Youths' criticism of counselors, however, and knowledge of the small proportion of students served each year by counselors, shows that most youths' needs for being known and cared about by some school adult are not being met by counselors or by anyone else.

An additional need students have is for certainty that they are engaging in the appropriate school program from among the available programs, which have become increasingly complex as to substance and diploma requirement. Is not assistance in this matter a traditional function of counselors? Yes, is the appropriate response, to be followed by two questions: Should counselors take time for so simple a need, and why do students face problems in this matter?

The principle undergirding the occupation of T-A is the same as that of all guidance team occupations. First state the objectives to be attained, find out whether they are being reached, and, if not, then find the best procedures to be used to attain them. Subsequently the school can either use present or create new occupations to carry out those procedures. Repeating another principle: the number and mix of positions on the standard guidance team are not bureaucratically set; they are determined by the assessment of youth needs for the school, and the number and mix of the standard team will be altered as subsequent surveys show the need. The kind and number of additional guidance team occupations is similarly determined. If the assessment shows that now it is appropriate for this school to solicit volunteer teacher-advisors and then train them and give them time to function, they will be added to the guidance team. Five years hence their use might not be warranted in this particular school.

And for the identified need there indeed might be other responses than the T-A, such as the employment of noncredentialed persons (Zerface & Cox, 1971) who quickly learn the advising function just as the continuing education technician would quickly learn his functions on the job. No new ritualistic response (teacher-advisor) is proposed here to replace an old ritualistic response ("That's a counselor's function"). An identified need does call for some response, couched in the suggestion that the guidance team concept is a more flexible way to respond to youth needs than is employing just certified counselors.[9]

Registrar

Inclusion of this functionary on the guidance team also permits a brief test of the separation of guidance program functions from school administration. A registrar is appropriate for and used in some schools that

---

[9] One illustration of counseling out-of-school youths with a broader intention than counseling only is described by Delgiorno (1970).

have a sizable proportion of graduates going on for continuing E/T. For that subpopulation numerous records must be prepared and sent to continuing E/T institutions. Counselors in the past have been involved in the process of helping students to select higher education institutions and the application activity perforce is associated with the selection activity. It thus became an easy matter for administrators, students, and counselors themselves to assume that application assistance also was the responsibility of counselors. And that assistance means transcript preparation among other clerical activities.

Because there are major guidance outcomes set up to contribute to each student's being graduated, counselors in some schools have become the functionary responsible for verifying that seniors have completed requirements for graduation. This assignment of a school administrative nature takes the counselor into the student record file again. For the several and continuing reasons why counselors use student records, it is no surprise to find counselors in some schools responsible for the collection and storage of data about students, or at least for a large portion of those data.

Occasionally one heard or could read that some Counselors preferred these or any clerical duties because they would not then have to work with students. In fact, surveys among counselors, and statements made by them in a variety of settings, have shown that most counselors have been dismayed about the large number of clerical responsibilities that devolved on them because those clerical duties keep them from serving students. The outcry against clerical duties has a long and continuing history. A first and common use of the unexpected funds made available to school systems for guidance by the National Defense Education Act (1958 et seq.) was for the employment of clerical assistance.

But clerical assistance is not enough, because transcript preparation and other facets of student record keeping are more than a mere clerical function. Thus the concept of the registrar. But whose registrar—the guidance team's or the administration team's? Is what a registrar does related to a guidance outcome, or is it a school management function?

To ask this question about the registrar is to raise a specific instance of a very general question. Although extensive treatment of the topic could be made, it will be treated summarily here with this statement: the culture of guidance has come to be cluttered by many nonguidance functions because counselors are available (there's that guidance = counselors equation again). Numerous counselors fill assistant principal functions now through accretion of such duties over the years. They do not receive half-time assistant principal pay, incidentally, although some counselors do receive a salary differential above the teacher salary scale.

In sum, a school's registrar can be attributed to either the administrative or guidance aspects, but, because that functionary is so closely associated with guidance outcomes, the position has been included here in the guidance team and associated with the continuing education technician as Figure 3 will show.

Peer Counselors

This recently developed practitioner is now a member of some schools' guidance teams and for that reason is considered here. I do not propose that this new functionary be included as a prospective position on the guidance team proposed herein, however, for a reason to be explicated after the arguments for it are presented.

We could again refer to youth needs as justification for peer counselors, but perhaps a different approach conveys the rationale better. This different approach starts with the axiom that adolescence is marked by the candid sharing of confidences and concerns among youths. Surveys over years (e.g., Grant, 1954; Zetts et al., 1973) have shown that youths seek out other youths with whom to discuss concerns of all kinds, while conversely counselors are not high on the list of persons whom students seek out for help.

Because it is natural for youths to seek out peers for counseling, the reasoning goes, why not turn this natural act into a guidance team asset by identifying students with whom other young adults would readily discuss concerns, and then for those youths so identified, and who volunteer to be peer counselors, provide interview skills. The evidence about the effectiveness of this use of peers as counselors has been slowly but steadily accumulating (e.g., Armstrong, 1969; Brown, 1965; Leibowitz & Rhoads, 1974; Lobitz, 1970; Stockdale, 1972; Truax & Lister, 1970; Varenhorst, 1974; Zunker & Brown, 1966). So too has the evidence about the substance and length of training peers and other nonprofessionals benefit by having and the effectiveness of that training (e.g., Andrade, 1972; Carkhuff & Berenson, 1967; Leibowitz, 1974; Pyle & Snyder, 1971; Ware & Gold, 1971).

With such good reasoning and evidence, why then is it that I do not encourage adoption of the concept of peer counselors on the guidance team? Because skills to be learned and used by a few can and should be the skills learned and used by all. Table 1 has a single guidance outcome in School Goal 3, and this outcome posits that all students will acquire the skills of interpersonal relationships, which are, of course, the skills learned by peer counselors.

If the concept of the training of the selected few that characterizes peer counseling were applied in other guidance areas, the guidance movement would continue to be marked by that condition for which it has been recently attacked. Recent critics, as noted several times before, have demonstrated that the benefits of guidance, and they more often than not mean the assistance of counselors, have been received by only a small proportion of students. If we seek to have a guidance program profit all students, it would make no sense to select a few students and train them in occupational decision making, for example, with the hope that they might help other students. The stance often stated here is that the attainment of guidance outcomes, such as decision-making skills, particularly as applied to careers, are goals for *all* students. By the same token, then, interpersonal relationship skills are taught to all students in the same group setting in which other guidance outcomes are attained. Peer counselors yes, in one sense. That sense is that *all* students are trained as peer counselors. Until a school is in a position to train all students, temporary use of a coterie of peer counselors is encouraged.

To disclaim a need for peer counselors, if all students receive the training, does not thereby speak against the use of students for a variety of forms of assistance in the guidance program. Such assistance not only benefits the guidance program, but also the participating students. For example, students have been used to assist career development technicians in a variety of functions (information evaluators, audiovisual technicians, aides in decision-making programs) and as aides to counselors (research assistants, aides in group activities). The latter group is illustrated by the use of high-performing, inner-city adolescents to raise the academic attainments of low-performing peers (Vreind, 1974).

THE COMPLETE GUIDANCE TEAM

Figure 2 portrayed the essential or standard guidance team. The material following that figure showed how and why other occupations are added to the guidance team, and this topic can now be concluded by an additional figure, showing the full guidance team of our hypothetical Real City High School, but matched, at least in part, by numberous real high schools.[10] Figure 2 was enclosed in a box, but Figure 3 is not. A true guidance team is not set off from the rest of the school (it is an open system), and, although the interrelationships of various team members to a

---

[10] This volume's concern is with high school guidance teams. College counseling centers have long histories of multiple staffing, that is, use of occupations other than counseling psychologists. An unusual example of this differential staffing is the employment of a lawyer at California State College, Los Angeles, during 1968–1969. His employment, incidentally, provides a good test of the concept stated in Chapter 1: the word counselor must always be modified, because a counselor always counsels from a discipline. A student going to the college counseling center could not ask just for "counseling." He would have to specify whether he meant psychological or legal counseling. Another college innovation related to this section is the establishment of a new guidance occupation at C. W. Post Center, Long Island University—that of a full-time academic counselor, a college equivalent of the part-time teacher-advisor.

72   Specialists in the Guidance Program

```
              BS      BS

         C      C       C

   CDT                CET ── R
                                     T-A
   CDA         CW
                         OC

              GAC
```

BS — Behavior Specialist
C — Counselor
CDT — Career Development Technician
CDA — Career Development Aide
CW — Case Worker

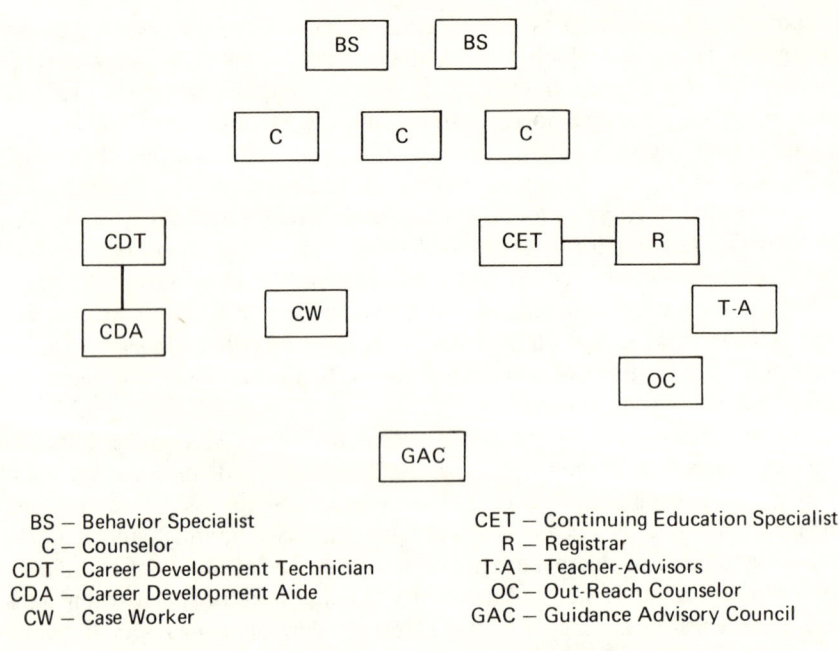

CET — Continuing Education Specialist
R — Registrar
T-A — Teacher-Advisors
OC — Out-Reach Counselor
GAC — Guidance Advisory Council

Figure 3.   *A complete team of guidance specialists.*

school's administrative staff, faculty, and students were briefly stated as the several guidance occupations were presented, readers are urged to visualize the practitioners in Figure 3 as permeating the school program.

Figure 3 also shows an additional guidance component, although it is not a part of guidance team practitioners: the Guidance Advisory Group, comprised of students, community representatives, administrators, teachers, guidance team members, and central office school officials. The regular meetings of this body, illustrated again in occasional schools, such as Annapolis High School, Maryland,[11] provide that kind of force or pressure

[11] The evolution of a guidance team in Annapolis High School, including peer counselors, teacher-advisors, and an advisory group, is the product of a joint field study of which several persons were originators and in which several bodies have participated. Officials of the Ann Arundel County Board of Education, along with Dr. George L. Marx, Chairman of the Department of Counseling and Personnel Services, University of Maryland, and Dr. John Jefferies, then Supervisor of Guidance, Maryland Department of Education, and now Supervisor, Pupil Services, began the project along with Mr. Joseph Mirenzi, then Principal. Other persons too numerous to acknowledge here gave ideas and energy to the project, but particularly deserving of note are Dr. Jane A. Stockdale, now Guidance Consultant, Pennsylvania Department of Education, Drs. Herbert J. Stern and David J. Rhoads, Department of Counseling and Personnel Services, University of Maryland, and Dr. Louis Levin, then a doctoral student, same department. I am grateful to those and other persons associated with

that results in a school, school system, and a community becoming and remaining permeated with and committed to the guidance movement and in the guidance program being a school program.

Parents as Members of the Guidance Team?

What could be the basis for raising *that* question? Is a school's guidance team to have hundreds of members? The answer to the latter question is No, even though this section's title is not without substance. More explanation is in order.

Parents are guidance workers. They have been so for thousands of years longer than formal guidance practitioners have been employed by schools. Surveys of youth show that for many major concerns they have they claim to turn to their parents for help. This section's thrust is that parents can become guidance workers—in their own homes, not in the school—with training. To that end I propose an activity, the value of which has been demonstrated by Shaw and Rector (1968) and which is gaining momentum today. The demand by parents for this kind of training is demonstrated in the success of a commercial program for that purpose, Parent Effectiveness Training (PET).

Medicine again provides the metaphor. Parents could be completely ignorant of health and medical first aid practices, and their children would suffer in consequence. The more parents have by way of formal knowledge about health and about first aid practices, the more their children benefit in both general and specific ways, but also the more likely parents are to use medical specialists when faced with a health problem beyond their capacity. The pay-off is healthier children. For school guidance practitioners to train parents who volunteer to learn about guidance procedures is to increase the probability of benefit to the children. No, parents should not be members of the school's guidance team. Yes, the school can contribute to the guidance effectiveness of parents.

CONSIDERATIONS FOR TRAINING

Whether or not the delivery of guidance services by specialists is considered from the team model described in this chapter, or the counselor-only model common to most high schools today, there is one facet about functions and training of specialists to which attention must be given.

---

the project for the opportunity to know the developments and outcomes of that inquiry. Ann Arundel County, under the leadership of Mrs. Anne Koehler, Supervisor of Guidance, is extending the findings of the Annapolis High School project to other high schools in the county.

Adequate thought about this facet requires that we look again at evolutionary steps in the development of the severally distinct occupations provided by schools under the typical title of "pupil personnel services": counselor, psychologist, and school case worker (a type of social worker).

Two of these occupations, psychologist and social worker, started in response to social needs in nonschool settings and were later borrowed for use in schools. At the outset there were distinctive goals and procedures for each of these two outside occupations, as well as for that occupation that was developed by and in schools, the guidance counselor. Training for each was carried out in three different university departments whose separate existence could be justified then because of the differences in academic discipline and applied methodology characterizing those departments.

If we choose for the moment the date of 1930 for a baseline, we find those disciplinary and methodological distinctions to be quite pronounced in the training departments and in the occupational graduates of those departments. Actually, there was no formal counselor education. Counselors came from the teacher ranks, and thus normal schools and teacher colleges were the source of the discipline and methods of counselors then. This distinction in preparation and function is represented in Figure 4, which shows three discrete occupations. The distinctions of the training and functions of each occupation are illustrated by the area within the broken lines projecting from the top of each rectangle.

If we pick a later period in time, and 1960 will satisfy, examination of the training and functions of the three once-separate occupations can be described with reasonable accuracy by Figure 5.

Figure 5 is an oversimplification and is presented only to establish the general point: there are fewer differences between the three occupations in function and preparation now than is commonly thought. New students in counselor preparation have illustrated that consistently. When asked to

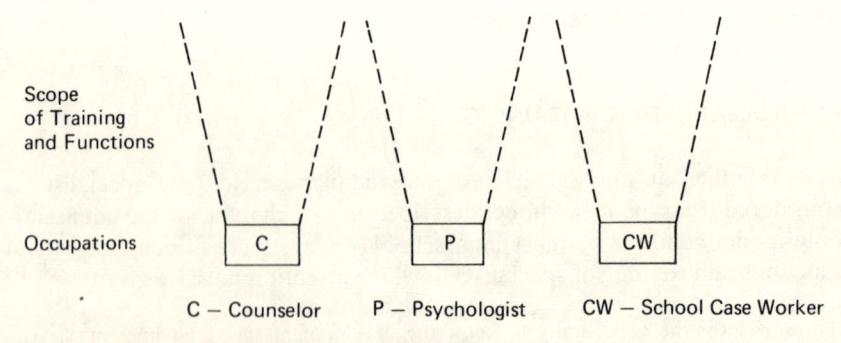

C — Counselor   P — Psychologist   CW — School Case Worker

Figure 4. *Discreteness of early professional training and functions.*

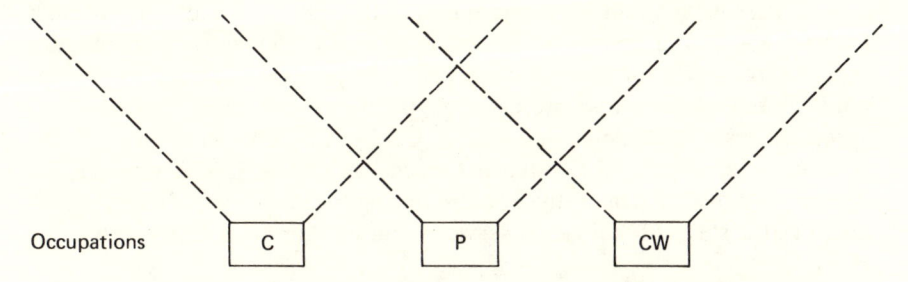

Figure 5. **Present overlap of training and functions of helping professions in the schools.**

write out the differences in training and substance and occupational function among the three occupations, they consistently attribute more uniqueness to each occupation than is the case. In another test of this inaccurate perception, I have presented the course of studies from one school of social work to groups of students, with slight modification of course titles so as to not give precise clues. The task for the audience is the designation of which of the three practitioners, psychologist, counselor, or social worker, was being prepared by this course of study. Their answers typically scatter among the three occupations.

That this last test produces the answers it typically does is a result of the changes in social work curriculums toward including study of the causes of behavior, and thus of how to change behavior, which are topics studied by counselors and psychologists. Psychologists' training has long since moved to consider the social influences on behavior, as is studied by social workers and counselors.

There is a reason why these separately titled but overlapping positions are continued when there is reduced reason for this to occur. Persons in common ventures set up organizations for the preservation and enhancement of that venture, thus the emergence of occupation-based societies. These interest or professional associations are part of the culture of the occupation, and their protecting and enhancing function serves to preserve facts-become-myths. The fact is that psychologists, counselors, and social workers at one time were practitioners of unique occupations; that is more a myth today than a fact. Shaw (1967) tested this by examination of the statements made by the professional associations of school psychologists, counselors, and case workers about the purposes and procedures of their practitioners. He found a preponderance of similarity of statements among the three associations, leading him to wonder whether one practitioner might not be prepared instead of three, at least on the strength of the statements made by the three associations.

Others gave attention to the question through proposals and through field studies of the concept of developing a practitioner for schools, designed particularly for schools, who would be prepared through interdisciplinary studies for cross-professional practice. The child development specialist was one such occupation. Berdie (1972), President of the American Personnel and Guidance Association (1970–1971), studied services as he traveled around the country during his presidency. His examination of the state of guidance services caused him to propose that by 1980,

> instead of having elementary school counselors, junior high school counselors, college counselors, social workers, remedial teachers, school psychologists, child development specialists, rehabilitation and employment counselors, or other such special personnel, that we develop a new profession, not to be added to these others, but rather to displace them.[12]

The proposal that an interdisciplinary practitioner can be prepared to carry out cross-professional functions has been heard with skepticism by some not familiar with the present-day commonalities of preparation and practices among psychologists, counselors, and school case workers. "If it takes 2 years to prepare a counselor (the APGA standard), 2 years to prepare a school psychologist, and 2 years to prepare a social worker (an MSW degree earner), won't it take 6 years to prepare this cross-professional practitioner?" is a typical question. The negative answer results not only from the fact of great overlap among the preparation programs, as noted, but because evidence shows that competence can be trained for in much shorter time than has been the prior assumption, additional evidence having been noted earlier in the discussion of peer counselors.

With a focus now on training as much as on type of practitioner, we can note that college-graduated women seeking employment but not trained in psychological counseling were trained by Rioch, Elkes, and Flint (1965) in a relatively brief program in psychotherapy. Magoon and Golan (1966) evaluated their effectiveness and found they gave credible counseling and psychotherapy services. These practitioners were offered for consideration for school employment, incidentally, but, because there was no teacher certification slot into which to fit them, they were not employed by public schools. The schools' loss was the gain of the mental health clinics and agencies by whom they were employed. The Magoon and Golan findings were later supported by Carkhuff (1968), and the clear conclusion

---

[12] I disagree with Berdie on the inclusion of the child development specialist in a list of "traditional" (my word) occupations. The CDS was developed for elementary schools to do exactly what Berdie calls for: replace a multitude of separate occupations.

from all such investigations is that important clusters of helping behaviors can be adequately learned in a briefer time than is reflected in typical programs and certification requirements.

It is tenable to conclude that the competencies of the behavior specialist and of the counselor, but particularly of the behavior specialist, should be of an interdisciplinary breadth not now common, and that competent levels of professional behaviors can be acquired by other practitioners in briefer times than had been formerly assumed to be required. Two years of preparation can result in a highly competent mental health practitioner and behavior mediator. One year of carefully designed and executed preparation can result in a practitioner whose competence, it is conjectured here, will exceed that emanating from customary 1-year counselor education programs. This conclusion applies not just to the advanced-level practitioners on the new guidance team model examined in this chapter, but also to the preparation of counselors serving in the traditional counselors-only schools.

COMPETENCY AND TRAINING SUMMARY

Because information placed on a table is more likely to be understood than if presented in prose, this information about similarities and differences in the competencies called for in the several guidance occupations and in the preparation programs for them is drawn together in Table 3. Not all possible guidance occupations are shown there, nor are all training topics or purposes, but most of each are.

The instructional advantage of this kind of table is offset by the table's being a less-than-valid portrayal of reality. The reduction of complex natures to one of five numerals, as in the competencies section, or to a brief phrase in the training portion, purchases simplicity at a price about which each of us needs to be cautious.

SUMMARY

At this point in guidance history two generalizations about staffing a guidance program appear warranted. One, some aspects of guidance programs are staffed by persons who are not guidance specialists, and two, there is need for a variety of guidance occupations, not just the single occupation of counselor.

The nature of youth development and concerns, partly reflected in the school's guidance objectives, calls for each high school to have a standard team of three guidance occupations: behavior specialist, counselor, and

Table 3. Competency and training levels, guidance occupations.

Guidance Team Occupations	Occupational and/or Educational Information — Knowledge of	Skill in Group Strategies to Build Behaviors	Psychological Assessment — Knowledge of	Skill in Group Strategies to Cause Students to Know Themselves	Interview Skills	Other Behavior Intervention Skills — Classroom Management Skills	Skill in Group Strategies, Social Competency, and Self-Management Domains	Skill in Removing Excess of or Completing Deficiencies in Coping Behaviors
Peer counselors	0	0	0	0	1	0	0	0
Teacher-advisors	1	0	0	0	1	0	0	0
Field counselors	1	0	0	0	2	0	0	1
Career development technicians	5 (Occnl)	2	0	0	1	0	0	0
Continuing education technicians	5 (Edl)	2	0	0	1	0	0	0
Counselors	3	5	3	5	3	3	3	3
Behavior specialists	2	2	5	2	5	5	5	5

Table 3. (Continued)

Guidance Team Occupations	Education/Training Level Prior to Guidance Preparation	Length of Guidance Preparation	Characteristic of That Preparation	Characteristic Field Experience in Preparation
Peer counselors	10th or 11th grade	6 weeks	Workshop	—
Teacher-advisors	A.B.	6 weeks	Workshop	—
Field counselors	A.B. or less	15 weeks	Workshop	Referral agency visits
Career development technicians	A.B.	6 weeks	Workshop	On-the-job supervision
Continuing education technicians	A.B.	6 weeks	Workshop	On-the-job supervision
Counselors	A.B.	1 year	Graduate school	Study of/in schools 100-hour practicum-internship
Behavior specialists	A.B.	2 years	Graduate school	500+hour internship in schools and other agencies

Competency Level Code: 0 = no competency required; 1 = introductory level; 2, 3 = average; 4, 5 = expert career development technician, by the titles used here. Although there may be some overlap in functions carried out by the practitioners in these three occupations, for the most part the functions associated with each occupation are distinctive.

When assessment of youth needs shows requirement of other occupations to be represented on the guidance team, they might be one or more of these: continuing education technician, teacher-advisor, registrar, out-reach or field counselor, case worker, and, on a temporary basis, peer counselor. As is appropriate for a systems-based structure, the proportion of practitioners among both the standard and complementary guidance team occupations is determined yearly for each school and may change from year to year as assessment of youth characteristics shows the need.

REFERENCES

ANDRADE, B. M. *An Experimental Investigation of the Feasibility of Training High School Students to Conduct Facilitative Interviews with Their Peers.* Unpublished Ph.D. Thesis, University of Maryland, 1972.

ARMSTRONG, J. C. "Perceived Intimate Friendships as a Quasi-therapeutic Agent." *Journal of Counseling Psychology,* 1969, *16,* 137–141.

BERDIE, R. "The 1980 Counselor: Applied Behavioral Scientist." *Personnel Guidance Journal,* 1972, *50,* 443–450.

BROWN, W. F. "Student-to-Student Counseling for Academic Achievement." *Personnel and Guidance Journal,* 1965, *43,* 811–817.

BYRNE, R. H. "For Elementary Schools: A Developmental Specialist?" *Educational Leadership,* 1967, *24,* 349–355.

BYRNE, R. H., "High School Counseling—Conditions for Change." In Margaret Ruth Smith (Ed.), *Guidance–Personnel Work: Future Tense,* New York: Teachers College Press, 1966.

BYRNE, R. H., et al. *Final Report, Elementary School Project.* University Park: University of Maryland, 1968.

CARKHUFF, R. R. "Differential Functioning of Lay and Professional Helpers." *Journal of Counseling Psychology,* 1968, *15,* 117–126.

CARKHUFF, R. R., & BERENSON, B. G. *Beyond Counseling and Therapy.* New York: Holt, Rinehart and Winston, 1967.

DELGIORNO, J. E. "A School for Out-of-School Youth." *Personnel and Guidance Journal,* 1970, *48,* 394–395.

GOLDMAN, L. "Help for the Counselor." *Bulletin of the National Association of Secondary School Principals,* 1967, *51,* 48–53.

HOPPOCK, R., & NOVICK, B. "The Occupational Information Consultant: A New Profession?" *Personnel and Guidance Journal,* 1971, *49,* 555–558.

KATZELL, R. A., KORMAN, A. K., & LEVINE, E. L., "Dynamics of Worker Job Mobility," *Research Report #1*. Washington, D.C.: Social and Rehabilitation Services, U.S. Department of Health, Education, and Welfare, 1970.

LEIBOWITZ, Z. *The Differential Effectiveness of Adult and Adolescent Trainers Using Reinforcement and Nonreinforcement Training Procedures on Social Skill Acquisition Rates of Adolescent Subjects*. Unpublished Ph.D. Dissertation, University of Maryland, 1974.

LEIBOWITZ, Z. & RHOADS, D. J. "Adolescent Peer Counseling." *The School Counselor*, 1974, *21*, 280–284.

LEVINE, L. S., GELATT, H. B., NOWLIN, L. G., LITTELL, W. M., & LAHADERNE, H., "The Use of the Child Development Specialist in the Elementary Schools." *Psychology in the Schools*, 1965, *2*, 3, 255–262.

LOBITZ, W. C. "Maximizing the High School Counselor's Effectiveness: The Use of Senior Tutors." *The School Counselor*, 1970, *18*, 127–128.

MAGOON, T. M., & GOLAN, S. E. "Nontraditionally Trained Women as Mental Health Counselors/Psychotherapists." *Personnel and Guidance Journal*, 1966, *44*, 788–793.

PIERCE-JONES, J., ISCOE, I., & CUNNINGHAM, G., JR. *Child Behavior Consultation in Elementary Schools*. Austin: University of Texas, 1968.

PYLE, R. R., SNYDER, F. A. "Students as Para-professionals at Junior Colleges." *Journal of College Student Personnel*, 1971, *12*, 259–262.

RIOCH, M. J., ELKES, C. & FLINT, A. *A National Institute of Mental Health Pilot Project in Training Mental Health Counselors*. Washington, D.C.: U.S. Department of Health, Education, and Welfare, Public Health Service, 1965.

SEIDMAN, E., et al., "The Child Development Consultant: An Experiment." *The Personnel and Guidance Journal*, 1970, *49*, 29–34.

SHAW, M. C. "Role Delineation among the Guidance Professions." *Psychology in the Schools*, 1967, *4*, 3–13.

SHAW, M. C., & RECTOR, W. H. *Modification of the Learning Environment through Intervention with Significant Adults*. Chico State College, Calif.: Western Regional Center, Interprofessional Research Commission on Pupil Personnel Services, 1968.

STOCKDALE, J. A. *A Study of the Effectiveness of Untrained High School Pupils in Helping Peers Deal with Personal Problems*. Unpublished Ph.D. Thesis, University of Maryland, 1972.

TRUAX, C. B, & LISTER, J. B. "Effectiveness of Counselors and Counselor Aides." *Journal of Counseling Psychology*, 1970, *17*, 331–334.

VARENHORST, B. B. "Training Adolescents as Peer Counselors." *Personnel and Guidance Journal*, 1974, *53*, 4, 271–275.

VREIND, T. J. "High Performing Inner-City Adolescents Assist Low Performing Peers in Counseling Groups." *Personnel and Guidance Journal*, 1974, *47*, 9, 897–903.

WARE, C., & GOLD, B. K. "The Los Angeles City College Peer Counseling Program." OEO/AAJC Report No. 2, The Urban Community College Project Series. Washington, D.C: American Association of Junior Colleges, 1971.

WHITLEY, A. D., & SULZER, B., "Reducing Disruptive Behavior Through Consultation." *Personnel and Guidance Journal,* 1970, *48,* 836–841.

ZERFACE, J. P., & COX, W. H. "School Counselors, Leave Home." *Personnel and Guidance Journal,* 1971, *49* (5), 371–375.

ZETTS, A., BYRNE, R. H., & CRABTREE, J. A. *Student Survey #1, Guidance Appraisal Project.* Gaithersburg, Md.: Gaithersburg High School, 1973. Mimeographed.

ZIMPHER, D., FREDERICKSON, R., SALIM, M., & SANFORD, A. *Support Personnel in School Guidance Programs.* Washington, D.C.: Association for Counselor Education and Supervision (APGA), 1970. Mimeographed.

ZUNKER, V. G., & BROWN, W. F. *Personnel and Guidance Journal,* 1966, *44,* 738–743.

4 Scientific Base of Guidance Technology

INTRODUCTION

This chapter, in effect, backs off the trail followed up to now and begins from a new starting point. The original trail has been moving us closer to an examination of the guidance practices employed to attain guidance goals. Those practices will not be offered in "how to do" fashion only, but, more importantly, as "why to do's." I hold that guidance practices can and must be rooted in principles that have their origin in behavior science, so the undertaking of the next four chapters is to establish those principles before offering a systematic examination of guidance practices.

The mission of Chapters 5 and 6 is to present those behavior principles. Chapter 7 sets out the social settings in which behavior is acquired, because such settings determine a large portion of behavior. Chapter 4's mission is more fundamental. It sets out a basis for judging whether or not any theoretical proposals about the origins, maintenance, and change of behavior qualify for our attention. It provides criteria for making those judgments. It provides the context within which the principles displayed in Chapter 5 must be set, starting off with consideration of the most fundamental topic of all—what theory is. Implicit in this chapter is the notion that a structure of concepts, of ideas, is a system. It is an effective system when the goals are clear, when feedback provides knowledge about the effectiveness of subideas in reaching those goals, and when the ideational system is modified on the basis of that feedback.

THE NEED FOR THEORY

A theory is an accounting for phenomena. The guidance practices of most school counselors, typically the single guidance practitioner up to now, have been based either on no theory, on nonscientific theories, or on a mishmash constituted of pieces of different theories. In contrast, the public health officer, whose array of community duties is similar in structure to the counselor's, has the good fortune to be standing on theoretical bedrock, on a single theory that is the same theory on which other health practitioners carry out their professional functions.

That the school counselor has demonstrated so poor a theory record partly represents the lack of empirically supported behavior theory until recently. Clinical psychologists and psychiatrists have been working within an equally confused theoretical framework. Neither the practitioner nor his preparation programs deserve to be faulted for this undesirable state, for history cannot be hurried. However, when history brings the potential for clearing up the theory mess, it is imperative that we respond with affirmative action.

The lack of disciplinary basis among counselors—their having only homemade, poetic theories to which they could be anchored, if they were anchored at all—has had a negative effect on their professional behaviors. When mediating a student's behaviors in a one-to-one setting, the counselor might engage practices based on one theory, but might turn to practices based on a different accounting of behavior when working with students in other settings. Or more vividly, within the one-to-one activity called counseling, the counselor might have demonstrated differing behaviors reflecting differing theories when meeting with each student. He would have been able to account for these differences in professional behaviors only on the basis of what he felt was the appropriate thing to be doing.

In the past the chronically poor state of the art of behavior mediation could be anticipated by instructors in counselor preparation programs, not just because of the absence of any researched, and thus empirically defensible, theory, but because of the plaints of their students. Not entering students—completing students. Here is a combined summary of these plaints: "I've studied so many theories of counseling, and they all make some sense; I don't know which to follow; I don't know what my counseling (behavior mediation) behaviors should be; my professor says that I must be authentic, I must do my own thing; to which authority should I give my credence, and by so doing, have my professional behaviors informed? Whom shall I believe?"

The need for these disturbances fortunately is behind us, thus we can forego wringing hands about the past, an activity that yields no useful crop.

It is fruitful, however, to attend to what the present and future can be, particularly because that which can be, when actually employed, will eliminate the confusions and nonproductivenesses of the past. This chapter seeks to offer to the prospective guidance practitioner the means for rooting his professional practices in a scientific theory. It does this by equipping the new counselor with criteria by which he can judge theories, thus determine which theory and practices are scientifically tenable from among the variety of theories and technologies he might study. The new student, then, will not be forced to plead for direction and will not need to ask the types of plaintive questions above.

This purpose is engaged by first studying the relationship among three elements: (1) phenomena, (2) theories that explain phenomena, and (3) technologies through which the phenomena are controlled.

THEORY AND TECHNOLOGY

Phenomena are events that occur in any portion of creation. Humans for all history have sought to control phenomena and to make them work for human benefit, including the phenomena of behavior. Said another way, humans have developed, or have continuously sought to develop, techniques to control phenomena. The event called wind is an example, and even though man has not yet been able to control the conditions for producing or eliminating wind, he did develop devices to capture wind so as to use it to run mills and move boats. Later the phenomenon of steam, including its generation, was controlled with even more usefulness to man. Similarly Rogers (1942) developed a technology intended to control the phenomenon of undesired behavior, as the psychoanalysts had done before him.

But man, being the intellectual, curious, creative creature that he is, just could not be satisfied with control or use of natural phenomena. He was and is driven to account for the inherent natures of phenomena, to account for why those phenomena occur, and how they occur. To explain them, in brief. Man knows, moreover, that when he can provide those accountings, he is able to exercise an even greater control over the phenomenon, well-illustrated in that area best described by the cliché, the harnessing of the atom. Those ideas can be condensed into the following list:

1. Phenomena are observed.
2. These phenomena are accounted for—are explained—by a postulate or related postulates, called a theory.
3. Application of the theory to concerns of daily life are made through techniques supplied by the technology that flows out of the theory.

In the relationship between theory and technologies we have noted that sometimes step 3 follows step 1 without step 2. So too does it sometimes occur that step 2 follows step 1 without a technology developing, although that is comparatively rare, and occurs only when a technology is not possible (e.g., controlling celestial bodies) or not needed (e.g., controlling rock formation).

The faulty cosmology of the ancient Greeks was subscribed to in the Western world for over 1,500 years, with techniques for controlling the cosmos neither needed nor possible. We can only guess that, if the ancient Greeks had a pressing need to use cosmological data and a more advanced technology for collecting that data, their faulty cosmology would have been corrected.

The nature of the three-part formula—observed phenomena, accounting, and technology—is testable with a more earthly, though not modern, illustration. In the centuries prior to the Renaissance persons were observed who showed the symptoms we label today as epilepsy. The explanation, the theory? Possession of the person by a demon. What technique of cure does this theory call for? Exorcism. Is exorcism a theory of cure? No, it is a technique of cure based on or stemming from the theory that accounts for the observed phenomenon.

We move to current times and address a similar question. Are there theories of civil engineering? No. Engineering is a technology based on theories, which in turn were developed from observing phenomena. Medicine is a technology based on biological theory, which in turn results from observing biological phenomena.

Behavior mediation practices, either one-to-one (counseling) or in groups, is a technology. Counseling behaviors are man-made technologies, like engineering technologies. There are no natural phenomena that have occurred for which a counseling *theory* is generated, thus counseling theory is a misnomer. There are phenomena that occur, human behaviors, that are accounted for by theories of behavior. The application of these theories to the day-by-day world requires technologies, which are man-made. One technology is counseling. There have been different groups of counseling techniques because there have been different theories of behavior, resulting in confused counseling preparation and practice. That is the problem attacked in this chapter.

The varying clusters of behavior mediation techniques, each a technology, instead of being called theories of counseling, are better called schools of counseling, in the parlance common to science in the Western world. Based on this use, the word "school" is also used to designate an institution where a technology is learned, thus schools of medicine and education, with the word "school" being part of the title (capitalized). In the case of a certain technology, say, homeopathic medicine, one is schooled in this medical practice in School A. To learn (be schooled in) allopathic techniques, a student must go to School B. School C, another hypothetical school of medicine, would do well to not hire graduates of both Schools A and B, for that way lies chaos for School C and its students, analogous to staffing the faculty of a new school of theology with Moslems, Jews, and Christians.

Translated into counselor preparation, there are some schools of counseling that teach a single theory of behavior, but, on the other hand, the faculties of a number of counselor preparation departments are staffed by graduates of schools in which theory and technique M are learned, by others who are graduates of programs where theory and technique N are propagated, and in the same department by still others from O-oriented schools. The inevitable result is confused students, those who must plead, "To whom shall I listen? Each of those theories and techniques sounds plausible; which should I follow?"

Not only are different technologies taught in single departments, but there are also taught a variety of theories on which those technologies rest, usually under the label "theories of personality." The difficulty will be compounded by the professor's effort at theoretical neutrality in teaching those theories, one that results in equal emphasis given to each position, as if each were an equally valid representation of the real world. The resultant confusion may be more vividly portrayed in this hypothetical figure.

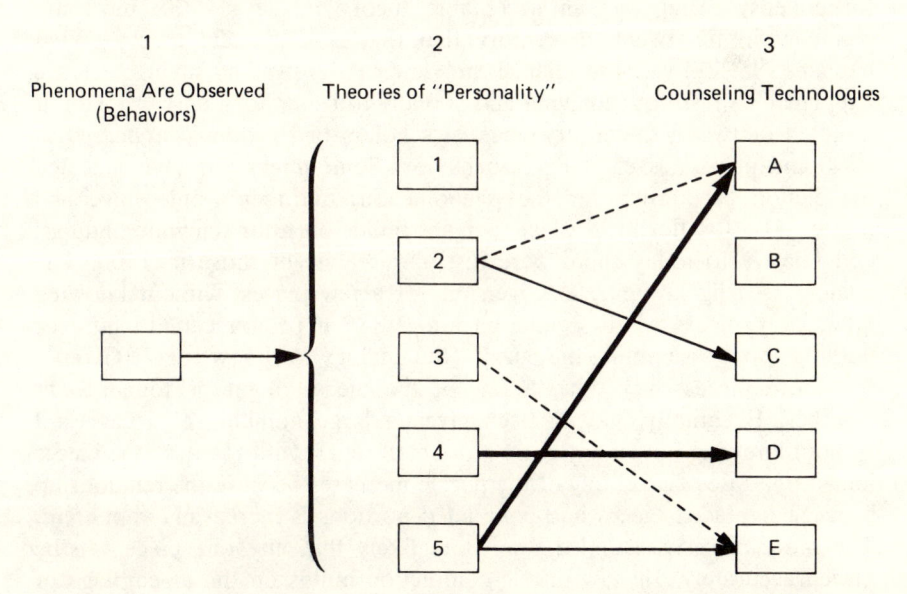

Figure 6. *Potential relationships between phenomena, theories, and technologies.*

Figure 6 intends to show that some theories, such as 1, do not lead to a technology, some technologies have no theory, illustrated by B, and some theories result in technologies that overlap with the technologies of other theories, as 5, A, and E. A variety of other vaguenesses and confusions is possible, but is not illustrated in the figure. The hope for this text in general and this chapter in particular is represented by the next figure.

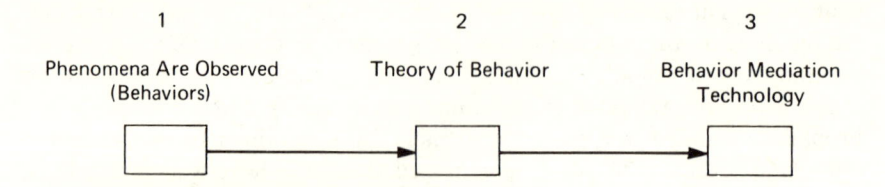

```
       1                           2                          3
Phenomena Are Observed      Theory of Behavior         Behavior Mediation
     (Behaviors)                                           Technology
    ┌─────────┐              ┌─────────┐                 ┌─────────┐
    │         │─────────────▶│         │────────────────▶│         │
    └─────────┘              └─────────┘                 └─────────┘
```

This lofty goal is next pursued by considering the characteristics of scientific theories, producing criteria that the new student can apply to the variety of theoretical materials he studies.

CHARACTERISTICS OF SCIENTIFIC THEORIES

An earlier illustration noted possession by a demon as an accounting for epilepsy. That was an acceptable theory in, say, 1400; most are confident in the twentieth century that that is an invalid theory. What happened in 500 years to change the view? To answer by saying "science happened" is just not satisfying and is really too simple an answer. What if a clutch of twentieth-century scientist scholars had suddenly appeared in 1400 and puzzled over epileptic behavior? Some might not have accepted the demon accounting for the phenomenon, but they would have had nothing else to offer in its place. Science builds on prior scientific findings, and relative to today there were just about none of those in 1400. The analogy is a jig-saw puzzle. Given one or a few pieces, without knowing how many pieces there should be altogether, a person can do little or nothing about assembling the puzzle (the analogy for knowledge). Given a few more pieces over time, a few of the pieces might be found to fit together. Eventually, having been given a large number of pieces (still without knowing how many there will be all told), with many of the pieces joined, the rate of assembly of the puzzle increases because the relationship between unplaced pieces and completed portions is increasingly apparent. The more pieces assembled, the more likely that any one piece can be placed accurately. Jig-saw puzzle completion builds on the assemblage of ever-larger portions of the puzzle. In 1400 there would have been no "pieces" of biological knowledge to build on, and in consequence scientists of that time could not counter the demon explanation for epilepsy with a tenable theory. There were no prior scientific findings (puzzle pieces) available for cues.

What those "instant" scientists would have said about the demon explanation, however, would have been in accord with the nature of modern scientific theory. They would have said, "We must submit this accounting (theory) to proof—to the test."[1] They would have thus engaged in the characteristic scientific behavior of controlled experimentation.

Proof and the Evolution of Theories

Why are new theories currently being generated and older theories being revised? Have we not long since observed and accounted for all existing phenomena? No. We are continuously observing new phenomena as a result of our improved techniques and thus must modify our theories. Older theories not only can be revised, but are revised because they need to be as a result of proofs, or because occasionally a creative thinker—Einstein, for example—develops an entirely new way of accounting for phenomena. The scientific theory of behavior has been even more recently expanded to a relatively complete accounting. Has it the validity of the demon theory? How can we know? Proof is the major answer.

The Ptolemaic accounting (theory) for the motion of celestial bodies (observed phenomenon) was accepted universally in the Western world for many centuries. Then Copernicus, holding that the Ptolemaic theory was an insult to God, thought out a different accounting. For about a half-century these two theories could attract and retain followers only on a logical basis because there was no way to test, to prove, either theory. Then Galileo developed the telescope and proofs of the two cosmologies could proceed. The proofs were positive for the Copernican theory and negative for the Ptolemaic. If a different theorist had proposed that a mysterious force, Wug, to which he alone had been introduced, was significant as an explanation of the observed phenomena, he might have gained followers because there are always persons around who will believe the most preposterous things. As with the explanation of demons for epilepsy, however, that proposal would be outside the pale of science because the hypothesized mysterious force known only to the proposer cannot be tested.

[1] "Proof," meaning test, is misused by the person-in-the-street. For him "proof," which might result in either negative or positive results in science, typically means only positive results. "This is a proven product" claims the advertiser, knowing that the average reader or listener will think that the product has shown its merit. The proof (test) indeed might have shown negative results. There can be proof positive and proof negative.

Orgone is one example of a Wug of the twentieth century in the area of behavior.

Because testing is central in science, one characteristic of a scientific theory is that it accounts for phenomena only with testable constructs. I anticipate a bit by asking you to ponder the testability of the constructs id, mind, self (other than body), and personality.

Testable constructs and adequate instrumentation permit validation of a theory. Once a theory's postulates have been validated, should not they now be called laws? Should not theory mean as-yet unvalidated postulates that account for a phenomenon? Persons-in-the-street, again, often hold to the latter view. And the same might be said for a parallel group, teachers-in-the-classroom. There is a phrase that has been stated for years, typically about proposals for teacher practices as made by professors in schools of education: "That's just theory. Don't expect it to work in your classroom." Or, "He has been out of the classroom for so long that he only knows theory and wouldn't know how to handle a class." The intentions of those statements may be correct, but their use of the word "theory" is not.

Usually a theory is comprised of a number of related postulates, some of which have been validated, others of which have not been thoroughly proved. Scientists are generally cautious about using the word "law" even for the validated portions of theories. The history of science in certain areas produced in the early days of that history that array of postulates that at that time seemed to be the final accounting for the observed phenomena only to find that tidy applecart upset a short time later. Thus today theory may connote three modes of assurance: (1) laws; (2) an accounting as yet completely untested; or more likely (3) an accounting, part of which is validated, and part of which is still either inadequately tested or metaphorical.

THEORIES "WORK." That the idea that theory is ivory-towered dreaming far removed from practice is commonly held does not make it any the less invalid. The single intention of scientific theory is to provide workable practices—to permit control of phenomena. In the early stage of development of a theory, an applied technology might not yet have been developed, as in the early days of nuclear physics, but because the theory was stated so that it could be proved bit by bit, it eventually resulted in mankind's most magnificent demonstration of control of phenomena. The more validated a theory, the more practical it is.

In fact some professors in schools of education are not scientists and might generate hypotheses about practice that are not couched in theory and are not tested. Only then would the experienced teacher in a course taught by that professor be justified in muttering to an experienced student,

"Don't pay any attention to that; that's just theory—it won't work in the classroom." On the other hand, the teacher who says theory doesn't work is wrong.

BEWARE THE ENSNARING METAPHOR. In building a theory a scientist might have to lean temporarily on metaphor, on the "as if" type of statement. The temporary usefulness of metaphors is that they help fill in a crude map for exploration, a basis for making tests (proofs) of a theory. Early atomic theory, early modern, not the ancient Grecian atomic theory of Democritus, was postulated around the metaphor (and analogy) that an atom is structured *as if* it were a solar system. Physicists now know that atomic structure is not like a solar system's. Having set up the metaphor, however, permitted certain "if . . . then" statements to be made that could be tested, the "if . . . then" statements being subportions of the main thesis, or in the Greek term, hypotheses. Continuous testing of hypotheses leads to proofs positive and negative, and slowly a theory's postulates are either given further credibility or are discredited. If one or two key postulates of a theory must be rejected, then the entire theory may have to be rejected, but, if not, at least considerably reworked.

One difficulty the new student faces is the metaphorical statement from which the "as if" phrase has been eliminated. When the poet states that the sky was latticed by the webs spun by Aeolian spiders, a reader might enjoy the imagery, but it is not expected that the reader will be moved to look for spiders in the sky or to view certain forms of cirrus clouds as being real spider webs. When the scientist or nonscientist leaves the "as if" phrase out of a statement, the new student is faced with a metaphor having been changed into a theoretical postulate that apparently should be accepted literally. "He is *as if* possessed by a demon" is a patently different statement from "He is possessed by a demon." We know the first statement is poetic, that is, metaphorical; the "as if" makes that clear. The second statement might have been intended as poetry, but, if that intention is not otherwise made clear, and if the person making the statement is revered or is otherwise possessed of attributes of authority, one should expect the statement to be accepted by some naïve persons as literally true.

An excellent example of metaphor gone mad is the much used hydraulic reference, which views the human as comprised of a variety of reservoirs. These references are most common in the behavior technology area and appear to have psychoanalytic origins. Note the gist of this statement: "He has a large pool of hostility that must be drained off before therapy can truly begin." Hostility thus conceptually becomes a thing, which it must be if it is supposed to have a fluid nature that permits draining off or out of the person.

The hydraulic figure represents more than metaphor; it illustrates analogy, although the distinction between metaphor and analogy are not agreed upon, not sharply delineated. The figure allows us to examine in more detail a pair of characteristics that may mark a theory: analogies and homologies. The characteristics of each of these are also not agreed upon by those who use them. Many use the word "analogy" only because they do not make a distinction for which two terms are needed and use analogy and metaphor interchangeably.

For those using both analogy and homology, an analogy describes the *relationship* of elements in one phenomenon by saying that that relationship is like or even identical with the relationship between elements of another phenomenon. Metaphors point out identities between things; analogies point out identities of relationships between the things of phenomenon X and phenomenon Y. In the hydraulic illustration, "pool" is a metaphor for "hostility," and that kind of metaphor permits the draining analogy, it describes the relationship among "things." In that statement hostility has been reified, that is, made a "thing."

For some persons use of the word "analogy" covers all classes of relationships. Others, however, distinguish between surface, apparent, nonsubstantive similarities of relationships on the one hand, calling these analogies, and on the other hand similarities of relationships that go beyond the surface or apparent. These latter would be similarities of the laws or substance between the relationships in phenomenon X and phenomenon Y in addition to similarities of an apparent or surface nature. Von Bertalanffy (1968) holds that "analogies are scientifically worthless. Homologies, in contrast often present valuable models" (p. 84). He sees analogies as meaningless resemblances, "superficial similarities of phenomena which correspond neither in their causal factors nor in their relevant laws" (p. 84). Homologies, on the other hand, may present different efficient factors, "but the respective laws are formally identical" (p. 84).

The comparison of atomic structure with a solar system used metaphors. Did it also present an analogy or a homology? When first offered it might have been meant as an analogy by some who acknowledged that the laws undergirding atomic structure were inadequately known. Other persons, however, may have meant that there was not only a surface similarity between atomic structure and a solar system, but that the same laws controlled the motion of the elements, that is, controlled the relationship among elements. Those speakers would have intended a homology, not an analogy.

Indeed a substantive point of this volume is offered as a homology: systems theory. The systems nature of physical phenomenon has been identified for many decades. The question to be asked about social phenomena, about institutions, is whether they only *appear* to have a relationship among elements similar to the relationships among elements of physical phenomena, or do social institutions behave more substantively like physical phenomena? In my view social systems are homologies of physical systems, not just analogies.

One damaging analogy, assumed by the naïve to be a homology, is the proposition that the medical model, which works for physiological functions, is an equally valid way to describe behavior. This analogy, which also contains metaphor and hypothetical constructs, states that certain external appearances of the body are to unsensed systemic states as certain behaviors are to "inner" psychological dynamics. For example, certain appearances of eyes and other externals express the inner or hidden medical condition of diabetes just as certain behaviors, such as hitting or speaking aggressively are the symptoms of an inner or hidden state of some unresolved psychological complex brought forward from childhood, or of a "pool" of hostility. The functional significance of this inaccurate analogy is that just as you do not treat the eyes of the diabetic but the essential diabetes itself, so you do not treat noticeable behaviors; these are merely "symptoms" of a buried or hidden complex, and thus you must treat the complex itself. The prevalence of this medical model until recently may account for the poor rate of cure among those technologies based on it. The hypothetical construct (the complex) and the metaphor (pool) have no operational or empirical referents. They cannot be tested. The analogy has not attained, and I propose cannot attain, status as a homology.

Use of metaphors and analogies does not necessarily mean sloppy theorizing. The solar system illustration from nuclear physics demonstrates the converse. But conceptualizing and dealing with the atom *as if* it were a solar system was to borrow, for dealing with the atom, an already validated theory, a law, an established accounting from another field. That is good metaphor and good use of metaphor in development of theory. This use is defensible in science; such metaphors can be tested in a new field of inquiry. Look, now, at a different kind of use of metaphor, not defensible in science, a fictional example that is also an analogy.

For this hypothetical illustration we must go back 2,000 years. Picture yourself as a Greek sage in ancient Athens. A trusting youth comes to you with a question neither you nor anyone has entertained before. The youth asks you how the sun goes around the earth. What would be the logic that leads you to an answer that was, in fact, actually given and accepted for centuries?

Your logic starts with the fact of motion and the likelihood that the sun has some weight. Now you ask yourself, how do we Athenians carry materials from one place to another? Well, slowly on slaves' backs, or more rapidly either by chariot or cart. But since the sun is a substance in the sky, it must be within the province of the gods. Gods, like superior mortals, do not ride in carts, let alone carry anything; they ride in chariots. The sun, therefore, must be carried around the earth in a chariot, which, needing a driver, would have to be driven by a god. Lacking one, you create one and name him Helios. Thus you account for a natural phenomenon, but with a theory which is not only completely a metaphor, but one that cannot be tested. In science that is bad metaphor. Good poetry and workable theology, but bad science.

It was noted earlier that some use the term "metaphor" to refer to a thing, a process, or both. The Greek accounting for the passage of the sun around the earth illustrates both uses. One modern and common use of metaphor to explain a process is found in the term "brainwashing," and it is not only persons-in-the-street who use the phrase quite seriously. Since the early 1970s there has been a spate of use of this term to describe youths who converted to a form of Christianity of which their parents disapproved. The youths were brainwashed, was the cry, and a person of national fame was and still is employed by some parents to restore their children "to their right senses."

From this and other uses of the metaphorical phrase "brainwashed" we find the important connotation of the term. If a person changes so as to act or think like I do, then he has "come to his senses." If the person moves in the opposite direction, he had been brainwashed. The term was first employed and attained its prominence in the Korean War to describe U.S. soldiers who were prisoners of the North Koreans, and who later wrote and spoke against the United States and for the North Koreans. Brainwashing was the metaphorical way of accounting for this change, because it was undesirable. We did not hear about North Korean prisoners of the United States who converted to our side, but, if there were any, then we could expect the report to be that they "came to their senses," or finally "saw the light."

Psychoanalytic accountings for human behavior are replete with metaphor and analogy. For example, certain behaviors exist in persons as if seeds (metaphor) lying latent (analogy) but under proper conditions for emergence, sprout out, thus become patent instead of latent.

BEWARE ANOTHER RUBBER CRUTCH. Beware also the untestable hypothetical construct. A hypothetical construct is a fabrication of the intellect (intellect is itself a hypothetical construct) to fill a void in a theory when no metaphor is available or because no metaphor could convey the concept needed by the theorist. The testable hypothetical construct can be as useful to the theory builder as the testable metaphor. It is the untestable hypothetical construct, the one without identifiable "empirical referents" (Marx, 1963, p. 31) that the prospective guidance worker must learn to identify as the soft spot in a theory. Phlogiston (remember?) long served as hypothetical construct in the theory of fire. It was discarded because it did not stand up under proof.

In original usage, "demons" is a hypothetical construct. It permitted ancient, unscientific humans to account for (to provide a tenable theory for) some human behavior and had theological support in all societies. The construct of demon is bad from a scientific standpoint because it is untestable. It was accepted for centuries by many—an expression of the "fifty million Frenchmen can't be wrong" fallacy—and still is accepted by many. It is not a testable construct.

Whether or not theories include hypothetical constructs seems to depend partly on personal variables of the proposers. Some persons are comfortable with an accounting for phenomena that includes only what has been established by proof positive, and nothing more. Others find it useful to gingerly propose hypothetical constructs to temporarily fill in the gaps in the theory, but expect promptly to engage research around those constructs. Still others seem to propose constructs simply because, unlike the first kind of person, these persons need a gestalt, a complete picture. They are uncomfortable by saying, in effect, "this is all that is known, and for now I am content with just that much."

Early cartography illustrates. In each society, hundreds of years ago, portions of the earth's topography were known. One mapmaker would be contented to record only what was known, and beyond that to mark the unknown areas as just that, *terra* or *mares incognita*. Other mapmakers, however, filled in what was unknown by hypothetical constructs of those areas and gave those areas equally hypothetically constructed creatures to inhabit them. These latter needed to show the complete world, including, for some, the elephants on whose backs the earth rested.

A hypothetical construct can be used metaphorically: "You are a demon," which translates as, "I accept as valid the hypothetical construct of demons, and you behave *as if* you were a demon." An invalid hypothetical construct makes an invalid metaphor, but it does not follow that a valid (testable, tenable) hypothetical construct makes a valid metaphor. "Atom" is a hypothetical construct, a valid, useful one. When would it not be validly used as metaphor? An illustration of that would be if someone were to hypothesize that intellect is an atom ("as if" an atom), with a nucleus and other atomic components. A good hypothetical construct would thus be badly used as metaphor.

What of id, mind, self (not the physical body), personality—how do they measure up as testable hypothetical constructs, as ideas that have "empirical referents"? Poorly, and thus they are not good science, and when borrowed for any theory, they are bad metaphor.

A particular danger of hypothetical constructs and metaphors, good or bad, is that of "reification"—making "things" of them, as if they really were things. Mind, for example, is a hypothetical construct that serves a useful, informal communication purpose, such as in, "I will keep that statement in mind because it may be on an examination soon." But, being untestable, mind is an undesirable hypothetical construct for use in the science of behavior.

When some persons who use the word "mind" have been challenged, they have responded that by "mind" they mean the brain. The counter to that is that there is already a word with most precise common meaning, so why use as synonym a word with such ambiguity? The cortex of the brain behaves electrochemically so that the human, as a result of that action, emits symbols, vocally and subvocally. Mind may be all right for the describing word for the person-in-the-street, but not for science or applied scientists.

Culture has made persons-in-the-street into dualists; they accept as fact that there is a "thing" that is called mind, and another "thing" for which the label is body. When persons-in-the-street prepare as counselors, however, it may be expected that they would no longer behave dualistically as a result of their training. But this is not necessarily so. Not when they will be studying in courses labeled Mental Hygiene or Mental Health. If mind is not a thing, only a poor hypothetical construct, then health cannot be mental. In fact that term has inhibited accurate thinking and actions about human behavior for a long time. It is a term also kept alive by medical groups, thus letting those groups claim behavior (which is social) as their professional domain as well as the body. But, of course, behavior cannot be the modifier of health because behavior illness or behavior health would be too bizarre a term, thus the construct of mind must be retained, so that medicine can claim jurisdiction over mental illness.

DON'T FALL INTO SYNECDOCHE—THE BLIND MAN'S BLUFF. Five blind men who had never before heard about or had any concept of the elephant were brought to one.[2] One felt a leg and announced that the elephant is like a tree trunk (an excellent use of a metaphor; scientifically valid too, because it would be testable). Another, feeling the trunk, announced that the elephant was like a snake, and so on for all five persons, each of whom felt a different portion of the elephant's anatomy, and drew a conclusion about the animal's nature from his perception of only that part.

I change the story and report that the blind men said, "the elephant is a tree trunk," and so on (leaving off the "as if" phrase, or its equivalent, "like"), and that is *synecdoche,* the blind men's error. No one who reads this new report about the elephant could know whether each implied a metaphor or meant literally what was said. That's bad science too—not

[2] In my days of childhood everyone knew this fable. It is astonishing to me that usually no more than 5 percent of graduate students have heard the story of The Five Blind Men.

making clear what is meant, but that is one of the risky characteristics of metaphors and hypothetical constructs.

The error, obviously, is in the fact that each reports a part as if it were the whole, synecdoche being the rhetorical name for that incorrect practice. The only valid blind man's report would be that which said, "I do not know all that an elephant is, but, for that part which I have explored, it is like a tree trunk. What else it may be like, and what that portion that seems to me like a tree truck really is, I cannot say. Also I wish to ask my fellow blind brothers what they have found." It is a good fable for us, because behavioral scientists are like (are "as if") blind men, no one of whom can ever see the whole element of behavior, thus must piece out the whole by sharing of ideas and research.

To whom do we listen? To those who carefully explore, use metaphors and hypothetical constructs only for temporary purposes, and only testable ones at that. They do not claim that the portion they have discovered is all there is to be described, and are eager to have other "blind men" compare notes about their exploration with them. For years, and even today, some counselors-to-be have been and are told in authoritative fashion in texts and by professors in training programs that self-concept is the cause of behavior. Stating that one part is indeed the whole thing would not only be synecdoche at best, and that is bad, but would be untenable as science because self-concept is an untestable hypothetical construct.

The meaning and danger of synecdoche are further tested by examining a different area of technology. To do this a fictional situation is first set up. Imagine that you have moved recently to a new place, and one of your children becomes quite ill. You have not yet acquired a healer for your family ("healer" will be used for a while as a neutral term), so you ask your neighbor, who has given other helpful suggestions and who has children of the same age as yours, to which healer he goes with sick children. The neighbor provides the information, and you go to that person with your sick child.

But wait a minute. In Western societies there are at least five major technologies about healing, each based on a different accounting of the cause of illness, therefore of the cure. The observed phenomenon is illness. Five theories are established to account for illness. Five technologies perforce ensue. Have you asked your neighbor which accounting (theory) is held by the referred healer, and thus which technology he will use? When addressing this hypothetical question to mature adults who are graduate students, the response is often wonderment, and the reply, "I just thought doctors were doctos!" For all that that statement represents ignorance of medicine, the fact is that some healers to which a large number of intelligent, well-educated persons go may not be called "doctor."

Among those who may be legally so titled, however, do you, as the person in the fictional predicament, ask whether the person practices medicine on the theory of homeopathy, allopathy, or osteopathy? Those three theories yield different technologies of medicine (although this story is weakened by the fact that over years the distinctions among them have lessened, for reasons that *are* important to this story). Those three labels take care of three of the "at least five" technologies. The other two? Chiropractic medicine is one, with some states permitting its practitioners to assume the title "doctor." But there is yet another healer, who does not use M.D., O.D., or D.C. after his name, but uses instead C.S.P.: the Christian Science Practitioner.

Without extending the fictional situation further, you can see that knowing which kind of healer your neighbor recommends does make a difference. For the thrust of this section, which has been attending to partial explanations for phenomena, it is to be noted that chiropractic, homeopathy, and osteopathy are synecdoches; that is, they account for the whole of illness with partial explanations. Christian Science practice is not a synecdoche; it is a wide perimeter theory, an all-encompassing theory, but despite its title, not scientific in the way that term is commonly used.

Attend to the allopath, because allopathy is to medicine as behavior principles are to counseling. Allopathic procedures seek the most complete description of the nature of illness, the one form of health practice based on a theory that is both parametric and scientific. It is ready to employ in its technology any procedure that produces the desired effect, a cure. In the past decade, for example, a team of allopaths studied the folk medicine practices of African tribes to find out what works. As scientists, of course, they sought out the precise cures and were able to eliminate the peripheral, noncuring properties of the treatment. A herb put into the mouth of an ill person brought to the medicine man, for example, is studied for its curative powers and then can be synthesized. The kind of mask and the dance form also used during the treatment would be found to be noncurative in a biochemical sense. They might, in fact, have considerable placebo effect for members of a particular tribe, but might have an opposite effect in our society.

Take the issue raised by the fable of the blind men and translate it to the concern new counselors face as recorded at the opening of this chapter: "Whom shall I follow; to whom shall I listen?" Let it be hypothesized that a student finds that person A, a counselor educator of some renown, has postulated that behavior is changed by doing M. The naïve student finds the propositions A writes about to be plausible, and that the evidence of effectiveness provided seems to be substantial. Therefore, concludes the new student, perhaps I am an Aian (a follower of A). We hypothesize further that the new student had short supply of those skills needed to see that A is saying, in effect, "Tree trunk is a complete and sufficient description of what an elephant is." The goal of this chapter can now be restated in different words: to provide the new student of counseling with some of the knowledge needed to make critical analyses of the multiplicity of statements, technologies, and (incorrectly labeled) counseling theories with which he is faced. One of those analytic competencies is the capacity to discern partial from complete theories, particularly when the partial theory is assumed to be a complete theory. Related to counseling, these are theories of behavior.

Philosophical Bases of Behavior Theories

It is a point of fascination to me that among the sciences only behavior theory faces a philosophical issue, one that the new student of behavior mediation must resolve for himself. When this fundamental issue is resolved for each new student other issues will fall more readily in line and be far more easily resolved. We confront this issue with two long questions.

Is anything you observe in the world really out there, whether you know it or not; does it exist objectively; does it have a structure that can be verified through scientific procedures and that can be known by all persons? Don't answer yet. Wait until the corollary but opposing question is posed. And that is, is it correct to say that "all any person can know is the everchanging impressions, images, and ideas of which he is aware; that he has no evidence, and cannot possibly obtain any evidence that there are external objects and events corresponding to, and causing his mental content" (Schell & Daubner, 1969, p. 508)?

The counseling student who recalls his knowledge of philosophy recognizes two extreme, basic philosophical positions reflected in those two questions. The first of these positions, labeled realism, postulates the existence of an objective world, discoverable and organizable, whether or not any person knows that reality. The second question connotes the second philosophical position, that of idealism. This position, in purest form, postulates a subjectivism that lets the knower know only "that there are shifting impressions, images, and ideas, and that there is an awareness of them which appears to be continuously connected with what he calls 'himself' " (Schnell & Daubner, 1969, p. 508).

So how do you answer those questions? A "Yes" to one means a "No" to the other. Or perhaps you cannot answer. Perhaps you never entertained any questions of this order, but, being faced with them here, align yourself promptly and quickly with the realists.

That would be no surprise. As an aside I wonder how many persons today, and of which categories, such as sex, education, or nationality, are either realists or idealists in such pure forms. How interesting if we had data reporting the distribution of the educated populace between these two, for each century since A.D. 1400. It is tenable to expect a massive increase in the proportion of realists following the Renaissance. Peruse any school text with the challenge to find any statement that even raises the question. To the contrary, school texts in general and particularly science texts, operate from the realist position.

The issue? To repeat it—behavior is the only scholarly area whose theories face realism versus idealism as an active issue, an issue that contributes to the confusion experienced by the neophyte student. It is the basic reason why there have been more than one accounting for behavior.

Yet the lines have been too strongly drawn here, as suggested by the words "extreme" and "in purest form." There are persons who see epistemological truth falling so as to encompass some elements of idealism along with realism, and some of those are persons who write about and practice counseling.

Those who espouse an idealist position as a counseling base, the phenomenologists, are not pure idealists, as a review of their writings shows. They readily acknowledge the existence of a reality—of a world "out there"—but minimize its importance, particularly as a cause of behavior. A number of those persons who present counseling "truths" from a realist perspective also postulate that a person's perceptions of the real world are important in behavior causes. They are thus saying that the inner functionings of the person, the subjective element, is an additional variable to be dealt with in counseling.

It is a matter of emphasis. "I am a Democrat who happens to believe that there is too much permissiveness in our society, fiscal irresponsibility relative to public funds, and not enough of the old-time virtues." "I am a Republican who happens to believe that our federal government must do more for the poor and must exercise greater control over the actions of massive corporations." A Democrat talking partly like a Republican, and vice versa. Just as there are conservative Democrats and liberal Republicans, there are realists with some phenomenological (idealistic) leanings, and idealists who attend to the objective world. Sometimes a Democrat becomes so conservative that he jumps the party fence. Sometimes a person who started as a idealist, faced as he might be with newer ideas and by research, jumps the philosophical fence into realism. I started as a realist, slid, rather than jumped, into being more of a phenomenologist—a fairly pure form of idealism—but have in recent years returned to my philosophical home base, realism. But I continue to see the need for counseling to include an individual's perceptions, under certain conditions.[3]

---

[3] Hitt (1969) examined this issue of behaviorism and phenomenology. One of his four conclusions is that there "appears to be truth in both views of man" (p. 657), a view that apparently accords with the view expressed here, that behavior principles applied to counseling not only do not require abrogation of phenomenological concepts, but indeed may require phenomenological technologies as a portion of behavior-based technologies.

OTHER EPISTEMOLOGICAL ISSUES. Realism versus idealism is one kind of epistemological question, epistemology being that portion of philosophy concerned with the question of what can be known, and how we know what we know.[4]

Further epistemological elements can be teased out by going again to cosmology. In that area of inquiry we are now asked, does the earth go around the sun (is our universe heliocentric), or does the sun go around the earth (a geocentric universe)? You and I answer affirmatively to the first question; we know that the earth rotates around the sun. How do we know that? Have we carried out proofs? Have we read the scientific reports? Indeed, how can we know the heliocentric position to be a fact when it is quite apparent to any person who looks that the sun rotates around the earth? Indeed, there is none among us who has not asked about or described a sunrise or sunset, phrases that show that we must know that the sun rotates around the earth.

But what is "knowing"? An ability to restate what I have heard, as Plato describes it? Doesn't knowing mean more than restatement? More than the ability to provide an explanation on the basis of empirical evidence? If we hold to the latter, then we speak in favor of science as the basis of knowing, which, of course, accords with the word "science" anyhow (L. *sciere* = to know).

There are four modal origins of what one knows, three of which have dangerous fallacies potential in them.

1. Experience. This produces the experience-is-the-best-teacher fallacy. I have read no history of astronomy that reports what the person-in-the-street said for many years after Copernicus' theory was proved positive, but it is easy to conjecture that such persons knew that Copernicus' theory had to be wrong because it went against experience. "Any fool can see that the sun goes around the earth!"

2. Authority of individuals *qua* individuals, which can result in the mommy-knows-best error. Children are taught that parents know, and the behaviors acquired in response to parents generalize to other classes of adults, such as teachers and religious leaders, even to all older persons. The practitioner of counseling synecdoche and the willing or unwilling new

---

[4] The word "idealism" may draw readers off into other meanings than the epistemological one appropriate for this chapter. Most of us will associate the word with "ideal." However, in its epistemological sense, particularly when paired with the word "realism," idealism is best associated with yet another form of the word, idea, and the correct form of the word is idealism. Idealism, then, in purest form (Mach, Pearson, Kant, Spencer) is a word which states that to know phenomena is to have *ideas* about reality, but only ideas; true reality cannot be known. "Between us and reality there is a wall of partition which no thinking man can ever penetrate" (Leighton, 1918). This is almost a complex topic, for which I stake no claim of expertise. It is a critical variable in an analysis of theories and practice, however, so it must be confronted by those of us interested in mediating behavior.

counseling technology guru can become with equal ease the "expert authority" whose statements are those which anyone of us can "know."

It is recalled that one of the new counselor's concerns is about which authority or expert he is to follow from among the numerous ones to which he has been exposed. For this concern Bertrand Russell had sage words: "(1) when experts are agreed, the opposite opinion cannot be certain; (2) *when they are not agreed, no opinion can be regarded as certain by a nonexpert* [emphasis added]; and (3) when they all hold that no sufficient grounds for a positive opinion exists, the ordinary man would do well to suspend judgment." Yet we must be cautious about the quality of the empirical evidence supporting ideas on which experts agree. For hundreds of years experts were in agreement about the correctness of the Ptolemaic cosmology.

3. Authority of groups, even more powerful than that of individuals, the essence of the 50-million-Frenchmen-can't-be-wrong fallacy. I might "know" for a while as a child that the earth is flat (I can make the Platonic restatement) having been so informed as a child by my parents, but as I live in the community that knows otherwise, I come to "unknown" that the earth is flat and come to know that it is globular. However, my parents, wishing me to retain the knowledge of the earth's flatness, might cause the family to live among only those persons who also know of the earth's flatness and might cause me to attend a school where that idea is propagated, among other approved but uncommon ideas. And this is the nature of culture, the common knowledge of a group and its efforts, even unto death, to retain that knowledge. The group can be an even more powerful authority than any individual in the group.

We know that the earth rotates around the sun, rather than vice versa, and contrary to our experience. How do we know that? We have been told so, first by individuals (parents, teachers), then by all members of the group in which we live. Most of us accept that fact solely on authority. But is it really true? Are the mommy-knows-best and the 50-million-Frenchmen fallacies operating, causing us to deny what our experience tells us?

4. Science is the fourth general source of knowing. It is the seeker of truth and accuracy and many times finds itself in direct and violent opposition to the dogmas of individuals and groups and contrary to individual experience. And it is science that lets you and me know that the earth rotates around the sun, and in fact most of us can at least loosely cite the proofs. Moreover, the Copernican theory has been demonstrated again and again in techniques of such massive complexity and interrelatedness that holding to any other view is just not possible for educated persons. On the other hand, there are those citizens of this country who "know" that no persons have landed on the moon; their cosmologies make that an impossibility.

That which the new counseling student must first study is how man comes to know anything and whether what does come to be known is adequately validated knowledge. The new student starts with epistemology and then moves to philosophy of science. Next he studies accountings of behavior, that is, *theories* of behavior. For this step, however, the adequately prepared student is equipped with the necessary armamentarium to criticize single postulates or groups of interrelated postulates and to identify the scientific theory from among the nonscientific. The student will be able to identify the metaphors, both the defensible ones (those already validated within field X and now borrowed temporarily for field Y but which are testable within field Y), and the poetic ones, those that never can be tested. He will note the hypothetical constructs and will accord credence to those deserving of it and withhold it from those that propose some equivalent of Wug, or those used for political purposes.

The student is then able to avoid the error of the five blind men and also will know to take the precaution of asking to be lashed to the mast while sailing within sight and sound of that deadly Siren, the guru, whether self-proclaimed or set up by the populace. After sailing through the sea of books, the rivers of journal articles, and having avoided Siren Shoals and blind Man's Reef, the student sails serenely into the safe harbor of a scientific accounting for observed behavioral phenomena (metaphor, trope, and simile galore there!). The subsequent technology to be acquired then is a relatively simple undertaking. The outcome: a guidance practitioner who does not need to wonder, "Whom shall I believe; what shall I do?" It is an outcome not as easily achieved as written about. For many it can be an outcome purchased only by the pain of unlearning (Feibelman's theory of unlearning [1955] merits detailed study).

Theological Bases of Behavior Theories

The science of behavior is not only beset with the fundamental philosophical conflict just examined, it also must face strong competition from theological theories about behavior.

Some sciences, such as geology and astronomy, had theological accountings for their phenomena before there were sciences, but they long since have moved away from the theologically based folklore that was their mark in prescientific days. Today a number of persons in Western culture hold that the earth is a few thousand years old, but the number who hold that the earth is the center of the universe is almost nonexistent. Those two "knowledges" were common for centuries in Western culture. Indeed, in Zion, Illinois, a few decades ago there was dispute about school texts that proposed that the earth was globular, which was contrary to what those particular citizens of Zion "knew," having been so informed by their theology.

Although certain tenets about the earth's age and its central position in the universe seemed to be axial to some theological systems, those systems were not shattered by surrendering those beliefs to science's documentations. Theologies concern themselves with mankind's relationship with God, and that concern is not vitiated if a theology has to abandon long-held tenets about the physical nature of the universe. Two hundred years after forcing Galileo to recant, the Roman Church accepted the Copernican cosmology as valid.

It appears that in this day religious leaders do not discourse about geology and astronomy from their pulpits, but they often do discourse about behavior, quite assertively, as is appropriate in view of the central concern of theology. And there are more persons in this nation who listen to religious leaders regularly than who study the science of behavior.

Thus the statement: the science of behavior has strong competition from theological positions about behavior among a great mass of persons. Look at this additional complication: no student entering the formal study of geology or astronomy enters that study with an array of metaphorical beliefs, reified hypothetical constructs, and theologically based assumptions about that area. Persons who enter the formal study of behavior do bring such arrays with them. They come to such study with such scientifically bad hypothetical constructs as free will, mind, and even the intervention of demons in behavior.

If they came to the study of geology with the conviction that the earth is a few thousand years old, they would face the need to resolve the conflict by either withdrawing from geology or by accepting their earlier beliefs as erroneous. But that confrontation doesn't happen; students generally do not enter geology with dissonant beliefs. Some students, however, do bring to the study of counseling a strongly entrenched parcel of beliefs about behavior—theological, unscientific theories that account for why humans behave in whatever way they do. Just another complication for those new students of counseling.[5]

[5] I have a vivid recollection of an event that occurred almost a quarter of a century ago. I was one of a panel of four persons speaking before a local professional association on the topic "My Philosophy of Counseling." One of the panel members was a nationally known teacher of behavior intervention theory and procedures who was also a clergyman. He readily observed that his science was often in disagreement with his church's teachings and that this presented severe conflicts for him. Another scientist and practitioner, a Conservative Jew, commented in a different setting that he had no difficulty in reconciling the accounting of creation as recorded in Genesis, on the one hand, and the geological and biological evidences about the earth's age on the other, because he interpreted "day" in Genesis to be a figure of speech, meaning an unknown period of time—each "day" perhaps being millions of years. Christian groups are ever in conflict between a strict and absolute reading of the Bible, each word meaning what it says, on the one hand (fundamentalists), and an interpretive reading, similar to the analysis of Genesis given by the Conservative Jew. Why and how persons come to live comfortably with different psychosocial ecosystems, when those ecosystems hold opposing views, can be explained by behavior principles.

FIRST SUMMARY

Four somewhat overlapping areas for the new student to attend to in evaluating what authorities say about counseling have been examined. They will be recapitulated now, but in a different order from that in which they were presented.

First, a theory of behavior and the technology that flows from it must be based on the philosophical base of realism. If humans are to control their own behavior, or assist others in doing so, it must be because all behavior is nomogenic and because there is a real world that is knowable.

Second, any technology proposed is rooted in a theory, and any workable theory about behavior has a technology. The postulates of the theory will not require metaphor, but, if they do, the metaphors will be few, will be clear as being metaphors, and their temporary function in the theory will be stated or implicitly understood. Hypothetical constructs will be avoided; but if they must be used, they will be few in number, will be identified as hypothetical constructs, will implicitly or explicitly be temporary within the theory, and most important, will have empirical referents.

Third, epistemologically the theory will not only be realistic, but it will have been developed from within the principles of the philosophy of science. The postulates of the theory will have been tested by the scientific community, and such proving will continue and be publicly reported.

Fourth, in order to merit our credence, the theory's postulates, if not parametric in scope, must at least be set in a context that covers all behavior. The array of postulates will be examined particularly to ascertain that the error of synecdoche is not committed, or that the proposed technology is not offered as applicable to all behavior mediation needs, whereas in fact it is tenable for only certain persons under certain conditions.

CHARACTERISTICS OF SCIENTISTS AND OF SCIENCE

Reverse the topic, as if looking at the other side of a coin. Instead of looking at characteristics of theories we examine characteristics of persons who develop theories. In what contexts and from what assumptions do such persons function; how do they behave?

Answers to these questions have been scattered through portions of the material above, or connoted there, but now answers must be drawn together. Let the focus first be put on the scientist, with the characteristics of scientists defined around four topics.

EDUCATION. The scientist has the greatest amount of formal education his field provides, or is working toward that level, and the essence of that education is experimental research and theory development.

ASSUMPTIONS. The scientist is a skeptic, needing to doubt even his own work to some degree. He works from no base of assumptions about the nature of nature except those that have been validated by other sciences. Scientists can be religious persons, but often are unchurched because church membership would call for acceptance of dogmas about the nature of nature that either are contrary to what the scientist knows, or that oppose the questing nature of scientific inquiry. These difficulties in church membership might befall the behavioral scientist more than others for reasons noted earlier.[6]

RESEARCH. The scientist spends a major portion of his professional functions in theory development and proof.

COMMUNITY MEMBERSHIP. In his experimentation, the scientist never works alone. He may be alone physically, perhaps, but he is always in written contact with other scientists through publication in scientific journals and in oral contact through local, regional, national, and international associations. This point, incidentally, is demonstrated in a fascinating fashion by the communications between U.S. and Soviet astronomers not only during World War II, but during the Cold War that followed. Politicians will wage wars, but some scientists will remain above wars and will continue basic research and maintain communications with other nonpolitical scientists in other countries.

Speaking to the main thrust of this section is the observation by Stevens (1963) that the work of scientists leads to propositions, and "only those propositions based upon operations which are public and repeatable are admitted to the body of science" (p. 53). Publication and paper reading, plus informal communications, among members of a scientific community meet at least the "public" criterion. The repeatability of a finding depends on the accuracy of the concepts and operations carried out by the scientist who is reporting.

---

[6] In my scattered knowledge of scientists I know that most were and are not those who prefer to describe themselves as atheists, or, in the Soviet sense, antitheists. Were that so, I would find that puzzling. Mankind deals with countless constructs and concepts, but only one that defies understanding: infinity. The answer to the question, "What is time/space/infinity?" has to be in the supernatural realm. It appears to me, therefore, that any person who entertains that question cannot escape acknowledgment of the supernatural, whether identified by the commonly used term "God" or however labeled.

Scientists and theory are inextricable. Scientists develop and test theories, and theories inform scientists, determining the direction of their experiments.

Theory and the Characteristics of Science

Scientists need theories in their work, and scientists behave professionally in accord with the principles of science. Theory, scientists, and the procedures of science are unitary, although it may be useful instructionally to examine each as a separate topic. But having said much about theory and scientists to this point, it likely suffices to say in sum that science is a procedure of controlled observations that are publicly reported, at least to the science community, the members of which test whether or not a given accounting for phenomena—a theory—is a valid accounting for those phenomena. Science, in sum, is conjectural, objective, scholarly, public.

Applied in unitary fashion, the characteristics of theory, science, and scientists form criteria by which the neophyte interventionist can sort out the position he should take. The stance to be taken regarding behavior mediation, the persons to be followed as those speaking the closest approximation of truth are identified by matching propositions and persons against these criteria.

ECLECTICISM AHEAD! ENTER AT YOUR PERIL. New Student: "I've just been studying what X, Y, and Z say about counseling, and each of them makes very good sense, even though their propositions conflict in numerous ways. Until I am competent to judge what is scientific and what is not, why shouldn't I use some of what X, Y, and Z say?" And, if the student has the word in his vocabulary, he might sum up with the challenge, "What's wrong with electicism?"

There are several kinds of eclecticism, and certain times when eclecticism is good. One undesirable form is ignorant eclecticism. Actually the adjective describes the characteristics of persons who engage in that type of eclecticism and not to the inherent properties of eclecticism itself.

Ignorant eclecticism can be specified through an analogy. We set the time as 1600 and refer to a hypothetical person named Ignosticus. When asked about the scientific cosmology he holds, Ignosticus states that he holds to the new Copernican concept of a heliocentric universe (thus demonstrating that he is "with it" in his journal reading), that he likes the Plutarchian concept of planet revolutions in circles (that's part of the cosmology on which he was brought up, and it is comfortable to have links to the past), and that a goddess, Diana, has influence on the actions of the moon (this appeals to his romantic nature). Being ignorant, despite occasional journal dipping, Ignosticus is unaware that the first two parts of his cosmology are incompatible and that the third part is mythology and is thus outside the pale of science and therefore has no place in a scientific cosmology. Had he really studied Copernicus' full theory, he would have found that it accounted for almost all cosmological phenomena, and that as a solid, parametric cosmology it had an attribute of any good theory: it prohibited certain other explanations. Copernicus' theory, as modified by Kepler, for example, makes planet motion in concentric circles an impossibility.

But can eclecticism be "good"? Yes, when there has been demonstrated that a new *technology* is effective, although the technology has not yet been set within a theoretical framework, one is nonetheless wise to use that technology. A primitive technology often precedes a science in an area, chemistry, for example, or engineering, but also behavior mediation. How any primitive technology is explained, however, is crucial for our consideration. Supposing new phenomenon X is observed in nature as a byproduct of some simple operation a person was carrying out. Oxygen was discovered somewhat like that, but let's deal with a hypothetical X for a bit. Let's say now that one person, A, discovered phenomenon X at the same time as person B also discovered it. Both A and B could merely state that X occurs, and not try to explain why, but human nature being as it is, it is unlikely that A or B would merely report the phenomenon without explanation.

Person A is a dilletante, who in his playing around discovered phenomenon X. But B represents a history of scholarly effort in the area within which X was discovered and, as a scholar, had long published results in his studies and had been in continuous communication with other scholars in the field. Who is in a better position to account for phenomenon X? Person B's accounting can be expected to hold more weight in the scientific community than A's.

But back to eclecticism. It may be correct to say that the usefulness of technique X is demonstrated, but an explanation of why it is useful, why X works, has not yet been published. So too with techniques Y and Z. X, Y, and Z work. They perform. They let applied practitioners do things. In the absence of all-inclusive (parametric) theories, that is, lacking a series of interrelated propositions or postulations to account for X, for Y, and for Z, the wise practitioner says, in effect, "I will use each of these three technologies when I judge that each is appropriate for the outcome I wish to attain." That is good eclecticism.

In the course of time, however, explanations of techniques X, Y, and Z are developed. The explanations for X are from within the scientific (scholarly) community; that is (and to repeat), they have been developed under conditions wherein findings and accountings are put to severe proof, published among other scholars, and thus proved again and again by other scholars. The explanations about Y and Z, however, are in terms that do not permit research, even though those proposing technologies Y and Z may publish their ideas. Techniques Y and Z, along with their explanations, remain the property of the individuals who proposed them and are labeled with their names. How eclectic should a practitioner now be? If the practitioner is prepared for his practice by study in a scientific community, the practitioner will come to see that one theory is the best scientific accounting and that it does indeed account not only for technique X, but also that techniques Y and Z can be explained in terms of the theory scientifically developed for technique X. The practitioner uses techniques X, Y, and Z, but is he therefore being eclectic? No. Another hypothetical illustration may show why not.

For this fantasy let us imagine that person M, just playing around, developed a magnet. At the same time person N, who has devoted his life to scholarly inquiry, has discovered the fundamental properties of electricity. Person M accounts for his magnetic metal bar by proposing that a mysterious force, Gez, is operating in the metal bar and says that Gez is the same force that pulls the souls of dead persons up into heaven or down into hell. Person N pursues his discovery of electricity and, based on previous scientific inquiry, accounts for electricity through the concept of electrons and their flow, with negative and positive charges. Person N, in our fantasy, has not yet addressed himself to magnetism.

Typically, any of us learns about the technological applications of M and N's work before learning of any theories offered as explanation. Thus we use magnets, and we use electrical flow, and indeed we, the uninformed appliers of technology, do not see any connection between magnetism and electricity, an understandable ignorance. We use both technologies because they work, and this is good eclecticism.

As N develops his theory of electricity, however, we can see that N's theory also accounts for magnetism. We still use magnets, and indeed by now N has come to use magnets to generate electricity, but we are no longer being eclectic, because we need not be. One theory is scientific, so we are rooted in that theory even though we will use technologies that were originally developed in a subjective, nonscientific way. But when we use the technology of magnets, we do not thereby give credence to M's proposition that magnets work because of Gez, on the one hand, and electricity works on simple, natural principles on the other. We account for magnetism in scientific terms. We are not being eclectic. When medical science adopts a technique from folk medicine, it is being pragmatic, not eclectic. It is also being scientific in that the folk medicine is analyzed for the reasons for its effectiveness, and then its effectiveness is accounted for in scientific terms.

SECOND SUMMARY

The first summary stressed four criteria for the new student to use in evaluating theories and technologies: (1) theory and its technology must be philosophically based on realism; (2) technologies must be rooted in theory, and the theory must not use metaphor or hypothetical constructs except under very controlled conditions; (3) to merit our credence any theory must meet all criteria of science; and (4) the error of synecdoche must not be committed by the theory or by a technology.

Between that summary and here two points have been made: (1) an imperative for theory is that it not include theological or other untestable assumptions; and (2) in resolving the theory/technology confusion that the new student might face, eclecticism must be recognized as risky business and until one is adept in theory analysis, is best shunned.

TAKING THE MEASURE OF BEHAVIOR THEORIES

The student of today is far better off than the student of 10 years ago. Then and for all times prior there were no findings of a parametric science of behavior to inform the student. Eclecticism was one route for the student of those days to follow, of course. More likely he learned about the variety of parascientific positions regarding behavior, common then and still prevalent, studied technologies stemming from those positions, and was told by professors to take his choice. After naming the several arrays of positions available to a student in 1954, Bernstein (1954, p. 33) stated that prospective behavior mediators "must choose the system which makes the strongest *appeal to their convictions, their experiences, and their personalities* [emphasis added]." For Bernstein, the chief instrument of behavior change was the behavior changer as a person, instead of any technologies stemming from scientifically tested propositions about behavior. The prime need of the neophyte counselor, Bernstein proposed, was self-knowledge, because "failure to acquire such self-knowledge means that the counselor will have to operate blindly" (p. 33).

Bernstein's admonitions are no longer valid. "Doing one's own thing" in the area of counseling is not only no longer necessary, it is no longer defensible, when empirically established principles of behavior are available to the new student of counseling.

As a conclusion we practice a bit of all that has gone before as a demonstration of what each student needs to do as part of his preparation activities. We apply as criteria some of the principles developed earlier to ascertain whether certain collections of propositions (theories) of behavior, and/or technologies of behavior mediation meet these tests of science. For this test we examine and apply our criteria to two theories and technologies that have had historical appeal to many in the area of behavior mediation: psychoanalytic views of behavior and phenomenonogical-perceptive (self-concept) views. Two proposers of note in each of the two areas are Freud and Rogers.

First, are these theories solidly rooted in the philosophical base of realism? Neither is. The phenomenological-perceptive position emphatically is not so.

Second, are metaphor and hypothetical constructs eschewed or used, if at all, in minor, temporary ways? No, both theories have metaphor and hypothetical constructs as the central framework, not temporarily, but permanently. The hypothetical constructs do not have empirical referents.

Third, do these theories meet the criteria of philosophy of science? Are they empirically supported by controlled experiment? No. Could they be? No.

Fourth, are they true parametric theories, or is either a synecdoche appearing to account for all behavior? The psychoanalytic position is comprehensive, but the perceptual-phenomenological is a synecdoche.

For a theory to fail any one of those criteria must cause doubts about its merit. If more than one criterion is not met, the theory and its technology do not earn our further attention.

Because adeptness in theory analysis is important for prospective guidance practitioners, an analysis of these two theories will be undertaken in a bit more detail. To this end we pose further tests in question form, the first asking: were these persons who accounted for their observations of human behavior, and who proposed a technology, operating from within the scientific approach to the study of behavior? Our answer is no. Each was an individual who in his own work observed natural phenomena and tried a technology. The technology worked in some cases. Each eventually proposed an accounting for these phenomena and thus for the workability of the technology. When Freud did his early publications, the scientific study of behavior was in its infancy and in many ways was not further advanced when Rogers shook the behavior mediation world in 1942.

We apply a second new test: has the scientific community, now well-established in the behavior field, accepted the postulations of these two original intellects and tested them? No, they are not testable. Did either of the two proposers carry out systematic research? No. Has *any* research gone on about them? Yes, but only at a technological, and therefore, assumptive level. No research establishes the postulates as valid, but then again how can the postulates be proven positive when they include metaphor and hypothetical constructs that have never attained substance?

If the psychoanalytic and perceptual-phenomenological theories are nonscientific, does that mean that their technologies must be abandoned? Not necessarily. Scientific approaches to human behavior and its mediation can account for the instances wherein the technologies of these two systems have been effective.

Take, for example, Freud's useful construct of defense mechanisms. He artfully described these behaviors and labeled them. Do we summarily reject them because they are the product of a nonscientist? No, defense mechanisms are still alive and doing well within the scientific community. The difference today is that they can now be accounted for by behavioral principles (Tucker, 1970) instead of merely describing what happens. Perceptual-phenomenological procedures are used in extinguishing anxieties and phobias and, as will be noted in Chapter 5, in helping a student to assess his coping needs. Also recall our fantasy about M and N, one of whom discovered magnetism, while the other discovered electricity. If M had only described magnetic behavior without offering an accounting for that phenomenon, N eventually would have accounted for it by scientifically determined principles. Person M, however, did account for the magnetic phenomenon by the hypothetical construct of Gez. The scientist can accept the fact of magnetic behavior without according any validity to Gez. For the scientific community to accept some of Freud's (and other related proposers') descriptions does not put the scientists in the position of "blessing" psychoanalytic accountings.

Pick any theorist about behavior or any person who proposes a technology of behavior intervention. Start by testing whether that person is working from a basis of realism and within the scientific (experimental, knowledge-accumulating) community or whether his proposals are made from a basis of private, solo observations. Ask other kinds of questions like those above. Save the last question as the best test: can the nonscientific, solo proposer's propositions be as well or better accounted for by the findings that come from the scientific community's findings about behavior and its mediation? You will be pleasantly surprised by the results.

A science of behavior has been marked out, has laid out the major benchmarks, and has mapped much of the terrain, all within recent years. The science of behavior is now filling in the gaps of knowledge, the last pieces of the jigsaw puzzle are being placed, to mix the metaphors. What is occurring now in behavior science was attained earlier in other sciences, what Kuhn (1962) calls a mopping-up operation. Learning to use the principles of behavior as the road map for pursuit of technical knowledge and skills is the first requirement of the prospective behavior mediator.

When they are fixed, and the technologies that flow from them learned, the prospective behavior interventionist will do well to study the history in this area so as to have the appropriate context for his knowledge and skills. Just as the physician-to-be, who never deviates in his study from learning the findings of science, studies the parascientific history of medicine—for historical and context purposes, but not because the body of pre- and nonscientific knowledge in medicine should be learned seriously for current applications. The workable from the pre- and nonscientific areas of medicine will have long since been studied by the medical scientists, proven positive or negative, and the outcomes of such proofs accounted for in scientific terms.

The ultimate issue posed within the pages of this chapter is whether or not the prospective guidance practitioner goes with science or nonscience. Or, if with science, then with just a fragment of science, or with the science of behavior in its full parameters. Those who manage going even with a fragment of empirically supported precepts will be able to expand to cover the full field. Those who enter the study of behavior with previous (probably unconscious) commitment to the philosophical position of idealism will be faced with challenges. Probably all students will be faced with some conflicts, because most of the nonscientific positions about behavior that students will read or hear of are the products of fine, persuasive persons, often ensconced in positions of high status, with trappings of prestige, and given popular adulation. There have been, and likely still are, more nonscientists in the behavior theory and mediation technology areas than scientists, thus the fragile student may be susceptible to the force of numbers, the 50-million Frenchmen false criterion mentioned earlier. A large number of persons makes a critical mass, and the force of numbers is difficult to counter. Accepting and defending a theory is not required in other applied areas, but it is in the behavior area. The task might be easy if the new student can quickly decide whether he goes with science or nonscience.

THIRD SUMMARY

Guidance technology can now be based on scientific findings. This has not been the case until the last few years of the history of the guidance movement. Competing with that science-based technology are pre-and parascientific propositions that still have much currency. The new student of guidance can discriminate among the welter of theories and technologies by applying to them the criteria that characterize science and the corollary criteria marking scientists.

The criterion questions to ascertain that the postulates of a theory are scientific are:

1. Is the theory based on realism and the philosophy of science?
2. Does the theory stand without use of metaphor, analogy, and hypothetical constructs? If any is used, are the metaphors and analogies borrowed from empirically based propositions, and do hypothetical constructs have empirical referents? Does the theory avoid untestable assumptions?
3. Is the theory parametric? If not, do its postulates avoid the error of synecdoche?
4. Is the theory one that has been studied from within a community of critical scientists and under systematic proving with public report of the proofs' outcomes?

Most portions of most theories undergirding guidance practices cannot pass muster against those criteria, thus can make no claim on the allegiance of guidance practitioners. Behavioral science has uncovered principles that prove out positively against those criteria, and it is those principles that constitute the footing for the guidance technologies reported later in this text. Chapter 5 explains those principles, and Chapter 6 elaborates on them.

REFERENCES

BARCLAY, J. *Counseling and Philosophy: A Theoretical Exposition.* Boston: Houghton Mifflin, 1968. Guidance Monograph Series II: Counseling.

BERNSTEIN, A. *On the Nature of Psychotherapy.* Doubleday Papers in Psychology No. 12. Garden City, N.Y.: Doubleday, 1954.

FEIBELMAN, J. K. "An Ontological Philosophy of Education." In N. B. Henry (Ed.), *NSSE Yearbook,* Part 1. Chicago: University of Chicago Press, 1955.

HITT, W. D. "Two Models of Man." *The American Psychologist,* 1969, 24, 651–658.

KUHN, T. S. *The Structure of Scientific Revolutions.* Chicago: University of Chicago Press, 1962.

LEIGHTON, J. A. *The Field of Philosophy.* New York: D. Appleton-Century, 1918.

MARX, M. H. *Theories in Contemporary Psychology.* New York: Macmillan, 1963.

ROGERS, C. R. *Counseling and Psychotherapy.* Boston: Houghton Mifflin, 1942.

SCHELL, E., & DAUBNER, E. "Epistemology and School Counseling." *Personnel and Guidance Journal,* 1969, 47 (6) 506–513.

STEVENS, S. S. "Operationism and Logical Positivism." In M. H. Marx (Ed.), *Theories in Contemporary Psychology*. New York: Macmillan, 1963.

TUCKER, I. F. *Adjustment Models and Mechanisms*. New York: Academic Press, 1970.

VON BERTALANFFY, L. *General Systems Theory*. New York: George Braziller, 1968.

5 Principles of Behavior

INTRODUCTION

Guidance specialists, in working to attain guidance objectives, are called on to mediate others' behaviors. The prospective guidance practitioner, therefore, needs to know the principles that account for the way behaviors are acquired and maintained and are thus also to be mediated (changed).

The substance of this chapter is a partial review of what you learned if you recently studied courses under titles such as Introduction to Psychology, Social Psychology, and Applied Psychology. The word "recently" is important and is defined as within the past 10 years, so great has been the mass of recent research. The need for recent study is compounded by the fact that courses, like textbooks, sometimes lag behind the accumulating evidences. If you have not engaged an Introduction to Psychology course recently, perhaps even ever, let alone some of the other courses mentioned, this chapter will not be an adequate substitute, and there will be a need to assess whether or not you should engage more extensive study of this topic than the scant treatment afforded by this chapter.

Subsequent chapters describe a variety of procedures carried out by the specialists on the guidance team, thus the significance for guidance practice of each topic of this chapter receives only terse treatment. Because the detailed guidance procedures that begin in Chapter 8 are based on behavior principles, however, a prior brief review of such principles is needed. The concepts, terms, and procedures that are used in this and other chapters are common among behavioral scientists, but not universal. The nature of this text does not allow examination of other positions, but the student of behaviors does need to examine them sometime.

Behavior principles are examined here first by noting in some detail the active nature of humans and the role that activity has in making learning possible. Activity permits respondent and operant conditioning to occur, two principles to be examined briefly, and these result in turn in the person's acquisition of a symbol system that mediates a person's behavior increasingly with age.

STIMULATION, ACTIVITY, AND BEHAVIOR DEVELOPMENT

The substance of this planet may be divided into nonliving and living materials. Living matter is cast along a continuum marked at one end by simple reactive matter, that is, the controlling variables over the life of such matter come from outside it, spore-bearing plants as an example. Toward the other end of the continuum we find complex proactive/reactive organisms, but the end of the continuum is occupied solely by humans. The human not only reacts to external stimuli, but initiates activity, although the human's first activities are random and purposeless. Through the symbol system that the human acquires, he learns to activate purposely, be proactive, and thus to use and modify the ecosystems into which he becomes locked by the chance of birth. Some of a person's behaviors are rewarded by some ecosystems he operates in, are unrewarded or even punished by others, and, of course, can be both rewarded and punished by a single ecosystem.[1] The adult human, through the agency of his symbol system, selects the ecosystems in which he will live, seeking pleasurable systems and avoiding painful ones. This latter statement, incidentally, is one quick way to speak of occupational choices: that is, selection from among the array of those occupation-centered ecosystems of that one type of occupation that is the key feature of a rewarding or pleasurable ecosystem for that particular human.

Personality

Each youth and adult is identified by behaviors that occur again and again. In common parlance these behaviors constitute a person's personality. Guidance team members typically are not interested in producing some

---

[1] The term "ecosystem" conveys some subtleties beyond the term "social system." Those connotations are dealt with in Chapter 7 where they properly belong. For dealing with this chapter, if the term "ecosystems" has little meaning for you, I suggest your substitution of the term "social system" whenever you come across it.

global description of an individual, therefore they are not interested in a construct labeled "personality." They are interested in specific patterns of behavior and in the specific patterns of stimuli that maintain those behaviors.

Individuals act in the main in specific rather than global terms; so it is, then, that the help a youth seeks, or a common developmental need identified by adults, is for establishing or changing a specific behavior or pattern of behaviors. Even if a guidance specialist did employ the construct "personality," and sought to change personality, he could not do so by some global approach to the person, but by changing specific psychomotor behaviors and cognitions of which a personality is constituted.

An additional reason why the guidance specialist does not find the construct of personality to be a useful one is that for many persons that term connotes an integrated organization of behaviors. In fact persons acquire behaviors and behavior patterns that conflict; that is, one stimulus pattern can elicit two conflicting patterns of behavior, an experience within all of our histories. Or one stimulus pattern elicits one behavior pattern one time and a conflicting pattern another time. If the construct and term "personality" could be used at all, it could not be used in singular number. A person has several personalities, not just one. In Chapter 6 an additional reason for not using the construct "personality" is given.

Infant Activity

At the outset of life the human is more reactive than proactive and is completely dependent on others for his existence. The infant's activity produces responses in other humans, and these responses in turn start to shape behaviors in the infant. Other events occur in the infant and child's life that establish and maintain behavior. These shaping responses and other behavior-establishing events are examined in the sections of this chapter that treat respondent and operant conditioning, followed by the section that deals with the cognitive or symbol system the human acquires, under the control of which so much of his behavior eventually comes. In this section, although occasional reference is made to respondent and operant conditioning and to the symbol system, our attention is on activity. Without activity, there could be no behaviors acquired, thus the topic of human activity acquires the need for brief separate examination.

Adults can say of infants, and, of course, of other humans, that they are active because adults can see, hear, and feel the infant be active. If a person-in-the-street asked, "Why are humans active?" an answer that "they are born that way" would probably suffice. For the applied behavioral scientist the answer is a bit more technical: the infant is stimulated by internal/external forces or drives, and the first responses to relatively internal stimuli are called arousal. In infants the internal states that arouse are physiological imbalances that have been labeled hunger and thirst. The aroused states from these stimuli produce responses to the infant from adults, and the infant is thus embarked on a life of acquiring instrumental (operant) behaviors, with some such behaviors persisting for an entire lifetime. Other behaviors, even if not persisting in their original form, affect whether and how other behaviors will be established and maintained. To repeat the theme of this section, in order for a human to acquire behaviors, he has to do something; that is, he must emit behaviors, he must be active. The rewarding or pleasing qualities of the response to the infant's activity determines which behaviors will become fixed (established) and which extinguished, and that process is called operant or instrumental conditioning. In addition, the human acquires other behaviors, or emotional colorations to behaviors, from human interaction and from sources other than the responses of others, through a process called respondent conditioning. In fact, respondent and operant conditioning more typically interact to form behaviors rather than function as separate influences.

The infant or child whose aroused states are not adequately attended to, or who is deprived of those many other nurturing behaviors summed up in the phrase "tender, loving care," can become withdrawn, or, in terms of this section, inactive. With reduced activity, the infant or young child is not acquiring useful behaviors, and indeed the ultimate effect might be death. If not that ultimate outcome, the result can be at least a state of slowness in acquiring behaviors for which the summing word "retarded" is used. In older children, differences in social systems in which they live relative to the external stimuli those systems provide have a less obvious but nonetheless highly significant effect on behavior establishment, a point expanded in Chapter 7 through description of maximum and minimum experience families.

Fondling is one form of stimulation for the infant, and how much and for how long an infant is fondled can have lifetime significance. One reason is that fondling apparently contributes to the development of the myelin sheath that must cover nerves and is not fully developed at birth. Incidentally, the quantity and quality of physical contact, culturally determined, is important for other behaviors and for a person's sense of well-being when older. Some behavior specialists conclude that the no-contact strictures of some subcultures of European origin in this country, as observed in a note at the end of Chapter 7, lead to deficient behaviors in some adults who are products of those subcultures. Those behavior specialists counter this "don't touch" behavior, which they hold to be unnatural and unhealthy, with a variety of deliberate physical contact activities in groups.

The combination of all stimulations for infants results in later behavior differences. Levine (as quoted by Tucker, 1970) reports that, in experiments he carried out on young animals, he found stimulated animals to be less timid, more aggressive as adults, and able to learn faster to avoid aversive stimuli than animals who were not stimulated when young. Moreover, "stimulation in infancy results in the capacity of the organism to respond more effectively to its environment: to exhibit an appropriate and motivating emotional response to threat and a diminished emotional response to novel stimuli" (Tucker, 1970, pp. 52–53). Levine is then quoted as holding that "tactile and kinesthetic stimulations in early infancy are crucial to the production of later individual differences in response to stress." The amount and kind of fondling, then, is but one of countless contingencies under which early behaviors are acquired, which in turn affect the learning of other behaviors.

Later in life, symbols acquire excitation or stimulus properties. This symbolic behavior is most frequently verbal, but still or moving pictures become a far more potent stimulus, a fact long known, as conveyed in the ancient observation that a picture is worth a thousand words. A verbal description of a natural catastrophe or some destructive event, like murder, can excite responses to which a person learns to attach labels. A still picture might elicit the same feelings as those stimulated by words, only at a more intense level, but a moving picture likely causes greater stimulation. Add music, assuming conditioned responses have been established by similar music being associated with similar pictures, and stimulation may be even further increased.

Music is one sound that can later acquire excitation and therefore learning properties. The generality to be put into the record (readers already know the fact, of course) is that hearing is a prime channel for transactions, thus for acquiring behaviors, and a wide array of deliberate or chance sounds stimulate infants and all other humans.

In the matter of chance sounds, a child might acquire behaviors labeled fear through the conditioning of the autonomic response naturally produced in a hearing child by a loud clap of thunder, when that autonomic response is associated with a mother's fearing behaviors. If the child does not hear the thunder and thus is not aroused, the behavior cannot be acquired.

Reference has been made to the significance of verbal symbols (words), the controlling properties of which are acquired partly by chance and partly by deliberate teaching. To grasp the relationship of sounds and their stimulus properties and therefore their significance in behavior acquisition, one has but to study the development of children who are deaf from birth. To do so lets a student of behavior understand why it has been said that if one had to choose between losing either sight or hearing, he should choose loss of sight. Loss of hearing is a far greater handicap, so vital is hearing for transaction in human ecosystems. It is essential for receiving and transmitting the oral symbols (words) necessary for humanizing, that is, for acquiring the behaviors that, in sum, are the distinguishing characteristics of humans.

As noted, aroused states as stimuli leading to activity are natural, are inherent in humans, and all humans respond to those stimuli. Stimuli in uncountable arrays impinge incessantly on the human with normal senses. The human, however, does not respond with activity (behavior) to all potential stimuli, but mostly to stimuli that have been conditioned as rewarding or punishing. In brief, the human can learn to be stimulated by a potential stimulus just as he can also learn not to be stimulated by it. A physician I know, when starting to build his practice, accepted night telephone calls at home. His wife received and acted on the stimulus of their children's crying when it occurred in the night. The physician husband did not acquire responding behavior toward night time crying and thus was not stimulated by that sound. He, however, responded to the sound of the telephone ringing, whereas the mother did not. A mark of an expert in any adult occupation is the capacity to receive and act on stimuli that are not received by persons who lack experience in that field. Sherlock Holmes frequently received visual and auditory stimulation that Dr. Watson did not, although the same stimuli were presented to both men.

Stimuli acquire culturally determined properties, and cultures as used here may be racial or ethnic groups, or cross-generational within any racial or ethnic group. Orientals are stimulated by musical sounds that leave Occidentals unsatisfied, and vice versa. My generation was stimulated by the popular music of the Swing Era. Most of today's youths are conditioned to respond to different sounds, however, and listen without stimulation, thus with puzzlement or boredom, to Granddad's music.

Inactive or withdrawn states are found in adults, and in so-called mental hospitals new techniques based on operant procedures are now available to start activity in persons who have become so severely withdrawn (inactive) as to require hospitalization. One of the more dramatic portrayals of the need for activity among withdrawn adults in order for health to be restored was offered in a television play of the 1950s. It vividly demonstrated the point and thus merits a brief resume here.

Visualize a ward in a military hospital. To this ward have been brought a dozen Korean War soldiers from a number of hospitals, soldiers who have reacted to their battle experiences by now being apathetic and withdrawn. The patients have been wounded and are bed-bound, and the scene lets us see not jocular, active humans, but depressed, inactive persons.

Their only medical contact is a nurse, although their physical wants are well cared for by orderlies. The nurse, to the viewers' consternation, is not only a socially and professionally cold human, she in fact treats each individual with a harshness not normal in any human, let alone a nurse. She sneers at her patients, labels them cowards, shirkers, malingerers. Slowly the patients "come to life," become active. Whereas the play started with apathetic individuals not caring to live and not interested in their ward mates, now we can see not only individual cognitive and physical activity, but a group adhesion developing around one purpose: to get revenge on the nurse.

The denouement of the play comes when we see for the first time the nurse out of the ward in conversation with the physician in charge of the ward. The nurse is in tears, and viewers are amazed to see that she is in fact a caring, solicitous human who has been aversive by design. The plan was to arouse each soldier through generating in him a reason for arousal and for joining with others to achieve a common purpose. Their hatred of the nurse led to their eagerness to give her her come-uppance, a design for which the soldiers had been brought together in one hospital. Once aroused, once having acquired not only an individual but also a common purpose for living, the soldiers were then open to other treatments, which returned them to normal behavior.

Looking at stimuli from a different stance, the question is asked, what is boredom? Defined objectively, it is a low rate of emission of behavior, which results from an absence of or minimal presence of events that have stimulus properties. What behavior results from a visit of a loved person not seen for a while? Behaviors labeled with the summing word "excitement," that is, a high rate of behavior emission. Excitement is the opposite of boredom, and because the sensations called excitement are pleasing, humans seek excitement. Extending that last statement we can say that humans like stimulation, thus we can also observe that stimuli not only serve as the necessary condition for the establishment of behaviors, but, to repeat, being stimulated results in the subjective responses that are given the summing description of pleasure. Although the pleasure response of stimulation is important, we limit our interest in stimulation here to its importance in the establishment of behaviors.

From birth to death, then, stimuli, both internal and external, with resultant activity by the human, both cognitive and motoric, are the sine qua non of development.

Significance for Guidance Practices

The prior section primarily has served an explanatory function related to general principles. There are rare cases when school guidance practitioners will need to counter apathy. Apathy does exist among a school population, of course, but more commonly as the temporary phenomenon each of us experiences from time to time. Adult accusation of youth as being apathetic again as they were in the 1950s is a social value judgment, conveying an estimate of a lack of interest by youth in matters of school or broader societal concerns. Students are not apathetic about other matters of interest, however; that is, they are not pervasively apathetic.

For the occasional generally apathetic youth who seeks assistance for removal of apathy, some procedures are noted in Chapter 8 for guidance practitioners to use.

RESPONDENT CONDITIONING

The establishment (fixing), maintenance, or extinction of behavior is a result of two kinds of conditioning, respondent and operant. The word "instrumental" is sometimes used instead of "operant." Respondent conditioning is the oldest documented form of behavior development, and Pavlov is the best known among the many who have identified the laws under which it operates. The following illustrations will demonstrate the essences of respondent conditioning.

Sights, sounds, smells, and touches incessantly impinge on us. For the infant and child most of these potential stimuli are not in fact stimuli; that is, they do not elicit a response. At first they are neutral sights, sounds, smells, and touches and can be stimuli only when they become "learned" as stimuli and therefore result in some response. Other stimuli, however, do elicit responses for the reason that response to such stimuli is built into every human. For our purposes here these will be called "natural" stimuli, although that is not the customary term. A sudden loud sound produces that uncontrolled, natural behavior labeled startle, or elicits those more extreme behaviors labeled fear. Food in the mouth produces saliva. Hugging and gently tickling an infant or young child produces a natural response. If any neutral stimulus is consistently present just before or simultaneously with a natural stimulus (a stimulus that naturally produces a response), the neutral stimulus takes on the stimulus properties of the natural stimulus. We say, then, that respondent conditioning has occurred.

Pavlov's well-known experiment with dog salivation is the classic example. A vibrating tuning fork does not produce salivation in animals or humans, but food does. Pavlov struck a tuning fork immediately before his experimental dog was given food and was therefore salivating, and eventually, after many repetitions, the sound of the tuning fork produced salivation. For the dog, then, the once neutral tone is now a natural stimulus, or, in technical terms, a conditioned stimulus (CS). The response of salivation on hearing the tone is said to have been *conditioned* to the formerly neutral stimulus of the sound of the tuning fork. In different words, salivation resulting from the tone is a product of respondent conditioning.

A formerly neutral stimulus that becomes a natural stimulus can now become paired with still other neutral (unconditioned) stimuli to result in higher order respondent conditioning. The tone now produces salivation, and, if a different unconditioned (neutral) stimulus, such as a light, is now consistently presented just before the tone is sounded, salivation can become paired to this new unconditioned stimulus (UCS). The light in turn takes on the properties of a natural stimulus; that is, the new UCS takes on response-producing characteristics as if it were built into the creature as part of its natural, involuntary responses. It is apparent that these compounding response conditionings can later result in behaviors that occur apparently without reason. Even if human behavior was established and maintained only by respondent conditioning, we could grasp that this form of fixing behavior alone is sufficient to account for the complexity of human behavior. In addition to respondent conditioning, however, instrumental or operant conditioning establishes and maintains behavior, and then later the human's symbol system, acquired as all behaviors are through respondent/operant conditioning, enters the melange of stimuli-responses and affects the establishment and maintenance of yet other higher order behaviors.

Visualize a lemon being squeezed, and what results? Even the word lemon itself without the visual imagery perhaps has caused you to salivate, in a simple illustration of respondent conditioning. Fondling results in autonomic responses, and for most persons these autonomic responses become locked to a person who later is labeled mother, thus there begins the emotional response toward mother for which the summing word "love" later is used.

Respondent conditioning typically occurs without the human's being aware that it has occurred, and it occurs sometimes with undesirable results as a matter of chance. For an illustration of the latter: a young child is engaging in a specific play activity in his yard and is attacked by a dog. The autonomic response of the child can not only respondently condition him against dogs in general, but can result in that specific play activity's becoming aversive. A loud and unexpected noise, such as thunder, produces autonomic responses. If the child's reaction is immediately associated with fearing behaviors on the part of the mother or other significant adults, as noted earlier, storm-fearing behaviors may become fixed and may be respondently locked into some other context associated with the autonomic response, such as night time, bed time, or being in a certain room, these now also being feared. How long these higher order conditioned fears will persist cannot be foretold. The subsequent experiences will cause them to extinguish rapidly in one child and to be reinforced in another.

Although more behaviors become established and maintained

through operant conditioning than through respondent conditioning, the respondent type of conditioning has more permanent effects, that is, is less open to extinction. This kind of conditioning affects what other behaviors can be established and maintained through operant conditioning. Autonomic conditioning results in the emotional coloration that internal and external stimuli have for humans and in the emotional coloration of many of their operantly acquired behaviors.

A study by Staats and Staats (1958) illustrates the potency of the intervention of a person's symbol system in higher order respondent conditioning. Six national names—German, Swedish, Italian, French, Dutch, and Greek—were separately projected on a screen, and accompanying such projection the experimenter called out a word such as happy, sacred, ugly, bitter. The result among the experimental subjects was positive or negative responses to each national name depending on the words paired with that name. From such higher order respondent conditioning racial, national, and ethnic prejudice are established. An ethnic label is a UCS, but when paired in higher order conditioning with other stimuli and responses, labels lose their neutrality and become conditioned stimuli (CS). Such labels do not need to be the pejorative ones developed by a society. In fact, a child can behave positively toward persons under such usually pejorative labels as wop, mick, spic, nigger, and kike. Of course, it is assumed that in a case like that the child would be ignorant of any negative effect those words might have on the persons addressed. We can speak of those five labels as intending to carry one's negative feeling to hearers and to be received (heard) negatively by the persons addressed. The opposite could be equally the case, that is, those labels could be intended and be received very positively, and, conversely, the formal labels—Italian, Irish, Puerto Rican, Negro, or Jew—could be used for and received (heard) as words of hate. Potentially, words are unconditioned stimuli. Whatever emotional loading words receive depends on the quality of the context in which they are used. Humans learn early in life to respond negatively to a derisive tone of voice. It is associating a label with a derisive or loving tone that produces its negative or positive loading.

We see, then, that any words as UCS's acquire a conditioned emotional response only when paired with other positively or negatively conditioned behaviors. Guidance team members may or may not deal with racial and ethnic higher order conditioned emotional responses, but they all do have to deal occasionally with such responses associated with occupational decisions and advanced education choices. "Community college" or "state university" have acquired for many students at least a weak negative higher order conditioning, whereas the names of status private universities have acquired at least a weak positive conditioning. The youth so conditioned who seeks to enter a profession for which a nearby state university has a superior training program is impelled to eschew the state university and conversely to seek an inferior preparation at far greater expense in a status private university.

Junk dealers can be wealthy. A youth with strong conditioning about occupational status who seeks an occupation of high income would be astonished and repelled if a career specialist or counselor were to recommend his being a junk dealer. "Junk" is a word with higher order negative respondent conditioning. An extreme illustration was used, but the process is the same one that produces any youth's list of interesting occupations and his list of unacceptable occupations.

In the matter of stimulus and response generalization, the child in the illustration earlier who was respondently conditioned by the attacking dog also demonstrates a more limited stimulus and behavior generalization. Because he is too young to discriminate, he does not fear this particular dog, but he fears the class of animals called dogs and indeed might generalize fearing behaviors to other animals. His, of course, is an instance of a more specific response conditioned to a more specific stimulus, but right now we are considering autonomic conditioning associated with multiple stimuli.

A child in a family that consistently responds nurturingly to him, and that stimulates him so that he engages in activities that are then operantly reinforced, likely will acquire seemingly diffuse desirable respondent conditioning to "the family," meaning the persons in it and the many conditioned and operantly reinforced stimuli it provides. Conversely a child who receives random, brutal treatment from both parents, the brutal treatment not being associated with any specific behaviors he emits but associated with any kind of behavior, will acquire diffuse and undesirable respondently conditioned behaviors.

Because the acquisition of later behaviors is affected by respondent conditioning of earlier acquired behaviors, one can predict with a high probability that the first child used for illustration, the nurtured one, will continue to acquire effective coping behaviors in our society. The child respondently conditioned by physical and social abuse, however, may never acquire acceptable coping behaviors, but instead might become one of those persons who practices destructive behaviors on others and who eventually merits the label "sociopath."

Only rarely will school guidance practitioners deal directly with respondent behaviors. One of those behaviors, however, is that pattern of responses known as phobias. Only a few phobias will call for mediation by some guidance practitioners, with school-related ones most likely to be the ones. The most general of these is school phobia, and a more specific one is test phobia. The guidance practitioner will employ counterconditioning to eliminate those phobic responses.

To repeat an earlier observation, a youth or adult's behavior is mediated by respondent and operant conditioning in ways that most often are inextricable, that is to say that that portion of behavior variance attributable to respondent and that to operant conditioning rarely can be extricated from each other. Because they are so intertwined, it behooves us to move now to highlights of instrumental or operant conditioning so that the more correct interaction of these two kinds of conditioning can be seen.

INSTRUMENTAL OR OPERANT CONDITIONING

Recall that respondent conditioning is the label given to learning wherein a stimulus acquires the ability to elicit a response that would not result naturally from that stimulus. This occurs when that behavior is present immediately before or at the same time as an additional stimulus that does elicit that behavior is paired with the first, nonarousing stimulus. Although the phrase "before or at the same time" was used, for mnemonic purposes we can fix on the word "before." Now operant conditioning can be associated with the word "after."

Operant or instrumental conditioning is the label given to learning wherein the *consequences* of a behavior have a pleasant effect, no effect, or a punishing effect. These three effects yield either: a high probability that the behavior will be repeated under similar circumstances, a high probability that the repetition of the behavior will not be affected one way or the other, or an increased probability that the behavior will not be repeated or will be extinguished if it already is established. What happens *after* the behavior is what determines whether the behavior will be strengthened or weakened. That "what happens" is the subjective reaction of the behaver. The defining question: is the consequence of the behavior pleasant or painful?

Reinforcers

Central to a presentation about operant conditioning is a word used often herein, with its several variations. The verb form is "to reinforce" and the primary noun form is "reinforcing stimulus." Variant forms appear with equal or greater frequency, however. Two commonly used variants are "reinforcer" and "reinforcing." Definitions of the word "reinforce" and its variants are terms that do not yet have precise agreement among psychologists, but I will define their use here.

To reinforce: to strengthen a behavior. *To be reinforced:* a behavior that is strengthened. *Reinforcing stimulus* or *reinforcer:* an internal and/or external result or effect of a behavior that strengthens that behavior by becoming a stimulus for that behavior. The word "strengthen" has several connotations. A simple one is the probability that that behavior will be continued. Another is that the behavior so strengthened might gain potency over a competing behavior, with the effect, of course, that given a need for a behavior pattern to be emitted, the stronger, the more reinforced behavior will appear with greater probability than the now weaker behavior.

Each of us has first-hand knowledge about that point. Let me illustrate with a case that many of us have experienced, one that many school guidance practitioners will be called on to help students with. A student is required by a course enrollment to do certain readings and complete a scholarly paper by the end of the course. Near the end the student finds himself running out of time and plans to use a weekend to complete his task. He begins his study and writing, but is invited by liked persons to engage in hedonistic activities. He responds toward the hedonistic activities and thus does not respond toward study. Study responses are weaker responses. In guidance practice, the technical question is how to strengthen (reinforce) that person's study responses so they will be stronger than hedonistic responses, given the need to produce materials by the end of the course.

Infant behaviors are reinforced by milk and other foods and liquids, by fondling, and by other soothing, attending behaviors. One of the first external stimuli (reasons for emitting behavior) is the discomfort caused by wet or soiled diapers, and the natural behavior used to respond to both sources is crying. The comforting parental behaviors directed to the child become associated with one or a few faces and voices, and the infant acquires recognition behaviors of smiling or even becoming quiet when the comforting stimulus, usually the mother, appears even though the behavior of crying was established first through its reinforcing consequences. In short, it is safe to state what reinforcers are for all normal infants. But not for older children, and less so for youths and for adults. The reason? Each person's learning history causes him to acquire likes or tastes and aversions through respondent conditioning, some of which are similar to other persons' likes, tastes, and aversions, but some of which can be very different from other persons' likes, tastes, and aversions. An Arabic youth's behavior will be reinforced by eating sheep eyes, an aversive food for Westerners. Touching one person on the shoulder can be a social reinforcer for him, while another person is offended (is averted by) the same touch. A day on which permission is given to be absent from school, a permission earned through accumulating points for many specific behaviors that a teacher wishes to reinforce, may be a permission eagerly sought by most children, yet one child may evidence those behaviors labeled "anxiety" if he does not attend on a session day. Being submitted to physical abuse is desirable to some persons, such as by those whose sexual pleasures or religious ecstasies are amplified by physical abuse, but such abuse is just painful to most others. Much of what becomes meat for one man and poison for another is learned.[2]

The contrasts are endless and have been sufficiently illustrated, enough at least to demonstrate that planned use of operant conditioning procedures requires identification of what reinforces a particular pattern of behavior and in which contingency pattern or context.

Here is an example of the matter of setting or context and its effect on the reinforcing properties of actions. A young male child enjoys being embraced by his father on occasions within the house, he finds his father's embrace aversive when given in front of peers whom the child is trying to impress with his manliness. To repeat, it is not always sufficient just to ask about a person, "What are reinforcers (reinforcing stimuli) for him?" The correct question often must be, "What has reinforced this or a similar behavior for this person in the past and in what context?" The guidance team member will be cognizant that numerous contingencies of a context itself, not one specific element in the context, may have been the reinforcer.

Persons learn how to learn, to repeat an essential cognition. Future behavior acquisitions depend on prior reinforcement experiences. A person can learn to move from a condition wherein there is a need for reinforcing stimuli to immediately follow an emitted behavior, to the condition of having reinforcements postponed, a fact that is of importance to guidance team members and other school adults.

A behavior is not likely to be a permanent part of an individual's repertoire just because it was reinforced the first time it was emitted or was reinforced after only a few emissions of that behavior. A behavior might not become established, or may extinguish with time unless further reinforcement occurs. Technical studies establish rules about frequency or time-interval rates of reinforcements, a facet that the guidance team member will study but that is not detailed here. To state that a behavior might need reinforcement over time in order to become permanent may suggest that all behavior is repeated only if external (extrinsic) reinforcement follows the emission of that behavior, even if it is only intermittent reinforcement. That is an incorrect conclusion. Many, if not most, behaviors become *established* by extrinsic reinforcers—those outside the person—but then these behaviors typically come under the control of, are maintained by,

[2] The selection of reinforcers for children with handicaps can be troublesome. An accounting of the difficulty and the solution to the problem of identifying a reinforcer for use with a deaf, severely mentally retarded 12-year-old boy is reported by Kahn (1970).

intrinsic "internal" reinforcers. For example, the first steps in acquiring the skills known as reading or piano playing may well be described as dull, chorelike activities. There is nothing rewarding per se in the behaviors of the first steps in learning to read or play the piano. These first behaviors, therefore, usually have to be extrinsically rewarded by simple praise, food, and other extrinsic reinforcers, such as orchestrating the more subtle reinforcement of status-in-a-group (competition and status seeking). Later, when the child can read or play, the consequences of the reinforcing stimuli are their own reward, and the activities are done for the intrinsic reinforcement they provide. The various subjective states, for which we can use the general word "pleasure," are the reinforcing stimuli that maintain the reading and piano playing.

The reader has noted my occasional use of old sayings. Let's try another: virtue is its own reward. Puzzling? Not when you apply to it knowledge about extrinsic-intrinsic reinforcements. Name a virtue. Modesty? Avoiding a definition of that word, we first can note that modesty is not an inherent behavior; it is acquired. This means that modest behaviors at first have to be extrinsically reinforced. Modest behaviors, and thus modesty as a generalized trait, are built through time and shaping. When a child emits those behaviors that fall within the summing term "modesty," the parents put a label on that behavior—they call that behavior "modesty." Thus that behavior is now partly under the control of symbols, a word in this case. In certain contingencies the human can cue off his own behaviors of modesty by the use of self-referent words (I am modest) and can be intrinsically reinforced by having engaged in those behaviors that at one time needed the extrinsic reinforcement of his parents. To behave in accord with the virtue called modesty is now its own (intrinsic) reward.

A part of the earlier learning-to-read example needs further analysis. This part is the matter of the reinforcing nature of the extrinsic rewards used to establish learning-to-read behaviors. The extrinsic rewards named were praise, food, and status in a group. In fact, for one person none of these may be reinforcing. The pleasure accompanying praise is learned, thus a child who has not learned pleasurable reactions to praise would not have his behaviors reinforced by it. Far-fetched possibility? Maybe yes, but let's ask a different question: what is praise? Phrases like "Good show!" and "Bravo!"? Yes, for some persons in some subcultures. "Good boy!" to a young black male might be offensive.

Food as a reinforcer? In most cases, yes, thus the frequent practice of giving small pellets of chocolate candy to children immediately following a desired behavior. One person might have an allergic reaction to chocolate, however. Thus to eat an intendedly reinforcing pellet will produce aversive results and may act to extinguish the desired behavior. It appears that there are fewer parents adhering to Grandma's law (eat this before you get that), and to the contrary, permissive eating of any food at any time is the mark of many reasonably affluent homes with well-stuffed refrigerators and pantries. In such families parents have lost one of the major reinforcers they could use to establish and maintain other desired behaviors. Families that permit children to eat while watching television likely are reinforcing television-watching in general. If the eating systematically occurs in correlation with a certain show, the children may develop a strong liking of that show.

Competition, with high standing in a group, as a reinforcer? Yes, for those who have learned competition as a desired behavior and have had competitively high standing reinforced. But not a child from one of several cultures of the indigenous persons of this continent—a Pueblo Indian child, for example. Chapter 7, which deals more systematically with social determiners of behavior, will show that some so-called Indian subcultures teach their children to avoid standing out competitively against their peers.[3]

The summation of this section up to this point probably is obvious: operant or instrumental behaviors are continued at first by extrinsic reinforcers, but what is an extrinsically reinforcing action or thing has to be discovered for each human, as do the intrinsic reinforcers. One other general point relating to reinforcement needs to be expanded: specific extrinsic actions and things can reinforce behaviors but the context surrounding these actions is important.

Reinforcing Contexts

Previous examples have shown that specific reinforcers have demonstrated value for maintaining relatively simple, early behaviors. Among older persons specific reinforcers may have the same effect, but more likely other conditions present constitute a reinforcement "package," of which the specific reinforcer is but a part. Said another way, in some cases a specific action or thing does not have a reinforcing effect by itself, even though, at one time, it might have been a reinforcer for that person. Packaged along with other contingencies as a context it contributes to an accumulative reinforcing effect. For example, a child learns to feel pleased

---

[3] As with any topic briefly presented in an overview text, this topic of the relationship of cultural differences to operant conditioning and contingency management later will be studied at length by the student who pursues a guidance team preparation program. For the student who wishes to briefly explore the topic now in general terms, it is recommended that he read Burger's (1972) article. For the student who wishes to examine the same question applied specifically to the American Indian culture, see Spang (1971).

by praise, and praise from either parent reinforces behavior. When the same child is a middle or late adolescent, praise from a parent given in the privacy of the home does not act reinforcingly. On the other hand, the same words of praise for the same behaviors given by the same parent but in a certain public context, one that is known to have some reinforcing properties for the youth, may have reinforcing effects. The acquisition of the reinforcing effects of popular music, used as illustration earlier, shows the reverse. At first the music has no reinforcing properties, but it acquires such properties in a complex social context. Then later, only listening to the music in the absence of the social context, that is, in the absence of the other contingency conditions, cues off some of the pleasure responses that accrued to the fuller contingency context.

Another musical illustration, although partially repetitious, conveys a clearer example of the role of context in behavior—in this case a simple behavior. If an album of a musical play is heard without having seen the play performed, the listener might speak of part of the music as "pleasant," referring to those parts that cue off responses associated with earlier music that had acquired the properties of pleasing, but in general that listener might be little stimulated by the album. Another person sees the stage production, and because the staging stimulated (it cued off responses learned in this person's behavior history), because the behaviors of the other members of the audience contributed to this person's stimulation, because he was in the company of a cherished other person (these and perhaps other contingencies being part of this brief ecosystem), the music acquired intense stimulating properties. This second person, then, in listening to an album of the production's music, is strongly and pervasively stimulated—the music has far greater stimulus effect on him than it has on the first person who did not see the actual production.

The sight and/or sounds of crowds can be stimulating. Watching a group athletic competition on television with the sound turned off is less exciting than hearing the crowd react. Stimulation by large numbers of persons requires proximity. The British acknowledge this fact in causing the House of Commons assembly room to have fewer seats than members, with the result that most sessions are packed.

Another facet of context important for the student and needing later study in greater detail is the concept of role: that array of behaviors a person acquires for use in a given context, several different arrays of behaviors being acquired for several different contexts, so that the person is spoken of as one who plays different roles in different situations. This situation is similar to the one that lets us say that a person does not have a personality, but has personalities.

Another way to address the matter of context in which behaviors become operantly conditioned is to reconsider such contexts under the heading of ecosystems, and in so doing, to add a reconsideration of the subtle and often unaware ways in which ecosystems reinforce or extinguish behaviors. This restates something that was noted earlier: much behavior is acquired not by gross or even deliberate actions toward a person, but instead through the subtle interactions of all the stimulus contingencies in an ecosystem. The total ecosystem can also be spoken of as a climate for each component element of that system. This climatic effect on humans is similar to the effect of an ecosystem on animals and plants. Consider a young slow-growing tree that has sprung up 10 feet from and on the north side of a fast-growing tree. The latter increases in size rapidly and starts to shade the slower-growing tree. The rapidly growing tree now not only shades the slower-growing tree, thus decreasing its functioning, but the increased root system of the rapidly growing tree takes more and more nourishment from the root system of the other tree. Relative to a model of a tree at its best, the slow-growing tree is deficient, not because it was intentionally acted against, but because of a subtle and natural outcome of transaction within the ecosystem in which it happened to be. A child's position relative to his siblings is a similar matter within the family ecosystem.

Let us now suppose that another element of the ecosystem works deleteriously against the fast-growing tree of our illustration, and it starts to die. As it loses its leaves and takes less nourishment, the slower tree begins to grow, and its growth increases the decline of the faster grower, and soon the latter is dead, and the former has been well reembarked on appropriate development, eventually approximating a model of a tree at its best.

Changing a person's social climate to change his behavior is a procedure probably as old as man and is institutionalized in law. Taking children from their own families and placing them in foster homes has been done through legal process for years in this country. It often results in its intended purposes: the child or youth with poor development (some desirable coping behavior not acquired, some undesirable coping behavior acquired) recommences desired development. Our interest in this illustration needs to go beyond the general point. Persons competent in understanding behavior need to and can specify the contingencies in the bad climate that prevent the development of desired behaviors, or cause undesired behaviors to be learned. They also need to and can therefore identify the stimulus and response contingencies that must be present in the new ecosystem, the foster home, so as to bring about the acquisition of desired behaviors and the extinction of undesired behaviors. Social workers with some probability, and lawyers with high probability, to speak of averages, do not have this kind of knowledge of behavior, and thus foster home placement commonly is carried out only in generalized and hopeful terms, rather than with technical precision.

Contingencies—Accidental and Planned

Foster home placement when carried out with attention to the specific behaviors to be changed and to the contingencies that are necessary in the foster home so as to change such behavior would be a somewhat loose example of planned mediation of contingencies, or, in technical terms, of contingency management. The example of the withdrawn Korean War soldiers is a more tightly drawn example of contingency management.

Contingency management is more explicitly treated in Chapter 8, but a brief comment is needed at this point. The contingencies to be managed are the outcomes of what a person does, desirable or undesirable. Through managing those outcomes that are associated with a person's behaviors, the person's behaviors can be changed in quantity and/or quality. For most of the lives of most persons, the results of behaviors are either chance, or, if deliberate, are not consistently so. In behavior management, a procedure based on operant conditioning, the outcomes are deliberately and consistently controlled by the management plan. Grandma's Law shows contingency management. "You get no dessert unless and until you eat your vegetables." Said otherwise, "Receipt of dessert is contingent upon your eating your vegetables." Grandma "means it" (it happens just as she says), and she says it every time her grandchild comes for a visit. The grandchild thus eats vegetables when visiting Grandma but does not at home, where no such contingency has been stipulated. If the parents wished the child to eat vegetables also at home, they would have to apply (manage) some form of contingent outcome.

Most ecosystems practice contingency management without knowing the technical term. Grandma's Law is an example of narrowly drawn contingency management. In the two extreme family illustrations in Chapter 7, those of maximum and minimum experience, we will find a description of pervasive contingency management in the maximum experience family. Therein we will see the behaviors resulting from contingency management, although the contingencies were not specified. The deliberate actions taken by the controlling or dominant feature of that ecosystem, the parents, to shape the behaviors of their children are contingency management, to apply the technical term. Shaping also occurs in the minimum experience family, but randomly or accidentally, not by design. Although we can speak of the behaviors of the children of the minimum experience family as being respondently and operantly reinforced, we cannot say that this occurred through contingency *management*.

Subtle Effects of Contingency Management

Contingency management is a procedure or technique based on operant conditioning, but it is not just another term for operant conditioning. Characteristics of the latter are great specifity of behavior, reinforcer, chaining, shaping, and schedules of reinforcing. Contingency management typically is a far less controlled use of procedures that apply extrapolations from operant conditioning.

Just as a youth's behaviors are shaped by the numerous unplanned or loosely planned contingencies in his several ecosystems without his being aware of the fixing or changing of his behaviors that is occurring, so are the results of contingency management equally subtle when contingencies are carefully and deliberately changed, as with the Korean War patients. Neither those patients nor children and youths in the maximum and minimum experience households, where contingencies cannot be described as managed if we are speaking with attention to accuracy, would be able to state that "this behavior I am currently emitting is under control of this particular stimulus-response contingency," and then proceed to describe the specifics of that contingency. In the management of contingencies carried out by a guidance team member, however, the person whose behaviors are mediated by that management might not only be aware that a behavior change is being sought, but indeed, we can assume, has sought out the guidance team member so as to attain the desired behaviors. The recipient of the benefits of contingency management, to put it another way, might be fully aware of the outcome and might have asked for it, but is not aware of the subtle way that contingency management produces the sought-after behaviors.

Significance for Guidance Practices

However much respondent behaviors color all other behaviors, and occasionally present conditions in a person's life requiring the mediating assistance of a guidance practitioner, it is operant behaviors to which the guidance practitioner must attend more often. This will be so when a person is ineffective because of excesses of coping behaviors. In a different condition, operant principles are employed to establish coping behaviors that are nonexistent or of insufficient strength. In the former instance a person who behaves angrily beyond the requirements of situations, for example, can have these excessive behaviors reduced through deliberate application of the same operant principles that nondeliberately caused the anger behaviors to become established in the first place. Most high school youths provide an illustration of the latter instance. They lack decision-making behaviors and particularly information-seeking behaviors as a subset of decision-making behaviors. These behaviors will be established through the application of operant principles. Countless other illustrations will present themselves to the extensive reader or to the experienced practitioner.

THE COGNITIVE OR SYMBOL SYSTEM

The considerations of respondent and operant conditioning necessarily touched on the development of a person's symbol system and the potency that system has for mediating a person's behavior, with mediation generated spontaneously by the person himself as much as from external sources. In this section additional information about the symbol system is offered.

Symbol Development

Behavior in all living creatures results from internal and external stimuli. In very simple forms of life, such as in the case of the earthworm, the external stimuli are relatively simple: light and touch. In more complex forms stimuli and behavior are brought under the control of sounds. A dog learns to respond to the sound "here," and his human master responds differently to the variety of sounds the dog makes. The dog produces an "I want to go out" bark, an alarm bark that is different in quality and intensity, and a "give me some of that food" whine.

Human behavior is mediated to a large degree by sounds other humans make, those sounds being fantastically differentiated into the complex pattern called speech. Each element of speech (words), and the way those portions are sequentially arranged into phrases and sentences have behavior-mediation intention for the developing human, as does the inflection with which speech is employed. As a human develops from infancy into childhood, adults cause children's behavior to be mediated by speech that has been changed to visual symbols for speech, which we call writing. Oral communication remains the paramount tool of transaction for most persons most times, however. The fact that speech is the chief behavior mediator is naturally of great importance for members of a guidance team, for speech is their chief tool too.

Words and sentences acquire connotations beyond the simple naming and commanding function. A direction given to a child, "eat your vegetables," for example, is simple and nonconnotative. For an example of the acquisition of connotative meanings to words let us look at a nonhuman illustration.

A dog learns to respond to commands. When he behaves correctly, his behavior is reinforced not only by food but by words, such as "good dog." And "good dog" is said with "pleasure" in the voice. The dog jumps on a sofa, where he is not to be, and on discovery is hurled off, struck, and the words "bad dog" are said with "displeasure" in the voice. Relatively soon, after a number of repetitions of "good dog" and "bad dog" when the dog's behavior is reinforced or punished, just saying "good dog" while the dog is lying absolutely still will produce tail wagging and other behaviors described by the summing word "pleasure," and just saying "bad dog" will produce behaviors we describe in sum as embarrassment and shame. The connotations of the sounds are now sufficient to produce behavior as a result of respondent conditioning. Because the value of life for humans is judged by their assessment of the quality of life's experiences, connotative meanings of speech are of paramount importance.

Symbols as Reinforcers of Specific Behaviors

Humans learn a wider array of far more subtle connotations to words, and for our concerns here and later in Chapter 8 we are more interested in the positive or affirmative words and sentences, such as "good," "you did well," "that's fine!" In operant or instrumental conditioning this kind of speech is called a "social reinforcer," with large significance for mediating behavior. What can be effective as a social reinforcer, like all behaviors, must be learned, as noted earlier. Said differently, those phrases that reinforce a person's behavior are acquired in a person's behavior history, as are the reinforcing or punishing characteristics of other stimuli. If a child develops in a family that does not cause an association between (does not condition) typically reinforcing phrases and behavior that is reinforced by other means, those phrases do not acquire the positive higher order conditioning they need in order to serve as reinforcers.

Numerous researches have demonstrated the function of social reinforcers in maintaining behavior. Two are reported here, and the behavior reinforced in both cases is oral. An ample supply of experimental data has shown how motoric behaviors, that is, motions or "doing" something, are established and maintained by social reinforcers, but these two experiments are closely related to the interview behaviors practiced by members of a guidance team and are thus closer to the core interests of this text.

In one experiment (Greenspoon, 1950), persons were asked to say a series of unrelated words, including plural nouns. When the persons said the plural nouns, the researcher gave a simple social reinforcer: he said "mmmm-humm." This oral reinforcer significantly increased the number of plural nouns spoken by the subjects of the experiment.

Greenspoon's study is informative per se, but it is recorded here also because it demonstrates how a counselor's verbal behavior can affect the client's verbal behavior. Verplanck (1955) demonstrated the same phenomenon related to opinions expressed by 24 experimental subjects. In lengthy conversation for a controlled period of time, experimenters reinforced opinion statements emitted by subjects and for other controlled periods did not respond to (made no effort to reinforce) emitted opinions. Experimenters' responses used with the intention of reinforcing the subjects' behavior of stating opinions resulted in maintenance of that behavior. In the period when no reinforcement was given for opinion stating, the behavior extinguished. The sum effect of experiments such as these that use social reinforcers lets us state the general rule that attending positively to a behavior will strengthen the behavior, that is, increase the likelihood that the behavior will be repeated.

Folk psychology has long recognized this and other behavior mediation facts. Said of a pestering child, "ignore him and he'll quit." Scientific psychology uncovers the rules by which such principles can be used with precision. For years parents have suggested to visitors to the family that they ignore the showing-off behaviors of the family's 4-year-old, an extinguishing type of behavior mediation, while at the same time seeking to involve the child in other activities, that is, reinforcing the child for engaging in other behaviors. Scientific psychology provides the laws that explain this and other folk psychology.

Control of Patterns of Behaviors by Symbols

Up to this point we have observed that when a person with reinforcing characteristics for the behavior of another person states specific positive phrases following specific behaviors emitted by the other person, those phrases increase the probability that such behaviors will be repeated. This is an important role of speech to be noted, but, in fact, it is a relatively minor function in adult behaviors. Adult behaviors come under the control of a symbol and cognition system so complex as to defy analysis. Short or extended labels that a person has acquired about himself function as determiners of behavior and become immensely potent when respondently conditioned. But so do labels associated with social phenomena. Behaviors by a person of one race antagonistic to persons of another race are the function of respondently conditioned symbols acquired by those persons, as we have seen. As such, of course, these symbols are most resistant to rational extinction and are changed with more sureness by counterconditioning or other techniques that deal with the autonomic responses to which those persons' labels, their cognitions, have been respondently conditioned.

Labels and concepts about a culture or subculture, used in a cultural or subcultural context, acquire stimulus potency through respondent and operant conditioning. They result in stimulus and response generalizations and specifics that favor one's own subculture, with its myriad ways of behaving. These labels and concepts also determine the type of behaviors to be shown to persons of differing subcultures. That portion of the symbol system that is about self and cultures starts to build slowly. Later, acquired components of that system, both as to what is learned and the quality of that learning, are mediated by the earlier acquired symbols and congnitions.

The potency of a symbol system contributes to the fact that the human is not a robot, to restate this erroneous charge against psychology's views. The label "robot" means that the human is reactive only to stimuli outside the human. The symbol system can permit ideation about futures, but, of course, only if the human has learned to conceptualize about futures. The model of a youth at his best held by some guidance team members may value youth behaviors of hard work and the foregoing of current pleasures (behaviors not being under control of present stimuli that otherwise could have the power to elicit behaviors immediately pleasurable) so as to attain a desired future. Indeed the presenting of behaviors oriented toward some future goal instead of toward immediate pleasures is commonly offered by developmental psychologists and mental hygiene experts as an indication of maturity and of good mental health.

To be alive is to be active. To be active in the animal kingdom means to engage in some observable behavior. To be active in the human kingdom means, in addition, to have cerebral and other brain and neural activity that may result in some observable behaviors, but often and importantly does not. If Rodin's sculpture *The Thinker* were alive, he would be called active in the most distinguishing way a human can be active.

Historically, counselors have sought to help persons only through engaging their symbol system in the abstract, that is, in an interview room in which the only behavior emitted and dealt with is speaking. The error of this historical position is in the synecdoche—taking the part for the whole. A symbol system is one route for mediating the behavior of youths and adults, but ignorance of how a person's symbol system has been determined by respondent and operant conditioning will limit the assistance the counselor can give, and working only with verbal abstraction about behavior instead of also with behaviors as they occur in their contingency settings is to ignore the facts about how behavior is formed and thus can be mediated. This ignorance results in the ineffectiveness of so many of the "talking to" procedures used by parents and other adults in attempts to mediate behavior. Said otherwise, this ignorance results in the common ineffectiveness of reasoning procedure as the sole behavior mediation. ("But I told him again and again why it wouldn't work and he still did it!" "I explained to him that he shouldn't feel that way about her because there was no reason to, but he didn't listen to me!")[4] In its fullest expression, the whole of behavior mediation as applied to an individual who wishes to change behaviors is first to engage that person's symbol system in the abstract setting, if oral interaction is appropriate at all. This is done to make the necessary analysis of the respondent/operant conditioning coloration of the components of that system where such conditioning is significant. Then the guidance worker's assistance moves out of the abstract, artificial setting of an office so as to mediate behavior through respondent and operant procedures in that behavior's natural setting, that is to say, through stimulus or contingency management in the day-to-day places where that behavior occurs. Some behavior is accessible to mediation by symbols alone because the symbols related to that behavior either have minimal conditioning, or, if conditioned, are so in a favorable direction. This will be the situation related to many youths who will come to the guidance center for occupational and continuing education planning.

Significance for Guidance Practices

Guidance practitioners can speak of the importance of rational procedures, procedures that focus on a student's cognitions of his own behavior and of the world around him. Such cognitions are a part of any person's stimulus-response pattern and thus must be accorded attention in behavior mediation activities, as implied in the earlier illustrations of guidance practices related to respondent and operant behavior mediation. All guidance practitioners will deal with a person's cognitions, no matter whether it is respondent and/or operant principles that may be maintaining a behavior to be mediated, or when establishing or strengthening a behavior. Engaging rational procedures (dealing with cognitions) is a guidance practitioner behavior that does not need be acquired. What must be acquired by the prospective guidance practitioner are other needed forms of interventions, thereby avoiding the common error of approaching all behavior intervention from a rational (cognitive) mode.

---

[4] The phrase, "He won't listen to me," is another common example. It is usually said with affect labeled by such words as anger, resignation, frustration, and irritation. The speaker is saying, in effect, "I am unskilled in behavior mediation. The only tool for mediating behavior I know about is reasoning, and I am ignorant as to why reasoning cannot work. Reasoning did not work with this person, indeed, but it is too threatening for me to admit my own inadequacy, so I have to project the error onto the person I was trying to help. The Judaic-Christian culture in which I grew up caused me to acquire the view that human behavior is an act of will, thus the ineffectual results of my efforts can be attributed to him as a fault, the fault being that he willed to not change." Strangely enough the person-in-the-street is now ready to accept that some behavior cannot be changed by reason, for example, the behavior of an alcoholic, but the person-in-the-street does not establish a general principle that lets him see that most behaviors are not accessible to mediation through reasoning.

THE PENULTIMATE WORD

This next-to-last word would be the first word you would engage in a systematic study of behavior. It has to do with the brain and neural structure. The person-in-the-street knows about the human brain and knows that a person "thinks with his brain," but is relatively ignorant of the structure and functioning of other portions of the central nervous system, of the autonomic nervous system, of glandular discharges, receptor and effector cells, and of how synapses function. Indeed his view of the brain is of a global entity, not of a differentiated organ whose several parts have unique functions.

A student of behavior has to start with this biology, thus the comment previously that this next-to-last word would be the first word in systematic study of behavior. In this text, however, only portions of topics are examined at best, with no exposition made of the topic of the brain and the nervous system, even though it is basic to understanding behavior.

A demurrer is posited that new students in the field will need to extinguish the cognition, if it has been acquired, that there is a soma (a biology) distinct from a psyche (a person's behaviors). The total, indivisible human behaves. He behaves as a result of stimuli, internal and external, received in the central and/or autonomic systems, not as a robot, but as a human, in that his symbol system is one of the sources of internal stimulation. There is no "mind." There is thought, and thinking is a biological function, the cellular activity of the brain.

The persistence of the error of dualism, that there is body *and* mind, is understandable, just as it is understandable why inadequately educated persons have believed for so long that the earth stands still and the sun circles it. The pervasiveness of the misconception has led to misunderstanding about behavior by the person-in-the-street and even by some who should know the facts, a misunderstanding frequently demonstrated by the common use of the word "will," but perhaps more frequently by "won't." For instance, the parent or teacher who says that a child "won't" do certain behavior, with the child's being held at fault on moral terms. Or, more specifically, "My child is a selfish ingrate who won't help around the house at all." "This youth won't do his homework or pay attention in my class or any classes. He is just a lazy good-for-nothing and the quicker we get him out of this school the better for all of us." If the parent and teacher in these illustrations knew that each human is an entity, not the two-part creature their misconception leads them to believe him to be, and knew how behaviors are acquired, they might say instead, "I have not created the contingencies by which my child could learn to help around the house," and "The school and other ecosystems with which this youth transacts have provided contingencies that cause the youth to find school subjects aversive, and those contingencies have not caused him to acquire the behaviors described as goal-oriented (motivating)."

Not everything that will ever be known about behavior is known now, including gaps in knowledge about the functioning of the neural component. Enough is known, however, so that understanding of behavior no longer requires poetic interpositions, metaphorical concepts, and the use of tropes as was found useful in the early days of scientific investigations about behavior. Some hypothetical accountings are still useful, but only within the now existing mass of empirical evidence.

An example of useful hypothesizing is found in the proposal that one source of difference among humans lies in the quality of connection between the cortex of the brain and the limbic system, the pleasure center of the brain. This accounting postulates that in those humans wherein there is a weak structural connection between these two portions of the brain, pleasures are sought by exposure to external stimuli, to sensuousness. Others, however, with stronger connections, have their limbic systems stimulated by the cortex, or in more common terms, are pleasured by thinking, by problem solving dealing with cognitions, with the symbol system. Adding that hypothesis to the fact that nervous system characteristics—the quality of the "wiring" and of the "computer" (the brain)—are inherited, even if it does not explain as yet how human behavior differs so greatly, at least lets us understand why it differs.

Guidance team members do not engage a youth's "mind" or any free-floating behavior. They engage an awesomely complex totality at whose core is an interlocked neural and cell structure, the nature and function of which requires some knowledge before other knowledge about behavior can be applied.

EVALUATING BEHAVIOR PRINCIPLES BY CHAPTER 4's CRITERIA

You are urged to apply the criteria of a scientific theory to behavior principles. The extremely terse presentation in this chapter permits some portion of that evaluation. The absence of metaphor and hypothetical constructs may have been apparent. No record was offered here of the generators of knowledge in this area to permit response to the question of whether or not they met and meet the criteria of scientists. Nor was there anywhere nearly enough exposition of the procedures followed in arriving at these principles to permit you fully to determine whether the criteria of a science were met. Hopefully your motivation is strong enough to carry you to other writing that will provide you with a sufficient portrait of those persons and the origin of these principles to permit that kind of evaluation needed by every conscientious student in the guidance field. I make patent what is otherwise obvious: it is my view that behavior principles, developed by scientists practicing scientific procedures, are the postulates on which guidance practice must be based.

REFERENCES

BURGER, H. G. "Behavior Modification and Operant Psychology: An Anthropological Critique." *American Educational Research Journal,* 1972, *9,* 343–360.

GREENSPOON, J. *The Effect of Verbal and Nonverbal Stimuli on the Frequency of Members of Two Verbal Response Classes.* Unpublished Doctoral Dissertation, Indiana University, 1950.

KAHN, W. J., JR. "The Case of Michael: Finding the Reinforcer." *Counseling and Student Personnel Journal,* 1970, *2,* 21–33. College Park: CAPS Department, University of Maryland.

SPANG, A. T., JR. "Understand the Indian." *Personnel and Guidance Journal,* 1971, *50,* 97–102.

STAATS, A., & STAATS, C. "Attitudes Established by Classical Conditioning." *Journal of Abnormal and Social Psychology,* 1958, *54,* 37–40.

TUCKER, I. F. *Adjustment Models and Mechanisms.* New York: Academic Press, 1970.

VERPLANCK, W. "The Control of the Content of Conversation: Reinforcement of Statements of Opinion." *Journal of Abnormal and Social Psychology,* 1955, *51,* 668–676.

6 Concerns About Applying Behavioral Science

INTRODUCTION

The science of behavior has produced postulates, and some of those essential for guidance practices have been explored in Chapter 5. The postulates and technology propounded by behavioral science have been validated by applications that have moved out of the behavioral science laboratory into real-life situations. Not all that will be known about behavior principles is now known; yet it is tenable to hold that the theoretical and practical foundations of the structure of this science have been placed, and the frame and walls are well under way.

The orderly, interrelated postulates comprising the theory of behavior are often labeled behaviorism. Behaviorism uses no metaphor or hypothetical constructs. It holds that the world is real, that the role of the scientist is to discover the laws under which the real world of human behavior operates.

As might be expected, some persons do not accept the findings of behavioral science, but there appears to be more opposition directed to the technology that is based on the principles. When that opposition focuses on unethical practices, which some may use, it is not only a useful but an imperative opposition. The practitioners of a technology may be at fault, but it is not correct on that basis to fault the underlying principles. It is understandable that that faulting of principles would occur, of course. Any new finding that goes against dogmas or myths that are central to establishments or to cultures must perforce draw opposition. To illustrate this point, let us look again at the area of cosmological theory.[1]

The Copernican theory of 1543 was empirically validated by Galileo Galilei in 1610. However, society's adulation and honors did not follow Galileo's magnificent feat; in fact, condemnation and ridicule were his allowance. His discovery of new planets, a by-product of his validation activities, was also ridiculed. Sizi scoffingly asked, Were there not seven of all important matters: cardinal virtues, mortal sins, sacred candlesticks, plagues, wonders of the world? Therefore "there can be no more than seven planets in heaven, and the new ones revealed by the telescope are an optical illusion" (Sizi, 1610, reported by de Santilliana, 1962). The main contempt, of course, was for Galileo's claim that the Pythagorean/Copernican statement of a heliocentric universe was correct. In 1616 a church commission found it to be utterly false, causing a "typical man about town, Monsignor Querengo" (de Santilliana, 1962, p. 119) to write in his journal:

> The disputes of Signor Galileo have dissolved into alchemical smoke, since the Holy Office has declared that to maintain this opinion is to dissent manifestly from the infallible dogmas of the Church. So here we are at last, safely back on a solid earth, and we do not have to fly with it as so many ants crawling on a balloon (p. 132).

Those two quotations give some idea of the reaction to Galileo's findings, where once again we see the operation of the dictum, "if the facts disagree with my opinion, something is wrong with the facts." It seems permissible, in view of those and other reactions to Galileo to summarize the views of the person-in-the-street (de Santilliana's "typical man about town") with a hypothetical quotation, one that could reasonably go like this: "Copernicus and Galileo have created a cosmos that is a bad cosmos because it puts man in an inferior position. Copernicus, Galileo, and their kind must be stopped from making up and propagating such ideas."

The point to which this has all been leading, the point that requires reemphasis, is that scientists do not "create" or "make up" facts; they uncover or discover them. Copernicus made up nothing; he uncovered the

---

[1] I make repetitive use of cosmological theories because they provide excellent instructional matter. Although they relate to so sweeping a mass of phenomena, they are relatively simple. They have always been an interest of man, if for no other reason than that they deal with phenomena all humans observe every day. There is another reason, of course, and that is man's historical association of nonterrestial bodies or space with his major questing about his relationship with God, god, or gods. Most persons know the bare outlines of the Ptolemaic/Copernican dispute, so cosmologies provide a wide base for illustrating matters relating to science and cultures' reactions to scientific findings.

laws by which the universe operates, and Galileo validated them. What man does with new, validated knowledge is another matter, as Alfred Nobel pathetically came to see related to his invention of dynamite.

The science of behavior has been committed to one goal: discovery of the principles that account for the establishment, maintenance, and thus the change of behavior. From Pavlov's time to the end of the 1950s is a brief time in man's history, but it is of incalculable significance relative to what man came to know about behavior through the discoveries of behavioral science. As with support for the Copernicus theory, as the data have come in, the opposition has also become greater. This differs from the fear aroused by Copernicus, which was a fear of ideas. If fear is the correct accounting for attacks on behaviorism, it appears to be more a fear of the technology, because it is the technology that is most vigorously attacked.

Behavioral science has not thought up new behavior-control techniques. Behavioral science has uncovered the principles by which man's behavior has *always* been established and maintained and has been and is controllable. Certainly the now vastly refined technology based on those principles can be employed for outcomes that some persons will deem undesirable; at the same time other persons will consider those same outcomes desirable. How man uses the technology is a mortal/ethical question, as it is with use of dynamite and atomic power, as it was with fast-burning powder, whose undesirable use is shown in its most common name, gunpowder. This chapter considers some of the general and specific concerns that have been expressed about behaviorism, but primarily about the technology based on behavior principles.

THE PLEASURE-SEEKING, PAIN-AVOIDING PRINCIPLE

No survey figures are known that tell how many persons are turned off by behaviorism because of this basic principle, but personal experience leads me to believe that it could be a large number. It appears to me that their turning-off is a result of two characteristics. One is a strong caring for humans and the human lot. As people who value caring, they are turned off to applications of behavior principles because they incorrectly attribute to those principles the characteristic of noncaring about humans or the human lot. They take for granted that behavioral science, because it is a science, must be cold about humans. The other condition producing the turning-off is ignorance of the principles. Let me offer a long, hypothetical statement here as if it were a quotation in order to catch up the essence of the misunderstanding about the pleasure-seeking, pain-avoiding principle basic to behaviorism.

You behaviorists are saying that persons are essentially hedonistic; that humans crave to satisfy animal-like pleasures of the body. Apparently you take that idea from brief moments in history that touched only a few persons, such as during the decline of the Roman Empire when certain practices were the mark of the few who were rich, but around whom the history of the times was written as if they were the many. In my experience, persons forego many pleasures and make many sacrifices. They deliberately engage in painful behavior, if you will. Thus I cannot accept the fundamental principle of behaviorism that man in general seeks pleasure and seeks to avoid pain.

That statement is a summing of genuine concerns often expressed to me and others. Its substance requires elaboration and clarification of the principle.

The take-off point is this statement of fact: most of a person's behaviors that provide pleasure or pain are learned behaviors; thus pleasure and pain, like beauty, are in the eye of the beholder.

The first pleasurable and painful experiences of the human are identical, inherent ones. The sucking/swallowing pattern of infant behaviors is pleasing and rewarding. It is a part of the baggage of reflexes every human carries at birth, reflexes that are required for maintaining life. Fondling is rewarding, a pleasure, and, as noted earlier, is important in development, if not in life maintenance. Sudden loss of physical support is frightening, and the accidental jabbing with a diaper pin produces a sensation of pain. Beyond these and a few other pleasurable and painful sensations common to all infants, those events that please and pain any person have been learned; they are patterns of responses unique to each person.

Certainly there were those in the Roman Empire who engaged in behaviors you and I consider undesirable, engaged in them because they gave pleasure, such as watching persons being devoured by wild animals, gladiators killing each other in brutal fashion, or the burning alive of humans—learned pleasures. What of Christians so killed? It is not accurate to say that they were seeking pleasure, but it is tenable to say that given the requirements of death by burning, their prospect of thus meriting quick entry into Heaven and a closeness with God accounted for the serenity with which some of them are recorded as meeting so hideous a death. If we can trust the histories of those days, it is recorded that some zealous Christians of the early church did indeed seek out occasions for early dispatch to a happy everlasting life. Would that be pleasure seeking?

We now place the focus on infants and readily recall the fact of their worldwide love of milk when given in the nursing (fondling) context. Move up to youth, and we find societies wherein youth are still pleasured by drinking milk, but others wherein milk is most undesirable. Youths in some societies are pleased with the delicacy of sheep eyes, given on special occasions. Those youths, it is safe to suggest, would be in gustatorial agony if forced to gnaw on raw blubber, which, at one time, was a delicacy in the Arctic. A chief taste pleasure of most of our own youth is the mass-produced hamburger sandwich, and there is little likelihood of sheep's eyes or blubber ever being on our school lunch menus. We see demonstrated again and again the culturally determined learned pleasures, not only in food, but in more complex and subtle behaviors, such as in music, dance, sex, and religion.

So too with pain. Here we must note as an aside that the precise use of the word means the unpleasant message to the brain, a message of which a person is aware when nerve endings are damaged or incorrectly used. Pain, accurately speaking, is a response to structural damage. The distress a person experiences as a consequence of hurtful social actions is as great or greater than the distress caused by true physical pain. In metaphorical usage, therefore, a person's reaction to psychological hurt has come to be called pain. And each of us has either experienced or is intimately aware of youths who suffer the most severe pain when rejected by other youths whose liking they crave, or adolescents whose appearance is, in their view, blemished by acne, obesity, protruding ears, or other conditions considered disfigurements in our particular society. Adolescence is a time of acute pain of this kind for many young persons.

The specifics of psychological pain are learned, as are the specifics of pleasure. These learned pleasures and pains are in a hierarchy at any one time, with some pleasure and pain responses more potent than others. Their potency shifts for a variety of reasons, and thus their place in the hierarchy can be different at different times. A fact complicating the understanding of a person's behavior is that persons emit behaviors that have both reinforcing and extinguishing outcomes at the same time. Ask a professional player of any body contact sport.

The basic ideas are tested by looking at Glenn, who gives most of his income to fiscally unfortunate humans. He enjoys the giving. Said in more precise terms, he is rewarded by the behavior pattern that is summed by the term "giving," and this learned rewarding response is a reinforcing stimulus of the behaviors called "giving." Glenn was not born with the behaviors to which our culture gives the positive valuing term of generosity. He learned those behaviors. One small behavior of that chain of behaviors known as generosity may have been emitted randomly and was reinforced. Other behaviors in that chain were either elicited, such as by modeling, or were also emitted randomly. However caused, they too were reinforced by rewarding each small behavior.

Charles, on the other hand, is described with the culturally negative label "stingy." Charles not only did not have reinforced for him the behaviors of generosity, if he ever emitted them, but did have wealth-retention behaviors reinforced. The differences between Glenn and Charles show that for some persons the chief pleausre they find relative to their wealth is to seek the opportunity to emit giving behaviors. For other persons, those who would find giving behaviors to be punishing, the pleasure-giving behaviors related to wealth are those that result in its retention.

Another fact to counter the misunderstanding of the pleasure/pain principle that was expressed in the hypothetical quotation is an extension of the first fact. There are many traits that can be learned, and are learned by many, that illustrate the class of those persons who do not seek "animal-like gratifications" or avoidance of displeasures. Such persons find doing things for the common good a pleasant experience. They seek out such experiences. Their behaviors, in the phrase of this topic's heading, are pleasure-seeking, but not hedonistic. The memory of any one of us is replete with knowledge of persons who engaged in exhausting, potentially self-harmful behaviors for the common good—the volunteer forest fire fighter among many, in the news as this is written.

In sum, the behavior principle of pleasure seeking, whether hedonistic or selfless, and pain avoidance, whether for self-protection only or accompanied by useful social outcomes, has always operated in every human life. To use the brief label "pleasure seeking" to name the principle, particularly in our moralistic society, appears to result in misunderstanding and rejection of the principle on the part of some persons. The guidance practitioner knows the meaning of the principle and brings the best assistance to a youth in increasing or decreasing certain of the youth's behaviors by first finding the pleasure/pain hierarchy that youth has learned. This was said in a somewhat different way under the topic of reinforcers in Chapter 5.

OPERANT CONDITIONING: NEW AND TRENDY?

Man's behavior has always been established and maintained by what we now call respondent and operant conditioning. The laws related to respondent conditioning were uncovered first, and only recently has science turned up the laws related to operant conditioning. The essence of the principles of operant conditioning has been known for ages, however, passed on for centuries in folk psychology. Some of the aphorisms of folk psychology have been noted in other places, but here is another. "Nothing succeeds like success." The technology based on behavior principles tells how to produce success: to attain a successful behavior, shape it by successive approximations, each of which is presented in such a way that the learner will be successful. Success results in rewards, which are reinforcing stimuli to continue the behavior or similar behaviors.

150   Concerns About Applying Behavioral Science

The scientific study of operant conditioning was begun over a half-century ago by E. L. Thorndike under the label "the law of effect," but only within the past two decades has the term "operant" (or "instrumental") conditioning become common. Persons who have never studied psychology are likely to know the term "operant conditioning," its use being reported in newspapers, books, popular magazines, and television with ever-increasing frequency. One illustration: the wide printed and televised reactions to the publication of *Beyond Freedom and Dignity* (Skinner, 1971). The untutored person, however, may falsely assume that some new procedure for mediating behavior has been developed recently and consider it a technological fad that will be replaced before long by another fad.

In fact, mankind's history is filled with references to the fact that it has long been known that the consequences of behavior are crucial in establishing, maintaining, or extinguishing behavior, even though other accountings for behavior, such as astrology, a faculty of will, angels and demons, and so on, competed at the same time. One homey illustration of the fact that people have known about the effect of consequences is found in Grandma's Law (Homme, 1970), repeated here several times, which is represented by a statement such as, "You won't get any dessert, Jane, until you eat your vegetables," a comment likely made in countless homes for countless years. What psychological science has done (mostly in the past 25 years) is reduce this law of effect into quite specific components so that there is now not only incredibly greater knowledge about behavior formation and maintenance, but precise procedures available for mediating all classes of behaviors.

One very important practical outcome of these recent findings, incidentally, has been the replacement of punishment, the technology of behavior control for thousands of years, by reward procedures. But here again science runs counter to cultures and to the behaviors of individuals in those cultures that use punishment as the primary control technique.[2]

The current rejection of the findings of behavioral science by some of the general populace, and indeed even by some who view themselves as applied behavioral scientists, appears to be the result of an assumed value

---

[2] Recall that Chapter 4 noted that behavioral science is the only science that has to compete with theological systems, and that is so in the applied field as well as the conceptual. Punishment provides a specific illustration, one which starts with a news event. A number of years ago a headmaster of a church-directed school in Maryland was taken to court for physical abuse of a student. The court hearings turned up the fact that not only the headmaster but all teachers often whipped their charges, practicing a God-directed behavior mediation procedure, they claimed. Their biblical authority was the directive, "Spare the rod and spoil the child." In court the headmaster stated that the only way to change undesirable behavior into desirable behavior is to follow God's direction and thus to beat children.

conflict, a conflict that is apparent rather than real, or is the result of respondent conditioning in the rejector. Let us look at one assumed conflict.

The "Humanism Versus Science" Nonissue

The swift rise to prominence, if not dominance, of behavior technology in the past decade or so has caused counter movements, including one within, of all places, professional psychology. Among such persons the nonissue of humanism versus something not clear but suggesting a cold, "mechanistic," noncaring for humans has been vigorously voiced and represents not only a misunderstanding of behavior principles but also of humanism. Thoreson (1973) finds it interesting that "many contemporary humanists now oppose the scientific world view" that was initiated by Renaissance scholars "as a reaction against the revealed truth of the Church and the dominance of Aristotelian thinking" (p. 386), those forces that had the sum effect of being antihumanistic.

Some who have a concept of themselves as humanists hold that these empirically validated laws of behavior devalue humans. This is not a valid position. If a person cares about humans, is humanistic, he surely will wish to work from the best possible basis for the benefit of humans. To illustrate, let us imagine an elderly physician or nurse whose training was done considerably in the past. We hypothesize also that this person has acquired behaviors toward patients that can be described as caring, solicitous, sentimental. This practitioner is aware that relatively recent medical research establishes the fact that a postoperative patient must sit, stand, then walk shortly after surgery so as to accelerate recovery. The professional behaviors of this hypothetical health practitioner, however, are more potently under the control of his sentimental behaviors about patients. Despite his knowing the validity of rapid postoperative motion, we hypothesize for this illustration that he encourages the patient to remain in bed until the patient can move without pain. This hypothetical practitioner might account for his professional behaviors by saying that his humanism does not allow him to permit the patient to suffer the pain that accompanies motion after an operation. The tenable position to the contrary would be that his humanism would require him to apply to the patient the established medical facts—that indeed, if the patient's welfare was his concern, his professional practices must come under control of the facts. The patient's short-run discomfort is necessary for long-run health. Short-run comfort will mean long-run disadvantage to health. It is a humanistic characteristic to hold, as some do, "that the use of reason and methods of science provide the best single means of solving human problems and improving the quality of human life" (Thoreson, 1973, p. 386).

Among some practitioners the rejection of the mass of evidence about behavior acquisition, strengthening, or extinction may be accounted for by their having been professionally prepared in some school of behavior theory that is based on metaphorical or poetic concepts instead of one based on science. A person who may learn to comfortably account for behavior through such metaphors may persist in their use. He has not studied the empirical results and thus does not come to know that accounting for behavior no longer necessitates using temporary, gap-filling metaphors. That person's avoidance of study of behavior principles, in turn, may be under the control of other invalid behaviors that are symbolized by such statements as, "Because I am a humanist and the emphasis in psychology on behavior defines humans as robots and treats humans mechanistically, I'll have none of it." The invalidity of the statement, of course, is in the minor premise—that the behavior emphasis defines humans as robots.[3]

Operant Conditioning: A Technique of Limited Applicability?

Some persons have expected operant conditioning to be a technique used by counselors and others, thus needing to be known by such practitioners, but other than this deliberate use, they would see operant conditioning as having no significance for mediating behavior. In analogy, certain medical specialists should learn surgical techniques, but such techniques have no significance for the day-to-day behaviors of the person-in-the-street. The error lies in equating surgery, which will not occur unless someone deliberately does it, with operant conditioning, which operates incessantly in all human lives as it has for all human history.

All human behaviors have always been established and are maintained by respondent/operant conditioning; they are under the control of patterns of reinforcing/aversive stimuli. Persons just starting formal study of behavior are often surprised by that statement because they have not been aware of the experiences that have shaped their behavior; for them this assertion is not supported by noticeable evidence from their own lives. Said another way, their own experience results in a strong competing response that serves to inhibit the acquisition of this cognition. No surprise in that; it is an example of the experience-is-the-best-teacher fallacy. For Galileo to give irrefutable evidence of the validity of the Copernican postulate about the heliocentric nature of our universe did not result in acceptance of this cognition among even the educated persons of the day,

---

[3] Ullmann (1970) presents a lengthy and lucid discussion of this "mechanistic" challenge. The reader who is not persuaded by the brief treatment given herein owes himself the reading of Ullman's article.

let alone the mass of humans who were uneducated. Among the latter, if not the former, Galileo's statement *had* to be false for the obvious reason that experience dictated otherwise. "Any fool can see the sun go around the earth!" A better analogy, however, is one that finds persons rejecting an idea, not because they seem to have strong competing evidence, but because they either have too little or no evidence and/or have taken on faith some other accounting for phenomena. The germ cause of illness was rejected by some because their experience did not support the idea of the existence of microscopic bodies, and moreover "we have been told by authorities" that physical disorders are caused by demons, or at least by sin. Or biological evolution is an incorrect idea because it contravenes history as recorded in the Bible, and moreover pictures of animals starting with those painted in caves of prehistoric men and on down through time show that all animals are as originally created, and man was separately created and is now as he was created. On the sole basis of that evidence, the concept of biological evolution indeed would have to be rejected.

The person undereducated about nourishment can think that vitamins are what one gets out of a bottle and are not a characteristic of foods normally eaten. Or that farm crops have either had chemicals put on them for fertilizer, or that, if not, the crops are "chemical free," being ignorant of the fact that "natural" soil is a collection of chemicals. A person undereducated about behavior can erroneously think that reinforcement is a technique occasionally applied to a person by an applied behavioral scientist but otherwise not a characteristic of normal daily living. In addition, because naïve motoric behavior quickly and permanently responds to operant conditioning, and because it is children who emit naïve, simple behaviors more than adults, demonstrations of reinforcement procedures can be easily and clearly conducted with children and, of course, with animals. Such demonstrations constitute a bulky part of the literature because they have been carried out for a long time and are relatively simple to do. It is understandable, therefore, that operant conditioning can come to mean a process that an applied behavioral scientist "does to" a creature, and the creature is either an animal or, if human, an infant or child.

Many of the relatively simple behaviors of a child can be readily fixed through reinforcement. One might be justified to use the figure, then, that behavior B in a child is elicited by pressing button A. So many adult behaviors, on the other hand, are fantastically complex. The adult has learned which stimuli to attend to, respondent conditioning has contributed to that attending and to orienting the person to other behaviors, reinforcements for one kind of behavior have sometimes been matched by punishments for the same behavior, or two competing aspects of a larger behavior have been reinforced, stimulus generalizations have been common, and so on. No "button A" for most adults, rather a melange of buttons, pushed with some randomness, to continue the metaphor, some producing a strong kick, others resulting in weak forces.

To continue in this vein, and at the same time to further extinguish the view that the human is only a reactive organism, the metaphor requires the statement that a large proportion of the buttons are inside the adult. Despite the complexity of human behavior, to know how it is formed and can be mediated produces simple procedures to follow, procedures that work—what works being the ultimate test of knowledge about natural phenomena. This is in contrast to older ideas about behavior, which, in the absence of adequate knowledge, had to be largely formulated around metaphors. Psychoanalysis, for example, is long, tedious, and difficult to practice, a metaphorically based complexity that often accounts for behavior in too simple terms. In contrast, the empirically supported positions recorded in later chapters provide relatively simple, short procedures for mediating complex behaviors.

Operant Conditioning Is Secretive and Manipulative

Yes and no. It would be interesting to accompany one reader of this book for a day, and from time to time ask him what are the elements in the pattern of stimuli that are causing the particular behavior patterns to be emitted at that moment. It is safe to assume that only a few could respond accurately, because as adults most of us are not aware of the reinforcing stimuli controlling our behaviors of the moment.

In any adult's life this lack of awareness might result from several causes. For one, reinforcers for adults are mostly subtle patterns of contingencies, although occasionally some single and apparent event can be discerned as having reinforcing properties. The regular paycheck illustrates one single and apparent reinforcer. Another general condition that prevents most adults from being aware of the reinforcing patterns that continuously affect their behaviors is embedded in their individual histories. This personal history has provided an array of behaviors that have been repeated so often that they are easily emitted by subtle stimuli, internal and/or external, of which the person is not aware. A simple example: a person is starting to learn to drive a hand-shifted car. He has to attend to (be aware of) a variety of stimuli, and successful shifting behaviors are reinforced through the car's responding in the desired fashion. Incorrect responses are extinguished because they result in the car's responding in an undesired or punishing way. Come back to that driver a half-year later. We note that he can go through complex traffic, shifting up and down faultlessly, all the time chatting about a topic in no way related to driving. His behavior remains under the control of reinforcing and aversive contingencies, but he has no awareness of that. The cues he receives that result in shifting are now so subtle as to be below his level of awareness. Of course, the entire array of orchestrated motoric behaviors related to driving are under control of subtle stimuli, even though only gear shifting was used for the specific illustration.

Another aspect of a person's history operates to make the person unaware that his behaviors are under the control of reinforcement contingencies. As we grow older we gain greater control over such contingencies. A high school youth has more control over contingencies than a child does, yet even he typically cannot select the high school he attends, as an example of some of his lack of control. If the contingencies in that high school happen to be more aversive than reinforcing of certain behaviors that are central to all other behaviors, he can escape the aversive stimuli only by withdrawing from school. This is a behavior that some youths cannot produce because that withdrawing behavior is prevented by even stronger parental contingencies. That is, the youth emits competing responses, and the stronger response will control his behavior. With full adulthood, however, the person now picks and chooses from among environments, and he chooses environments that continuously and unobtrusively reward, and he avoids environments that are aversive. This fact, incidentally, is a central consideration in occupational and marriage decisions, which sum to seeking rewarding environments and avoiding painful ones. The selection of environments (of ecosystems) by adults produces two outcomes of note. First, as a person ages his characteristics can become amplified; he may become a purer distillate of what he was at an earlier age. The other outcome is one that has been posited just above: repeated contingency patterns and a history of speedily emitted repeated behaviors that follow cause the person to be unaware of the fact that his behavior is under control of such contingencies.

The findings of Copernicus and Galileo were rejected because they countered established myths. Operant conditioning is opposed by some persons because the concept includes the fact that much of a person's behavior is formed by others without the person being aware of it, which runs counter to the myth that anyone can do whatever "he has a mind to do." If modern medical science demonstrates that a river held sacred for thousands of years and believed to have curing properties actually is a trough of disease-bearing microbes, then those who propagate the myth may be obliged to assail medical science. To assail medical science does not change the facts. It does emphasize the continuing need for examining values and ethics. Advertisers now know the laws of operant conditioning and employ them widely, whether in selling gasoline, a deodorant, or a president. Our citizens are constantly bombarded by "hidden persuaders," meaning that consumers are unaware of being "sold." Behavior specialists employ the laws of operant conditioning for others' benefit, not exploitation, even though at times the recipients of such assistance are unaware of its application. It is pointless to inform (make aware) an infant or young child who has acquired self-destructive behaviors that he is about to be subjected to operant conditioning procedures to replace those behaviors with self-enhancing ones. If the nurse treating the Korean War veterans in the illustration in Chapter 5 had announced that she was going to employ arousing procedures, there probably could have been no desired change in the soldiers' behaviors. In other instances, however, not only is there no need for secrecy about contingency management activities, but they should be explained for ethical reasons and also because the effect of those procedures will be greater when their nature and use are known by the persons whose behaviors are to be changed.

As with some of man's inventions, natural laws can be used for man's good or evil. Those who uncovered the laws of operant conditioning did not invent a procedure that includes "unaware manipulation" of others. They have simply identified with precision what has always occurred in human life. They have made it possible for skilled behavior practitioners to use this knowledge for human good, just as in the converse they have made it possible for skilled human exploiters to use this knowledge for their devious ends.

Manipulation is an ugly word for some. In this context it means the deliberate forming of another person's behavior with that person remaining unaware that his behavior is being formed, and it is intended that the behavior so formed is for the benefit of the person doing the forming or shaping as much as for the benefit of the person whose behavior is being manipulated.

All parents have been manipulators. Always they have tried to make their children behave in certain ways, defined by such terms as "a good (Methodist, Jew, Muslim, Hindu, Catholic, agnostic)," or "a good (Italian, Ethiopian, Paraguayan, Sioux)." Parents have forever sought and always will seek to transmit prized cultural ways and will constantly stress to eliminate as much free will as possible.

For example, we assume that a set of parents has a refined definition of honesty and wishes to have this trait expressed by their child in all manners of his behaviors. Without using the terms, they shape their child's behaviors by reinforcing procedures. Their intention is to produce that kind of young adult of whom they can say, "My child is completely honest; no matter what temptations to be dishonest he will face, he will be honest." In answer it is proposed here that the parents have as their goal that their child can never choose to be dishonest, but rather that they will have so determined his behavior that he shall always choose to be honest. He shall have no free will about honesty. The outcome of such training is a person with choices whose range has been conditioned and could be reconditioned, but not a person who is a robot.

To ponder these ideas may be to put such terms as "manipulation" and "free will" into a valid perspective. To ponder these terms is also to cause us to see again how in the past we have needed to describe natural human events with oversimple, untestable concepts.

For all man's history operant conditioning has been used to manipulate the behavior of infants, children, and youths, but always for the intended good of the youngsters, in the parents' view. The guidance practitioner, however, mediates behavior only on request of the adolescent, and then he explains what is happening. It is the applied behavioral scientist who now can use operant conditioning in a nonmanipulative, nonsecret way.

REFERENCES

HOMME, L. *How to Use Contingency Contracting in the Classroom.* Champaign, Ill.: Research Press, 1970.

DE SANTILLIANA, G. *The Crime of Galileo.* New York: Time Incorporated, 1962.

SKINNER, B. F. *Beyond Freedom and Dignity.* New York: Knopf, 1971.

THORESON, C. E. "Behavioral Humanism." In C. E. Thoreson (Ed.), *Behavior Modification in Education,* Part 1, 72nd Yearbook, NSSE. Chicago: National Society for the Study of Education, 1973.

ULLMANN, L. P. "Beyond the Reinforcement Machine." In S. H. Osipow & W. B. Walsh (Eds.), *Change in Counseling: Readings and Cases.* Englewood Cliffs, N.J.: Prentice-Hall, 1970.

7 Principles of Development

INTRODUCTION

The guidance aspect in education is the mustering of school resources to facilitate individuals' development and their movement into a satisfying adulthood. Although all members of a school staff have guidance interests and therefore carry out some guidance functions, most guidance specialists need to have greater knowledge than teachers about the several variables that affect human development. A major variable in all human life is the influence of a number of social systems on development. Said differently, the noticeable differences among individuals are partly attributable to the differences among the social system that each individual is or has been a member of. Not only does an introductory understanding of the guidance movement require attention to this variable, but those who will become professionals will need to attend to this variable in greater depth than considered here. Without that knowledge, the guidance specialist would be less effective.

The essence of behavior principles was set out in Chapter 5 and to some degree elaborated on in Chapter 6. Therein the social nature of learning, of acquiring behavior, was treated indirectly. This chapter focuses on the significance of social systems for development, and for behavior acquisition.

Variables other than social systems bear on the quality and direction of an individual's development, of course. The patterned changes in behavior we call development are partially organic, for example, and thus mostly independent of all other variables. Even if it were possible for a person to live in complete isolation from all other humans, physiological differences among humans that are born into each would result in greatly different behaviors among them.

Most human behavior results from socialization, however. The behaviors of interest to the guidance specialist are those specific ones that result from students' being members of specific societies, rather than interest in behaviors in general. For his assistance to individuals the specialist needs to know the principles that define how societies affect behavior in general. Mostly, however, the specialist needs to be able to ferret out the meaning for each individual's behavior from his transaction with his several social systems. It is a student's specific behaviors, including his conceptualizations about the future, with which a specialist deals when essaying assistance to that student.

This chapter's first concern is with social systems in general, examined under the concept and term "ecosystems," and with the specific behaviors that result from differences among ecosystems. Then the significance for individuals' behaviors of these general principles is examined by a longitudinal look at development, to which are added effects on behavior from variables other than ecosystems.

SOCIAL SYSTEMS AND HUMAN DEVELOPMENT

The phrase "social system" is frequently used, but apparently it is often used without the writer or speaker's understanding or explaining the significance of the word "system" in that phrase. That word means that any social institution operates on those principles relating to systematic guidance examined in Chapter 2. An institution operates on systems principles whether or not humans see that. Our solar complex operated in a systematic way whether or not humans understood its laws.

Essential to systems theory, to review the point, is that elements of the system are locked into each other so that the system, when healthy, operates as a whole. The living elements of the system, these would be humans in a social system, are in that kind of intense and thorough interlocking with each other and other aspects of the system that the word "transaction" was created to convey.

Pursuing the idea more specifically, we can first look at an older phrase that was used to describe that relationship: the individual *and* his environment. This phrase showed the ignorance of those days about the nature of persons and environments. Another phrase is a better approximation of the reality: the individual *in* his environment. But that still is not adequate, and the frustrating reality is that the psychological fact cannot readily be described by a short phrase.

The greatly inadequate term, "the individual and his environment," permits the inaccurate visualization in Figure 7.

Figure 7.   The individual and his environment.

The better phrase, though still inadequate, "the individual in his environment," permits the type of visualization in Figure 8.

Figure 8.   The individual in his environment.

The adequate visualization of an individual and his environment at the moment of looking at him, whether that environment is family, school, or other social system, lets us see him not as an entity discrete from that environment (even if "in" it), but diffused with the environment somewhat as in Figure 9.

This last visualization, for which no brief phrase can be an adequate representation, conveys that a person and environments are transacting. They are locked into a system. One analogy, often used to convey this locking is that of magnetic forces and a metal object. A metal object is seeable as a separate entity from a magnet to which it is attracted, and the magnet, of course, can be seen as a discrete entity from the attracted metal

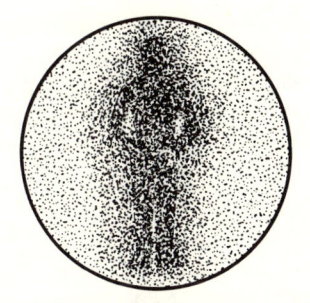

Figure 9. *The individual and environment in transaction.*

object. Yet the unseen magnetic force makes the metal object and the magnet a single entity, a system.

The introduction stated the desirability of examining social systems and individual development as but a single topic, a need demonstrated by the simple illustration of the magnet and metal object. The behavior of the metal object, nonliving, of course, cannot be understood outside of the system into which it is locked. Understanding human behavior, inestimably more complex in contrast to the metal object, requires the same consideration of occurrence, and not just in one system, but the numerous social systems with which the individual is in transaction. With this repeating of the need for synthesis so that you can be made more alert to that need, we now move to the more separate examination of the two concepts, focusing first on the school as a social system.

The School as an Ecosystem

The heading of this section uses a term that is more accurately descriptive than just "system" and in many instances is a better term than "social system." "Ecosystem" conveys subtleties that the term "social system" might not convey. It is a term borrowed for human concerns from biology, and in that field, according to Smith (Esposito, 1971)[1] it refers to:

> a naturally occurring assemblage of plants and animals that live in the same environment, are mutually sustaining and interdependent, and are constantly fixing, utilizing and dissipating energy. The interacting populations are characterized by constant death and replacement and usually by immigration and emigration of individuals. The populations are always

---

[1] The material on the following pages, including the quotations from Smith and Barker, is quoted from Esposito's (1970) address. Dr. Esposito's address crystallized my thinking about ecosystems and his willingness for me to quote his presentation at such length is herewith acknowledged with thanks.

fluctuating, with seasonal and environmental changes. The community depends upon and is influenced by the habitat, the specific set of conditions that surround the organisms, such as sunlight, soil, mineral elements, moisture, temperature and topography. The biotic (living) and the abiotic (nonliving) interact, thus creating an ecological system or *ecosystem*.

Moving over to psychology, the discipline that undergirds counseling and other types of helping services, Barker (1968) observes:

> Ecological psychology deals not only with events involved in a player's catching a ball in a ball game, but also with the playing field (its size and shape), the other players (their number and skill), the rules of the game, and other ecological phenomena that affect the consequences for subsequent behavior of catching or not catching the ball. The subject matter of ecological psychology . . . must be represented by circuits that incorporate the behavior of persons with objects and events of the ecological environment to form interdependent units.

The person concerned with assisting another person and doing so from an ecological stance about behavior must deal with understanding, predicting, and controlling the interdependent relationships between and among the behavior of persons, objects, and events in an environment. And he is aware that the same environment provides different inputs to different persons and different inputs to the same person if his behavior changes. The environmental input also changes if its structural and dynamic properties are changed. (This latter fact is the reason the helping practitioner must acquire strategies for mediating an institution's social system. First he must know about social systems.)

The fallacy to be prevented by these observations is that characteristics of environment A result in behavior B in person C. The ecological position requires the statement to read: the transaction of environment A and person C produce behavior B. The significance of this statement is that the helping practitioner does not focus his understanding techniques solely or even primarily on the person he seeks to help. Instead he seeks to understand the systemic properties of the social system *and* the characteristics of the individual in the system so as to mediate the individual's behavior. The practitioner's function requires this synthesizing of the human and nonhuman domains of the natural environment and the behaviors of the individual. To this end data of a multidisciplinary nature are collected and analyzed. Said another way, the practitioner's professional functions are not limited to interacting with the individual to be helped, but require concern with the systemic or organizational characteristics of the helpee's natural environment.

In addition to requiring the integration of the physical, psychosocial, and social-cultural milieus, the ecological rubric necessitates viewing these interactions from evolutionary principles that stress the *process* of human development.

Any ecosystem, either field biological or psychosociological, might have one characteristic or element that determines most other properties of that system. A discernible and prime element of all those ecosystems we label "school" is the adults, although that primacy diminishes during adolescence (high schools) and in young adulthood (postsecondary education or training). Biological ecosystems, however, differ as to their prime element. When we speak of a forest, we are employing a shorthand term for an ecosystem comprised of many different living elements whose existence and interrelationships are determined by the prime element, the many tall trees that we call "forest." "Swamp" is the name we give to an ecosystem with forms of life and interrelationships among them determined by the primary condition of always wet ground. The ecosystem of a freshwater swamp differs from the ecosystem of a saltwater swamp or marsh, and the ecosystem of either kind of swamp found in northern climates differs from the ecosystem of either type of swamp in the tropics.

It is adults who, to a major degree determine the other elements of the school as an ecosystem, as noted, and each ecosystem (each school) must be studied ideographically. To know one school as an ecosystem is not to know all schools because schools differ as to the kinds of adults and students that are their populations. The way humans differ is a major variable in causing the differences in schools' ecosystems.

Think for a bit what it means to adults to be part of the ecosystem called school, and what it means differently to youth. For adults the school is an end, an occupation that constitutes the linch-pin holding together most other components of their individual lives. To "be" a teacher, principal, or whatever, means something more than helping students learn. In some circumstances a student who disrupts a class might be objectively viewed by a teacher as a young human who needs special thought and assistance. In more common circumstances the disrupting student is viewed as a threat. He threatens the psychological well-being of the teacher. That kind of student is, in effect, a public statement that "this teacher cannot teach, cannot control his class," and is privately viewed as an enemy, albeit an impersonal one. The disruptive student can be aversive not only because he frustrates the teacher's immediate professional behaviors, but, particularly if the teacher is not yet tenured, because he is a threat to the teacher's career, and thus to his economy, and to his entire being. If the teacher is fired, his life might well come apart.[2]

---

[2] Fuller (1969) studied the research in this area and found reactions of threat (self-protection) characteristic of teachers early in their careers. She found, however,

For students, school is a way-station in life and it cannot have the meaning for them that it does for teachers even if it is thought of as the setting of a temporary full-time job. At best it is a pleasant experience that will be exploited for such personal gains as good marks and maybe therefore college admittance and even a scholarship, for the pleasure of athletics or music, for the usefulness of learning a trade or other employable skills, and so on. At worst it is a painful, meaningless experience, a mass of aversive stimuli to be escaped from no later than the birth anniversary that legally permits withdrawal. For youth at both of these extremes school is a temporary point in life, coinciding with the surge of exquisite sense of self that comes with adolescence. The teleological gap between the adults and youths is massive, and the power of the adults is supreme. To know the school as an ecosystem requires, if nothing else, an understanding of the interaction of the adults in the school, along with community cultural variables.[3]

This knowledge of the school's adult social system requires that study must be made of the interactions of the adults. Inquiries of the following kind are useful:

1. What teacher groups are there?
2. For each group
    a. What is the primary bond that attracts and holds members?
    b. What are the demographic variables: (age, geographic origins) and cultural variables (social class, religion, ethnic commonalities) of the group members?
    c. Career characteristics: commitment ("I am a professional teacher" versus "teaching is just a temporary job for me"), length of service, career path, and ambitions in education?
    d. Behaviors of the group relative to the school's principal: submissive, equal, dominating, admiring, fearful? Is the group sought out by the principal for advice and socializing, or shunned by the principal?
    e. Behaviors of this group related to other groups: to which other group does it behave aggressively or submissively? With which other does it socialize or avoid social interaction? What is its general professional standing with other groups?

---

that data appear to support the idea that experienced teachers are more concerned about pupils. It can be hypothesized that tenure laws can mitigate the threat a teacher might feel when a disruptive youth misbehaves.

[3] This point is clearly demonstrated by Mitchell (1968). He studied 11 metropolitan area high schools using Stern's High School Characteristics Index and found large differences among schools along some dimensions of the HSCI. He concludes that for these school characteristics and their interactions to be understood there is need to recognize "the influence of larger social, psychological, and institutional forces" (p. 528).

Some of these questions or modifications of them can be addressed about individual teachers, of course, and should be. This is so either because not all teachers are members of groups, or are members of several groups, or have independent influence regardless of group membership. Because of the potential prominence of the principal as a dominant feature of the ecosystem, particular study is made of him. Much will be known of the principal's transaction with the other adults, of course, as an outcome of the study of cliques and of individuals. A unique characteristic of the principal's transaction requires particular study: his communications. Because transactions in a human ecosystem are instrumented primarily by words intended to affect behavior through informing and directing, through arousing autonomic reactions, through instrumental conditioning, both positive and negative, and through punishment, the principal's communication behaviors, both formal and informal, written and oral, require study.

The principal's influence on the ecosystem needs attention around the variable of his power over staffing. It is through this variable that a principal has long-range effects on the school ecosystem because he affects in the school what is called, in a field biological ecosystem, the balance of nature. If a principal has hiring power, teachers who leave the school through normal attrition are replaced with teachers who are in accord with the principal's ideas. An aggressive principal can make life unpleasant for dissident teachers who would not normally leave, but who therefore apply for a transfer.[4]

If a new principal of a school that has minimized athletics is a former school and college athlete and is convinced that a school's athletic program makes a school, he will convert that school into one that maximizes its athletic program. Not only will the new staff he hires help do that, but the focus of fund-raising activities he instigates, and the manner in which he uses his discretionary funds raised by those activities will accord with his athletic interests.

In an overview text such as this, topics can be examined only briefly, thus we put aside further attention to procedures for examining adult behaviors that are used to understand the school as an ecosystem. The student who pursues further study of the guidance movement will be given occasion to learn more of the concepts and processes of this topic.[5]

---

[4] I have observed this phenomenon, and principals have also reported to me their success in changing school staffs, including one who recently managed the change from a tradition-oriented faculty to an open-school-oriented faculty in 2 years. Studies at the Bank Street College of Education in New York City have shown that changing a faculty is typically slower, usually 5 years after a new principal takes charge.

[5] A good starting point is Snyder (1971), who covers numerous basic topics in this area.

THE SCHOOL'S GOALS, PROGRAM
REGULARITIES, AND BEHAVIOR REGULARITIES

An ecosystem in field biology differs from a psychosociological ecosystem for the obvious reason that the latter system deals with humans. But there is one characteristic of that kind of psychosociological ecosystem with which guidance practitioners deal, that is, schools, which may not be characteristic of other kinds of psychosociological ecosystems. This characteristic is the existence of formal and informal statements of purpose for setting up and maintaining the ecosystem. Schools, as noted in Chapter 2, typically have statements of purpose, often incorporating the type of outcome they seek to bring about (their effect on students). Schools are an example of a formal ecosystem, and that formality is expressed, among other ways, by formal statements of purpose and goals and by the deliberate selection of guidance practitioners for the stated aim of helping the school attain its purposes.

A family, on the other hand, even though it is an ecosystem, is likely to be a far less formal one. Its purpose is formally but ambiguously stated in the marriage contract, which only rarely is written and typically attains no further formal statement of purpose. The interdependency of the humans of the family is not formalized in writing, and the use of the material resources or components of this type of ecosystem typically are equally informally determined and often function within the ecosystem on an ad hoc basis. This relatively informal functioning is desirable for a family, and this absence of a formal document on which to base the transactions of the family members places a family about midway between a formally organized ecosystem, such as a school, and the completely unplanned ecosystem of field biology.

To understand the school as an ecosystem, therefore, we need to know not only what its formal purposes are, as shown in its goal statements, but also its informal purposes. Both purposes theoretically form the base of the institution's culture and also theoretically are controlling principles in the operation of the agency as a formal and informal social system.

Theoretically again, the statement of goals would be the first step in creating this system, followed by the formal establishment of the institution. Then the controlling persons of the institution would set up a structure—the program—of the agency so as to carry out its purposes. The program is in reality comprised of numerous program regularities, that is, systematic procedures that permit the institution to function. These regularities describe the authority flow, the communications plan, the substance of the school's activities (the curriculum of studies), the manner in which that substance will be carried out ("open" nongraded schools as against graded, self-contained elementary classrooms, as an example), and so on.

Program and Behavior Regularities and Ecosystem Intervention

In Chapter 2 the connection between school goals and program and behavior regularities was established in concept. That concept is given further substance through more illustrations with their significance for ecosystem intervention noted. That connection arises from the need to ascertain that a school's program regularities result in the behavior regularities called for by the statement of goals. Although the guidance practitioner is concerned with guidance program regularities and their resultant behavior regularities, illustrations related to general school goals are also useful for testing the idea.

If, for example, school goals were so specifically drawn as to include as outcome that its students shall become increasingly cooperative, then we should be able to find program regularities that have been established to attain that goal. We could then evaluate the behavior regularities of the students to see if indeed there is a consistent increase in cooperation, accompanied by an attempt to determine to what degree that increase can be attributed to the program regularities. To illustrate this last point, with a patently unreal example, a school's goal statement might call for one of its outcomes to be an increase in the height of students. A program regularity designed to attain this goal is that every day, five times a day, each teacher is to ask all students to imagine themselves becoming taller. Growth is demonstrated at the end of 1 year. It was not the program regularity that produced that growth, of course, and that program regularity can be classed as a superstition. The illustration was described as being patently unreal and extreme, but there are other program regularities carried out by numerous institutions that also are superstitions. "A purpose of this school is to develop good citizenship," and one program regularity designed to contribute to that goal is the daily pledge of allegiance to the flag. In the absence of empirical data, this program regularity is a superstition. That does not mean that the daily pledge is devoid of desired effects. Rubbing a rabbit's foot when faced with a problem or danger can have desirable effects for the rubber. The need is to distinguish between the true and useful effects of that behavior regularity of rubbing and the falsely ascribed effects which are of a superstitious nature.

If a school has stated that one of its goals is the development of citizenship among students, a person wishing to know the attainment of that goal first would have to describe the behavior regularities that define citizenship. Then he would seek out what program regularities the school has established to attain those objectives. At the same time he would look to see if other behavior regularities in fact work against an increase among students in attitudes and practices of good citizenship. For example, the school, may not have established any program regularities that permit student participation in decisions, and indeed it may have program regularities that deny students the safeguards of due process, thus resulting in a behavior regularity in opposition to the stated goal.

To carry out this task with an orientation to guidance, we would need to identify program regularities and their effects on student attainment of objectives that are consonant with the guidance movement. These could include, we saw, that all students acquire social competency, self-management behaviors and knowledge and skills that will enable them to become employed upon graduation, or to enter postsecondary education and training that, when completed, will permit employment. If an assessment of this kind were made by the guidance team, and the assessment showed that such behavior regularities were too few, then it would be incumbent on the guidance team to change the program of regularities in the guidance field.

Existing program regularities need to be assessed for their effectiveness, too. Much ecosystem energy might be expended on Career Days, for example, a program regularity in many schools set up to contribute to reaching guidance objectives in career development. The question must be asked, to what degree does the Career Day produce results that justify the energy expended on it? Said again in another way and in more general terms: each program regularity must be held accountable in terms of the quantity and quality of its ensuing behavior regularities.

The practitioners on guidance teams will be more able to mediate behaviors if they examine the school as an ecosystem through its formal and informal statements of goals, identify the program regularities established to attain goals important for effective development, and study the transactions of the adults. In addition there is another component of the ecosystem that requires identification and understanding if behavior mediation efforts are to be successful: the subcultures of the students.

Subcultures of Students in the Ecosystem

An individual is in transaction with other humans in several social systems, and there might be conflicts between goals and program regularities among the several systems of which one individual is a member. In analogy, imagine a shrub of a certain type growing in a tropical saltwater swamp. Imagine the effects on that shrub if it were transplanted to a northern saltwater swamp, then later to a freshwater swamp, then back again to the tropical saltwater swamp. If the shrub did not die, as well it might, its development would be adversely affected. Yet this kind of transplanting occurs to many children and youths every day, not in the same physical sense as in the hypothetical shrub, but in a cultural sense. The conflicting ecosystems can result in conflicts in behaviors in an individual.

A family is a subculture, and likely the family's neighbors are other families of nearly the same subculture, a fact that can be quickly confirmed by visual inspection of neighborhoods. Real-estate values are similar in neighborhoods, partly as a function of similarity of the ages and occupations (incomes) of the adults, and classes of occupations (incomes) are associated with distinctive life styles. If the subculture of a family differs from the subcultures of the adults and the dominant number of children in a school, a child of that family is, in effect, transplanted 5 days a week to an ecosystem, the school, whose dominant features, the adults, might determine an ecosystem that differs in significant ways from the family and neighborhood ecosystems from which the student comes.

Illustrations of the phenomena are countless, but one pronounced example will be useful, not only because it illustrates the point, but also shows the kinds of subcultural variabilities in this country to which guidance practitioners have to attend. This illustration lies in the fact that the culture of certain tribes of indigenous inhabitants of this land (for example, the Pueblo Indians) causes its members to behave in those ways for which Westerners use the summing term "cooperation." Conversely, its members are caused to avoid those behaviors Westerners call "competition." When a youth of this culture is transplanted to a school that rewards competitive behaviors, then at least the guidance specialists of the school must be aware of this cultural transplanting and its effect on that youth. (When a school is staffed by autochthones and serves only indigenous children or youths, as in some schools run by the Bureau of Indian Affairs of the Department of the Interior, then the cultural shock that results from the daily transplanting of children is not present.)

A typical school is populated by students from varying subcultures, a condition more pronounced in high schools which draw their populations from a wider area than elementary schools typically do. Important as subcultural differences are in an elementary school, their importance is magnified in high schools. Children are relatively passive, reactive and present-oriented. In consequence, some behaviors established by their subcultures might be relatively latent during childhood, but will become pronounced and have significance during adolescence. Youths in high school, having entered or passed through the psychological changes accruing to the biological changes producing sexual maturity, are relatively independent and self-determining, thus active and future-oriented, and for them subcultural characteristics then become prominent. To know a school as an ecosystem requires knowledges of the subcultures represented by the students. This need is amplified when a member of the guidance team is seeking to assist an individual. The assistance given will be less effective, and perhaps even ineffective, if the team member does not attend to subcultural characteristics of the individual, and the interaction of those characteristics with the school as an ecosystem.

STUDYING SUBCULTURES. Knowing the subcultures from which groups of students come is relatively easy, with some rather obvious entry points. Likely the best is observation of the student population, using as the filter around which such observation is conducted some questions like those used when studying the adults of the school.

Youth populations in some schools are relatively homogeneous, but in other schools they are found to have highly polarized subcultures. One basis of this polarization in some of those latter schools is race. In other schools where the race variable is a constant, the prime basis for polarization is around life style. This latter variable is satisfying for a gross assessment, but for a more precise understanding of the student population this variable can be broken down further into the subvariables of wealth, intelligence, and conservatism-liberalism differences.

The youth of some schools populated almost entirely by whites have been observed, when race was a constant, to cluster into three groups, called by the youth in those schools the freaks (formerly hippies), squares, and greasers or rednecks. In those schools these groups are quite noticeable because of obvious associations, appearance (hair, clothes), and the visibility they attain through trying to influence school policy or by participation in school-sponsored or -condoned activities.

Most high school students in these continuing studies are identifiable as members of a group or several groups, but a sizeable number of youths are loners—the silent minority. The assessments of youth subculture includes the views of students, scarcely an objective source of data. The names (freaks, and so forth) can convincingly be used about archtypical members of a group, the small inner core, but long hair, jeans, and beards are not limited to freaks, for example, although more freaks have them than not. Some freaks-in-spirit have short hair, and some youths, otherwise conservative, have long hair.

In one school the freaks might be the intelligentsia, in another the squares might be. In some schools the brighter students were found both in the freak group and the square group, although the squares were achievers and the bright freaks were more desultory about academic attainments. Rednecks might be youths of lower income families, or might just be anyone disliked by the youth who is describing the school's subcultures. In short, information received by interviews with youths is imperative, but needs to be balanced against more objective and current data. The titles above (freaks, and so on) were current in one region at the time of the preparation of this book. The same subcultural characteristics might be labeled differently in the same region at a different time, in a different region, or the same label might connote different subcultural behaviors elsewhere. Moreover, even at the time of this writing those carrying out these assessments were reporting changes among youth subcultures in high schools reflecting, among other forces at work, the changes occurring in the larger society.

One manner of this assessment is observation. Who sits with whom in the cafeteria and socializes elsewhere on school grounds? Who comes to rock band concerts? Who publishes the school paper, or the underground paper, if it continued after their common time in the early 1970s? More complex assessment is needed to determine how much school policy apparently is affected by different youth subcultures, and the part parents of such subcultures play in trying to influence school policy. Examples of the latter: "We insist that you (tighten/liberalize) the dress code." When data from these and/or other assessment procedures yield a reasonably comprehensive picture of subpopulations, identifying persons in such groups can be done, at least on a sampling basis. Then cumulative records can be consulted for other demographic data to increase the factorization of subcultural variables.

The capping inquiry in knowing the school as an ecosystem is to assess the effect on youth behavior of the transactions of each of the several youth subcultures, the several teacher groups, individual teachers, and, of course, the principal. Inquire as to the similarity of the behaviors of youth in one subculture to those behaviors called for in the goal statements of the school or in its philosophy statement. Think about that activity in these analogous terms: a country's absolute monarch is converted to a certain religion and he declares his new religion to be the state religion; all subjects must follow its precepts or they will be punished. That religion prescribes codes of behavior, and an observer examines all subcultures of that country with the intention of identifying the degree along a continuum to which each subculture at present has behaviors least like the new codes of behavior to those subcultures that now have behaviors most like the new precepts. The observer can predict, therefore, which subculture will adapt best and have behaviors rewarded by the monarch, and which will be in difficulty with the monarch.

Schools in general can be described as oligarchies of adults, and in rare instances as autocracies, with the principal as the autocrat. Nonetheless student say in the governance of the school is more and more tolerated, if not actively encouraged. A school's goals/philosophy/purpose statement is usually promulgated by adults, sometimes only by school administrator, and it is seen as applicable to all students. Some youth subcultures have behaviors that are in close agreement with that goal statement, whereas the behaviors of other youth subcultures are not congruent with it.

It is not the statement per se that is the important consideration; the important matter is the degree of similarity of behaviors on the part of each youth subculture on entry to the school with the behaviors called for by the program regularities that emanate from the purpose statement, and, perhaps of even more importance, the accord of such behaviors with the program regularities that flow from certain unpublished positions taken by the faculty or even by the principal alone. Are athletics the prime feature of the school, with all the attendant reinforcement of behaviors associated with athleticism? If so, freaks may be an inferior order in that ecosystem. Many freaks will be discomfited by program regularities, such as school assemblies, which glorify jocks (their name for athletes) and athletic activities, and they will avoid behaviors that reinforce athletic activities. On the other hand, behaviors of most of the squares will likely be in accord with athletics-enhancing program regularities.

The subcultures of youth when race is a constant are complex, and assessment of them is difficult. Mixes of races and ethnic subcultures magnify and further compound the need for assessment of the effects on behaviors of the transactions of youth subcultures and the school's adults. For a student to be in a subculture whose members are actively trying to preserve their ethnic identities, such as the Hispanic or so-called Indian subcultures, and for that student to attend a school staffed by Americanized (assimilated, homogenized) adults, no matter what the cultural origins of those adults might be, is to create conditions for development problems. The student's transactions with those adults will require behaviors that differ from those expected by his ethnic group.

In assessing race as a subcultural variable, wherein black youths are a minority in a school, the error of expecting blacks to constitute a single subculture must yield to the fact that there are subcultures of black youths. Black youths from economically middle and upper classes are culturally more like their white counterparts from the same economic levels than they are culturally like blacks from poor families.

To summarize: although adults of a school, even though differing among themselves as they do, are a relatively uniform component of an ecosystem, the students might represent a great variety of subcultures. One of these youth cultures will be similar to the subculture of school adults, but others might be different. Transactions of all components constitute the ecosystem that must be known by members of the guidance team, if by no other school adults, for the reason that assistance in development which team members provide for individuals requires knowing each youth through his behaviors. These behaviors are the product of these transactions and the transactions of the youth in the other ecosystems into which he is locked, such as his family. Separate pieces of data about a youth, such as yielded by standardized testing, are part of the knowledge of the youth to be used in helping him in his development. It is more important to know the subcultural dynamics of his life, because these are the elements that hold him together as a psychosocial being. To know these dynamics lets the guidance team member understand the behavior outcomes of those cultural components of the youth as they transact with the variegated culture that marks the school as an ecosystem.

THE COURSE OF DEVELOPMENT

The thrust of the prior section has been to the school as an ecosystem, with the corollary significance that ecosystem has for knowing any youth at a particular moment of observation—in a way of speaking, a horizontal cut across any and all students at a given moment. In this section we attend to the vertical dimension—a brief look in a longitudinal fashion at how behaviors are acquired over time, and at some other variables in development.

It can comfortably be said that much is known about behavior in general and youth development in particular. The task now faced is further distillation of this mass of knowledge into a section of this chapter. These demurring comments are made so that an unwary person will know that what he reads here is the description of but a few peaks of the vast range of mountains of knowledge about this topic.

Humans the world over and through all time have some behaviors that are common. The majority of behaviors, however, is culture-specific, and persons of similar cultures share many more behaviors in common than they do with humans the world over. Ultimately each individual represents mutations of the behaviors common to his culture and subcultures because each individual is a unique biosystem, with autonomic responses conditioned in a way unique to that individual, and instrumental behaviors acquired in patterns not duplicated in any other human. In a few ways, each human is like all other humans, in many ways he is like some other humans, and in some ways he is like no other human.

The concern of the guidance movement in education is the facilitation of development toward a satisfying future of each of these unique, unduplicatible individuals. But referring to an earlier point, each person's behaviors have some commonality with those of others from his culture and subcultures because most of his behaviors, like those of all members of the culture and same subcultures, are generally determined by those cultures. Language is a clear example.

Genetic Resources and Growth

On the average, one-sixth of life is spent as a child, that is, as a relatively passive, reactive, receptive, present-oriented, dependent organism, relatively unaware of self. Glandular changes programmed into each body start sometime after age 10 and are completed by age 18, with an earlier starting mean for females than males and variability of the start and completion of such changes among individuals. The single and major physiological outcome of these changes in sum is that the organism can carry out the reproductive function. As important and central in human development as that capacity is, guidance team members will be attending to the other, more important behavior outcomes associated with these physiological changes. The former child is now an active, self-directive, self-conscious, future-oriented, independence-seeking person, thus marked by qualities that constitute the original and continuing purpose of the guidance movement: to help youths sort out appropriate futures from the confusing array of possibilities, to help them learn the complex routes to those futures, and to help them deal with the conflicting assortment of behaviors that mark the child-adult. These in turn mean helping extinguish outworn and self-defeating behaviors carried over from childhood and helping establish and maintain new self-constructive behaviors.

But what will a youth bring to that rebirth after 12-to-15-year gestation period as a child? Indeed what does he bring to his first birth as an infant by way of native endowment? The nature-nurture question remains active and at this writing, is boiling and quaking around reports of recent studies that let the researchers conclude that blacks inherit less intelligence at conception than whites in this country. Two comments, one lesser and one major, are appropriate. The first and lesser comment is that the issue is far from settled, and as a corollary issue each reader has to decide for himself whether he agrees with those who say that such research should not be carried out right now during times when major race readjustments are needed. The more important comment points directly at the work of guidance team members, and the substance of this comment is caught by the terse question, "So what?" The built-in answer to that question says, in effect, that whether a child has inherited or learned (or both) the physique, intellect, or other significant characteristics that distinguish him is not a germane question. Members of the guidance team assist each youth *as he is;* thus for us it is primarily an academic question as to how much nature or nurture contributed to his characteristics. Persons responsible for organizing social institutions can profit by knowledge generated by genetic research, and such responsible parties include school officials at the higher echelons, but helpers of youths do not need to know which characteristics were inherited in order to assist a youth.

Whatever the proportions of influence of heredity and environment on learning, the important fact is the learning a child brings with him at the time of school entry, because all later learning is built on early learning. Children from families where parents take time to teach them—a middle-class behavior no matter what the race or ethnic origins of the parents—are likely to learn, at a geometric rate, those materials prized by schools. These children will be measured as having medium to high IQs. In the absence of parental nurturing of preschool learning, there is likely to be poor readiness by children to undertake the learning tasks of the school and to achieve over the years. These children will do poorly on IQ tests. Whether or not children from these latter families are genetically more impoverished, the fact is that a child with such learning deficits does not catch up with his more advantaged peers. Indeed because of the nature of institutionalized learning as found in typical schools, he might even regress over a span of school years from earlier levels of achievement.

Whatever the academic significance of the genetic/cultural question related to ability to achieve in school, it is far exceeded by the pragmatic significance for guidance specialists of the learning behaviors of a person as he is at the moment of assistance.

Behaviors Emerge and Are Maintained

In a person's earliest day as an infant certain behaviors are reinforced, and learning begins. Certain spontaneous vocalizations of sounds are reinforced. The infant says, "Da," is enthusiastically reinforced, and Mother excitedly calls Father and says, "Baby said his first word today!" Other nonsense sounds are not reinforced, and the baby is encouraged to model his sounds around those he hears spoken. Thus language develops. The toddler's language becomes instrumentally reinforced, so that he learns that certain sounds produce desirable effects: diapers are changed, water and food given, cuddling supplied. Crying produces cuddling, which is desirable; thus crying, a natural behavior, is reinforced and maintained beyond its natural function. In early childhood this is apparent in the instance of a child who receives a minor hurt, or is offended by someone while at a distance from mother. Crying starts, but in the absence of mother the crying is not attended to and thus is not reinforced. The child stops crying, therefore, and goes to seek out his mother. As he gets close to mother he starts to wail again and receives the cuddling and solicitation he has been taught that crying elicits. Incidentally, the procedure for extinguishing crying in a child who cries too much is relatively simple: ignore it. The difficulty in this procedure is with the parent whose learned behavior is to comfort the crying child.

Much of a child's behavior is acquired in that fashion for which "modeling," referring to imitative behavior, is a common summing term. Some of the obvious modeling behaviors are imitations of instrumental acts of the mother: playing at ironing, washing dishes, and the like. Other such behaviors are dressing up in adult clothes and playing mother and father. These are obvious and valuable imitations, but some of the harmful modeling is not so obvious. Fear is readily learned and is difficult to extinguish. The mother's reactions to the numerous phenomena that come into daily life have a high probability of being acquired by the child. If the mother fears electric storms (behaves in fearful ways), the child might not only behave that way, but the excitation of the autonomic nervous system will be associated with those behaviors, and the child thus might acquire a strong emotional fear of electric storms. Thunder and lightning produce an autonomic response that in turn causes the overt behaviors labeled "fear" through the learning process called respondent conditioning.

By school entry time, the child has acquired many complex behavior patterns, most of which will bear on his success in school as measured by gettting along and by the quality of his cognitive development. It may be useful to contrast some of the behavior repertoires of children from those subcultures that make it possible to acquire a maximum array of such coping behaviors with those of children from subcultures that provide a minimum acquisition of these coping behaviors.[6] (See table on pages 177–179.)

Digression: Are Humans Robots?

With this much about development set out, it is crucial to engage again an issue considered in Chapter 6 before continuing the longitudinal theme. This issue can be differently addressed by asking several rhetorical questions.

Is human behavior learned solely by respondent and operant conditioning and through modeling? Is the human only reflexive—a robot responding to external stimuli? Am I excluding those behaviors for which there are such summing terms as striving and rising-above-circumstances, behaviors that seem not to be under the control of identifiable contingencies? These questions partly contain their own answers, and they are a sampling of reactions that sometimes come from persons who have not systematically studied human behavior. Let us nail them by starting with the last question first.

This is done by first observing that anyone who could believe that the

[6] An authoritative yet brief (86 pages) work addressing the characteristics of some minimum-experience families is *Low-Income Life Styles,* edited by Lolo M. Irelan (1967). The descriptions therein, well-documented by research, are disturbing. Focusing on poverty's outcome on youth is an excellent volume titled *America's Other Youth,* edited by Gottlieb and Heinsohm (1971).

	Behaviors of Children from Maximum-Experience Families	*Behaviors of Children from Minimum-Experience Families*
Language	Large number of words used for things, abstractions, and actions (verbs). Verbalization in great quantity.	Very few things experienced, and little attention for labeling those things. Few or no abstractions labeled. Verbs are simple commands. Little verbalization.
Numbers	Child counts because he has been deliberately exposed to counting contingencies and reinforced for counting.	Little or no attention to counting other than few numbers, and little or no opportunity to learn numeric abstractions (subtracting, multiplying).
Dexterity	Child cuts, assembles complex toys bought to teach dexterity, has many manipulable toys, such as train sets, wheeled vehicles, simple tool sets. Parents spend time with child in these activities, often with sex typing. Mother teaches girls to sew; father teaches "boy" skills to males, including skills for later athletic competence. Children have skates, different kinds of balls for different purposes (they learn subtle distinctions need to be made in equipment). Space perception high.	Child's time is spent mostly with television (reinforcing inaction), has few, if any, toys to manipulate, no wheeled vehicles. Parents do not participate in teaching games and sports, and no equipment is available and no room to use it if it were available. No money for skates and other frivolities. Parents "too busy" for children and punish them if they "get in the way." Space perception low.
Relating to others	Sharing behaviors are taught, cooperation through games, ethical behavior (no stealing, no sex activity, love others, respect elders, correct manners, do not hear taboo words), birthdays and other times for being honored and for honoring others. Parents' good relationships with each other and with many others can be modeled. Racial and ethnic tolerance practiced by parents are modeled by children. Older children help younger. Problems settled by discussion.	Relatively ignored child is not presented with contingencies for learning a variety of behaviors related to others. Parental relationships and relationships with others are quarrelsome, selfish, and child learns that other persons are to be exploited, by force if necessary. Stealing condoned. Words that are taboo in school are part of vocabulary. Other races and ethnic groups acted against. Older children bully, or at best ignore younger. Problems settled by force.

	Behaviors of Children from Maximum-Experience Families	*Behaviors of Children from Minimum-Experience Families*
Aesthetics	Children exposed to good music, observe older children in family practicing music, family singing, own musical instruments, directed by parents toward enriching musical and other artistic experiences. Provided with drawing and painting materials, taken to concerts, museums, plays, galleries. Learn rhythm, notes, and to enjoy variety in music. Learns about "sense of situation"—that is, on this occasion we do this, but not on that occasion, wherein we do something different.	Television primarily, and programs watched are those that most powerful person determines (another occasion for learning that "might makes right"). No variety in music, if any is heard. No musical instruments. Few drawing materials, and no teaching by parents or older children. No visits to cultural institutions.
Knowing the world	Much reading done to child who by school entry is doing some reading on his own. Family travels to many and varied spots: Disneyland, recreation spots, motor boats used, nature centers and zoos visited, family camping (child learns more about cooperation and how to cope with different environments), visitors to family from other parts of world.	Life limited to home and immediate neighborhood. No books. Television primary source of world, and thus impression is of the unreal, violent nature that marks programs selected for viewing by the parents or older siblings.
Sum effect	Child enters school which is for him a familiar environment. The program regularities are similar to those with which he has lived. Biggest adjustment needed: to do things when told and to meet schedules. He readily adapts. He has lived in a timed environment (he can read a clock and has learned to deal with timed abstractions such as "we eat in 10 minutes," "you may watch television for 1 hour," and he has been expected to	The child enters school and is faced with program regularities unlike those in his family. He has little sense of time (no clock in the family), and behaviors demanded of him were on impulse, not on a time basis. He went to bed when he wished, ate when he could, rather than as a family. In school he is expected to behave in a timed, rhythmic way, engaging cognitive, dexterous, and aesthetic activities for which he has no readiness. If he enters a typical

Behaviors of Children from Maximum-Experience Families	Behaviors of Children from Minimum-Experience Families
do chores regularly). The school he enters may be well supported financially, have the best teachers, and a great variety of equipment.	elementary school, there is a fixed, timed curriculum. Those who learn do, those who do not, will be passed to the next grade anyhow, and the gap between those who entered school equipped to cope and children not readied will increase. In addition his school may be ill equipped both as to teachers and material resources.

human is not a striving person, that a human's behaviors show him to be under the control of only present, noticeable contingencies, just has not observed human behavior. Conversely, almost any person-in-the-street can attest to the striving nature of man, that the human is not just reflexively responding to such immediate visual-auditory-tactile stimuli as those that control a bird's behavior, for example. Nor are the low-quality behaviors that were established by contingencies in a person's past fixed for his life. The answer to both the last and next-to-last questions, those about humans being only reflexive, and thus about striving behaviors being excluded, is an emphatic No.

Then what is the issue? It is simply that some persons with minimal experience in formal study of behavior misinterpret the effects of respondent and operant conditioning so as to produce questions of that kind. Those persons, probably without thinking in exactly these terms, are asking in effect, Are not robotized, permanent behaviors the natural outcomes of respondent and operant conditioning? Without deliberate or chance intervention in a person's behaviors, those may be the outcome, but, because change can occur, by chance as well as by plan, the most accurate answer must still be No.

Yet the answer to the first question, "Is human behavior learned solely by respondent and operant conditioning and through modeling?" is *Yes,* except for a few reflexive behaviors shown in early infancy. For some this may seem to contradict the prior paragraph, and the three questions and answers then demonstrate the critical nature of the issue. Here is the reconciliation of the answers.

Man is striving; he is not a robot. Think about a youth who is in the maximally experienced subculture identified earlier. Let us identify him as living in a family with a strong musical emphasis. His early musical efforts, modeled on others in the family, are reinforced, both autonomically and operantly. The more he is reinforced, the more he engages in music, and the better he becomes in music (we shall say it is piano playing). The better he becomes, the more he is reinforced, not only by other humans but by music itself, which has become intrinsically reinforcing.

His parents also came from maximally experienced families. Thus they know how to cope, to use resources, to be effective in this society. And they too have ambitions, including some for pleasure. They have spoken for quite a while of the pleasures of owning a houseboat. The family, at a family council, agrees to save for that end; and in a year that goal is achieved, with the down payment made, and the boat received. Many similar events of looking to and planning for the future have occurred.

The youth, therefore, has experienced how future goals, even if big, can be attained. His parents' demonstration of future-oriented behaviors (forego some pleasures now to save for later enjoyment) are among the many parental behaviors that he models, imitations that provide one cause for this kind of behavior to become established and maintained, thus increasing his repertoire of satisfaction-producing responses.

In addition to modeling, other conditions have permitted him to acquire a history of future-oriented behaviors, such as the first major purchase he made when 11, a motorized model airplane, a purchase made possible by summertime earnings. Because earlier earning and saving behaviors were reinforced, both socially by parents and by attainments of desired goals, it is within keeping of the youth's history that his now larger earnings are saved for the eventual purchase of a piano. He is a striving and goal-oriented person. He often moves in a direction opposite from his present contingencies, from his moment-by-moment conditions of living. There are many demands on him to use his savings for present short-run pleasures, but he does not react reflexively to those stimuli; his behaviors are not robotized. Instead of reflexive, unconscious responses to the immediate-gratification stimuli, he chooses at a conscious level to act as he does. Between stimuli and his response to them comes the intervening operation of the unobservable but most human of all human behaviors—thought, and also the mediation of his self-cognitions. Additional learned symbolizations mediate this decision, including the history of the way his immediate behaviors have been brought under the control of symbols (thoughts, imagery) related to his future.

We fictionalize the appearance of another kind of behavior clearly outside the robot category: his increased musical competence moves clearly into a creative direction and now he is composing musical pieces. This behavior too is consonant with his behavior history. He was reinforced throughout childhood for imaginative, creative activities. He was often building contraptions, many of which did not work for the purpose intended. Nonetheless he was applauded for making the effort. Indeed when he was 8, he was asked to compose a song in honor of his newborn sister.

His behavior-aware parents were killing two birds with that stone, incidentally. They were encouraging creativity in a field in which he had already shown exceptional competence and getting him to be a partner in accepting his baby sister, instead of imagining her as a threat to his well-established position of eminence as the sole child.

The more he created, the more he performed well, and the more his creative behaviors were reinforced. We find occurring in this youth that development that marks integrated adults: the older a person becomes the more he becomes "like himself"; that is, behaviors that are compatible become stronger and other behaviors that are incompatible wither away. Said differently, strengths become stronger, and conversely, as a person learns to avoid contingencies that produce his weak behaviors, the weaknesses atrophy. Each becomes a more pure distillate of himself with the passing of months and years—each who has distillable strengths to start out with.

The hypothetical youth of our illustration shows behaviors that are a composite of early learned behaviors, modified or strengthened by later learning through respondent and operant conditioning and mediated by his symbol system. His behaviors can now be summarized as abstractions by such terms as self-actualized, striving, autonomous, spontaneous. The person knowledgeable about behavior does not denigrate this youth or the human lot by acknowledging that these and any prized behaviors are learned. Spontaneity is an endearing trait and is no less endearing when it is acknowledged as a learned trait. To act spontaneously generally requires a history of reinforced behaviors, if not identical to the current spontaneous behavior, then approximating it.

Childhood and Adolescence

Throughout childhood children experience a fantastic mix of contingencies that reinforce (strengthen) or are aversive to (weaken or extinguish) behaviors. Many of these contingencies are unplanned or chance, but whether occurring by design or chance, they may have a long-lasting effect on development, and they often generalize to other contingencies, thus producing inappropriate behaviors for those other contingencies.

Sometimes contingencies are planned by adults for a child's good, but they may have an opposite effect. For example, assume parents who think that sending their shy, awkward child to a summer camp is just the ticket. They are nonselective. They generalize the word "camp" and take their neighbors' word that Camp Upandatem is "wonderful; our boy just *loved* it when he went there!" Thus the shy boy is enrolled in a camp wherein highly skillful behavior in athletics and games is prized and rewarded. His inability to play is devastating to him. He is treated aversively by the campers and the counselors, and the situation does not let him use such compensatory skills as he has to claim attention. The trauma is so severe that he runs away from the camp, and "camping" becomes a generalized aversive stimulus—all his life he might hate camping.

Children from maximum experience families learn to label their behaviors, with the effect that their behaviors can be brought partly under the control of symbols (words) by themselves and others.[7] Conversely, children from minimum experience families have fewer symbols for their behavior and for contingencies, acquire fewer abstractions about life, thus are less well equipped to vicariously engage their behaviors vis-à-vis their contingencies and their ecosystems.

In living in this society, then, children daily experienc a wide array of chance contingencies and program regularities in their homes, schools, and other settings. They arrive at adolescence with the array of conflicting behaviors that mark typical youth; that is, one contingency might elicit two or even more incompatible responses struggling against each other for expression as the behavioral response to that contingency. They begin adolescence with some pronounced skills, perhaps condemned in one ecosystem, praised in another, and are painfully and consciously aware of their need to find a place in the sun. Whatever the behavior repertoire at the

---

[7] This facility with symbols is a potential obstacle to full humanness. Children from maximum experience families can become so skillful with words that they increasingly intellectualize the world of experience, including other humans, and decreasingly engage the world of experience, including other humans, with openly experienced emotion and spontaneity. In addition they may be admonished against touching other persons, so that aloofness in interpersonal relationships is not only emotional but physical.

Although the origins of overly intellectualized (verbalized) and physically aloof behaviors have not been sufficiently documented, the popularity of group experiences generically entitled "human potential activities" have vividly shown that many persons have become dissatisfied with their overly intellectualized, dehumanized behaviors vis-à-vis other humans. Likely most readers know of the existence of such group activities under terms as T-groups, encounter groups, or sensitivity groups. Persons experiencing either the older form of awareness or sensitizing activities as sponsored by the National Training School at Bethel, Maine, or the newer more radical forms, such as those practiced at the Esalen Institute in California, report what is in effect a reemergence as humans after years of emitting overly intellectualized, unaware, ritualized behaviors related to other humans. Their new humanness includes an eagerness, sometimes as overeagerness, to give and receive physical contact.

Ironically, persons who grew up in minimum experience families are recorded as being informal, emotionally open, and spontaneous in relationships with other humans. There may be more romanticising than reporting of reality in such statements. On the ethnic variable, however, there is more common acceptance that some national groups (southern Europeans, for example) are more emotionally open and ready to make physical contact with humans than persons from more northern European cultures. One specialist in counseling Spanish-speaking Americans told me that a Spanish-speaking child or youth will be distressed if a counselor does not make some physical contact during an interview, so essential is physical contact as a sign of acceptance among the Spanish-speaking.

end of childhood, adolescence makes it a new ballgame. Now sexuality must be dealt with, and not just the physiological immediacies, but what sexuality means for a new form of relationships with others, and for one's standing in the world.

Some of the paperback literature recently addressed to adolescents concentrates on the liabilities of society. A record of society's faults is a distortion of reality and can scarcely facilitate the adolescent's already difficult tasks. Stressing only our country's deficits is to ignore the continuing suffusion of the principles of the Declaration of Independence throughout our social institutions. To focus on those adults in and out of various governmental and financial establishments who fight the suffusion of those principles is to ignore the massive victories won for those principles in our country's brief history.

In contrast to prior times, youths today are kept continuously aware of social deficits and are enjoined to be skeptical, to doubt not only society's institutions but even that the good life can ever be attained. Some hear and heed; others are skeptical of the skeptics. Uncertainty is magnified when there is so much more to be uncertain about, more occupations from which to choose, more credentials to be acquired, more hard decisions to be made earlier—all this at a time of life when new behaviors of independence have to be matched against emotionally colored ties with family, when the delicate etchings of new kinds of interpersonal relationships are smudged by defeats. The child-become-adolescent, even from the maximum experience family, has left the easy-going, on-top-of-it-all state and at best is puzzling to parents who remember their perfect child and forget their own adolescence. Even worse for some parents is the threat to their importance ("My child no longer needs me"), to their values ("Why does he have to dress that way, run around with those persons, speak disparagingly of our institutions?"), to their time investment ("After all we've done for him, he turns out *this* way").

Some desired behaviors acquired in childhood may fissure, if not crumble; other behaviors must be dropped from their repertoire if responsible adulthood is to be attained. The family will become a far less significant ecosystem for the adolescent; parents of a 17-year-old have far fewer contingencies to manage, so, if certain behaviors were not established or inhibited during childhood, it is likely too late for parents to establish or inhibit them now. The minor intimacies of childhood, shared then with parents, are now major intimacies and are shared only with peers. Confidence and doubt surge and submerge like sunshine and shadow passing over a field on a cloudy, windy day, even for the advantaged youth. The adolescent from the minimum experience family may rarely see the sunshine of confidence. He may see nothing ahead of himself except a series of empty tomorrows. He is the most likely one to have dropped out of school, thus losing even that small bit of regularity, of steadiness, which the contingencies of schooling might have contributed. But our first concern is with those youths still in school, with helping them with the fascinating, depressing, joyous, anxious, exciting eternities that are an adolescent's days and with the difficulties in deciphering the future.[8]

The school's program regularities reinforce some of a student's behaviors and may be aversive to other behaviors without changing them, or on the other hand may result in changed behaviors. Some have learned to seek out persons of similar behaviors, because therein lies comfort, and thus they are seeking contingencies which make them more sharply defined persons of the kind they have been; others have great problem with attaining identity. Prior learning has given some a capacity to deal with the future in long-range terms, or perhaps at the other extreme others' histories may have been futureless ones, ones in which day-to-day living has been the best that they could work with. The future-oriented youth may or may not be ready to work out that future with a member of the guidance team; most squares will, many freaks will not because they expect such planning will have to be cast around society's givens, and the prospect of that is unwelcomed by establishment-skeptic youths.

A final word: an observation or illustration referenced to a single person may be true of most persons of that class, but not of all, or may be true of some, but not of most. Illustrations are a device to help you learn principles, and hopefully the principle is now fixed that individual histories vary so much that one can speak in general only about how behavior is formed and cannot safely generalize about specific behaviors. Folk psychology, so often correct, is again correct on this point: "One man's meat is another man's poison." What reinforces one person's behavior extinguishes another's. To help humans means to help individuals. For the guidance specialist to help individuals means to know how the behavior of all individuals is formed and maintained, the nomology. It then means knowing any individual as a discrete behaving entity—what his behavior history is, what reinforces *his* behavior, and therefore what portions of the several ecosystems he lives in are reinforcing to certain behaviors and aversive to others. Ultimately it means to conjecture with him about the nature of the future he might seek and to help him plan for and move toward that future.

---

[8] Of the painful moments in text writing I find one of the most painful to be the choice of topics to be included and excluded. Adolescents are the focus of this volume, yet are not systemically treated. I can but urge readers to seek out other writings. The best brief review is provided by Shertzer and Stone (1976). A few among the more extensive and recommended treatments are those by Coleman (1961), Erickson (1968), Friedenberg (1959), and Hollingshead (1949).

THE HIGH SCHOOL

Up to and throughout this chapter the underpinnings of guidance practices have been set. Yet there has been a topic notable for the omission of systematic treatment—the high school setting. That topic will not be treated here, but this chapter could not be ended without at least a head-nod in its direction. There can be maximum and minimum experience high schools as well as families, which is but another way of saying that characteristics of high schools, the subtle more than the obvious, bear on behaviors that are acquired, strengthened, or weakened.

Differences among high schools are enormous, thus the student of guidance cannot view himself as knowledgeable about them only through remembering the high school from which he was graduated, or by being familiar with the one currently employing him, or a neighborhood one. Only in a superficial way do high schools in suburbs resemble similarly named institutions in the portions of large cities inhabited by the poor. All kinds of high schools are deemed to be inadequate for youths today by recent blue-ribbon commissions which have studied the role of secondary schools in our current society (Passow, 1975). The professional guidance practitioner is perforce bound to be a social critic, particularly of the institutions of public education, as well as being knowledgeable about the more general principles that account for the formation, maintenance, and mediation of behavior.

Guidance objectives and practices are for youth no matter what the label of the institution, and no matter what divergences among units operating under a single label. They belong in the most conventional, conservative junior and senior high schools, in those populated by the children of wealthy suburbanites, in free-form schools, street academies, slum schools, reform schools, mobile schools, private academies, comprehensive schools, specialized schools, schools without walls. Wherever youths are found in institutions, there must be guidance services and guidance practitioners who know the effect that institution has on the individuals who transact with it.

REFERENCES

BARKER, R. G. *Ecological Psychology: Concepts and Methods for Studying the Environment of Human Behavior.* Stanford, Calif.: Stanford University Press, 1968.

COLEMAN, J. S. *The Adolescent Society.* Glencoe, Ill.: Free Press, 1961.

ERICKSON, E. H. *Identity, Youth, and Crisis.* New York: Norton, 1968.

ESPOSITO, D. *An Ecological Approach to the Theory and Practice of Guidance.* Address presented to the annual convention, American Personnel and Guidance Association, Atlantic City, N.J., 1971. Mimeographed.

FRIEDENBERG, E. Z. *The Vanishing Adolescent.* Boston: Beacon Press, 1959.

FULLER, F. F. "Concerns of Teachers: A Developmental Consideration." *American Educational Research Journal,* 1969, *6,* 207–226.

GOTTLIEB, D. & HEINSOHN, A. L. (Eds.), *America's Other Youth: Growing Up Poor.* Englewood Cliffs, N.J.: Prentice-Hall, 1971.

HOLLINGSHEAD, A. B. *Elmtown's Youth: The Impact of Social Classes on Youth.* New York: Wiley, 1949.

IRELAN, L. M. (Ed.), *Low-Income Life Styles.* Washington, D.C.: U.S. Department of Health, Education, and Welfare, 1967.

MITCHELL, J. V., JR. "Dimensionality and Differences in the Environmental Press of High Schools." *American Educational Research Journal,* 1968, *5,* 513–530.

PASSOW, A. H. "Reforming America's High Schools." *Phi Delta Kappan,* 1975, *56,* 587–590.

SMITH, R. L. *Ecology and Field Biology.* New York: Harper & Row, 1966.

SNYDER, D. U. "Guidance and the School as a Social System." In D. R. Cook (Ed.), *Guidance for Education in Revolution.* Boston: Allyn and Bacon, 1971.

SHERTZER, B., & STONE, S. C. *Fundamentals of Guidance,* 3rd ed. Boston: Houghton Mifflin, 1976.

8 Mediating Behavior

INTRODUCTION

The professional behaviors carried out by members of the guidance team are intended to result in the attainment of guidance objectives. These professional behaviors or guidance practices, based on principles of behavior, receive the attention of this chapter. In more conventional terminology, the topic of this chapter would be labeled "counseling," with which label no fault is found. The phrase "mediating behavior," however, conveys a more precise meaning than counseling, as will be seen, and is a more fitting phrase for the theoretical position of this text.

Guidance practices are designed to benefit individuals, but only sometimes in a one-to-one situation, that is, one guidance practitioner with one student. In most schools for most times past the view has been held among professional guidance practitioners, rarely any occupation other than counselors that the delivery of guidance benefits must be to individuals one by one, and only to those who request assistance. A different position has been built here. This position holds that attainment of guidance objectives by all students will result only from scheduling *all* students in guidance program *group* experiences. Beyond those group experiences, individuals will still receive attention from guidance specialists on a one-to-one basis, but the group approach will greatly reduce the need for the one-to-one approach.

Whatever the setting, guidance practices will alter a person's behavior so that he[1] can more effectively cope with conditions met day by day, can

---

[1] At this point I repeat the essence of an earlier footnote in case it was missed: I use the masculine pronoun to represent both sexes with great reluctance and

more adequately make decisions about his short- and long-range future, and can monitor and mediate his own behavior. These alterations of behavior might be in the nature of adding new behaviors or increments to present behavior or reducing or extinguishing some behaviors. "Behaviors" in this statement refers not only to those visible actions a person carries out, but also to that paramount human activity, thinking, or, in different terms, to the use of symbols—the use of cognitions.

"Behaviors" also includes that class of reportable as well as noticeable responses that are typically described by the word "emotions." What this means, in the words of Chapter 5, is that guidance practices result in the addition, modification, or removal of operant and respondent behaviors, and in changing the elements and processes of ratiocination. To produce such changes means improved competence in managing daily life and in moving toward the future.

These changes induced by the guidance program and by guidance specialists are directed to those points where a person's life is inextricably intertwined with a psychosocial ecosystem. Because so many guidance practices come into "the middle" of those transactions of the person and a social system, they are referred to here as "behavior mediation."

The use of the term "mediation" in labor-management disputes provides a somewhat useful simile. Therein a mediator enters the institutional life of a body of workers in transaction with the employing social system. The mediator in this instance, an outsider, engages not only the behavior of the workers, but also the behavior of the employing social system. Thus does the guidance practitioner also not only enter or mediate the behavior of an individual, but in understanding and affecting that behavior, he must also frequently mediate the behaviors of a social system, because the individual behaves in transaction with social systems. Certain guidance practices do not require the mediation of a system's behaviors, an example being that valuable assistance given to a youth who is making a career decision. In this type of guidance concern, some individual's behaviors might be mediated by the relatively simple procedure of helping him acquire and assimilate career information. The important variable in this instance is tense. In this instance the youth is engaging a decision about the future, involving social systems with which he is not yet in transaction. In many other behavior mediation practices, however, the guidance practitioner is mediating behaviors of an individual whose behaviors are locked presently into a social system. The specialist's behavior mediation practices, therefore, must account for the individual's behaviors and also those of the social system with which he is transacting.

---

in contradiction to my practice in other contexts. Current publishing conventions bearing on ease of reading cause me to engage in this most uncomfortable behavior.

There is a wealth of detailed information about guidance practices based on behavior principles. In this text, which is introductory to the guidance field, there is room to present only a sketchy overview of procedures for mediating behavior. I suggest that readers who wish to examine mediation practices in more detail consult the brief exposition by Vernon (1972), and then a more extensive offering, such as those by Bandura (1969), Reynolds (1968), Sulzer and Mayer (1972), or Tharp and Wetzel (1969). In this chapter we look at the general activities of mediating behavior that are employed by different guidance practitioners in a secondary school.

CHARACTERISTICS OF GUIDANCE PRACTITIONERS

Members of guidance teams are characterized by traits other than behavior mediation knowledge and techniques. They are characterized first in general by being a certain kind of person, with the fundamental description being "caring." "Caring" here connotes an eagerness to assist youths in maintaining or attaining a satisfying current existence and in moving toward an effective adulthood by dedication of at least one's employment energies to those goals. Some guidance practitioners' nonremunerated energies also are given to the same outcomes—they volunteer time and energy in those causes.

On the other hand, it will be recalled, some past and present counselors were described as not being unusually caring about youth—that their functions were or are carried out with no more dedication to youth than that of any other class of adult. This contradicting observation will come as no surprise to anyone who has known a population of students entering counselor preparation programs. There one occasionally finds the person who candidly states that he seeks to be a counselor in order to escape from a now-aversive classroom situation. Obviously this is only intended to be self-serving; if it is also youth-serving, then it is only by luck. A proportion of the nondedicated to those who are dedicated cannot be given, but there is no reason to suspect any different proportion among counselors and other guidance practitioners than would be found among physicians, for example, or politicians. All occupations have saints and sinners.

Caring can be more finely specified now than a decade ago. As a result of continuing research about interview effectiveness, several behaviors or at least characteristics have been documented as defining the concept. Some of these are attentiveness (Ivey, 1970) and accurate empathy, nonpossessive warmth, and genuineness (Truax & Carkhuff, 1966). The behaviors of attentiveness are specific, such as eye contact and attentive listening, and the behaviors summed by the broad terms "empathy," "warmth," and "genuineness" have been reasonably described. It deserves note, however, that behaviors denoting these characteristics can be learned as techniques by some noncaring persons and presented at will by them despite the absence of the feeling inside that those behaviors are supposed to represent. These persons too are probably in tiny proportion.

The guidance team member, caring as he does, is eager to know about youth, and thus studies about youth not as a certification requirement, but because of high interest. He is most knowledgeable of the currents crossing through youth subcultures and of such specifics as their heroes and demons; the radical-conservative thrust; their seekings, graspings, and repellings; and the events of joy and the causes of despair among each of the youth subcultures. Because he cares and has benefitted from professional preparation, the guidance practitioner acquires the capacity to make only professional judgments. Despite great differences among youths in values and ensuing behaviors, the guidance team member accepts students in all their varieties, seeing them as products of their societies, as persons to be aided to make sense of a fractious world.

In addition to knowing principles of behavior and their techniques and having caring characteristics, the guidance practitioner also knows how humans develop, knows the small portion of givens that affect all youths everywhere equally, and the major portion of variance carried by cultures and subcultures in the development of any youth. He knows about the primary business of the school—cognitive learning. Not the lesson-plan, How to Teach, Don't Rock the Boat components, but the psychology of learning. He knows about the sociology of schooling, because the evidence about how children and youths acquire learning shows the need for him to know. He will come to recognize that his actions to implement best procedures are sometimes thwarted by school and community forces led by individuals who have other fish to fry instead of seeing that the community's schools have the best structure for learning.

All these prior characteristics yield one other characteristic of the team member: he is active, he reaches out, he evaluates the effectiveness of his school in providing the greatest amount of learning for each youth, as such learning is consonant with the abilities and ambitions of youth. He seeks out students, he arouses them to care about having a say in their own destiny, he searches out (Baker & Cramer, 1972; Dworkin & Dworkin, 1971; Matheny, 1971). His caring is communicated not by his pious protestations, but by his actions. Ombudsman maybe; advocate always.

But unless he has skills, the unique skills of mediating behavior, his caring, active behaviors will result more in wheel spinning than in mileage gained. It is his array of behavior intervention skills, the topic of this chapter, that gives the guidance team member his potential for success.

BEHAVIOR MEDIATION—A COMPLEXITY

A person wishes to paint a room with a precise shade of green. He mixes into white paint a finely measured portion of yellow and blue pigments, an equally well-measured small portion of black, and a modicum of red, and then fully mixes the paint. Problem: inspect the paint and identify the yellow, blue, black, and red pigments. Solution: none. It cannot be done. The paint is a metaphor for some behaviors. Those would include a long-existing complex behavior, or pattern of behaviors, having been formed, as all behaviors are, by respondent/operant conditioning and then "mixed" with symbols. These components of behavior are blended in a fashion that makes identification of the elements impossible in some instances and difficult in most cases. On the other hand, behavior sometimes is readily analyzable as to origin and components. Phobic behaviors, for example, often permit analysis as to the respondent conditioning that established them. The components of the behavior of rational thinking can be identified, such as in the rational thinking related to mathematics. Illustrations of less scrutable behaviors abound, however. Consider the behaviors of a youth in a group engaging in some community turbulence. His observed behaviors are rock throwing, taunting police, addressing the protesters in a speech urging them to further violence, and providing a logic in that speech as to why violence must be used. His motor behaviors show respondent/operant conditioning mediated by a cognitive system that was also respondently/operantly formed, but exists now in a mix that defies analysis. Consider the youth who shows to a guidance team member oral behaviors with conflicting emotional coloration as he discusses his schooling and his thoughts about his future. He also shows, in a less dramatic example, behavior blends whose components cannot be analyzed by quick inspection.

Mediating behaviors in many instances, therefore, is not the simple matter of an easy analysis of the components of that behavior and then the employment of procedures for each of the analyzed components. The guidance team member usually has to deal with complex behavior patterns. This latter statement, however, needs to be promptly countered with the observation that analysis of components, including original causes, is not necessary to mediate much behavior. The green paint of this section's opening paragraph can be changed to other tints or colors without analysis of the amount of original pigments, nor of how nor when they were added. This point is also illustrated by another example from field biology.

In the several references and illustrations made in this volume to ecosystems, it is important to stress the "system" portion of that word. A system refers to interlocked (transacting) parts that operate as a whole—change one significant part, and you change the whole. In this field biology illustration we hypothesize a gross change identified in an area of a few hundred acres. Changes in flora are noticed first, then subsequent changes in fauna. Of the several effects on humans that could be added in this fictional illustration, one is stated: a person's economy has been dependent on a crop consistently harvested from this area, and with the changes no harvestable crop can now be grown. Economic hardship falls on that person. An agricultural consultant is engaged. He identifies why this great change has occurred: modification of the earth's surface at some distance from the area has resulted in a dramatic and continuous rise in the water table in the area. Indeed the area is on its way to becoming a swamp. The cure identified by the consultant: cutting deep drainage ditches along a low part of the area. The result: as the excess water is drained off, the original ecosystem is restored.

Behavior too is a system, interlocked and maintained by feedback in social ecosystems. To mediate some behavior—to produce change in only one characteristic, perhaps a change in stimulus contingencies, in operant contingencies, or counterconditioning a respondent behavior—results in changes among other behaviors or behavior patterns. This is one critical point to remember as examination is made in this chapter of the different strategies of behavior mediation used by guidance team members.

Numerous Strategies, and Treatment-of-Choice

Members of the guidance team have numerous strategies available for mediating behavior, not a single strategy as erroneously believed for a long time, that single strategy having been the counseling interview in which a type of relationship was considered essential, and a narrow array of procedures followed.

The availability of several strategies for mediating behavior conforms with the concept of multiple occupations on a guidance team. They provide each team member with an array of helping techniques, or in other phrasing, they provide an array of treatments-of-choice, to borrow a medical term, appropriate for each individual. As the physician demonstrates his professional competency by deciding which treatment should be applied to a particular patient at a particular time, so too does the guidance team member, particularly the counselor and the behavior specialist, each display his professional competence by choosing from among a variety of behavior mediation strategies that one or combination that constitutes the treatment-of-choice for leading a group of students to reach guidance objectives, or for helping a single student at a particular time.

TWO MODES OF MEDIATING BEHAVIOR

The strategies for mediating behaviors appropriate for a school's guidance team can be analyzed differentially around different variables. One such analysis shows two modes of strategies. One is that class of verbal procedures used directly with individuals, either as sole individuals or with individuals in a group. The other class is that of mediating behaviors that deal with stimulus- and/or response-producing characteristics of an ecosystem. Of course, instances are frequent when procedures from both classes are used in mediating a person's behavior. Additionally, there are procedures for mediating behavior that are well outside the province of the practices of a school's guidance team. For example, psychopharmaceuticals are gainfully used in treating severe behavior imbalances, but they are beyond the scope of school practitioners. School adults, however, may be involved in modifying severely imbalanced behaviors in the case of a youth who is undergoing out-of-school treatment although he still attends school. Contingency management or psychopharmaceutical programs for that youth may be set up to be carried out in school in conjunction with the out-of-school treatment and in collaboration with the out-of-school practitioner. So too might teachers and parents manage stimulus and/or response contingencies of a more typical youth for whom such management plans have been devised by a behavior specialist on the school's guidance team.

DIRECT VERBAL MEDIATION PROCEDURES

Reasoning

The most commonly used procedure in direct verbal mediation is reasoning, or in different terms, a rational process is employed.

A value in our society, extending from the principles stated in the Declaration of Independence, holds that individuals are important and have the right to determine their own destinies within society's relatively loose ethical limits. The individual makes decisions about his life's course. To make decisions he needs knowledge about himself—some awareness of and minimal conflict in his behaviors—he needs knowledge about the world, and he needs the capacity to deal rationally with these data. In other words, the youth must have the ability to engage in the decision-making process.

For example, a youth is with a counselor. The topic of concern is an occupational choice to be made by the youth, with corollary schooling significances. The counselor is confident that the youth is defined by prominent nonconflicting behaviors, but finds the youth relatively unaware of the occupational world and inexperienced in making decisions about himself. For this youth the counselor's first procedures are to provide training in decision making and to ascertain as the youth gains that competency that he also acquires continuously increasing knowledge about the occupational world.

The training in decision making, assuming that the absence of such behaviors were not caused by some negative respondent conditioning or by conflicting behaviors, would be carried out rationally. In simple terms, it is private teaching—tutoring—in this needed skill, in which any decision-making behaviors of the youth are reinforced. The occupational information that is acquired in the Career Center with the help of the career development technician and then discussed with a counselor also involves well-known rational procedures.

Before going on, an important aside must be considered, this being the observation that private teaching around outcomes common to all students cannot be defended as a typical guidance practice. In fact, the student in our example should have learned the decision-making skills he needs in a group of fellow students, not in the unnecessary, wasteful individual conference manner.[2]

Reasoning is the historical counseling process. As the new student in the guidance area studies beyond this introductory text he will come to know the writings of E. G. Williamson (1950, 1965) wherein reasoning procedures in all their mutations are well set out as they relate to helping persons develop tenable life-course patterns.

Well and good when youth are characterized as the hypothetical one above is: he has nonconflicting behaviors, but is unskilled in decision making and is deficient in knowledge of occupations; a youth whose self-data are at a workable level of awareness and in minimal conflict. Let the illustration be changed: another youth has decision-making ability and does know the occupational world reasonably well, but his behaviors of self-reference are in conflict, and these cause other competing behaviors to be emitted. For some it would be outside tenability to expect that the competing behaviors of a youth so characterized could be mediated by reason. Indeed in Chapter 5 the ineffectiveness of telling and explaining was noted. For others, however, deficiencies in self-reference can be mediated by a

---

[2] Of the numbers of statements holding to this position, one of a particularly authoritative nature is that by Prediger, Roth, and Noeth (1974). They studied career development through a sample of 32,000 youth. Certain of their findings are germane to later portions of this text and will be reported there, but one conclusion their data force them to draw should be noted here: "we firmly believe that the traditional one-to-one counseling model for helping youngsters 'choose their life's work' can no longer be justified" (p. 103).

form of reasoning. The deficiencies may be statements contrary to fact, such as an able person saying of himself, "I am unable." They may also be in a lack of self-reference behaviors when there is a need for them, or in conflict among self-references, such as holding that "I am a responsible person" at the same time stating that "I don't do the things I should do." Altering self-reference statements and their associated behaviors is not just by telling or explaining, it must be noted, even though these are reasoning processes.

The rationale and process for arguing a person out of inadequate or conflicting self-references has been honed to a fine edge by Ellis (1962). That this process is tenable rests on the basic fact that behavior relating to major human interactions and to life-course actions, even if originally acquired at an unconscious (unsymbolized) level through respondent/operant conditioning, comes partly under the control of the person's cognitive (symbol) system. Thus, as noted in Chapter 5, the starting point in mediating most youth and adult behaviors is with the symbol system relating to those behaviors. Behavior mediation starts out with and continues with words, even if other unwordy processes are also employed. The behavior specialist on the guidance team, therefore, acquires cognitions about and skill in rationally manipulating the symbol system of a youth with conflicting or other deficient self-references. Of course, the behavior specialist goes beyond this reasoning process by also developing contingency-mediating schemes for the youth.

In sum this section informs us that some members of a guidance team primarily use rational procedures solely of an academic nature in their behavior mediating activities. Such team members include the career development and continuing education technicians. Counselors use the same kind of rational processes and in addition will engage some youths with minimal self-reference conflicts in that kind of rational process that is emotionally toned for those youths, as just described. The behavior specialist will have advanced competencies and experience in this latter process and thus will be assisting youths whose needs are beyond the counselor's level of competency.

Excitation

Some youths will be identified whose behaviors generally are reactive; that is, they are as a twig on the stream, floating through the school, satisfied with dependent behaviors, complaisant about having others make decisions about them, and receiving minimal stimulation from the array of potential stimuli. Let us assume that such a youth has been identified first by a teacher-advisor, and the youth agrees when the teacher-advisor suggests a conference with a behavior specialist. In conference with that member of the team the youth expresses bland envy of other assertive students and is again agreeable to the specialist's proposal that the specialist might bring some changes into that youth's life style.

Although direct verbal procedures alone will not be sufficient in this instance, the specialist will focus on arousing, exciting procedures. The specialist, of course, will be attending to immediate reinforcers to be used in these individual interviews, and to reinforcers applied in contingency procedures he plans and implements with teacher assistance in the many normal school activities this youth engages. But, as with the Korean War veterans earlier, the first need for this youth is to get him moving again, or maybe for the first time, that is, to arouse him so that he is open to the establishment of desired behaviors. The specialist's interview procedure is verbal, but it is not reasoning, or, if partially reasoning, then the use of procedures in addition to reasoning is what is important.

Operating on the principle that nothing succeeds like success, the behavior specialist might use group procedures, probably incorporating students who demonstrate the desired behaviors to serve as models for the youth who needs those behaviors. The students' presence might arouse this person to demonstrate assertive behaviors, which will then be reinforced. The group setting thus permits both presentation of arousing stimuli and the reinforcement of desired behaviors emitted by the detached person. In brief, the youth experiences success, the taste of which is pleasurable, and is thus motivated to seek out a larger serving of that succulent dish and to try other items on the success menu. These items might be coaching in specific behaviors, following, of course, established principles of shaping; use of other live or filmed models both for stimulation and to help in the establishment of assertive behaviors; and other schemes that any creative behavior specialist might invent for specific goals.

Another fact about stimulation will be known by all members of the guidance team: with rare exception it is stimulating for a youth to be singled out by one or several adults whose behavior toward the youth is characterized by such summing words as caring, attentive, interested, and helpful. When these attentive behaviors are applied by the person-in-the-street, there is no less stimulation, of course. Guidance team members, however, know the behavior processes that occur, know reinforcement principles, or, to say it in brief, know what to do about the aroused behaviors for the student's long-run benefit, whereas the person-in-the-street doesn't. For example, the creative behavior specialist, the one who invents specific procedures based on behavior principles, might, in order to reinforce social behaviors, arrange for a conference between the youth and some status adult such as the principal. The principal, of course, would be party to the reason for the conference, as perhaps even the student might be.

Supportive Counseling, and Facilitative
Procedures Used as Limited Densensitization[3]

Sometimes when a youth is engaging in comprehensive, productive behaviors directed to his future, such as decision making and related planning, those behaviors can be inhibited by undesired competing behaviors. More to our interest, however, is the fact that the smaller productive behaviors necessary for a person to cope satisfactorily with day-to-day living also commonly fall prey to unwanted competing behaviors. Such day-to-day response conflicts are not grossly devastating; that is, they do not bring productive behaviors to a complete stop. Small conflicts they may be, but they have much undesired effects, nonetheless. An analogy might show the distinction between major and minor behavior conflicts, and their relative effects.

For the analogy, think of a group on a long hike. One person develops a blister on his foot. The behavior of limping competes with the larger desired behavior (steady, fast walking) and thus with the hiker's attainment of a desired goal. It also produces the undersirable "internal" state called pain. If the blister is not attended to, it may become infected and even more serious outcomes could result. A blister is not a devastating medical condition and is relatively common. A torn ligament on this march, however, is much more devastating, and relatively rare compared with blisters. A pebble in a shoe can be equally inhibiting of the desired marching behaviors and goal attainments, but is more readily remediated than the blister. Life for youths and adults can include many psychological blisters and pebbles-in-the-shoes—the fears and anxieties that, as compet-

---

[3] This popular term is of medical rather than psychological origin. Its popularity stems from the research and writing of Joseph Wolpe, an M.D. Other terms, such as reciprocal inhibition (also a Wolpe term), counterconditioning or deconditioning are labels consonant with psychology and are very close in meaning to desensitization. Wolpe's bold experiments and wide clinical experience have been extensively reported in psychological literature, of course; thus the medical label "desensitization" has come to have acceptance among psychologists. It is used here for that reason, although readers are sometimes reminded of this note by putting the word counterconditioning after desensitization, even though they are not quite technically the same.

Desensitization is actually the extinction of a behavior, but the word focuses on the stimulus pattern rather than the person's behavior. It gives importance to what causes a behavior rather than to the removal of a behavior. Beyond extinguishing a behavior, no matter what term is used for that process, and there are different terms for different processes, the reader must be aware that often behavior is extinguished not just by deliberate efforts to reduce or remove behavior, but by causing those behaviors of a higher order of probability of emission to be learned. Here Wolpe's term, reciprocal inhibition, serves to connote not only extinction of a behavior, but doing so by establishing new behaviors, or at least by increasing the potency of existing behaviors.

ing behaviors, sully hopes, impede useful behaviors, and consume energy in nonproductive ways. They come in surges and ebbs, with such tidal action mediated, of course, by the varying ecosystems with which the youth or adult transacts.

Many of these undesired competing behaviors of mild strength will be ameliorated or removed by procedures for which several different labels have been proposed: facilitative (Delaney & Eisenberg, 1972) and helping (Benjamin, 1974).[4] Supportive counseling (Osipow & Walsh, 1970) is a purpose of counseling, and no specific procedures are given by the authors for attaining supportive counseling outcomes, but the intentions of supportive counseling and the outcomes of facilitative or helping procedures are the same—the reduction of a counselee's respondent behaviors, thus permitting constructive behaviors to dominate. This type of behavior change is the one examined in this section as an appropriate treatment-of-choice, and to avoid the clumsiness of multiple titles, the word "facilitative" is selected to index the particular kind of detailed procedures that have been used under different names as far back as 1942 (Rogers, 1942, 1951).

The fears and anxieties that compete with constructive, coping behaviors can be mediated by the counselor's verbal behaviors, those verbal procedures having the effect of desensitizing (of extinguishing) the client's behaviors related to the cuing stimuli. In short, the verbal behaviors of the facilitative interview and of a limited type of desensitization are identical. The limited nature of the desensitizing actions written about in this section needs to be restated for empasis, because there are other desensitization activities that go quite a distance beyond those soon to be described. The earlier analogy may again help. A person on a hike may be immobilized by blisters as effectively as one who is immobilized by a torn ligament. Both require medical treatment, but the treatment for the blisters is of a more limited medical scope than the treatment of the ligament. The desensitization procedures examined here are of a quite limited nature usable for mild fears and anxieties.

Skilled Use of Words in a Facilitative Interview

The procedures used in the facilitative interview, which are an elementary form of desensitization (counterconditioning), represent the zenith

---

[4] Benjamin (1974) provides the most detailed exposition of this class of interview behaviors, but does so within the context of a theoretical stance not compatible with the position taken here. Choosing Delaney and Eisenberg's term, facilitative, to represent this class of professional interview behaviors acknowledges that their procedures, although presented with less detail than Benjamin's, are offered from a theoretical position compatible with the one used in this volume.

of a practitioner's verbal skills, one of the three distinguishing components of the trained practitioner. The major component is his knowledge of how behavior is formed and maintained. The second component is his knowledge, through supervised experience, of a variety of strategies to use to mediate behavior, and the third is the ability to determine which strategies should be applied, and when, in order to mediate a person's behavior. When the strategy required in a particular instance is limited desensitization, the practitioner's moment-by-moment skilled use of words comes to the fore.

There has been an erroneous assumption prevalent about the trained, traditional school counselor: that the difference between a counselor and any other adult in school lies only in their subject matter, in their academic knowledge, with the counselor's knowledge (subject matter) being the world "out there" instead of traditional subjects like mathematics, French, music, or shorthand. Many persons, furthermore, hold that any intelligent adult already knows the subject matter of counseling. It can follow from that contention, therefore, that "any teacher can be a counselor; the only difference between being a teacher and a counselor is having time set aside to counsel with students." I have heard this kind of statement numerous times, and it explains why it was not uncommon ten and more years ago for a teacher to be appointed as counselor with no preparation, solely on the basis that the teacher "gets along well with youth." Or, let's face it, in other cases because the person was not an effective teacher, perhaps got along poorly with youth, thus causing student and parent complaint to rain on the principal. The only route for the principal to follow in "getting rid of" this ineffective teacher was to appoint him as counselor. Although instances of this action are known to me, they were rare by the early 1960s and remain so.

The argument up to this point has been that the counselor and other guidance specialists need cognitions beyond those that any educated adult has. Now we are adding the point that specific interview skills are needed as well as the knowledge of how behavior is established, maintained, and extinguished, and how life-course decisions are made. One skill that distinguishes the trained behavior mediator from the person-in-the-street is use of words in a highly skilled way. And that latter statement leads us to face another dilemma: skilled use of words in behavior mediation often is contrary to the way persons learn to use words. And *this* statement leads us to the next dilemma: teachers, having practiced one kind of word usage that is opposite from the kind that counselors use, may be among the *least* likely persons to appoint as counselors without training! Said yet another way, programs to prepare teachers as counselors need to extinguish types of verbal responses built into and reinforced as teaching behaviors and replace them with a competing array of verbal behaviors. It can be hypothesized that it is easier to prepare an educated person-in-the-street in these desired specific verbal behaviors than to undo the verbal behaviors acquired in some occupations, such as teacher or minister, and then rebuild with the desired behaviors.

We will examine these verbal skills by first looking at the skill of deliberate nonverbalization: silence. It is better to speak of attentive, silent *listening,* with occasional quiet utterances such as "um-hmmmm" viewed as not being a breaking of silence, than just silence. The skill is actually that of listening carefully and letting the other person speak without interrupting.

Silent, attentive listening is a learned skill and is contrary to the customary verbal behaviors everyone learns. Socially we learn to be uncomfortable with silence when in the presence of another individual, particularly if the setting in which one person is with another is identified as a setting in which the one person is supposed to help the other. Socially this means that the helping person is expected to talk to the helpee, especially if an older person is helping a younger one. The more the younger person is quiet, the more the older is socially obliged to talk, and therefore the less likely it is that the younger will talk. The phenomenon is expected of any adult, but may be pronounced in teachers, whose essential occupational behaviors are those of explaining and telling, of trying to make something clear. The trained counselor, on the other hand, is quite comfortable with silence, but more importantly he knows the behavior mediation effect of silence and uses silence with deliberation for immediate counseling goals.

In thinking about silence, we have been considering one behavior the typical prospective guidance practitioner has not learned to emit, but must learn to. Another common verbal behavior represents the converse condition; that is, it is a behavior that has been learned and that must be brought under stringent control when the appropriate behavior mediation strategies are those of the facilitative interview or elementary desensitization. This is the behavior called questioning or asking questions. Here again is a socially learned behavior that impedes professional behaviors, thus guidance worker preparation acts to bring this behavior under control, along with all other types of reflexive oral behaviors. When the prospective guidance practitioner has learned to be in long conference with a student in supervised training without asking a question, he can be comfortable that his future use of questioning will no longer be reflexive, that is, uncontrolled, but will be professionally deliberate, used when appropriate for the attainment of counseling goals.

Learning about categories and titles for kinds of verbal use is of less importance than knowing what the intermediate goals of the behavior specialist or counselor are, for which ends the types of verbal expression being examined in this section are the means. The practitioner is communicating by his behavior that he is a caring person, and it is this pattern of behaviors that supports or desensitizes. The person-in-the-street may care about another person, but there is no assurance that he has the skills for showing that caring. Thus he may impede counseling in bumbling fashion by anecdotes of his own related experiences, by the police-sergeant routine of questions, and by unintentionally degrading the other person's concerns through efforts to reassure. He might also impede good results by never getting to understand the meaning of events for the other person and thus not actually desensitizing the other person, no matter how sincere his desire to be of help. The trained person avoids the gaucheries, knows how to stand in the other person's shoes and see the world through the other's eyes. He is skilled in conveying his apperceptions of the other person's feelings. For the prospective guidance practitioner to know *what* should be done is not enough. Instrumental behavior is rarely changed by cognitions about that behavior. The alcoholic who knows that his alcohol consumption is damaging to himself physically, and psychosocially damaging to his family, does not through that cognition alone stop his alcoholic intake. Prospective practitioners can readily state the cognition that silence is golden and reflexive questioning is undesired, yet still be unable to change their interview behaviors. By now you know how such interview behaviors are to be changed: in a training program that shapes these behaviors through use of instrumental conditioning.

This chapter's needs are served by just this much examination of the kinds of verbal procedures used in facilitative interviews or limited desensitization counseling; others will be treated in Chapter 10. Relaxation procedures, probably well-known to readers, yet not customarily used, are additional verbal approaches to mediating behaviors, and these approaches more explicitly result in altered somatic functioning, thus reducing the need for the unwanted behaviors that compete and surge over productive behaviors.

Before leaving this section, it is appropriate to make readers aware of several other facts and defensible opinions.

One fact is that the verbal procedures of the facilitative interview partially portrayed here and popularized by the followers of Carl R. Rogers (1942, 1951) have been taught in many counselor training programs for almost 20 years as the sole manner of counselors' verbal interactions, and likely those early Rogerian procedures have been the ones learned by most high school counselors of recent decades. It is tenable to hypothesize that adherence to this one procedure for mediating behaviors, instead of having a number of behavior mediation strategies available from which to select the treatment-of-choice appropriate for each counselee, is a cause of the increasing dissatisfaction with high school counselor effectiveness on the part of students, educators, and parents. There has been a mystique attached to this early, commonly taught mediation procedure, but this has considerably lessened today. One reason for this lessening is that analysis of these procedures by behavior principles causes those procedures to be seen partly and simply as use or withholding of reinforcers (e.g., Truax, 1966). It likely is apparent that it is undesirable to embue procedures with a mystique, for then a practitioner of those procedures is unaware of the moment-by-moment effect his interview behaviors have on a client.

The verbal procedures of the facilitative interview alone are effective for certain purposes, but inadequate for mediating other behaviors. They are useful, indeed almost necessary, in any first interview, no matter what other strategies are to be used to help a counselee. They might be appropriate during subsequent interviews, being woven in and out of many conferences. As with any mediation strategy, the prospective member of the guidance team learns the contingencies that dictate when these procedures should be the treatment-of-choice.

OTHER PURPOSES OF FACILITATIVE INTERVIEW BEHAVIORS. It was noted earlier that the procedures that typify the facilitative interview are sometimes the only behavior mediation strategy used. Osipow and Walsh (1970) observe that they might be used when "the client's difficulties are so pervasive that the counselor finds it difficult or impossible to identify and/or deal with the antecedents" on the hope that, by using these helping procedures, "further deterioration can be avoided" (p. 58). The authors go on to observe that these verbal procedures are "adopted at times when no other approach seems cogent." When in doubt, be supportive, or, in another term, facilitative.

The use of these procedures is recommended by two researchers in behavioral counseling, Krumboltz and Thoreson (1969), who observe that

> the counselor begins by listening carefully to the client's concerns. The counselor tries to understand and assess the client's thoughts and feelings. He first tries to see things from the client's point of view. He communicates his understandings to the client and attempts to determine if he is accurately perceiving the client's thoughts and feelings. [p. 8]

Digression: Desensitization in Schools?

In equating the very commonly used verbal procedures of the facilitative interview with those of a limited or elementary form of desensitization, I am, in fact, stating that high school counselors have often been desensitizing youth through counseling interviews without using that term. To say that is to acknowledge that a tenable question, if not a challenge, might have emerged in some readers. "Desensitization—in a school? What justification is there for a school employee to engage in an activity of that kind?" The validity of the question is acknowledged, and in the next few paragraphs a rationale that applies not just to desensitization but to other procedures described later in this chapter will be presented.

It is premised that society establishes schools so that its youth can learn. Society has not only increasingly asked that schools relate education to occupation, but is now becoming downright insistent about it. Thus the word "learn" no longer means just abstract intellectual content, but also future-oriented useful content, including skills that are in demand in the occupation marketplace, skills acquired by all students.

Against that premise let us cast a youth who cannot learn to the degree appropriate for his ability and society's wishes. What is the school's stance about such a student? It can be elitist and autocratic, of course, and say by its actions, "Either you do or get out." Statist values are not unknown in this country, but the majority of the citizenry and schools appear increasingly committed to the humanistic values of the Declaration of Independence. They believe in the supreme value of individuals, with the state therefore in the position of servant.

Because individuals are important, and schools are maintained to help individuals learn, it follows that the school must be concerned when an individual is not learning. School adults seek to lessen the power of inhibitors of learning, if unable to eliminate them. But now this statement must be tested, and to do so some challenging questions are posed. "If a child has poor eyesight, it is the school's responsibility to give him glasses?" "If a youth cannot attend school because of poor health, which could be cured by an operation, does the school establish a hospital, or at least pay for the operation?"

The implied answers are "no," of course. If for no other reason than treatment of physical deficiencies by custom are handled other ways. But there are other reasons. One of them is that not only are there supposed to be easily accessible community resources for physical restoration, but also schools do not employ health practitioners of the kind needed in the two cases above. The youth absent from school because of illness of course *does* have school *academic* services either in hospitals or at home. In that case the school continues to carry out its obligation about learning.

But those comments do not yet address themselves to whether or not the school should provide desensitization and other behavior mediation procedures. In moving toward an answer, the health analogies used earlier provide a basis for contrast. There are many health practitioners available to most persons, either on a fee basis or free, but behavior mediation practitioners in most communities are rare, whether for fee or free, and particularly for free, except in schools. But this scarcity is not the chief reason for schools to provide behavior mediation procedures such as desensitization.

To ferret out that reason we need to again make a contrast with health problems.

Organic health deficiencies, in contrast to psychogenic ones, do not depend on transacting with other humans for their cure, and here we will exclude medical treatment as a transaction, even though it involves two persons. A tumor of the lung requires medical treatment, not a readjustment to the way one relates to other humans. Human relationships have nothing to do with the development of the tumor, or of dental caries, curvature of the spine, and a vast list of other physical deficiencies. But (and I am hopeful that you have anticipated what follows the "but") we recall that behavior is learned from transacting in social ecosystems, and it is within such systems that behavior must be mediated. Some social setting, some form of human transaction, is necessary for nonorganic behavior change. Even if there were many free behavior mediation practitioners provided by a community, to be as effective as our knowledge of behavior now permits, the practitioners would have to mediate individuals' behaviors within ecosystems. If they were private practitioners, therefore, they could be of relatively little value to as diverse a population as is found in a school.

There is yet an additional point, again using a contrast with health practices for making that point. The cure of organic problems often requires lengthy, very complicated procedures and equipment, with an array of specialists. On the other hand much behavior is amenable to mediation by relatively brief procedures carried out by one practitioner, or with the assistance of others who need only minimal training.

The four arguments in sum:

1. A variety of behavior mediation procedures is appropriate for schools because those procedures need to be carried out in that kind of setting to be effective.
2. Practitioners can be readied to carry out such procedures maximally with no more lengthy preparation than that called for by the American Personnel and Guidance Association as needed by a competent counselor (two years of training), the practitioner spoken of here as a behavior specialist.
3. Schools are an ameliorative type of social institution.
4. Because schools have been established for learning, schools should use resources that are theirs by custom so as to lessen the impediments to learning.

More Complex Desensitization
Purposes and Procedures

Returning the expository focus on desensitization as a procedure, we pick up the thread by recalling that in the early part of Chapter 5 there was used for illustration of respondent conditioning the case of a child frightened by a dog, and that the child might then fear the class of animals called dogs, not just the dog that frightened him.[5] It was also observed there that, if that fear were not deliberately extinguished, or if it did not extinguish by chance experiences, and as a result the child went through life fearing dogs, at times he would be greatly inconvenienced, but otherwise could lead a normal life. But what if he learned to fear humans, or schools, or open places? His functioning would be reduced to an unacceptable level. Desensitization procedures are used for rapid change in those fearing behaviors. What are such procedures and why do they work?

Recall the axiom: the human acts as an entity. A human is not the sum of two separate parts, physiological and psychological domains. Fear, therefore, is not psychological. Fear is human. It is a behavior of the entire person and is both patent and hidden. Noticeable behaviors identified as fearful (anxious, concerned) are only part of the behaviors of fear. Some can be reported by the person; others neither are apparent nor in the person's awareness. The fearing person might be aware of heartbeat changes, but not of other heightened or reduced autonomic responses. He may be aware of extreme sweat excretions, but unaware of abnormal blood pressure and skin conductance states. Cortextual and striated muscle activities associated with the fearing state may have some secondary and observable expressions, but the person will be unaware of much of this activity. Changes in brain waves occur, but can be detected only by electroencephalometric devices.

Desensitization procedures, as portrayed here with somewhat less than technical accuracy, are carried out to interrupt the undesired effect of autonomic responses on coping behaviors. Counterconditioning is subsumed here under desensitization, although with greater technical accuracy it should not be, in the opinion of some. Counterconditioning causes the establishment of a desirable behavior in competition with an undesired behavior and in such strength that it replaces the undesired behavior. Although technically different from procedures more justifiably called desensitization, counterconditioning has an effect similar to desensitization: undesired behaviors are replaced by desired behaviors.

Lang (1969) defines desensitization as

> an operant training schedule, designed to shape the response "I am not afraid" (or a potentially competing response such as "I am relaxed" or

---

[5] Actually this is not the best terminology. "Fear" is a hypothetical descriptive construct, thus in fact does not exist. There are certain behaviors commonly emitted by persons in the presence of certain stimuli, and there are subjective (internal) behaviors also commonly reported as well as observable behaviors. These constellations of behaviors have been given the summing label "fear," but it is important to be aware that an abstract fear does not occur, although specific behaviors do. Use of common terminology is made in instances such as in the referenced paragraph because it allows smoother reading.

"I am angry") in the presence of a graded set of discriminative stimuli. When well learned, the response [has] the status of a set or self instruction, which can then determine other related behaviors. [p. 187]

In this definition we see the significance of the person's symbol system. Fear reactions can be reduced by psychopharmaceuticals, but such procedures may have only a temporary effect. When fearing behaviors are the product of autonomic responses that the person has labeled, attached to stimuli that the person also has labeled, change in the undesired behaviors requires changes in cognitions. In the absence of cognitive controls over fearing behaviors, procedures for changing cognitions are obviously not necessary.

Let us look at an illustration of the latter circumstance—that is, no change in cognitions needed. In the case reported earlier of a girl who developed school phobia after a traumatic summer camp experience, return to school was efficiently and quickly attained by a simple, noncognitive procedure. Her parents worked out with a guidance specialist a procedure that included a precise schedule. On the first day she was taken by her mother to the school grounds after school sessions were over for the day. After a few days of walking outside, eventually going inside briefly during sessions, all in the company of her mother, she entered her classroom for brief periods, again with her mother. Her stays in the classroom were lengthened on schedule, her mother became more removed (for a period staying in the corridor while the girl was in the classroom), and within days the girl attended school in customary fashion with no fear.

This is a useful example of the work of a school counselor not only because it shows the role of a guidance team member in removing obstacles to learning, but because it demonstrates behavior mediation occurring without counselor-student interaction because the child's cognitive processes were not a potent factor in her undesired behaviors.

Lang's definition is now attended to, particularly focusing on one of the cognitions he identifies as a response that competes with undesirable responses: "I am relaxed." A common desensitization procedure is trained relaxation in the presence of aversive stimuli. Relaxation procedures are found in a range, from simple ones the counselor uses to more advanced ones the behavior specialist uses.

Relaxation results from the way the counselor uses words. This skilled word use in the counseling interview might appear to an untutored observer to be a typical social conversation, but in fact it is a delicate use of words in a deliberate effort to produce relaxation. The behavior specialist's desensitization behaviors, however, go beyond typical word use as found in a normal counseling situation and in relaxation exercises. By systematically associating muscle relaxation with fear-producing stimuli, he reduces or eliminates the reaction of fear to those stimuli (Bugg, 1972).

For an illustration of the counselor's desensitization activities, let us consider Edna, a high school junior. Edna has coped with life in a typically effective way through her middle school years, but has been increasingly dissatisfied with life in the past 2 years. She has become somewhat withdrawn, in comparison to her junior high school years, is often despondent, is earning lower and lower grades, and has asked her parents' permission to withdraw from school. Their response was to state that this request could not be honored until she conferred with a counselor, and that is the reason she has now asked for consultation. (An all too common state, regrettably. Edna said that she did not think of conferring with a counselor prior to her parents' insistence because "counselors just help you pick courses and colleges, and since I want to quit school, I don't see why I should go to a counselor.")

The counselor became aware right at the outset that Edna's behaviors were response generalizations to school, and that she, the counselor was probably included among the aversive stimuli, that Edna did not have sufficient stimulus discrimination to react to the counselor differently from other school stimuli that were truly aversive. The counselor, recognizing the problem, attempted differentiating herself from truly aversive stimuli. If she could not, the probability of the counselor's being of help would be severely inhibited. Her relaxing approach contributed to this immediate goal and, of course, was to be a prime procedure for attaining the intermediate goal of desensitization.

The counselor knew too that desensitization procedures carried out in counseling interviews would not be sufficient and knew that interventions in the ecosystems in which Edna was locked probably would have to occur. Social system intervention would be intended to retain Edna in school long enough for these other steps to occur, for desensitization activities to continue, and for new coping behaviors to be established.

The earlier illustration of the girl being desensitized to school as an anxiety-arousing stimulus showed desensitization that does not call for a verbal approach primarily, or for counselor-student interaction. The behavior mediation procedures used with Edna, on the other hand, illustrate the case of a student who would be helped by counselor-student verbal interaction, with desensitization being one goal of those procedures.

In her interviews with Edna the counselor was an attentive listener for much of the first interview. She practiced that difficult-to-learn technique, silent attention. There was less counselor silence nearer the end of the first interview and in subsequent interviews. When the counselor spoke, her sentences showed that she understood how Edna felt (the counselor was desensitizing Edna by employing reflection and other behaviors of conveying her empathy), and after a time the counselor no longer attended to

Edna's references to her unhappy state and did attend to (reinforced) statements of a positive nature.

One outcome or counseling goal, determined mutually by the counselor and Edna in the first interview, was achieved. This was a reduction in negative responses by Edna to herself and to the school as stimuli. That is, Edna could increasingly engage cognitions about herself and schooling in a positive, constructive manner because the counselor's behavior desensitized her to school as an aversive stimulus.

But that was only half the battle won. Even if Edna can now engage self and school symbolically, that is, talk about self and school without being upset by doing so, and "feels better," this is only a readying of Edna for the more important task. This task is an analysis of Edna's life course, the role of schooling in that life course, and a detailed analysis of Edna's specific behaviors in specific school situations, particularly in her subjects. Her constructive cognitions are no longer inhibited by negative respondent reactions. She is fruitfully stimulated by the attentiveness of the counselor and eager for and ready to engage in a rational analysis of her schooling.

As Edna speaks with the counselor, we can imagine her being aware of some feelings, and perhaps wondering whether she should express such feelings that are common among youth: confusion, guilt, and anger, for example. These feelings are a critical part of many youths' concerns, and, unless these feelings are brought to a higher level of awareness so that their existence can be known by the counselor and thus dealt with, they may impede constructive behaviors.[6] This observation leads us to the second reason for counselors and behavior specialists to use verbal behaviors of the kinds described as desensitizing: they create the conditions through which the student can become aware of his feelings and is able to speak of them. This comes about because the counselee learns, although likely unaware of it, that it is all right with the counselor to have negative feelings and to express them. He might feel guilt about "letting his parents down,"

---

[6] The word "feelings" is used here with reluctance. "Feelings" is a hypothetical construct; a feeling is not something real. What is real in "feelings" can neither be seen nor directly sensed, unlike the secretions of the endocrine system. Other unobservable behaviors resulting from those secretions can be sensed by the person, however, and, when they are, when the person is aware of those behaviors and has learned labels for them, he can then report those behaviors as "feelings." The guidance practitioner can learn about some of the person's respondent behaviors from such reports, and it is these behaviors that are mediated, not "feelings," when a counselee requests assistance because he does not like his feelings. Change the behavior and the feelings will change.

Within facilitative or helping interview procedures, it is desirable at the outset of an interview for the interviewer merely to reflect a person's feelings rather than to attempt to change the underlying behaviors. Through this reflection the interviewer conveys to the counselee that the interviewer is aware of the counselee's feelings. It is this interview skill that is recognized in this section. It is an important skill for desensitization purposes.

or anger at one or several teachers. That there might be these feelings, we will assume, would be unknown to the counselor or behavior specialist when a student seeks help around a seemingly academic matter. The guidance team member's conitnuous sensitivity to the possibility, however, and his skilled verbal behaviors increase the probability that such feelings will be expressed and thus be considered in the other procedures used by the team member.

There is another asset of silence, of attentive listening: sometimes that behavior, with occasional minimal verbal response is sufficient in and of itself to result in desired outcomes. Not only is this result of attentive listening frequently observed in varieties of literature, but many of you may have experienced its "lifting" or "releasing" effects. Someone to talk to is a commonly expressed human need, and perhaps expressed more by youths than adults. In the terms used here, the need is expressed as "someone who can listen attentively and caringly," and, implied in that statement, "also nonjudgmentally," in a moralizing sense. The reason why attentive, caring, nonjudgmental listening works, that is, why in some instances it is sufficient to restore a person's coping sense and reduce a sense of panic, can be described in respondent/operant conditioning terms, although this explanation is not ventured here. This statement is entered in the record, however, so that the reader does not suspect that after all there *are* some behavior mediation procedures that are mysterious, metaphysical, and extralegal. The statement *is* saying that sometimes the counselor or behavior specialist serves adequately who only listens caringly, but that these behaviors still are consonant with empirically established laws of behavior.

CONTINGENCY MANAGEMENT

Direct oral techniques for mediating behaviors comprise one class of procedures to use, one among the array of treatments-of-choice, and have been sketchily examined in the prior section. In this section we attend to the other class of procedures—those that manage stimulus/response contingencies. This class of procedures brings control to a portion of or a complete ecosystem and alters the responses of a selected person within that ecosystem. Contingency management is based on operant conditioning but technically is not operant conditioning. In operant conditioning a specific behavior is spontaneously emitted, followed by a specific reinforcing stimulus. Stated with more technical precision: a specific desirable (pleasant) stimulus that follows a specific, spontaneous behavior increases the likelihood that that behavior will be emitted again. A general reminder about respondent and operant conditioning is appropriate: in respondent conditioning the stimulus to be conditioned must occur *immediately before* or along with the start of the unconditioned response. In "pure" operant conditioning, and therefore in contingency management which is based on it, the behavior is conditioned not through pairing it with an unconditioned stimulus, but by the consequences, the pleasure or pain, that result or follow from a behavior. Another reminder: operant conditioning is rarely pure. It more frequently is accompanied by respondent conditioning.

The contingencies that are managed are the desirable conseqeunces of behaving in a certain way, as if a person were told "Your receipt of this reward is contingent upon your doing these certain things"—Grandma's law, in other words. In some cases undesirable outcomes are also used in contingency management.

One technical difference between operant conditioning and contingency management is that the former assumes a spontaneous behavior, not a coerced or solicited one, whereas contingency management, as the word "management" implies, assumes that a person or someone other than the person decides that a behavior should be acquired or eliminated. Following on that decision, either stimulus contingencies or response contingencies are managed so as to call out the behavior, or to reward, thus reinforce, a behavior that has been described to the behaver. Grandma's law again, but using more technical words: "The likelihood and/or strength of the behavior of eating your vegetables will be increased because that behavior will be followed by the reinforcing stimulus of a piece of pie," with the inference of no vegetable eating, no pie getting. Of course, "Grandma" is not interested in vegetable eating just this one time, so the contingencies are managed that way other times until the behavior of eaing vegetables is established and intrinsically maintained.

ILLUSTRATIONS OF CONTINGENCY MANAGEMENT

A widely used motion picture that demonstrates contingency management procedures shows an eight-year-old severely retarded girl who has never walked learning to walk in a few hours. This is indeed a dramatic illustration of the power of operant conditioning, with ice cream used as the extrinsic reinforcing stimulus. After she learned to walk, walking was intrinsically reinforced, that is, the behavior was maintained because walking provided the pleasures of being stimulated by endless new and different sights. Reading similarly comes under the maintenance control of intrinsic pleasures (stimulation) and thus is maintained without extrinsic reinforcers.

Next consider a potential academic achiever who has not learned to achieve. Contingency management can establish achievement behaviors for him. The reinforcers will need to be determined, of course, and, for a child in some situations, might indeed be ice cream. In an elementary school classroom, however, it might be some activity or time-use that the child can select from a "menu," an array of rewarding experiences from which a choice can be made. If the child is enjoying the reading of an exciting adventure novel on his own during reading period, for example, and not doing well in arithmetic, extra time is given for reading contingent on successful solving of arithmetic problems. In terms of Grandma's law, the dessert of extra reading time can be had only after eating the vegetables of arithmetic.

Shift the scene to a high school. A parent confers with a guidance team member about her daughter's undesired scholastic behaviors. In addressing this situation we first must face a corollary question, who is the client? It is now fairly customary to refer to an individual who has sought assistance from a guidance team member as a "client," but erroneous practice in the illustration now being considered would be to call in the student of reference and then think of her as client. She is not; the parent is. To be of assistance, the guidance team member can instruct the parent in contingency management, and the team member's involvement could end there. More likely, however, the guidance practitioner would confer with the student, who still is not thereby a client, to see if the student is willing to have the team member directly help the student as well as the parent. If the student agrees, she will also be a client. The team member has helped, or will help, the parent; he now seeks to see if the student wishes his more direct help because, if that is so, then not only through family-managed contingencies but also through school-managed ones, the team member will increase the probabilities of old behaviors extinguishing and the establishment of new behaviors.

Establishing new behaviors typically means shaping. If a teaching task is to make a basketball player out of a person who is devoid of any basketball-playing behaviors, the teacher does not view his task as producing some global activity, but instead as establishing numerous small behaviors, each of which builds on prior behavior, and which eventually lead to basketball playing. The teacher shapes and chains behavior, in short. He starts with the most elementary tasks and causes each to be established by the rewards they produce, then moves to increasingly advanced tasks, which naturally include the earlier tasks. If a youth does not study, and the task is to establish the behavior of homework on school topics, the contingency management plan may start with reinforcing a number of 5-minute periods of sitting at a desk—just sitting. The next step in the plan may call for sitting at the desk with a school book open. Times are lengthened, that is, the price for attaining the reinforcers goes up, and additional behaviors are required, such as explaining first just one page studied, then an increasing number of pages. The reinforcers? On the Premack (1959) principle, they will be those activities that have a reinforcement history for this youth—the strong behavior will pull up the weak behavior. Money is obvious as a reinforcer, but there can be television watching, car use, opportunity to earn a musical instrument through acquiring point values— "1,000 points and the drum set is yours." In any case, attaining that reinforcer is firmly and remittingly contingent on engaging each new, more comprehensive behavior. Rather typically such agreements are written— made a contract signed by youth, parent, and sometimes the counselor or behavior specialist when one of them has been involved in the process.

Bribery? No, bribery is paying persons to engage in illegal or immoral behavior. It is no more bribery than "Eat your vegetables, dear, so you can have some of this yummy pie," or "If you come to work on time, you'll not be docked any pay," or "Those who want to earn an 'A' in this course will have to do a term paper in addition to the other requirements."[7] Recall that all behavior is established and maintained by pleasure getting/pain avoiding, whether it is the behavior of writing poetry by candlelight in a freezing attic, shoplifting, being a medical missionary, manipulating stocks even if the poor widow loses all her income so the manipulator can become rich, making flawless furniture for sale, or becoming a counselor with the view of avoiding the pain of the classroom. All behavior has a payoff in pleasure (much of what pleases is learned) and in avoiding pain (social pain is learned). Contingency management first calls for identifying what pleases a person and then using those pleasures to establish and maintain other behaviors. In our context, of course, the behaviors to be established, if not socially useful, are good for the person who is the subject of the management plan. In another context the behavior to be established might be a social evil and damaging to individuals. Dickens's Fagin used contingency management to train homeless boys to be thieves.

Thievery among one stratum of children and youth was a fact in nineteenth-century England, as Dickens recorded. It is also a fact among subcultures of youth today, whether it is shoplifting among affluent children and adolescents, or that plus other forms of stealing among other subcultures. Thinking of young persons caught and sentenced for stealing lets us report an illustration of contingency management that is valuable both for its personal and socially significant results, and because it demonstrates several contingency management components. As the illustration unfolds, we can learn more about each of these management components.

Think first of a population of a prison for very young adults, whatever may be its official title or intention. If the intention is reformation or be-

---

[7] Tharp and Wetzel (1969) observe that in the ordinary nomenclature for rewarding behavior, other terms are used, such as salary, commission, praise, approval, or the hope of heaven.

havior correction, so often expressed in official titles as "Reformatory" or "Youth Correction Agency," the bald fact is that the adolescents in them are not volunteers. They are sent there by courts, and, as in any prison, they are restrained from leaving. The population is young persons who have committed crimes. They commit crimes because their criminal behavior is reinforced in the society in which they live. The dope addict steals to buy dope, and buying and taking dope are reinforcing—the payoff, the reinforcer for stealing. "Reformation" or "correction" has to mean extinguishing some behaviors and establishing and maintaining others. What are traditional procedures for reforming or correction as carried out in such institutions? Primarily confinement, based on the premise that confinement is punishing (is painful) and thus a youth will not again engage in crime so as to avoid punishment. Specific procedures in those institutions, such as schooling modeled on that provided for regular populations and training in trades, are intended to equip the youths for useful lives when they get out. Typically these youth populations are poor learners of academic subjects, and their average academic achievement is significantly below that of regular student populations, as are their results on so-called intelligence tests. The recidivism rate is high, on the average over 50 percent, and thus it is doubtful that the traditional youth prison "reforms" or "corrects" at a socially and personally useful level.

Operating on laws of behavior establishment and maintenance, reformatories can reform, correctional institutions can change (correct) behavior, as the illustration we are approaching demonstrates.

The illustration is taken from an extensive report by Cohen and Filipczak (1971) of a contingency management program carried out at the National Training School for Boys, until recently a federal institution for youths in Washington, D.C. The adolescents confined there committed crimes against federal statutes. Cohen and associates

> planned rehabilitation by inculcating new academic and socially appropriate behaviors under a schedule of reinforcement, while extinguishing inappropriate, antisocial behaviors by a schedule which was either competing or nonreinforcing. [p. 2]

The activities they established focused on specified academic attainments so as to program for success the individual inmates who participated in them. The youth had

> long histories of failure—both at home and in school. The punishing aspects of failure to perform in these environments produce not only school dropouts but dropouts from life. . . . The standard educational environment is aversive and punishing to a student with a limited history of success and a small academic repertoire.

The basic premise of this project, labeled with the acronym CASE,

> was that educational behavior is functionally related to its consequences and that—by setting up a situation in which appropriate consequences are made contingent upon changing behavioral requirements—these behaviors can be established, altered, maintained, and transferred. [pp. 5–6]

The essence of the contingency management program was the status of the youths in the program: they were employees of a "corporation," and were paid, both in money earned through accumulating points and in acquiring intellectual wealth. The money earned could be used in many ways, such as buying better quality food, clothing, and lodging; entertainment of visitors; and special highly desirable leisure time activities. If they were not to earn these, they would eat institutional food, sleep in bunks in large dormitories, wear institutional attire, and have only the usual visiting and recreational privileges. The investigators report that they were informed at the outset that the population of this institution

> consists of "con men and freeloaders" and that given the choice of free lodging and food or earning better quality food, lodging, and clothing, they would choose to go on relief [relief here meant the free food and lodging given all inmates]. This was not so. No student spent more than four weeks on relief during a fifty-two week period—and never more than two consecutive weeks. [p. 6]

As to the use of money as the generalized reinforcer, the investigators comment that an important reason devolves from the reinforcement principle postulated by Premack (1959) that

> given two behaviors, one at a low probability and the other at a high probability, the more probable behavior can be used to reinforce the less probable if [the less probable] is made contingent on [the more probable]. By providing money, we were making the more probable behavior which money can buy contingent upon less probable educational behavior. Eventually, through appropriate programming and environmental support, the educational behavior may come to be reinforced by non-monetary rewards. But it is a principle of programming that we distinguish between our terminal requirement, or goal, and the current repertoire of the student whom we tie into. We may not always wish him to work for money, but we start with his value system—just as we begin with his level of knowledge and skills—and work from there. . . . We developed a system of extrinsic reinforcements which were already strong in these students' repertoires and which lent themselves to being altered gradually into the generally more desirable form of intrinsic reinforcers. [pp. 7–9]

Money as such was not used, but points earned for academic achievement were. With points earned (bookkeeping was an essential part of this contingency management program) the students could rent a private room, purchase furnishings for it beyond the minimal essentials with which it was originally equipped, rent a private shower stall, select noninstitutional food in a cafeteria, purchase clothing and care for it in a coin-operated washer, purchase entry into a recreational hall, entertain visitors with food, and purchase magazines, room decorations, and other commodities from a CASE store. The student determined how his income was to be employed.

Points were earned for academic attainments. The inmate did not have to do academic work, but that work was the only means he had for earning points. The academic program each engaged was individualized after assessment of his academic competencies at the time of entry into CASE, with the substance of each student-inmate's courses engaged through programmed materials. Points were earned by such means as correct answers on these programmed materials and attainment of certain levels of achievement on tests.

> The major behaviors for which points were given were the educational behaviors whose establishment and maintenance were the primary aims of the project. The students had so many academic deficiencies that a variety of options were available for programmed materials and classes they could take. . . . [Students could] progress from pre-arithmetic through geometry on programmed materials. [Premack, 1959, p. 11]

Money (points) was not the only reinforcer. Outstanding performance was acknowledged before the group which provided social reinforcers by spontaneous expressions of admiration and congratulations. Beyond money and group accolades, however, the total environment constituted a respondent/operant program with the subtle, pervasive effects that social ecosystems have on persons. Unlike typical school activities in similar institutions, the student-inmates did not experience contingency management within one aspect of institutional life (academic) but otherwise lived as typical inmates. They were given options through the money earned to lead a life that was normal except for being restricted to the institution. They learned to make decisions about themselves, experienced privacy, control over room decoration and the use of their leisure time, freedom from regimentation, and other conditions rare in institutional living. Along with academic skills they learned for the first time those behaviors and reinforcing stimuli of the normal world to which they were being readied to return. Their academic experiences were intimately and inextricably tied in with the good life (relatively speaking). They experienced academic success and found that success of one kind is associated with other pleasures, other successes.

The results? You may be motivated to study the Cohen-Filipczak report in detail, not just to find the results, but because it is a comprehensive exposition of contingency management principles and procedures. There was outstanding academic success, and "violent social behavior lessened to a surprisingly high degree despite the decrease in traditional punishment" (page 15).

One response emitted to this report might be stated like this: "Well and good, but those investigators had money and could control the complete environment. We have no money to use in our school, and even though I as one teacher would like to use contingency management procedures, I know others would not. They would view those procedures as mechanistic, insidious, '1984' dehumanizing procedures. What can *I* do?"

This dolorous complaint is not unlike those I hear from time to time. The response starts with another old saying, "Half a loaf is better than none." Ideally a school would be organized around contingency management procedures for learning but, if it is not, any one teacher can organize his class that way—but only after checking with the principal and taking other precautionary steps. The National Training School illustration was around general academic attainment in a total environment sculptured to attain that goal, but contingency management procedures are used to attain almost any kind of goal and only rarely involve many persons. They are used to establish music skills or eliminate shyness, to establish responsible behaviors or extinguish hostile behaviors, to establish study habits whose pay-off is academic achievement, or to reduce obesity. They can be used by just one set of parents, or just one teacher in a school, or just one school in a whole school system.

If the complaining teacher who made the hypothetical statement has a student in his class who is not achieving, a behavioral contract worked out with the student's parents can mediate that behavior. The teacher does not go it alone, but uses the resource the school system provides just for such instances—the guidance team. From what the teacher could learn about a contingency plan for this one youth, he could learn how learning occurs (he likely did not learn how people learn in his teacher preparation program, but only learned "how to teach"). He could thus change his entire classroom procedures, thereby affecting learning by all youths in his class.

CONSULTATION IN BEHAVIOR MEDIATION

This section briefly brings together for emphasis and clarity those observations made from time to time about guidance team members working with other adults. This kind of activity is known as consultation, although a sound case can be made that the term "counseling" is just as appropriate. In this section the word "consultation" is used to minimize digressions.

Mediating behavior typically means entering a person's life at the point of contact that person has with social systems. The determining force in many social systems into which youths are locked are the adults of that system. To mediate behavior, therefore, often means directing attention to the social system, thus the adults, which brings us full circle to the term "consultation."

Consulting behaviors with both teachers and parents are carried out modally for several purposes, although two or more of them usually occur in any one consultation. One purpose is to acquire information or data that result in knowing more about a student's behaviors—what is holding those behaviors in certain patterns. Another purpose is to solicit the assistance of teachers and parents in a contingency management program related to the youth and teaching about such procedures. Another purpose is the converse—responding to a request for assistance made by parents and/or teachers related to a student. Falling in between these is the relatively simple, almost social conversation in which a guidance team member explains in general terms a youth's behaviors to parents or teachers, providing career information, or engaging in other consultations typical of PTA contacts.

A cognition to remember should be repeated in this record: in soliciting help from parents or teachers, or responding to their requests for assistance, the guidance team member is bound to engage in teaching those adults about behavior, and this can be one of the best services he can render to students. It is one activity within that general purpose of the guidance movement: nurturing the adequacy of development on the part of all youths. The more that teachers and parents know about the "cause and cure" of behavior, it is hypothesized, the greater the likelihood that social ecosystems will be more supportive of good development.

PRINCIPLES APPLIED TO GROUPS

In this text a central premise related to guidance strategies is that they are to be applied in group settings. Examples used in this chapter so far to illustrate behavior principles applied to guidance practices have been applications of those principles with sole individuals. Their application to individuals in groups is essentially the same. Facilitative interview behaviors, for example, are human interaction behaviors and thus are not dependent on any particular setting in which they are applied. One major activity with groups of students will be the development of decision-making skills among the individuals in the group, and the strategies for that objective are largely rational. Contingency management procedures, one type of behavior modification strategy, have been demonstrated as being eminently successful in changing the behaviors of individuals in group settings. In sum, behavior principles apply to behavior; the settings in which those principles are applied vary greatly, but the principles remain the same. In the school concerned about all students' attaining guidance objectives, groups will be a featured setting in which behavior principles are applied.

SUMMARY

The professional behaviors (technical practices) of guidance team members flow from a vast pool of knowledge about behavior. There is no single process or technique used for helping other persons, but instead there is an array of strategies from among which the practitioner chooses the appropriate treatment-of-choice in each instance.

These strategies fall into two modes, direct verbal mediating procedures (the "direct" meaning face-to-face with the person assisted) either with single individuals or among individuals in groups, and contingency management activities, typically set up by a guidance specialist but carried out by others.

The verbal procedures generally described were (1) two types of reasoning ("typical" reasoning and Ellis's rational-emotive procedures), (2) excitation, and (3) that process that requires ability to see cause/effect in others' behaviors as well as high-level verbal skill. For this latter procedure Delaney and Eisenberg's term "the facilitative interview" was used. This latter process is employed (1) sometimes for "holding" or supportive purposes; (2) sometimes to desensitize; (3) at the outset of any interview, no matter the eventual strategy employed; (4) at numerous times in any person-to-person conference with youths and adults, again no matter the main treatment-of-choice selected; and last (5) when no other strategy can be determined to help a particular person at a particular time. The kinds of behavior that guidance team members mediate will differ among them; thus the array of strategies differs somewhat for each team occupation. The career development and continuing education technicians use rational procedures almost exclusively. Other team members, including teacher-advisors, have some competencies in supportive counseling for which facilitative procedures are used, but it is the counselor and behavior specialist who use such procedures deliberately for desensitization. The behavior specialist, furthermore, has desensitization competencies well beyond those of the counselor.

Although the counselor might plan a contingency management procedure for mediating relatively "simple" behaviors, a greater part of the behavior specialist's time will be given over to behavior analysis, the establishment of contingency management activities based on that analysis, and the deployment and supervision of those activities among controlling persons in social ecosystems. In some instances the contingency management activity is directed to assisting a single youth. In other instances, however, the competencies of the behavior specialist are used pervasively in an ecosystem so as to benefit a large number of youths or even all who are in that ecosystem, such as done by Cohen and Filipczak.

REFERENCES

BAKER, S. B., & CRAMER, S. H. "Counselor or Change Agents: Support from the Profession. *Personnel and Guidance Journal,* 1972, *50,* 661–665.

BANDURA, A. *Principles of Behavior Modification.* New York: Holt, Rinehart and Winston, 1969.

BENJAMIN, A. *The Helping Interview,* 2nd Ed. Boston: Houghton Mifflin, 1974.

BUGG, C. A. "Systematic Desensitization: A Technique Worth Trying." *Personnel and Guidance Journal,* 1972, *50,* 823–828.

COHEN, H. L., & FILIPCZAK, J. *A New Learning Environment.* San Francisco: Jossey-Bass, 1971.

DELANEY, D. J., & EISENBERG, S. *The Counseling Procress.* Chicago: Rand McNally, 1972.

DWORKIN, E. P., & DWORKIN, A. L. "The Activist Counselor." *Personnel and Guidance Journal,* 1971, *49,* 748–753.

ELLIS, A. *Reason and Emotion in Psychotherapy.* New York: Lyle Stuart, 1962.

IVEY, A. E., NORMINGTON, C. J., MILLER, C. D., MORRILL, W. H., & HASSE, R. E. "Microcounseling and Attending Behavior." In S. H. Osipow & W. B. Walsh (Eds.), *Behavior Change in Counseling: Readings and Cases.* Englewood Cliffs, N.J.: Prentice-Hall, 1970.

KRUMBOLTZ, J. D., & THORESON, C. E. *Behavioral Counseling.* New York: Holt, Rinehart and Winston, 1969.

LANG, P. J. "Mechanics of Desensitization: Laboratory Studies." In C. M. Franks (Ed.), *Behavioral Therapy: Appraisal and Status,* New York: McGraw-Hill, 1969.

MATHENY, K. "Counselors as Environmental Engineers." *Personnel and Guidance Journal,* 1971, *49,* 439–444.

OSIPOW, S. H., & WALSH, W. B. *Behavior Change in Counseling: Readings and Cases.* Englewood Cliffs, N.J.: Prentice-Hall, 1970.

Osipow, S. H., & Walsh, W. B. *Strategies in Counseling for Behavior Change.* Englewood Cliffs, N.J.: Prentice-Hall, 1971.

Prediger, D. J., Roth, J. D., & Noeth, R. J. "Career Development of Youth: A Nationwide Study." *Personnel and Guidance Journal,* 1974, *53,* 97–104.

Premack, D. "Toward Empirical Behavioral Laws I: Positive Reinforcement." *Psychological Review,* 1959, *66,* 219–233.

Reynolds, G. S. *A Primer of Operant Conditioning.* Glenview, Ill.: Scott, Foresman, 1968.

Rogers, C. R. *Counseling and Psychotherapy.* Boston: Houghton Mifflin, 1942.

Rogers, C. R. *Client-Centered Therapy.* Boston: Houghton Mifflin, 1951.

Sulzer, B., & Mayer, G. R. *Behavior Modification Process for School Personnel.* Hinsdale, Ill.: Dryden Press, 1972.

Tharp, R. G., & Wetzel, R. J. *Behavior Modification in the Natural Environment.* New York: Academic Press, 1969.

Truax, C. B. "Reinforcement and Non-reinforcement in Rogerian Psychotherapy." *Journal of Abnormal Psychology,* 1966, *71,* 1–9.

Truax, C., & Carkhuff, R. *Toward a More Effective Counseling and Psychotherapy.* Chicago: Aldine, 1966.

Vernon, W. M. *Motivating Children.* New York: Holt, Rinehart and Winston, 1972.

Williamson, E. G. *Counseling Adolescents.* New York: McGraw-Hill, 1950.

Williamson, E. G. *Vocational Counseling.* New York: McGraw-Hill, 1965.

9 Career Development

INTRODUCTION

The ultimate goal of education, and thus also a goal of the guidance movement, is the molding of persons who find satisfaction and zest in life, and who contribute to others' satisfaction and to equality of society. Because each person's occupational career is central to the quality of that person's life, a major intermediate guidance goal is developing students who have acquired the behaviors needed to be successful in an occupational career. The term that sums up these outcomes is career development, an aspect of the school's program of career education in which guidance goals and performance objectives are prominent. It is through guidance procedures in this domain that society provides all persons with the sole, systematic, and formal means of assistance in attaining these outcomes.

Even though much has been said earlier in these chapters about career development and the relationship of the guidance movement to it, this chapter and the next are given over to a systematic and detailed exposition of the topic. To some degree Chapter 12 provides additional coverage.

DEFINITIONS

The terms used in this chapter do not have meanings agreed upon by all who use them. The meanings in this section represent some consensus, and in any case derive from the context in which they are used.

Occupation. An array of related work tasks carried out by one or more persons (usually many persons), for which one or a variety of titles are used. For example, baker, lawyer, stonemason, psychiatric nurse.

Job. An occupation as found in a specific company or employing unit. The job title in the company or unit may be the same as the usual title for the occupation. For example, one of the occupations found in the Hical Baking Company is the job of baker. Lawyer is one of two jobs in the legal firm of Cantwin and Tortloss, the other being secretary.

Position. This term refers to each single expression of a job, that is, a station, within an employing unit, thus filled by one person. For example, each of the three bakers in the Hical Baking Company holds a position as baker in the job of baker in that company in the worldwide occupation of baker. Each attorney in the U.S. Department of Justice holds a position in the job of lawyer in that employing unit, in which each carries out the work functions of the occupation titled lawyer. Incidentally, there is some agreement about these technical distinctions between job and position, but in typical parlance the word job is used to mean position, as in job hunting, taking a job, jobs available. Unless there is need for a distinction to be made, use of the word job in this and the next chapter might mean either job or position in more technical terms. The context will make the use clear.

Career. In the view of some there can be several careers, such as occupational and marriage careers. Our concern here is the occupational career, and the term in this use means, simply, a person's occupational history. Ideally it connotes a series of related occupations, jobs, and positions through which a person planfully moves—a "good" occupational history. Each change represents improvement in status and income because each is a planned progression in demands for greater skill and responsibility. A military career clearly illustrates.

Vocation. Originally this word meant only a calling from God to enter a religious occupation. The meaning broadened during the Reformation to mean God's calling to any occupation, and now this term is used most ambiguously. It is used here to refer to a person's patterns of behaviors that are significant in an occupation. "Occupation," then, refers to impersonal work functions described, for example, in the *Dictionary of Occupational Titles,* and "vocation" refers to the person, thus the two terms are complementary. A person has vocational behaviors that he applies to an occupation.

Vocationalization. This is a natural extension of vocation (it is Crites's [1958] term). It is a subtle concept implying society's efforts, chiefly school efforts, to mediate a person's development in ways to permit smooth, wise movement into and through a career. Vocationalization, thus, is the outcome of career education. Because vocationalization subsumes many facets of individuals' lives, it is seen as "a refined corollary of socialization" (Herr & Cramer, 1972, p. 28). "The process of vocationalization . . . speaks to the . . . psychological, sociological, cultural, economic [inputs] which result in such outcomes as effective vocational behavior, decision-making ability, and vocational maturity" (p. 29).

Vocational development. A more advanced conceptual step, this refers to the programmatic steps that lead to vocationalization. It conveys here the same ideas as career development, and since that latter term is the more popular one as a result of federal support, "career development" will be the term more frequently used in this text.

Career education. This is a new and sometimes misunderstood term. It refers to structuring complete school programs so that they attend to the vocational or career development, thus the vocationalization, of each student. The frequent error is to equate career education with *vocational education.* The latter is a historical effort to vocationalize youth, but in the historical accidents of public education, vocational education was required to be appended to other kinds of education going on in schools, thus benefitted only a small proportion of youths, those who entered vocational education. Career education, as noted, refers to making *all* school program regularities affect all students' career development by establishing behavior regularities of career benefit in all.

Career guidance. May become popular as the guidance contribution to vocationalization. Gysbers (1973), then president of the National Vocational Guidance Association, proposed that it could be a unifying term, one to replace those common modifiers of the word guidance that I see as useless and deceptive, "educational, social/personal, and vocational." Because a person's career is much of everything that a person is, career guidance is assistance to the totally behaving human, and as such is a term consonant with the thrust of this text. Career education and career guidance, however, are also seen as temporary promotional terms. Schools are rapidly moving toward providing career education, and when schooling and career education are synonymous, the word "career" will not be needed. If we were to use the term career guidance for a while, the modifier could also be dropped from that term when guidance came, eventually, to mean career guidance. Until then, however, career guidance must refer to all guidance functions, and not be just another term for "vocational guidance," thus imply activities added to other "kinds" of guidance.

CAREER DEVELOPMENT IN SCHOOLS

As implied in the word development, a school program in this area properly begins in each person's elementary schooling and continues throughout the school years. The end of high school brings a youth to an important step in his history of career development: either entry into a first position in a correctly chosen occupation, or continuing education/training. Perhaps both. In an adequate high school assistance in entering a first position is a natural extension of a history of career development and career-related actions sponsored for each youth by the school system. Thus in the guidance perspective this important step would not even be called position placement (usually called job placement); it is occupational or career entry.

The differences between the terms "job placement" and "career entry" are not important per se, but are important in the concept they might connote. For most persons "to take a job" connotes taking a step that is an end in itself. There is no connotation of movement through a career conveyed in the term, no suggestion of a dynamic, developing life. To take a job suggests taking what employment is at hand. To enter an occupation, a career, on the other hand, connotes the commencement of a futureful course in an area of work chosen after deliberation. Of course, one begins practice of an occupation through taking a job. Career or occupational entry is a broader dynamic term, however, and thus is selected for use here. Within the context of career development that begins in elementary school, occupational entry through taking a job is the smooth, natural step noted above, one that has been anticipated and planned for.

Those last words might acquire an incorrect inference, incidentally. They might suggest that career development, starting as it does in elementary school, means early decision about an occupation instead of this decision happening close to high school graduation (for those not continuing education). In fact, in a career development program a student does start early to learn about himself and the world of work, and how to make decisions that incorporate these data. But he is also subjected to other actions that cause him to postpone occupational commitment because an early commitment might arrest development. The guidance position is to help a youth maintain flexibility by postponing a commitment to an occupation until commitment is imperative, thus maximizing his options and development.[1] Eventually the high school student who will start his em-

[1] This decision postponement position appears to be supported by examination of youth development within our complex society, but has more substantial support from early findings of Super and Overstreet (1960) based on the now-completed

ployment history upon his imminent graduation has arrived at the time when he must choose among the options he has kept open. Even then guidance practitioners will help him see that this first occupation may be but a step in his development, not a final goal.

Assisting youths to move consistently toward a satisfying, socially useful life is done by some families and by other social agencies, but assistance there often is casually and informally given by nonexperts and not based on empirical data, whereas the practice of the guidance team member is expert and empirically based. Families and other agencies can and often do help a youth find a job, but simply to be placed in a position is not a goal of guidance. Entering a first full-time job occurs at a point in a life, and the guidance movement is not concerned with that point as an objective. It *is* concerned with each person's life as a nonending process of fulfillment, with movement through a career. Thus any one event cannot be viewed as a final attainment, but only as one step in a person's life course—a step that is either in accord with the evidence as being a good step to take, or to the contrary extreme, a defeating, time-wasting, nonproductive step. Guidance procedures are designed to help reduce the amount of error and of wasted time, money, and effort. But that is putting it negatively—stating what guidance procedures seek to avoid. The effort is not directed toward avoidance; avoiding such waste results from attending to the positive—helping the individual plan out the best future as far as can be foretold, and helping him attain the life style for which he has opted.

School guidance practitioners enter a person's life course, his occupational career, only in readying for that career, and at its outset at best, and in many cases not even then. In this latter group are those youths who go on to degree-granting institutions without a firm career plan, other than the plan to attend a college. They expect that the temporary delay in occupational commitment, particularly in view of the counseling help usually available in degree-granting institutions, will result in a wiser decision made later. It takes a well-prepared and experienced guidance practitioner

---

20-year Career Pattern Study conducted by Super. Their study presents documentation of the vocational immaturity of ninth-grade boys. Yet other data appear to present contravening evidence. Mezzano (1971), for example, reports that a study of 1,495 students in grades 7 through 12 shows that "ninth grade boys were most concerned about their future vocational and educational plans (page 44). For tenth-, eleventh-, and twelfth-grade boys also, concern about their future was their paramount concern. These data might appear to conflict with the idea of postponement of occupational and career decisions, but in actuality they do not. Concern among ninth-grade boys about their vocational future does not mean that they should make a career decision at that time. There is a natural interest, and that interest is a motivation for schools to offer and for ninth-grade boys to engage in activities in which they acquire career decision-making behaviors. Career commitment is postponed until a student is developmentally ready to make a selection, or at least until such contingencies as economics or family pressures force him to make a decision even if he is not developmentally ready.

to know when to encourage a college-bound high school youth to attain a career commitment while in high school, and when to encourage postponement.

The High School: One Ecosystem Influencing Occupational Decisions

The views of this section are speculative and extrapolative. They posit a large sum out of small parts. To state this position we refer to part of the substance of Chapter 7 where we saw that the effects of biological ecosystems are more subtle than obvious, and mostly are accidental. A milkweed seed blown into a dense pine wood will not thrive, because of the subtle effects of shade. A social ecosystem has its subtle effects, but such ecosystems might differ from the purely biological ones in that some of the effects may be deliberate, that is, some features of the ecosystem are present by intention. A youth of certain characteristics who is moved by chance into an ecosystem not tolerant of those characteristics will not thrive psychologically. Were a public high school to have only a college preparatory curriculum, a youth who was scholastically inept or not interested in learning of that kind, who otherwise entered the high school out of a desire to earn a high school diploma, would be in an inhospitable social ecosystem and would likely die, educationally speaking.

The point? If it is to be a fact that the school contributes to the career development of each youth, the school, an ecosystem, must be marked by those interrelated characteristics that nurture career development. The prime characteristic of a social ecosystem is its dominant members, and no more so than in schools. Thus it is the adults of the school who will determine whether the school as an ecosystem nurtures, is neutral toward, or works against the career development of all youths in the system.

High schools historically have emphasized academic attainments. The traditional view held that what students did with the knowledge they acquired, so far as a career was concerned, was of no concern to school personnel. Said another way, the traditional attitude of school systems about the youth who passed through them was concern about transmitting knowledge, not about what a person made of his life. The guidance movement partially reverses those values. It places primary importance on individual development. If what is learned in school and how such learning is managed are not entirely tailored to fit each individual's uniqueness, at least some measure of academic content and methodology is adapted to individuals in a guidance-oriented school. The guidance movement seeks to cultivate idiosyncrasy,[2] not just for a person's high school years, but more particularly for his life course. To be guidance-oriented, in short, is to be career-development–oriented. That is a term that describes a school that has created that kind of ecosystem that nurtures work values, skill and knowledge development, and the acquisition of decision-making competencies, particularly in the career area.

It is an oversimplification to refer to schools as being either guidance-oriented or not. Some high schools profess a guidance orientation and parade a cadre of counselors as testimony of their concern. Because tradition dies hard, however, some of those schools retain attributes of statist-type education, perhaps out of ignorance of how to be different. Most high schools have multiple curricula, but some cannot attain flexibility among curricula, let alone abandon curricula in favor of giving students free choice of study (in determination with a counselor) as practiced in rare high schools. There are degrees of guidance orientation, then, running from its complete absence, as in the highly authoritarian, statist school most of us know or have known. Degrees of guidance orientation then runs through all kinds of mixes of behaviors toward students, to those school practices at the other end of the continuum that are all oriented toward individual development. These practices are maximally expressed in individual progress through a curriculum resulting in cognitive knowledge and motor skill as developed for each student.[3]

Perhaps the most untenable employment position for a counselor is to be in a school where most employees take a feeble stance at best about human development, particularly in its career expression. In such schools the concept of counselor-as-advocate of individuals has little chance of expression. It is tenable to guess that those data that report youths as seeing counselors only as administrative agents of the school system, concerned only with not rocking the boat, were obtained in schools of that kind. It is equally tenable to fear that some counselors in such schools did, and do, fill roles of squeezing and shoehorning youths to fit them into academic Procrustean beds, and even enjoy doing so. Indeed from time to time one reads justifications of this stance, rooted in the premise of loyalty to the school as an institution and as an employer ("We take their check, so we should do what they ask us to do").

---

[2] A term coined by an eminent philosopher-scholar-educator Harold Benjamin (1949), and used as the title of a too-little known paper, *The Cultivation of Idiosyncrasy,* given as the Inglis lecture at Harvard University.

[3] Ten years ago innovative high schools were so rare that the few there were were so noticeable as to warrant attention in the public press and identification in texts of this kind. In 1976 the number of high schools managed around the hub of individual development is much greater, and therefore better-known to many readers.

A common but erroneous procedure for a school to follow in carrying out its commitment to career development is to function in a traditional fashion related to curricula and teaching procedures, but then to employ counselors on the premise that career development is their responsibility. (Recall that the guidance team is an emerging concept and practice, with the common practice still being the employment of one or more persons titled "counselor" who are equally prepared and certified and who engage in similar functions.) Why erroneous? Would it not be erroneous to state that student ability to read and use speaking and writing practices is the concern only of a school's English Department? Professional educators as well as community adults expect the entire school to be committed to effective communication, with English teachers employed for maximum technical learning in communication in their work with students and as consultants in communication in their work with colleagues.

Adequately prepared counselors are the school's experts in career development and thus are the school's resource persons in that area, the ones best qualified by training and experience to evaluate the quality of the school as a guidance-oriented social ecosystem. But career development, including occupational decision making, is a school concern, not just that of the counselors or the guidance team. And more than a secondary school concern. It is a school system concern because there is an important role in career development to be carried out in elementary schools, using the expertise of guidance team members to coordinate the elementary and secondary portions of the program.

These introductory comments have been intended to reinforce justifications established earlier for a school system to be concerned with career development by committing schools to the concepts and practices of career education. They can be summed with these reminders: most of life, for typical adults, is primarily twofold—an occupational career (recall the observation about a person's occupation: the watershed down which the rest of life flows), and an intense, intimate, and theoretically permanent involvement with a mate and children. A typical person's life, male and female, then, is a two-sunned solar system, all his purposes and identifying behaviors revolving around occupation and family. Thus occupational and family careers have to be the primary concern of schooling, which is supposed to ready all citizens for life, and of these two careers, the occupational one is that with clearest justification for school programming. The last comment, and the one of greatest importance, is that career development is not an occasional practice done only by student and counselor conferring together. Career development is an outcome of both the subtle and pronounced interactions of adults, programs of study and skill acquisition, and the system through which these are managed. It is the outcome of the nature of the school as a social ecosystem. In the ultimate, career development is a kind of behavior regularly emitted, resulting from program regularities.

OCCUPATIONAL DECISION MAKING

Of all the ways career development can be examined, a most useful one is to examine the process of occupational decision making and the teaching of those skills systematically to all students.

Role of Developmental Factors in First Occupational Decisions

The decision about the first occupation a youth will enter, or at least the entry occupational family, is one of the major career decisions a person makes and is thus of immense concern to guidance team members. This decision is the start of a journey, to use a time-worn figure. If the entire journey is to be the most efficient one that it can be, yielding maximum satisfaction, then each portion of the journey should be the best action it can be in light of the known factors at that time.

There are numerous inputs into this journey, the school system being one of those inputs. The role of the high school is to serve as the sorting-out and decision-teaching agent, resulting in refined and crystallized occupational decisions, at least for those not continuing their education. Whatever a youth's high school experiences, major inputs into occupational decisions are the behaviors he acquires in other psychosocial ecosystems, particularly the family.

An individual acquires behaviors in infancy and early childhood that have a bearing on later occupational career decisions. Recall the children and youths reared in the maximum experience and minimum experience families. The probability is high that children from the maximum experience families have had their inquisitive, reaching-out behaviors reinforced, and later their behaviors relating to successful school achievement were also reinforced. The probability is high that such reinforcement has occurred to a far less degree at minimum experience families, partly because some of the behaviors never were emitted in the first place. More often such behaviors, if emitted, may not only have been ignored, but indeed may have been punished because those behaviors might have been annoying to some parents. In consequence such youths arrive at career decision moments less ready to plan a career (Ansell & Hansen, 1971).

Another variable is likely operating in these two different types of families that also has occupational significance for children of those families. Parents in maximum experience families, on the average, are more intelligent than parents in minimum experience families, *other things being equal,* and so are their children. And, of course, other things often are *not* equal. Bright parents who happen to be black, American Indian, or from a Spanish-speaking subculture might be forced by society's denial of equal economic and social opportunities to maintain a somewhat minimum experience family. To whatever degree brain capacity and neural structure are inherited, and thus the degree to which the potential to behave intelligently is inherited, children of minimum experience families might be as bright as any in a maximum experience family. But since intelligent behavior is learned, it follows that the potentials of children in such families are denied. This view is supported by experiments that have raised the intelligence of children from minimum experience families through providing for such children those kinds of experiences that are common in the maximum experience family, but found far less often in minimum experience families. This is a delicate and controversial topic, with evidence only recently sought; thus no firm, empirically validated statements can yet be made. Unvalidated positions are still rampant, of course, some of them based on ethnically or racially prejudiced respondent conditioning.

Whether from either extreme of minimum or maximum experience family, or from a type of family that falls somewhere between the extremes, the child with his inherited brain and neural structure and his behaviors relating to coping, to exploration, to controlling his environment, also interacts with larger subcultures. In addition he is acquiring cognitions about self and about life. Thus by the time the child is a high school youth, he has acquired complex behavior patterns (including cognitions about self and life through which he manages to seek out pleasure and avoid pain, and to anticipate how he can manage the future so as to maximize pleasures further and to continue to avoid pain. Pleasure seeking, it must be recalled too, is not simple sense gratification, thus time-measured in hours or minutes. To find the best career for expressing talents and personal values as an example of seeking pleasure, and here we are time-measuring pleasure in decades, or even the entire life span as an adult. Pain avoidance in careers is to make decisions and engage in other behaviors so as to not find oneself in a demeaning, dead-end occupation that permits little or no employment of aptitudes, little or no expression of personal values.

For humans, pleasure seeking means seeking out and associating with persons who reinforce one's behaviors. Pain avoidance, by the same token, is avoiding associating with persons who punish behaviors, usually not deliberately, but the punishing effects on a person come from the myriad small behaviors that are foreign or antithetical to the person. Occupational satisfaction is not found solely in the occupational tasks carried out, but in associating with persons of similar life style. The persons who reinforce behavior are not culturally neutral individuals, but persons from similar subcultures. When black youths eat together and otherwise socialize in a biracial high school, and the whites behave in the same fashion, we see a simple, obvious illustration of this seeking out of persons who comprise a compatible environment.[4]

Race is a variable in seeking out persons who reinforce behavior, but other subcultural characteristics are also of as great or greater significance, a point elaborated in Chapter 7. A major one of these other characteristics is economic class membership. Thus in a high school populated by only one race, the economically privileged youths socialize, in general, and exclude economically poorer youths. These latter students would not want to socialize with economically privileged youths because that subculture is punishing, whereas the subculture of youth of their own economic class reinforces behaviors. Other subcultural variables cause further subdivisions of grouping.

Youth arrive at the time of a major occupation commitment, then, with complexes of behaviors, including a history of decision making, the extremes there being, on the one hand, a long history of successful decisions of great significance made, and, on the other hand, no decisions, with likely no opportunity for decisions. They have knowledge of occupations, again extremes being thorough knowledge at one end and almost complete ignorance at the other, and they have cognitions about self, marked by the extremes of ample, valid, positive cognitions at one end, and few, mostly negative, and perhaps invalid cognitions at the other.[5] They come with a history of experiences with others that lets the deciding person know which other kinds of persons doing which kinds of things will provide the most pleasure (be most reinforcing), and which other groups of persons doing other things are painful (are punishing).

The Substance of Occupational Decisions

A person's occupational decisions, assuming a capability to engage in such decision making, must include knowledge of the tasks performed in an occupation and the aptitudes needed to perform those tasks, among other matters. Occupational decision making must also include a consid-

---

[4] The most thorough analysis of work satisfaction is that offered in *Work in America,* a product of a special task force of the Department of Health, Education, and Welfare. This report is now available in book form.

[5] The study of 32,000 youths by Prediger et al., (1974, p. 103) informs us that youth show "both a lack of knowledge and a substantial amount of misinformation. For example, 53 percent of the 11th graders believe that *more* than one-third of all job openings require a college degree; 41 percent of the 8th graders believe that few women work outside of the home after marriage; and 61 percent of the 11th graders believe that *most* persons remain in the same jobs throughout their adult lives."

eration of the values to be expressed and the life style the person seeks to attain, which might mean selection of a social ecosystem that propagates and reinforces those values and that life style. Whether or not the concept of social ecosystems is a useful one in some instances of occupational decision making, the concept of birds of similar feather flocking together is appropriate. To choose carpentry is a decision not only to practice the skills of carpentry, but also to associate with other carpenters or craftsmen, be housed as they are, be in a labor union with them in a common cause, and practice other common aspects of a life style in a reinforcing way. Change the word "carpenter" to almost any other occupation, and the specifics are essentially the same, although instead of labor union, for example, the term appropriate for some occupations will be professional association. Holland (1966) succinctly summarizes these ideas by describing occupational decision making this way:

> People search for environments and vocations that will permit them to exercise their skills and abilities, to express their attitudes and values, to take on agreeable problems and roles, and to avoid disagreeable ones. [p. 11]

To use different words to repeat an essential cognition, the occupational-decision behaviors recorded above would not be shown by all persons. They do describe the nature of the process for those persons who have had histories of experiences resulting in development of knowledge, skills, insights, decision making, and a future orientation. Some persons at the opposite position do not have integrity among their behaviors, have inadequate cognitions about self, and have minimum knowledge. They have few, if any, skills that can be developed to a job-appropriate level, let alone a career, and present other behavior deficiencies that result in their occupational decisions being of a far lower order. Such psychologically ill-formed humans are less likely to decide among occupations and life styles associated with occupations, but, being faced with the need for sustenance, they seek employment in any available job. This latter group is represented in sharpest illustration by those adult males standing on certain street corners in certain cities hoping that someone will drive by and offer them a day's work as laborers and by the uneducated, unskilled females also equipped only for taking day labor jobs. Or such males might find employment along another route: running numbers, or robbing and stealing, and such females in renting their bodies instead of their labor.

Between these two extremes is at least one other mode of behavior related to occupational decisions—indeed it might be the most common mode. In this mode are reasonably literate persons, let's say at least high school graduates, with an array of low-level skills only. Their first and maybe only occupational decisions are made "on the basis of expediency and situational factors rather than on the basis of any long-term life plan" (Slocum, 1965 p. 862). That this is so understandable. Many youths graduated from high school have been in subcultures wherein occupational decisions were not made, but employment decisions were. In such subcutures the common reply to inquiry about working after graduation has been "I'll go over to the X factory (or the Y plant); I hear they're hiring." Such persons are quite ready to have an employment officer of an industry or business decide what occupation they shall enter, expecting to be trained in the skills needed for that occupation if they do not have the appropriate skills. Once trained in an occupation, and now identifying with that occupation, the person may later decide to take a position in that occupation in a different industry or business, or even to set up shop for himself. These are more accurately spoken of as job decisions, however; the occupation does not change, the original occupational decision having been made for the person by someone else. In some factory employment the assigned occupation may be only little removed from those occupations classified as labor; thus there is no skill acquired that results in occupational identity, career mobility, or occasion to barter for a better occupation in another industry, or in setting up one's own business. Many assembly-line jobs are of this kind, such as in the auto industry, where, incidentally, job dissatisfaction is high (Henle, 1975), and mental health low (Kornhauser, 1962).

It is important to acknowledge here that these generalizations about the necessary components of occupational decision making have their exceptions, and the role of the scholar pursuing study in this area as he prepares himself for a guidance occupation is to examine the enormous and ever-increasing body of empirical data related to work, decision making, and the meaning of occupations. For example, about two decades ago, Super and Bachrach (1957) analyzed research findings and made this conclusion:

> For persons who enter high-level occupations the occupation itself tends to be the focus, but for those who enter many middle and lower-level occupations the work situation and the kind of personal relationships which it permits or prescribes are more important. [p. 120]

This observation, in the words of the generalizations made earlier, says that questions of life style and choices among ecosystems are of less importance for persons who are heading for or are in professional or top management positions. Not unimportant, just less so.

This writing attends only to broad questions of career development, thus of occupational decisions and potentials, and the role of the high school in these, particularly the role of guidance team members. It cannot attend to most specific questions in the career development and decision-making domain. Thus the oft-stated prediction will be repeated: the scholar will be studying these specifics if he should pursue further training in the guidance field. He will likely study, at some point in his inquiry, Crites's (1969) bench-mark record of concepts and research, wherein many career topics are treated in depth.

Behavioral Theory Applied to the Career Decision-Making Process

An effort is made now to put a theoretical foundation under the preceding portion of this chapter. The science of behavior has generated principles that account for human actions no matter the arena in which they are observed. Career actions are as readily explainable by behavior principles as are any other kinds of behavior.

To present this picture I lean heavily on a recent offering by Krumboltz (1974), a person largely responsible for inching guidance practices off the theoretically sterile ground on which they have rested for years over onto scientifically generated tenets.

Krumboltz's analysis of the career decision-making (CDM) process produces four factors that influence CDM. He labels these (1) genetic endowment and special abilities, (2) environmental conditions and events, (3) learning experiences, and (4) task approach skills. These factors I call the raw materials that go into CDM, and generally they are understandable by their titles, I suspect, the concepts having been covered in earlier chapters. Respondent and operant conditions, as you might expect, are included in the learning experiences factor. Krumboltz labels them associative and instrumental learning experiences. Task approach skills is a different label for material covered earlier and requires a brief examination.

Such skills are those behavior likelihoods that every person brings to each new task. They are comprised of

> a set of skills, performance standards and values, work habits, perceptual and cognitive processes (such as attending, selecting, symbolic rehearsing, encoding, reflecting, and evaluating responses), mental sets, and emotional responses. [p. 20]

These skills applied to the new task affect the outcomes of that task, and those outcomes in turn affect the person's array of task approach skills.

These four factors, then, are always interacting and result in two more refined components of CDM. They are (1) self-observation generalizations, and (2) task approach skills specific to career decision making

(CDM). Krumboltz's self-observation generalization term connotes approximately the ideas covered earlier under the terms that I used, self-reference behaviors, although Krumboltz adds an emphasis on preferences as a component of self-observation generalizations.

The task approach skills specific to CDM include

> value clarifying, goal setting, predicting future events, alternative generating, information seeking, estimating, reinterpreting past events, emininating and selecting alternatives, planning, and generalizing. [p. 23]

These two components of CDM result in some type of action, specifically concerned "with *entry behaviors*. Those actions which represent an overt step in a career progression" (p. 23).

The Krumboltz chapter closes with the presentation of theoretical propositions. Some are quoted or paraphrased here. You will identify in them a number of the behavior principles given in Chapter 5, even if reworded for specific application to CDM.

The first of these propositions relates to preferences, an aspect of self-observation generalization that Krumboltz attends to. Preferences are defined as evaluative self-observation generalizations "based on those learning experiences pertinent to any career task" (p. 31). Some theoretical propositions that apply to preferences follow.

The likelihood is increased that a person will express a preference for a course of study or for an occupation if that person has

1. *Been reinforced for emitting behaviors the person associates with success in that course of study or in that occupation,*
2. *Observed a valued model being reinforced for emitting those behaviors,*
3. *Been reinforced by a valued person who models and/or advocates engaging in that course of study or that occupation, and*
4. *Been exposed to positive words and images associated with that course of study or that occupation* [condensed from pp. 31–32].

After offering theoretical propositions that account for a *reduced* likelihood that a person will express a preference, or an increased likelihood that he will express a *rejection* for a course of study or occupation, Krumboltz then presents theoretical propositions that account for the acquisition of decision-making skills.

"An individual is more likely to learn the cognitive and performance skills and emotional responses necessary for career planning . . ." if that person has

1. *Been reinforced in the past for emitting those behaviors,*

2. *Observed real or vicarious models engaged in effective career decision-making strategies, and*
3. *Access to people and other resources with the necessary information* [condensed from pp. 34–35].

Again there are offered propositions that predict a reduced likelihood that a person will acquire CDM skills. There next follow theoretical propositions about "entry behaviors into educational or occupational alternatives" (p. 37).

"*An individual is more likely to take actions leading to enrollment in a given course or employment in a given occupation or field of work if that . . .*" (p. 37)

1. *Individual has recently expressed a preference for that course, occupation, or field of work,*
2. *Individual has been exposed to learning and employment opportunities in them, and*
3. *Individual's learned skills match the educational and/or occupational requirements* [condensed from pp. 37–38].

As before, the referenced chapter offers propositions accounting for a reduced likelihood that such actions will be taken.

Description of Adequate Career Decisions

Krumboltz's analyses adequately define the career decision-making process, both as to the elements that comprise it and the theoretical propositions that explain it. I close with the rewording of material that offers three descriptions of what a human being is like who has been readied to make career decisions. The sum effect of the descriptions accords with the values about humans to which this society is committed in the Declaration of Independence.

When the human ideally arrives at any decision point related to his career, he is characterized

1. By a history of managing his own life through making important decisions about himself, and thus has a repertoire of decision-making behaviors.
2. By sufficient, valid cognitions about his values, interests, abilities, and competencies, and how these can be implemented by certain occupational careers particularly the psychological significance of such careers—and this means that he knows the world of work as well as his unique characteristics.
3. By a history of varied work experiences, even if only brief ones, and even if not commensurate with full-time, appropriate occupations when adult-

hood and independence are attained, those work experiences have provided a real test of his cognitions of self and of the working world.

For such youths, a counselor or behavior specialist serves the role of ontopsychologist (ontos: being), a kind of homemade term toyed with in Chapter 1. He serves to help the youth in being, now and in the future— in helping to make decisions and make plans that are appropriate for the youth in pursuit of happiness, in being a maximum kind of person. The plans and decisions to be made are among the variety of large and small ecosystems of choice, and among the various next steps to be taken toward entry into such ecosystems—keeping commitments relatively loose so that options exist for changing directions should the increased maturities of late adolescence and young adulthood make such changes appropriate.

For some other youths, greater in number than the kind just described, the formulations of ontopsychology are not less valid, but are of less immediate significance in that these youths have fewer of the three characteristics, or have them in less mature form. For yet even other youths, regretfully, the ontopsychological concept is so advanced as to be inoperative. These youths, described at several prior points, are bereft of the three characteristics, and, if they are not in a guidance-oriented school system, the best that can be done for them may be simply job placement. For this latter, underdeveloped subpopulation, career development needs will have to be served later by some other team of community human resources practitioners.

REFERENCES

ANSELL, E. M., & HANSEN, J. C. "Patterns in Vocational Development of Urban Youth." *Journal of Counseling Psychology,* 1971, *18,* 6.

BENJAMIN, H. *The Cultivation of Idiosyncrasy.* Cambridge, Mass.: Harvard University Press, 1949.

CRITES, J. O. Address to Annual Convention, American Personnel and Guidance Association, 1958.

CRITES, J. *Vocational Psychology.* New York: McGraw-Hill, 1969.

GYSBERS, N. "Career Guidance: A Unified Point of Departure." *NVGA Newsletter,* 1973, *12,* 1–2.

HENLE, PETER. "Worker Dissatisfaction: A Look at the Economic Effects." *Personnel and Guidance Journal,* 1975, *54,* 2, 152–154.

HERR, E. L., & CRAMER, S. H. *Vocational Guidance and Career Development in the Schools: Toward a Systems Approach.* Boston: Houghton Mifflin, 1972.

HOLLAND, J. L. The Psychology of Vocational Choice. Waltham, Mass.: Ginn Blaisdel, 1966.

KORNHAUSER, A. "Toward an Assessment of the Mental Health of Factory Workers." *Human Organization,* 1962, *21,* 43–64.

KRUMBOLTZ, J. D. "A Social Learning Theory of CDM Career Decision Making." In A. M. Mitchell, G. Brian Jones, & John D. Krumboltz (Eds.), *A Social Learning Theory of Career Decision Making.* Washington, D.C.: National Institute of Education, Report NIE-6-74-0134, 1974.

MEZZANO, J. "Concerns of Students and Preference for Male and Female Counselors." *Vocational Guidance Quarterly,* 1971, *20,* 42–47.

PREDIGER, D. J., ROTH, J. D., & NOETH, R. J. "Career Development of Youth: A Nationwide Study." *Personnel and Guidance Journal,* 1974, *53,* 97–104.

SLOCUM, W. L. "Occupational Careers in Organizations: A Sociological Perspective." *Personnel and Guidance Journal,* 1965, *43,* 858–866.

SUPER, D. E., & BACHRACH, P. *Scientific Careers and Vocational Development Theory.* New York: Bureau of Publications, Teachers College, Columbia University, 1957.

SUPER, D. E., & OVERSTREET, P. *The Vocational Maturity of Ninth-Grade Boys.* New York: Bureau of Publications, Teachers College, Columbia University, 1960.

10 Guidance Occupations and Programs in Career Development

INTRODUCTION

Adequate programs in career development can be set up simply by using the wide variety of published materials now available. A program will be better, however, if it is also based on an assessment of the career development of students in the school. The need for student assessment here parallels the need in another facet of guidance programming, that of staffing. It has been proposed that some of the problems in the guidance movement result from the premise that there is but one kind of guidance practitioner needed, that all practitioners carry out similar functions, and that all high schools should have the same student-to-counselor ratio. In fact, the needs of a particular school can be determined only after an assessment of the students, and the kind and number of practitioners, along with the functions to be carried out, must be redetermined occasionally, through additional student assessment.

School personnel can expect that the student populations of different high schools will vary in their career development maturity, requiring unique program aspects in each school. Specific requirements will be revealed by student assessment.

There are a variety of approaches to making such an assessment, including school generated instruments as well as commercially published ones. Two commercial aids are the *Career Maturity Index* by Crites (McGraw-Hill), and the *Assessment of Career Development,* developed by the American College Testing Program and distributed by Houghton Mifflin Co.

Table 4: Synthesis of inputs to vocationalization.

Approximate Ages					
Preschool	5–9	10–14	15	18	19–25

Formation of self-concept → Translation of self-concept into vocational terms → Implementation of self-concept

Developing preference or anticipation → Choice → induction → reformation → integration

Fantasy → Tentative → Realistic

Trial (with little more commitment) → Trial (more commitment) → stabilization → advancement

Awareness of the need to crystallize (orienting) → SG Use of resources (exploring)

S_2 → Formulating interests ─────── S_1 Relating interests and capacities ─── Relating interests and capacities to values

S_2 → Developing a vocabulary of self ─────→ SG Awareness of factors to consider in formulating a vocational preference

S_1 → Developing a vocabulary of work ─────→ S_1 Awareness of contingencies which affect vocational goals

→ Rudiments of basic trust in self and others ──→ SG Differentiation of interests and values Preparing for marriage selecting a mate

→ Rudiments of initiative ──────── Awareness of present-future relationships Developing capability for intimacy

S_1 → Rudiments of industry ──────── Accepting oneself as in process starting a family

S_1 → Knowledge of fundamentals of technology ──→ SG Relating changes in the self to changes in the world Becoming a productive person

→ Differentiating self from environment ────→ S Acquiring basic habits of industry Mastering the skills of an occupation

→ Identification with a worker ────────→ S Learning to organize one's time and energy to get work done Moving up the ladder within the occupation

→ Developing sex social role ──────── Learning to defer gratification, to set priorities

S_2 → Learning rudiments of social rules ────→ Achieving personal identity

S_1 → Learning fundamental intellectual, physical and motor skills

S Acquiring knowledge of life in organizations

S Preparation for role relationships

S Preparation for level and kind of consumption

SG — Preparation for an occupational career
SG — Formulation of generalized preference
SG — Possession of information concerning the preferred occupation
SG — Planning for the preferred occupation
SG — Choosing and preparing for occupation
      Achieving more mature relations with peers of both sexes
      Achieving emotional independence of parents and other adults

Developing planfulness
Developing decision-making strategies   Independence of choice

Role-playing ⎫
Identification ⎬ ⟶ Role-playing, curricula exposure ⟶ reality testing ⟶ work-study
              ⎭   attitudes of others ⟶ identification ⟶ self-appraisal

---

Source: Edwin L. Herr and Stanley H. Cramer, *Vocational Guidance and Career Development in Schools: Toward a Systems Approach.* Boston: Houghton Mifflin, 1972, p. 119.

An assessment of student needs in career development, or in any other area, cannot be made abstractly. One does not go to students and ask, "What are your needs?" Instead, such assessment is rooted in a development model or paradigm, that is, in a laying out of the tasks of normal development. Assessment relative to developmental task attainment is carried out, then, to see to what degree students are short in completing such tasks. That is the nature of need assessment.

Developmental paradigms have been set out by a number of persons. I chose for this volume that offered by Herr and Cramer (1972), which is reproduced as Table 4.

The resources required to accomplish developmental tasks, which are, in other words, inputs to vocationalization, are to be found in a number of agencies and institutions, particularly in families and family life. The school also can be a major contributor to the accomplishment of a large number of these tasks. To Herr and Cramer's original table I have added S's to show those development concerns to which the school can deliberately address itself through specific curriculum activities, with the S_1 showing higher curriculum priorities. In the center column the additional letter G shows a specific role for the guidance team. The absence of an S is not to suggest that the school has no role in that developmental need. That absence says only that the need is not addressed by organized curriculum activities but rather is attended to more by pervasive and subtle ecosystem characteristics.

Table 5 demonstrates some curricular and other activities that a school system can provide to help achieve these developmental goals. The contents of this table, which shows samples of activities, are structured in a way that also deserves special note, in that this structure is consonant with principles posited in this text. The samples Herr and Cramer demonstrate are prepared as behavior objectives. This text has emphasized the development and maintenance of desired behaviors, and Herr and Cramer's table illustrates how school activities can be designed to this end through behavior-shaping experiences. The additional observation is made that all intended school learnings should be cast in behavior objective terms, as indeed they are in some schools. Readers will do well to study the three chapters in the Herr and Cramer text that amplify the school system's strategies in vocational guidance in elementary, junior high, and senior high schools.

To view the objectives in Table 5 simply as samples suggests that any school system that employs these samples in each schooling level probably has a thorough program of career development, one that would result in the vocationalization of all youths who passed through this system. If only the high schools, or even only one high school of a system had so comprehensive a performance-based approach, or if a number of youths

Table 5: Sample objectives to facilitate vocationalization at different educational levels.

Elementary School	Junior High School	Senior High School
In an oral exercise, the student can identify at least six of the types of workers who contributed to building his school (C, K)	The student lists correctly the different educational areas both in the immediate and distant future that are available to him, the nature and purpose of each, the possible outcomes of each in terms of levels of occupational activity (C, C)	The student reality tests his broad occupational preference by systematically relating it to his achievement in different courses, part-time work, extracurricular activities (A, O)
In a flannel-board presentation, the student can label because of their tools or clothing ten different types of workers found in his community (C, K)	The student verbally differentiates his self-characteristics (e.g., interests, values, abilities, personality traits) and expresses tentative occupational choices that might provide outlets for each (C, C)	The student analyzes his present competency in skills necessary to his broad occupational preference and develops a plan by which these can be enhanced where necessary (C, An)
In an oral exercise, the student can state how different workers contribute to his well-being and the welfare of the community (C, K)		Given a part-time job in school or out of school, the student is able to list the advantages and disadvantages it might offer to him in terms of his interests or values (C, C)
After viewing a movie, the student can identify most occupations in his community and describe how they support each other (C, K)	The student can appraise accurately on a written profile his measured ability, achievement level, and current interests (C, An)	
The student can check vocabulary items correctly as being names of interests, aptitudes, abilities (C, K)	The student can place on a skilled/unskilled continuum twenty occupations about which he has read (C, K)	From a series of case studies about working conditions as they affect individuals with different characteristics, the student can identify patterns of coping behavior and discuss their implications for him under similar circumstances (C, E)
From a list of fifty occupations, the student can identify those which occur primarily indoors or outdoors (C, C)	From a dramatization portraying five different ways of valuing different methods of handling daily events, the student can	

(cont.)

Key: (C, K)=Cognitive—Knowledge; (C, C)=Cognitive—Comprehension; (C, Ap)=Cognitive—Application; (C, An)=Cognitive—Analysis; (C, Sy)=Cognitive—Synthesis; (C, E)=Cognitive—Evaluation; (A, Re)=Affective—Receiving; (A, Re)=Affective—Responding; (A, V)=Affective—Valuing; (A, O)=Affective—Organization; (A, CC)=Affective—Characterization by a value or a value complex.

Source: Edwin L. Herr and Stanley H. Cramer, Vocational Guidance and Career Development in Schools: Toward a Systems Approach. Boston: Houghton Mifflin, 1972, pp. 127-130.

Table 5. (Continued)

Elementary School	Junior High School	Senior High School
The student can select from a list of ten alternatives the five best reasons for planning his time (A, Re)	consistently identify and describe the value set with which he feels most comfortable (A, V)	The student executes plans to qualify for an entry-level position by choosing appropriate courses at the high school level (A, V)
The student can list correctly major breakdowns of the occupational structure: e.g. communications, manufacturing, distribution, transportation, or professional/skilled/semiskilled/unskilled (C, C)	The student can weigh alternative outcomes from different kinds of work against the public welfare and rank order his view of these outcomes (A, O)	The student produces a plan of alternative ways of accomplishing his educational (occupational) goals if his first choice is not successfully implemented (C, Sy)
The student can prepare a graph showing the different educational alternatives available: junior high school, high school, community college, area vocational technical school, college, apprenticeships, armed forces (C, Ap)	The student observes five films and then lists the major differences of the technological processes he has observed (A, Re)	Given ten choices, the student decides upon a broad occupational area to study in depth. He is able in a written proposal to outline the resources he will need to develop this study, the plans necessary to gain access to these resources, and the particular outcomes he desires to obtain (C, E)
The student can arrange in appropriate rank order the number of years of schooling normally associated with different educational alternatives (C, C)	Using the *Dictionary of Occupational Titles,* the student can identify ten occupations which are ranked highest in dealing with people, things, or data (C, Ap)	
	After a field trip to a factory, the student can tell in his own words the differences in work conditions or procedures he observed in different parts of the plant (C, An)	The student can differentiate between the major occupations that make up a broad occupational area or a job cluster in terms of (1) the amount and type of education needed for entrance, (2) the content, tools, setting, products, or services of these occupations, (3) their values to society, (4) their probability of providing the type of life style he desires, (5) their relationship to his
The student can classify the titles of courses available in his junior high school and senior high school and the types of content with which they are concerned (C, C)	The student is able to assess tentatively in rank order the value to him of each of ten occupational clusters (C, An)	
The student can choose from a list of twenty occupations those offering salaries within particular ranges (C, K)	The student can describe in essay form how knowledge and skills acquired in different subject matter areas relate to performing different work roles (C, Ap)	

Table 5. (Continued)

Elementary School	Junior High School	Senior High School
The student voluntarily discusses the importance of work and how education helps one to work effectively (A, Rs)	The student can identify and define ten forms of continuing education following apprenticeships, on-the-job training, correspondence courses, armed forces service schools, evening schools, reading (C, C)	interests and values (C, E)
The student can select from a table models of tools or instruments used in ten different occupations (C, An)		The student considers five different categories of post-secondary education, chooses one, and defines his reason for choosing it (C, C)
The student can role play three occupations which he thinks most interest him (C, Sy)	The student completes an assigned job analysis according to instructions and on time (A, Rs)	The student develops a plan of access to his next step after high school, either educational or occupational, listing possible alternatives, whom to contact, application dates, capital investment necessary, the self-characteristics to be included on a resumé (C, Ap)
The student can demonstrate how certain knowledges and skills acquired in different school subjects are applied in different work roles (C, Ap)	The student can compare correctly the social roles which describe a supervisor and a follower (C, Sy)	
	The student can tell a story in his own words about how an individual suffering a particular limitation can overcome his weakness and maximize his strength in education or in work (C, Sy)	
The student can identify the skills in which he feels most confident and role plays workers who might need these skills (C, E)		Given an identified social problem—e.g., air pollution, rehabilitation of drug users, the development of new uses for materials, creating by-products of fishery harvesting—the student can create a lattice of occupations at different levels which might contribute to resolving the problem. (The student may use as a reference the *Dictionary of Occupational Titles* or the *Occupational Outlook Handbook*) (C, E)
The student can role play his interpretation of the values workers might hold in four different occupations (C, E)	The student can identify, locate and describe the use of five directories listing post-secondary educational opportunities at college, junior college, and technical levels (C, Ap)	
The student is willing to share with others the planning and presenting of a play about work and being a worker (A, V)	The student can identify in a gaming situation future decisions he must make in order to reach different goals (C, Sy)	
The student discusses the importance of team work in different work settings, cooperates with others in order to reach a common goal, and can express the	The student can identify, assess, and defend his analysis of possible steps he might take to	The student makes adjustments in planning, use of resources, and exploratory experiences

Table 5. (Continued)

Elementary School	Junior High School	Senior High School
importance of his contributions and that of others in reaching a common goal (A, O)	minimize his limitations and maximize his assets (C, E)	necessary to maintain progress toward achievement of goals (A, O)
The student during his school activities expresses or demonstrates a positive attitude toward self, others, education, and different types of work roles (A, CCV)	The student continuously explores and synthesizes the relationships between tentative choices and demonstrated abilities (A, V)	The student verbalizes feelings of competence and adequacy in those tasks which have relationships to his vocational preference (A, CCV)
	The student is able to select two persons from history and discuss why he would like to emulate them (A, V)	The student is able to define the congruence between his aspirations, values, and preferred life style (C, E)
	The student can produce a list of resources or approaches available for learning about and assessing the world of work (C, E)	The student is able to use the ratings of him by teachers and peers to confirm his self-perceptions of competence or preference (C, Ap)
	In a role-playing situation, the student can project or portray the personal and social significance that work might have in the lives of individuals at different levels within the occupational structure (C, E)	The student takes specific steps to implement a post-secondary vocational preference (A, CCV)
	The student can describe possible personal and environmental contingencies that could impinge upon his future decisions (C, E)	The student demonstrates his ability to judge his choices in terms of situations, issues, purposes, and consequences rather than in terms of rigidity or wishful thinking (A, CCV)
	The student can differentiate between the several broad occupational areas in terms of (1) a potential satisfaction each might offer to him, (2) the nature of the work tasks performed,	

Table 5. (Continued)

Elementary School	Junior High School	Senior High School
	(3) the future impact technology could have on particular occupational areas, (4) the future demand for workers in broad occupational areas (C, E)	
	The student can demonstrate judgments about how different types of work can be better made to meet individual needs (A, O)	

transferred into a high school from out of the system, then the vocationalization of these and some other youths in that system would be in arrears. The high school would need "make up" activities to compensate for the vocational immaturity of those youth. The principle on which the prior statement is based merits retelling: beyond an occupations/career development program of standard components, based on common youth characteristics, a school system or single school needs to expand existing program components or add such other components as a career development assessment of youths shows to be the need in that system or school.

Helping Students Acquire
Decision-Making Competence

Table 4 can be also described as including some inputs into the process of decision making in the area of occupations. The idea of attending to decision making is not new, going back at least to John Dewey's analysis of problem solving, with his urging schools to produce problem-solving activities for children to work on. What is new is the refinement of Dewey's ideas into workable techniques, with a focus on acquiring decision-making skills in the career area, starting in elementary schools.

What is proposed here, in effect, is teaching decision making.[1] This

---

[1] The College Entrance Examination Board (888 7th Ave., New York, N.Y. 10019) has developed a program for use in junior and senior high schools to help students learn decision making. Two publications are included in the program, *Deciding* or *Decisions and Outcomes,* for use by students, and *Deciding: A Leader's Guide.* The program was developed by Gordon P. Miller of the Board's staff, and

proposal may strike some as bizarre, those who assume that a person "just decides, and that's that; all you need is accurate information and you can decide." In fact, one does not either have decision-making skill, or not have it. Assuming that everyone has some decision-making history, thus has demonstrated some skill, the important concern is whether the person has a history of making decisions about major, life-significant questions. No data are known, but the guess is that most youths do not. Everyone has a history of deciding such simple questions as what clothes to wear, whether to go one place or to a different place, whether to complete the essay tonight, or wait until study-hall tomorrow. These are bush-league decisions compared with occupational/career decisions.

Few high school students know the several steps employed in making life-significant decisions, nor how to order those elements into an attack hierarchy—that is, where to start, and what comes next. It can be a dull, tedious business and thus a chore easy to put off in favor of more immediate and pleasurable activities, even if a youth did have some idea about how to attack so large a decision.

But youths can know how to do it. They can have pleasurable decision-making histories if the school has provided guidance program regularities that result in such behavior regularities. Students acquire decision-making skills, not just for their first occupational choice, but for all kinds of decisions, so that they have "the ability to live in a world of insecurity in which one is always adjusting and never adjusted" (Wrenn, 1962, p. 125). To come full circle, this point is summed up in the prediction that a school with a career-development ambience will result in almost all youths acquiring through practice those skills needed in occupations/career decisions. Such a school is guidance oriented.

Career Development Activities and the Guidance Team

A high school vocationalizes its students through two modal activities: first, career identification and decision activities and students' planning that ensues from them, and, second, activities that provide knowledge

---

H. B. Gelatt of the Palo Alto Unified School District, now of the American Institutes for Research. The American College Testing Program (PO Box 168, Iowa City, Iowa, 52240) has published two minicourses, Exploring, for grades 8–11, and Planning, for grades 12–13, which are decision-making programs. The general purpose and value of causing students to acquire occupational decision-making skills is well laid out by another of Katz's articles (1973), and the roles of groups and individual activities in facilitating vocational development are set out by Smith and Evans (1973). The evidence supports the logic offered here: group procedures are imperative. But that assertion does not eliminate the need for some individual attention. The analogy: groups in guidance are like men's ready-to-wear suits—they fit most males. Some suits require small alterations to achieve a perfect fit, at a much smaller cost than tailor-made suits.

about self and occupations and about advanced education. This section presents some illustrative practices and examines the professional behaviors of guidance team members in these activities.

At the outset I repeat my awareness of the fact that in most high schools there is not now a guidance team but only a single type of practitioner whose title is probably counselor. Persons in this one kind of occupation have to do what they can in the cause of vocationalizing youth, this cause being the basic reason why the occupation of counseling in schools exists. Indeed, if his occupation is new to a high school that has not heretofore been guidance oriented, the counselor's task will be immense. Our examination, however, will be of more optimum practices in those guidance-oriented schools employing the multiple practitioners of a guidance team.

THE CAREER CENTER. We begin the examination with the Career Center. At best this will be a room or suite of rooms designed for this purpose, of which Figure 10 is an illustration.[2] The Career Center is as readily usable as the school library and may be physically associated with the library, although managed by the career development technician (CDT). As such it is a place to which students can go frequently, and, being open beyond class session times, will also be accessible to teachers and parents.

An ideal physical layout is but a means, of course, the immediate end being the presence in the center of readily usable, quality information about occupations and advanced education in the quantity needed. The ultimate end is student knowledge about occupations and advanced education, and thus plans for a Career Center are not completed until schemes are put into practice that result in students acquiring information-seeking and decision-making behaviors.

The Occupational/Educational Information Component of the Center

In the matter of the quantity and quality of information, and its attractiveness to students, the school will attend to the fact that printed material is less attractive than audiovisual materials (Laramore, 1971). Laramore examined the attractiveness and substantiveness of a newer type of easily acquired and used occupational information, a type that also appears to be tenable for advanced education information. This new

---

[2] This figure is reproduced from a report by Jacobson (1972), who shows two other center plans in his report. Jacobson issued two further reports in 1975, both valuable contributions. *A Study of Career Centers in the State of California* provides a needed data foundation in that area. Of greater breadth and significance is *The Master Plan for Career Guidance and Counseling,* which includes an exemplary array of performance objectives.

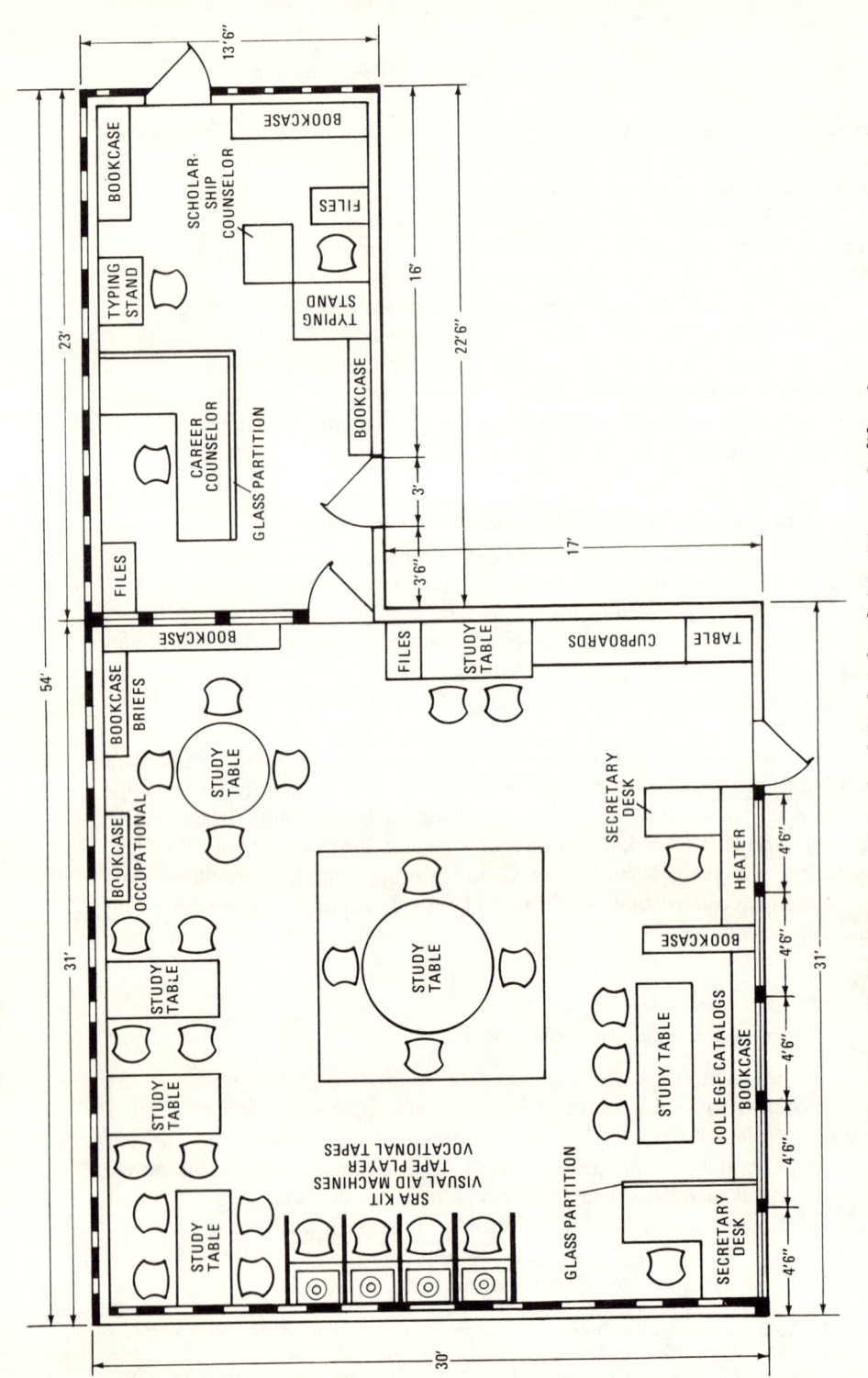

Figure 10. Career Counseling Center, Crawford High School, San Diego, California.

type material is in the form of colored slide photographs and accompanying tape descriptions, material that a student can select, mount on equipment in the Career Center, and use at his convenience. An additional asset in such material stems from locally acquired photo/tape material, in that it describes a local example of any occupation or advanced education institution. Printed occupational material from commercial publishers is less valuable because it has to provide information that is applicable countrywide. Some state education departments, through guidance section publications, Ohio for example, give a regional focus to printed information, which thus has some advantages over national information. Not to be overlooked as an asset is the fact that this slide/tape type of material can be student-generated, with the advantages that accrue to student activity.

Although the extensive topic of occupational information need not be treated fully here, a few additional observations are appropriate so you can understand the breadth of the topic, and have an entry-level familiarity with terminology and essential literature.

In selecting materials for inclusion in the Career Center's library, the CDT and his associates will attend to the quality of such materials. Material received is not automatically stored, but is studied first to see that it meets the criteria of acceptable information. The topic of evaluating materials is treated in a number of texts that focus on careers, such as the Herr and Cramer text referenced earlier, and a text by Isaacson (1971). The basic reference for the topic is *Guidelines for Preparing and Evaluating Occupational Materials* published by the National Vocational Association (NVGA), these guidelines often being incorporated into texts on occupations.

The standard reference for naming (classifying, and describing all occupations in the United States is the *Dictionary of Occupational Titles,* published by the U.S. Department of Labor, and its Volumes I and II will be a starting point not only for acquiring information-seeking behaviors by high school students but also for study of the occupational world by those preparing for a guidance team occupation.

The sources of printed materials are numerous. Isaacson (1971, pp. 390–391) lists 28 commercial publishers and five indices of printed and other materials (p. 395). One standard reference is the periodical volume of the *NVGA Bibliography of Current Occupational Literature,* and another is the listing of materials in each issue of *The Vocational Guidance Quarterly* (VGQ), a publication of the NVGA. Materials reported in the VGQ are not only listed but coded as to type of information, and, most important, evaluated.

A school's Career Center personnel will never be short of information, much of it free. The problem faced by the CDT and his staff is the time required to winnow out the one-sided or otherwise undesirable materials, thus keeping the library up to date (changes in occupations occur rapidly), and to acquire local information to supplement national descriptions.

A newer form of career information is of a kind that is less cognitive and more experiential: work samples. These are kits through which a student carries out some of the job functions of a person employed in that occupation. Thus he gains occupational knowledge of greater psychological impact than from material in which he just reads about an occupation (Krumboltz, Baker, Johnson, 1968). Use of work-sample materials is not just to give a partial work experience to students who have an interest in any occupation, but to stimulate interest in occupations to which the student may not have been attracted through want of any contact with or prior motivation to examine such occupations.[3] The value of work-sample material is illustrated in Johnson's (1971) findings that use of an x-ray technology work sample kit with eleventh-grade girls stimulated general occupational exploration by them.

No matter what the quantity, quality, attractiveness, and utility of information, however, it is not correct to assume that it will be appropriately employed by youths. If high school students have not acquired information-seeking behaviors through their elementary and middle school years, the high school has to offer particular help to overcome that inadequacy. One investigation (Biggers, 1971) warrants the conclusion that high school seniors are as limited in their ability to use information in vocational decision-making as they were in the fourth grade. Biggers's findings corroborate both 1960 and 1970 findings of Project TALENT, an extensive longitudinal study of high school youths throughout the United States. In his Division 15, American Psychological Association, presidential address, John C. Flanagan (1971), director of the project, stated that data reveal "very clearly that students do not have the necessary information either about themselves or the world to formulate personal goals and plan a program aimed at individual fulfilment." As some evidence for this point, Flanagan reported that five years after they were in their respective grades, only about 19 percent of high school seniors and about 14 percent of juniors were looking to the same career as they were expecting when they were in those grades.

The meaning of such data might be debated. If they were seen as evidence that most high school aged youths are too immature to make lasting vocational decisions, then guidance procedures are efforts poured into a leaking barrel. The arguments on the other side are far more convincing: high school youths not only need to but are fully able by normal

---

[3] Motivation to study careers can be generated much earlier than in high school. Interested students will profit from knowing the details of the excellent career motivation program in the Lincoln School, Dayton, Ohio, 45402, for kindergarten through the sixth grade.

developmental maturity to make occupational decisions that will stick. The missing ingredients are lack of decision-making training and, as Flanagan reports, lack of knowledge of self and of the occupational world.

Flanagan's study is another and heavy weight on the scale showing need for the guidance team to build information-seeking behaviors in all students through combinations of any techniques supported by empirical data, or suggested by behavior principles. One unusual technique is reported by Stewart (1969), involving a different use of models. The effective use of individual models live and on tape had been previously reported, but the investigation Stewart reports embodied two changes: using of a group of four student models, and presenting the behaviors to be modeled on audiotape rather than on videotape so as to reduce the excess and sometimes contradictory cues provided by video presentations. The particular procedure was to have three of the models genuinely assist a fourth student to acquire and use information within a decision-making process. The tapes, then, were used with groups of students, with successful outcomes.

The relatively terse treatment given here to the information element of guidance programs does not reflect its great importance. Creating program regularities to cause all students to acquire the behavior regularity of seeking validated information is a major guidance imperative.

CAREER DEVELOPMENT TECHNICIAN. A brief exploration of the career development technician's function was made in Chapter 3 and earlier in this chapter, and now is carried out in greater detail. First we assume that either student help is used in the Center, or perhaps an additional adult is employed to be librarian. This supplemental staffing of the Center is reasoned from the job activities of the CDT, activities that require his absence from the Center for long periods (see Appendix A for an extended job description). He will be working with teachers in career-related activities so that their students will learn the occupational and career significance of interest and competence that students might have in the several school subjects. One of these classroom activities might be occasional displays, including temporary occupational libraries in the classrooms. Basic to these possibilities is the assumption that the school is guidance oriented, and thus that each teacher is occupationally knowledgeable in his own field. If a school is assessed as not being sufficiently guidance-oriented, a way to increase that characteristic is to involve teachers in career information activities. In addition to the briefer participation of all teachers, some schools use subject areas engaged by all students for extensive systematic investigation of career-decision procedures and for shaping students' information-seeking behaviors (Hamilton & Webster, 1971). This latter component of this all-student learning counters the deficiency referenced in the prior section (Biggers, 1971), that students have to learn how to use information—that learning does not just happen.[4]

As observed earlier, local occupational information is featured in the Career Center and is but one index of a general local (regional) occupational thrust that may be expressed in other ways. However expressed, it is controlled by this undergirding principle: the specifics of a school's occupations/careers program are built around student needs, and thus an assessment of student characteristics comes first. If that assessment shows that almost 100 percent of a high school's students take advanced education away from the locality and do not return there to live, then localizing information will not be so important. Nationwide, on the average, high school dropouts and graduates remain in their home area for advanced education as well as for employment. It will be assumed here, then, that in a typical high school local information is of great importance.

This assumption brings us to another modal activity of the CDT that takes him away from the Career Center: he spends time in the area, visiting with employment specialists in the state employment service and in businesses and industries. He is, in brief, the single most important continuing liaison between the school and the area's employers. This liaison results in this specialist's role in curriculum revision and development, in improved occupational information materials and activities, and ultimately in increased probability that more students will attain higher levels of satisfaction through better identification of and entrance into compatible environments.

The CDT's continuing community liaison results in two specific activities that can replace Career Days, an activity of doubtful outcome. The typical Career Day begins with a census of student occupational interests. From that census a small portion of occupations of greatest numerical interest is selected, and a practitioner in each of those few occupations is sought to speak to a group of students during Career Day. Usually occupational presentations are timed around the school's usual class schedule; thus each representative may make five or six presentations to five or six groups of students.

Of the several inherent deficiencies in Career Days, two are pronounced. Even if as many as thirty different occupations are covered, that touches on only a small proportion of a high school's occupational interests. Many youths are required, therefore, to attend five or six occupational sessions in which they may have limited or no interest, or may even find aversive. The other major deficiency is found in the occupational representative. This difficulty rises from the assumption that a person in an

---

[4] The Seattle public school system offers occupational information at all grade levels, integrated into every subject of the school curriculum. For a report, see Hedrich (1971).

occupation, even a renowned expert, is a good person to inform students interestingly and organizedly about that occupation. Many readers will recall studying in university courses taught by unbearably boring experts of international repute and indeed may have found a first course in a topic so aversive that they were turned off from further inquiry into the subject. A master plumber or brain surgeon may be expert in the technical elements of his field, but may not be able to convey to youth what that occupation is as the core of an ecosystem, as an environment, as a determiner of a life style.

To replace these and other inadequacies of the Career Day, the career development technician identifies occupational experts who are also good teachers, and who are willing to confer with youths at school on an individually scheduled basis (in contrast to the all-at-once schedule of the Career Day that gathers some uninterested youths into each session). Or, when appropriate for the occupation, to confer with youth at the place where the occupation is carried out, a procedure that results in youths' not only learning about the factual skeleton of the occupation, but in their learning about the far more important aspect of the occupation; that is, what the total occupational environment may be like, what life style is to be expected for one in that occupation, what values can be expressed.[5]

The role and functions of a career development technician's team (a subteam of the guidance team) can be only generally defined here because of differences among localities and schools. As noted earlier, the fullest array of CDT practices is conveyed in the job description in Appendix A.

COMPUTER ASSISTANCE. Examination of Figure 10 does not show a computer terminal in Crawford High School's Career Counseling Center, but place for one can be readily imagined. Research around the role of computers in guidance has been steadily going on over the past 10 years with sufficient results to warrant inclusion of a computer terminal in a career center when funds permit and a central computer is available. Even if there were no evidence to demonstrate how computers attract many users, reasoning from human preferences in general would let us assume that students would be stimulated if they could engage a computer in the process of decision making. In fact, a computer is a useful tool in teaching decision making, and this makes computer use of extra importance in those secondary schools populated by numbers of youths from minimum experience families and subcultures.

---

[5] A most readable, puckish, iconoclastic, and accurate description of fourteen occupations has been written by Peter M. Sandman (1969). I hold this out as a model against which other stuffed-shirtish occupational descriptions can be judged and found wanting.

A detailed examination of computer use cannot be undertaken here, but a brief illustration is warranted. This is of an experimental project conducted by Donald E. Super and Roger A. Myers of Teachers College, Columbia University, and Frank J. Minor of IBM (Minor, 1970). Entered into the computer are profiles of student characteristics (grade and test records, and an occupational inventory record), an occupation and education data bank, and an advanced education institution data bank. The student engages the computer system by telling it his cognitions about his abilities, achievements, and interests. The computer replies with a comparison of the school data as retained in the computer, and these cognitions of self. With or without any reference to a member of the guidance team, the student can analyze these comparative data (the computer-stored objective data and his own perceptions) and perhaps revise his perceptions when appropriate. If he chooses to proceed to interact with the computer, he has several options. He might next

> browse through a number of occupations before analyzing any occupation in detail. He does this by indicating to the system:
>
> 1. His personal preferences for working with people, data, or things,
> 2. The kind of work conditions that are most appealing to him,
> 3. The minimum education level which he expects to complete. [p. 41]

In my terms, the student is thereby making a partial identification of the features of a compatible ecosystem.

The computer then searches through the data of 1,600 occupations for those that resemble these specifications. The student can alter his requirements, or tighten or loosen them, and browse again, as often as he wishes. The printed results again may be studied by the student alone, or discussed with a guidance team member, parent, friends, or anyone.

If and whenever he arrives at one or a few tenable occupational choices, he can reengage the computer system to receive detailed information about each occupation, including a work sample when appropriate. That an occupational choice is one of an ecosystem as well as of the specific behaviors required by an occupation is caught up in this information-receiving step. The student does not just receive data, he reacts to the data.

> As he performs the work sample and reviews the duties performed, he responds to various questions such as:
>
> 1. Would you like the environment in which this occupation is performed?
> 2. Would you like the kind of duties that are performed by a person in this occupation? [p. 42]

Again, when ready for an advanced step, the student can interact with the computer, which is programmed for conversational-type responses, so as to explore advanced education institutions appropriate for the occupations of his choice, receiving specific data about each institution, such as tuition fees and living costs, housing, and so on.

Minor concludes:

> The student should be able to sharpen his focus on goals, thereby making his high school course selection and curriculum more meaningful to him. His educational and vocational planning generally should be more efficient with the aid of effective access to personally relevant data, which improves his use of counselor time.
>
> The system should enable the counselor to work at a higher level of individualized and diagnostic problem-solving with each student, since the students should be aware of and better prepared to deal with personal problems of educational and vocational planning. The system should help the counselor identify students who may need immediate personalized attention because of unrealistic planning. The counselor should therefore be able to devote more of his time to professional counseling activities and less time to maintaining and operating a general educational-occupational information library.
>
> The same system could also be of service to the school administrators who must plan the curriculum. By reviewing students' inquiries and plans recorded in the system, administrators should be able to gain new insights into how well the curriculum being offered meets their needs. [p. 45]

The student who wishes to know more in general about computer use, and know about places where computers are being used in guidance activities has several good starting references. A U.S. Office of Education publication (Document OE-25053), *Computer-Based Vocational Guidance Systems* (1969), reports the twenty-seven papers presented at the fourth symposium on this topic convened by the U.S. Office of Education. *Technology in Guidance,* a special issue of the *Personnel and Guidance Journal* (1970, *49,* 3), offers eight articles, featuring ten examples of the present use of technology, along with reviews of guidance technology books. Educational Technology Magazine (PO Box 508, Saddle Brook, New Jersey 07662) has published a special report titled *Counseling Technology* (1969), with fifteen articles, some illustrating where technology is currently in use in guidance programs. More recently (1973), the NVGA has issued a twenty-four-page booklet, *Tested Practices: Computer Assisted Guidance Systems,* with guidelines and bibliography (APGA Publication Sales, 1607 New Hampshire Ave., N.W., Washington, D.C. 20009, 95 cents).

CONTINUING EDUCATION TECHNICIAN. It has been proposed here that every high school guidance team have a career development technician as part of its core of practitioners. It has also been proposed that practitioners in addition to the core are added when the assessment of student needs shows it to be necessary. If the proportion of graduates engaging education or training beyond high shcool is miniscule, a school may decide that a continuing education technician (CET) is not necessary, although a case can be made that the opposite conclusion is thereby demonstrated. This competing argument states that advanced education, at least at the community college or technical institute level, is warranted for a sizeable proportion of high school graduates. If one school has a significantly lower proportion of graduates engaging advanced education, the indication is that countering measures are required, and thus a CET may be all the more required in that school. On the other hand, if a school has a computer system that operates in the way described by Minor, the core guidance team might not need to be supplemented by a continuing education technican.

If a CET is employed, there is one occupational behavior this person can engage that cannot be duplicated by a computer. This behavior is similar to a behavior of the career development technician, namely, conferences away from the school. In the case of the CET there are conferences with admissions officers of advanced education institutions for several purposes, including the axiom that the personal touch can do wonders for troublesome admissions questions. Moreover, because advanced education institutions are complex ecosystems, and subtle data relating to this characteristic are difficult to put into a computer data bank, the CET can acquire information of this kind from that school's graduates who are in those institutions and from articles published in the public press which are then filed. An example is an extensive article on Franconia College, N.H., which appears in the June 12, 1972, issue of the *New Yorker* magazine.

The strongest case to be made for a continuing education technician extends from this need by youth for much information about higher education institutions not in catalogues and not computerable, as evidenced by numerous studies of college success and failure. The word "college" is used here as shorthand for advanced educational institutions, but means any kind of extensive postsecondary study.

A CET on the guidance team might cause elimination of poor higher education information procedures traditional in guidance practices. The continuing education counterpart of the Career Day is the College Night—held at night so that parents can meet with college representatives. These county fair–midway type activities are staffed by barkers selling their wares, scarcely a sound way for students or parents to acquire objective college information. Carline (1974) reports an excerpt of a survey of high school juniors as to the best sources of information about colleges. College catalogues were found to be the best source, despite their gross inadequacies, and visits from college representatives were rated the poorest. Recently colleges have started to forego individual school visits, using a regional approach, a college-fair type of offering to an area. One held in 1974 for the Washington, D.C., metropolitan area drew praise from youths attending, showing that a crust of bread may be a banquet for a starving person, so poor is the diet of higher education information in typical high schools.

Katz (1963) offers a review of issues and data relating to college completion and dropping out and quotes Summerskill's (1962) observation that "studies ranging over the last 40 years consistently indicate that about one-half of all college admissions are 'wasted,' in the sense that students drop-out before obtaining their degrees" (p. 43). Katz, referring to a study by Barton (1961), notes that adequate knowledge about college requires these "organizational outputs to be measured: inputs, outputs, environment, social structure, attitudes, and activities," and observes that virtually none of these is available in literature from colleges. He then observes that

> if we accept the notion of differentiating colleges according to those characteristics that may make an essential psychological difference to the student, we can see that the student needs more help than he can get from reading [college] publications. [p. 46]

In the stance taken in this text, these comments are translated to mean a need for colleges to be described as ecosystems. A quotation from Freedman (1956) by Katz, with some additional ellipses of mine, summarizes this idea in this contention:

> The [college] student body as an entity may be thought to posses characteristic qualities of personality, ways of interacting socially, types of values and beliefs, and the like, which are passed on from one "generation" of students to another . . . like any culture. . . . We contend, in fact, that this culture is the prime educational force at work in the college, for . . . assimilation into the student society is the foremost concern of most new students. . . . The scholastic and academic aims and processes of the college are in large measure transmitted to incoming students or mediated for them by the predominant student culture. [p. 55]

This subtopic of college information is closed by a last word from Katz. He asks how we can open up these realms of information, on the reasonable assumption that they are pertinent for college choice. "The colleges themselves have studiously avoided furnishing a single red tab, conspicuously marked 'pull here,' that will strip away the protective wrappings at once." It can be done, however, because

> the persistent counselor can find little shreds of evidence here and there that he may be able to grip with his fingernails and thus breach the glossy cellophane at one point or another. [p. 56]

Figure 10 also does not show office space for a continuing education technician as part of the Career Center. Although inclusion in or proximity to the Career Center might seem to be relatively unimportant, it has more importance than may appear at first glance. The CDT and CET do not actively engage in the psychological behaviors of decisions; they are not counselors in the usual sense. They are not persons who are seen only when there is a problem, as more likely is the case with conferring with a counselor, and definitely so when conferring with the behavior specialist. Students confer with the CDT and CET casually and on a random access basis around very specific information and process needs. These similarities warrant their being physically in close association, and both somewhat separated in space from the counselors and behavior specialists so as to minimize confusion in their roles that might occur among students were all team members closely and nondiscriminatingly placed. Some can argue that engaging continuing education does not necessarily mean that the intention is to acquire occupational knowledge or skills to be useful for employment immediately following graduation from an advanced education institution. Those so arguing would claim that a person goes on to earn a bachelor's degree, as in the European tradition, to become liberalized—that is, to be educated in the broad meaning of that term. To have the CET be part of the Career Center is to give the incorrect view, therefore (in these persons' judgment), that advanced education must have occupational intention and component.

No dispute with the philosophical issue is offered here. A realistic stance is taken, however, holding that most students seeking advanced education in this country are doing so also with occupational intentions. They are at least seeking training as well as education and many wish training only. Thus it is highly appropriate to associate continuing education decisions with other occupational career considerations. Likely the student wishing to follow the European tradition will make a college decision in consultation with his parents only and will seek enrollment in a private liberal arts institution. This type of student will not be adversely affected by locating the continuing education specialist in the Career Center.

REGISTRAR. One of the continuing complaints of high school counselors is that much of their time is taken up with clerical duties, and, in schools where a large proportion of graduates seek advanced education, a predominant clerical chore is preparation of transcripts and endorsements and with accumulating and recording other data requested by such institutions. This can indeed be a very time-consuming activity, one that can scarcely be justified as appropriate for counselors who can carry out far more useful functions related to human maximization. For counselors to be required to give so much time to this necessary chore may be one source of the complaint by teachers, students, and citizens that "our counselors give time only to those going to college, while the student who will enter the labor market after graduation is ignored."

Some high schools now have registrars, usually associated with the school's administrators. As observed previously, no stand is taken here that registrars ought to be in the guidance team instead, only that they should be employed when made appropriate by the number seeking advanced education or training, whether the occupation is affiliated with the administration team or not. Insofar as the registrar is also responsible for all student records, his placement in the administrative team can be additionally supported. There is, conversely, a strong argument for the registrar's more immediate supervision by the guidance team, those persons who are charged by the school with concern about the total educational-occupational life and plans of students.

JOB DEVELOPMENT TECHNICIAN AND OUTREACH COUNSELOR. These two possible members of the guidance team have been noted before in somewhat different contexts. These positions are repeated here briefly to complete the picture of a school's full array of occupations/career activities.

The functions of a job development technician may be carried out by a CDT when the need for job development in an area is relatively minor. When the need is so great that a separate occupation is set up, the job development technician is probably best located as a member of the career development technician's team.

The outreach or field counselor, when there is community needs as demonstrated by a noticeable number of truancies, dropouts, or squeeze-outs, is a school-based roving counselor who seeks out youths who have left school before graduation. His duties are rather patent: help the youth return to high school if the school and youth can adapt themselves to each other, and help other youths to use community resources, particularly to use training programs in the case of undereducated, unskilled youths, if it is not appropriate or possible for them to return to school.

PLACEMENT OFFICER. This guidance team member was not mentioned previously, but his functions would be obvious. A large high school with many youths seeking employment while in high school and after withdrawing or graduating may need not only the two specialists of the prior section but also a placement officer. In other high schools a job development technician might also serve placement functions, and in yet other schools the career development technician might serve the three arrays of functions.

Job placement is an important goal for youth, and in some high schools a major portion of counselor time has been put into job placement. A caution about a school's engaging in job placement must be repeated: job placement should not siphon off efforts that should go first into career development. If a school's primary guidance expression was a placement service, the school may judge itself as successful if it matches person with job in a one-time step taken near the end of schooling, a go-for-broke occupational choice. Tennyson (1970) observes that the preoccupation of counselors with this kind of choice "has imposed functional constraints which have limited the potential influence counselors might have upon students' vocational development" (p. 262). A school's participation in job placement, when carried out within the guidance contact, is but one step, albeit an important one, in a person's continuing development. The guidance movement is concerned with the years that lead up to this first placement, with the role that placement will have in the person's continuing development, and with what role that first job placement has, therefore, in that person's career future.

Any decision about employing a placement officer has to be made after considering the kinds of service and availability of placement persons in local offices of a state's employment services and other job placement services that might be available in the community. For numbers of Maryland high schools, for example, local branches of the state employment service offer a placement service that is similar to what the school would offer if it had a placement officer. It has long been a policy of the U.S. Employment Service that the state units shall work out service plans with local schools, but the quality of such liaison is mixed countrywide. Some school systems have recently formed placement services, while others have a long history. For example, the Baltimore school system's placement service, managed by the Guidance Department, is 50 years old.

Other Guidance Team Members' Functions in Occupation/Career Activities

This topic may better be addressed by starting with youth. One of the activities, inferrable but not explicitly stated in Tables 4 and 5, but explicitly noted in the computer activities described by Minor, is the submission of each youth to an inventory of interests and other characteristics related to occupational decisions. Inventorying these characteristics has been extensively researched, as might be expected in light of the long history of the guidance movement in assisting youth with occupational decisions. Among the several interest inventories with which the guidance student will eventually become familiar is a newer one that is noted here because it not only works for its intended purposes, but also because it is consonant with theses posited in this text. This is the Self-Directed Search (S-DS) by John L. Holland.

Despite the potential complexity of the position held by Holland and this writer that occupational decisions are a seeking-out of compatible environments, the S-DS is, in Holland's terms, "a simple-minded instrument," or perhaps better, a simple instrument for assessment in a complex area. Holland designed the inventory so that intervention by a counselor is not needed. He describes it as a self-administered, self-scored, and self-interpreted vocational counseling tool.

Holland et al. (1972) find several imperatives that call for a self-administered instrument like the S-DS.

> As always there are not enough counselors to provide vocational guidance for all, and it is unlikely that sufficient funds for this traditional form of help will ever be available. Also, the major alternatives to traditional vocational counseling possess major weaknesses. For example, new and old comprehensive test batteries provide massive amounts of information, but they still require a counselor for each student. And the computer-based guidance systems still suffer from serious deficiencies. They are relatively expensive to develop, operate and modify. Ironically, computer-based systems may have less flexibility than the present paper system.
>
> In short, counselors need a vocational guidance system that will multiply their time and talent so that a single counselor can cope with a large population of students or adults. The extension of vocational help to all who need it must be accomplished at the lowest possible cost in materials, equipment, and training time. And, equally important, any new system should possess a high degree of scientific validity and client-effectiveness. [p. 1]

The assumption of this illustration, then, is that all youths have been invited to take the S-SD whenever each wishes (it will be available for taking anytime in the Career Center), and most youths will indeed decide when it is appropriate to take it and will do so. Other youths will need to be encouraged by a guidance team member, including teacher-advisers, to take the inventory.

It potentially yields several specific and related occupations that the student can explore in detail in and out of the Career Center, with or without the help of the career development technician. Or the student can confer with that specialist or a counselor. Some youths will need to confer with a guidance team member because conflicting occupations, instead of related ones, have been yielded by the S-DS. The point to be emphasized is that there is no ritualistic treatment of the inventory results, there being in fact several options open to the student, including going it alone.[6]

Counselors' functions, as defined in this text, primarily are the use of strategies of decision making, including assistance to a youth in working out any behavior imbalances he has that are impeding such decisions, to the degree that the counselor feels qualified to give that assistance. Likely the student with more frustrating behavior imbalances will already have been in a helping situation with a behavior specialist on the team. It is tenable to expect, however, that in some instances that kind of assistance may be offered only after a youth has engaged some such inventory as the S-SD, has been puzzled by the findings, and then has sought the instantly available assistance of the career development technician or the youth's teacher-adviser, who in turn causes him to seek the assistance of a behavior specialist. Of course, this assistance might have been sought from a counselor instead, but the instance explained here is of a youth with that kind of behavior imbalance that the Counselor sees himself as unqualified to mediate, and therefore a Behavior Specialist must be involved.

Parenthetically it needs to be noted that the statement just above deliberately avoided such phrasing as "the youth was *sent* to a behavior specialist." It may not be a critical issue, but the writer's clinical instinct, informed early by Lloyd-Jones (1949), is that "centrifugal guidance," that is, sending a person successively to different practitioners in an outward-spiraling fashion, diminishes the probability of useful assistance, and that the converse approach, "centripetal guidance," is more likely to yield the results sought. This latter stance means spiraling specialists toward the center, which is, of course, the individual being helped. Thus in this instance the first member of the guidance team who assesses the youth's needs as calling for the expertise of the behavior specialist causes a joint conference to be set up among the three, the effect being that the behavior specialist is "pulled into the center." After this first conference has been under way a bit, the referring team member can leave.

The functions of the counselor have been only sketchily outlined here. They are of such importance that more detailed descriptions are provided in Chapter 12.

SPECIAL CAREER DEVELOPMENT CONDITIONS

Somewhat peripheral mention has been made from time to time about persons who either have never adequately developed, or, if having begun adequate development, were later extruded from it. The guidance movement is not oriented to typical humans, because that is a *class* of humans.

---

[6] The most complete picture of Holland's research and proposals are to be found in his 1973 volume.

The guidance movement stresses individuals, and its procedures are cut to fit individual needs. At the same time individuals who have special career development concerns do occur in noticeable numbers, and the needs and problems of these subpopulations merit special scholarly inquiry and unique procedures developed from that inquiry. Individuals victimized by development disparities can be better helped through knowledge about problems faced by others with similar disparities.

Rehabilitatees

Vocational rehabilitation has a fifty-year history of federal sponsorship. As stated, rehabilitation procedures, including counseling, were oriented toward handicapped World War I veterans, and thereafter to adult workers who became disabled and could not continue their occupations. The intention of rehabilitation was to help such persons learn a new occupation and be placed in it.

Intervening years have seen the vocational rehabilitation movement reach downward to age sixteen and broaden to include such categories of persons as prisoners with certain handicaps and persons who have been afflicted by certain behavior disorders, including mental retardation. For high schools the point of interest is assistance given to physically handicapped or otherwise qualified students who are of high school age. The high school guidance team, therefore, is occasionally supplemented by a visiting rehabilitation counselor from the state education agency, which is the unit through which federal rehabilitation funds are channeled.

Racial, Ethnic, and Regional Minorities

The latter half of the 1960s brought strong federal direction to the problems faced by subpopulations whose career development had always been thwarted by poverty and prejudice. Three groups have been highlighted by these efforts: the poor living in the Appalachian Mountains, impoverished blacks, and the poor section of Spanish-surnamed citizens. A fourth group, equally as poor and discriminated against, again was bypassed in public attention, that group being the natives of this land, the American Indians.

As is to be expected, modifications in school guidance procedures must be made to give individuals from these subpopulations their rights as promulgated in the Declaration of Independence, these altered guidance thrusts added to other societal changes that at long last have been instituted.

Prospective guidance team members can begin their study of concerns related to these subpopulations through special issues of the *Personnel and Guidance Journal: What Guidance for Blacks?* (1970, *48,* 9), *Counseling and the Social Revolution* (1971, *49,* 9), and *Culture as a Reason for Being* (1971, *50,* 2). Also meriting attention is a special supplement to the

Vocational Guidance Quarterly, The Vocational Counselor and Social Action, by Joseph Samler, 1971.

Females

Despite the long history of the Women's Bureau of the U.S. Department of Labor, common awareness of disparities falling to a person who happens to be female is relatively recent. The issue is complicated in that, unlike the four subpopulations mentioned in the prior section, females are not of a common view that they are in an occupationally disparitive condition.

As each of us guidance practitioners examines and modifies his model of the human at his best, does any of us find that there are two models needed, one for males and one for females? As we serve on a guidance team, do we propagate the historical view that there are male occupations and female occupations? What if a counselor's response to the last query were to be, "*I* don't hold to that view, but society does, so why should I hurt a female counselee by encouraging her toward a male occupation?" That sounds plausible, but so was the statement a few years ago that "I don't think airlines should discriminate against blacks as hostesses, but, since that is the fact of life, I would tell a black female student to not plan for that occupation." That appeared plausible less than a decade ago, but was it ever a defensible stance for a counselor? One counselor thought not, and his efforts in breaking the race barrier in that occupation produced results that can now be useful for many black females. A passive counselor who acknowledges only the status quo does not qualify as a counselor-as-youth-advocate, as will be expected of one committed to maximization of each individual. The career role of females is one about which present and future guidance team members might well be pensive and suspicious of their own acculturation into stances that are in opposition to the guidance movement.

The countering of developmental inadequacy of individuals because of poverty, race, sex, regional, or ethnic characteristics is not charged solely to guidance practitioners, but, if individually or collectively they are not active in countering those societal forces, the least that can be hoped for is that they do not contribute to their continuance.

Adults

An impression may have been acquired, through the emphasis on youth in this text, and from Herr and Cramer's developmental paradigm in Table 4, that once an occupational career is well launched in early adulthood through application of career decision procedures of the kind described here, the large career developmental tasks have been met. The idea may have been acquired that from here on out, except for occasional patching or slight changes of course, all is to be smooth sailing. Not so. Even with the greatest of care and with a long history of solid preparation for career decision making, major occupational changes can occur throughout life and, indeed, will occur for most people at that period known as retirement.

This fact of expectable career changes throughout life is being acknowledged by the increasing attention given to adult counseling needs in the professional literature, attending to adult concerns right to death. To obtain information about this adult emphasis, and thereby complete the full human development picture in regard to careers, the reader should see with two brief articles by Schlossberg (1975a, 1975b).

SUMMARY

Educational goals can be stated in grandiose terms. In refining these to more specific goal statements, one common educational goal is stated in terms of students' occupational effectiveness. It was in the occupations area that guidance programs came into the school, and it is in this one area that guidance programs are currently faulted.

The earliest guidance concepts and practices in the occupations area are insufficient for today. Guidance programs started out with a job selection and placement orientation. Today the guidance movement is concerned with career development. A concern with process rather than with event.

Career development is carried out in a school that is oriented toward career education. The school constitutes itself as a psychosocial ecosystem that nurtures and reinforces those behaviors that have been identified as being associated with career decisions and effectiveness, thus as contributing to individuals' attaining a satisfying life style. Program regularities are employed to produce behavior regularities needed by students for adequate career development.

A school that employs only one type of guidance practitioner, the counselor, can have an adequate career development program, just as the school that has no formal guidance practitioners can be oriented toward career education. Employment of counselors improves the likelihood of attaining the school's goals in this area. In like manner, having other guidance practitioners in addition to the counselor provides increased probability of success in goal attainment in the career development area.

Guidance practitioners, following principles of behavior, are expert school resource persons in the career development area. They attend to the behavior histories of youths, supporting those students who have decision-making competencies and ample knowledge of occupations. The practitioners particularly attend to those youths whose subcultures have had a minimizing effect on the behaviors that are important in occupational decision making and success. These practitioners know the psychology underlying career decision making: in simple terms, the seeking out of a compatible environment in which to live out a career.

REFERENCES

BARTON, A. *Organizational Measurement and Its Bearing on the Study of College Environments.* New York: College Entrance Examination Board, 1961.

BIGGERS, J. L. "The Use of Information in Vocational-Decision Making." *The Vocational Guidance Quarterly,* 1971, *19,* 3.

CARLINE, E. T. JR. "How Students Find Out About College." *The College Board Review,* 1974, 90, p. 25.

FLANAGAN, J. C. "Presidential Address, Div. 15." *Educational Psychologist* 1971, *8,* 2, p. 1.

FREEDMAN, M. B. "The Passage through College." In N. Sanford (Ed.), *Personality Development during the College Years. Journal of Social Issues,* 1956, *12.*

HAMILTON, J. A., & WEBSTER, W. J. "Occupational Information and the School Curriculum." *The Vocational Guidance Quarterly,* 1971, *19,* 3.

HEDRICH, V. "Seattle's Concentration on Careers." *American Education,* 1971, *7,* 12–15.

HERR, E. L., & CRAMER, S. H. *Vocational Guidance and Career Development in Schools: Toward a Systems Approach.* Boston: Houghton Mifflin, 1972.

HOLLAND, J. L. *Making Vocational Choices: A Theory of Careers.* Englewood Cliffs, N.J.: Prentice-Hall, 1973.

HOLLAND, J. L., HOLLAFIELD, J. H., NAFZIGER, D. H., HELMS, S. T. *A Guide to the Self-Directed Career Program.* Baltimore: Center for Social Organization of Schools, Report #126, The Johns Hopkins University, 1972.

ISAACSON, L. E. *Career Information in Counseling and Guidance* (2nd Ed.). Boston: Allyn and Bacon, 1971.

JACOBSON, T. J. "Career Guidance Centers." *Personnel and Guidance Journal,* 1972, *50,* 599–604.

JACOBSON, T. J. *The Master Plan for Career Guidance and Counseling.* La Mesa, Calif.: Grossmont Union High School District, 1975.

JACOBSON, T. J., et al. *A Study of Career Centers in the State of California.* La Mesa, Calif.: Grossmont Union High School District, 1975.

JOHNSON, R. G. "Job Stimulations to Promote Vocational Interests." *The Vocational Guidance Quarterly,* 1971, *20,* 1.

KATZ, M. *Decision and Values.* New York: College Entrance Examination Board, 1963.

KATZ, M. "The Name and Nature of Vocational Guidance." In H. R. Morrow (Ed.), *Career Guidance for a New Age.* Boston: Houghton Mifflin, 1973.

KRUMBOLTZ, J. D., BAKER, R. D., & JOHNSON, R. G. *Vocational Problem-Solving Experiences for Stimulating Career Exploration and Interest: Phase II.* Stanford, Calif.: School of Education, Stanford University, 1968.

KRUMBOLTZ, J. D., & THORESON, C. E. *Behavioral Counseling.* New York: Holt, Rinehart and Winston, 1969.

LARAMORE, D. D. *A Study of the Effects of Three Methods of Presenting Occupational Information on Selected Behaviors of Ninth-Grade Students.* Unpublished doctoral dissertation, University of Maryland, 1971.

LLOYD-JONES, E. "Centrifugal and Centripetal Guidance Programs for Children." *Teachers College Record,* 1949, *51,* 7–12.

MINOR, F. J. "An Experimental Computer-Based Educational and Career Exploration System." In D. E. Super, *Computer Assisted Counseling.* New York: Teachers College Press, 1970.

SANDMAN, P. M. *The Unabashed Career Guide.* New York: Collier, 1969.

SCHLOSSBERG, NANCY K. "Career Development in Adults." *American Vocational Journal,* 1975, *50,* 5, 38–40.

SCHLOSSBERG, NANCY K. "Programs for Adults." *Personnel and Guidance Journal,* 1975, *53,* 9, 681–685.

SMITH, R. D., & EVANS, J. R. "Comparison of Experimental Group Guidance and Individual Counseling as Facilitators of Vocational Development." *Journal of Counseling Psychology,* 1973, *20* (3), 202–208.

STEWART, N. R. "Exploring and Processing Information about Educational and Vocational Opportunities in Groups." In J. D. Krumboltz, & C. E. Thoreson (Eds.), *Behavioral Counseling.* New York: Holt, Rinehart and Winston, 1969.

SUMMERSKILL, J. "Dropouts from College." In N. Sanford (Ed.), *The American College.* New York: John Wiley and Sons, 1962.

TENNYSON, W. W. "Comment." *The Vocational Guidance Quarterly,* 1970, *18,* 261–263.

WRENN, C. G. *The Counselor in a Changing World.* Washington, D.C.: American Personnel and Guidance Association, 1962.

11 Self-Management Skills and Social Competency Behaviors

INTRODUCTION

Guidance objectives are a subset of school objectives leading to attainment of educational goals, or to distinctively guidance goals. Chapter 2 showed how the broad educational goal of career development had guidance objectives because guidance goals could be identified as relating to that educational goal. Even if there were not a school system goal in career development, there would have to be a guidance goal in that area because this has been the traditional main thrust of the guidance movement.

This chapter examines two guidance goals and their objectives that are less likely to come out of broad educational goals. These are the goals that all students will demonstrate self-management skills and will improve their social competency behaviors.

SELF-MANAGEMENT

Self-reliance, independence, or managing one's own destiny are similar descriptions for a goal that has been prized by most parents in this society.[1]

---

[1] At this writing there are roilings in some communities about public school textbooks. One type of text against which a small number of parents declaims is that which teaches children to be analytic, make judgments, see alternatives. In statements made in the public press those parents take an unequivocating stand that their children are not to make judgments or decisions—their parents will tell them what to think. This group comprises only a small portion of public school parents, but their actual

Policy literature about public education and the public statements of educators also hold that goal to be desirable.

Is that goal, under whatever description, actually attained, and do schools contribute to its realization? A fuzzy concept like "independence" defies adequate measurement, so it is difficult to answer the first part of the question. Even if we could know the degree of realization of a goal such as independence, it is still difficult, if not impossible, to specify the proportion contributed to its attainment by schools.

In response to the first part of that question—Is the goal attained at all?—we can agree that it is because we see children who once were dependent of their parents grow into adults who act independently. The answer to the second part—Have the schools contributed to this independence—evades sure response. Without ever going to school, adults would show some degree of independence as an outcome of physiological development, and because other attributes of the culture would produce some independence. Behaviors representing the goal addressed in this section are imprinted on the genetic ballast of every human, although the specific manner of its realization is dependent on cultural variables.

And we must be nagged by yet another question: Is the independence, the self-reliance demonstrated by most adults in our society the best that can be shown? Likely not. Likely there is a far higher level of this characteristic commonly attainable just as biofeedback research shows that the academic attainments of typical persons could be much greater if the resources of the brain and nervous systems were more efficiently harnessed.

This question was asked earlier in an analogous context. Therein the observation was made that high school and college graduates choose occupations and become employed without guidance. That being so, how can one justify expensive proposals about guidance programs in the occupations area? The answer, of course, lies in the view that guidance programs are not concerned with persons just entering an occupation. Guidance programs are concerned with individuals' quality of living and thus are designed to assist individuals in maximizing that quality through best occupational decisions and thus best employment.

---

number is far greater. The larger number is not heard from on this issue, however, because their children are not in public schools. These parents, seeking the same goal as that small proportion of public school children's parents, that is, dependence of thought around political, religious, or cultural orthodoxies, always have had nonpublic schools to which their children are sent. There is no need, therefore, for that large number of parents to protest texts that reflect the public schools' goals of self-reliance, independence in thinking, and managing one's own behavior. Their children are not challenged by such texts because their schools are designed to foster the opposite values of unquestioned acceptance of the authoritative statements of parents and other adults. Recall earlier comments about parents seeking to reduce the exercise of free will by making certain that their children will behave in predictable ways.

Shift this last idea over to and restate it for the issue of independence or self-reliance. The guidance movement, the individualizing thrust in education, does not abide by the attainment of a goal merely to the degree that might occur accidentally. It is concerned with individuals' reaching the best levels of that goal. The guidance thrust is for the *optimal* in occupational decisions, in educational attainments, in social competencies, in independence or self-reliance, and in any domain that is marked out as a guidance concern.

Causing all students to acquire decision-making behaviors can be hypothesized as also causing all students to attain higher levels of independence or self-reliance. At the same time the reaching of independence goals need not be left to be a secondary outcome of another goal. The guidance program can directly address and magnify behaviors of independence, and it is this section of this chapter that considers how this can be done, carried out under the term "self-management."

Self-management is the deliberate application of behavior principles to one's self by oneself—enabling each person to be his own counselor (Nye, 1973; Kahn, in press). Self-management is sometimes referred to by an older phrase, self-control, and by other newer ones, such as self-help or self-discipline. Whatever it is called, self-management is not a recent discovery, but, as with other applications of behavior principles, the technological specifics have been recently uncovered.

The oldness of self-management likely can be demonstrated by each of us. Most of us can report one or several persons who wished to act in a way in which they had not acted before, or wished to stop or reduce a behavior, and whose behavior was changed without intervention by others. The procedures employed to bring about the change came from the person's own resources. In days prior to our current knowledge about how behaviors are formed, maintained, and changed, this self-managed behavior change process most likely would have been attributed to the exercise of will power, with will seen as a human faculty. Present knowledge lets it be said that the attainment of the choice or wish was through the intuitive application of principles of behavior to himself by a person, particularly a reward/punishment schedule. Both the choice made and the procedures followed to effectuate the choice are accounted for by such principles. Illustrations in our personal histories showing the application of behavior principles to self-management are similar to those of the intuitive application of behavior principles in other areas for uncountable millennia. Recall here Grandma's law as a folk example of the application of intuitively perceived behavior principles to the forming of others' behaviors.

There is no longer need just to hope that some persons may discover by chance how they might apply principles of behavior to the management of their own lives. The principles are now empirically established, and the technical procedures are available for deliberately causing persons to acquire these competencies. An incidental favorable outcome can be predicted: because the learners will know how behavior is formed, maintained, and changed as part of learning self-management procedures, they will be aware also of how others might be seeking to manage the learners' behaviors. Those who learn self-management will be less likely to be unaware subjects of deliberate but unannounced behavior management programs run on them by others. The learners' independence and self-reliance will be furthered not only because they are competent to control their own behaviors, but because they are less susceptible to intentional or unintentional management programs carried out on them by others that would act to reduce that independence and self-reliance.

THE PROCEDURES OF SELF-MANAGEMENT

The procedures of self-management are the ones that would be applied when helping another person to change behavior; thus their presentation here will be familiar from illustrations used earlier.

Identifying the Target Behaviors

The first step in self-management is precise identification of what it is that has to be changed. Sometimes this might be a specific behavior that a person wishes to lessen or extinguish. Or it may be a behavior that is not established and that a person wishes to establish, or is only weakly established and needs strengthening. Watson and Tharp (1972) name some of these, and show how some are changed through self-management. Their list includes smoking (such as "I wish to cut down or stop smoking"), knuckle cracking, and nail biting as behaviors that some persons might wish to be lessened or extinguished.

Sometimes the wish of the person is stated as a general condition that needs changing, such as reducing overweight, overcoming a lack of success in acquiring friends of the opposite sex, or improving relationships with parents, which are paraphrases from the same list. What any person involved in self-management must come to see is that each of these conditions is an effect that results from the presence or absence of a number of specific behaviors. To change the general condition, therefore, requires the establishment or extinction of those specific behaviors. Those specific behaviors are the target behaviors.

The two paragraphs above convey an important difference. In the illustrations of the first paragraph the person has identified a specific behavior to be changed. In the second paragraph the person identifies a general goal to be attained, but has not identified the specific behaviors that constitute the goal. In this latter case the contributing behaviors, or the lacking behaviors, must be identified before self-management can begin. It might be that a person would describe poor health as a condition that he wishes changed. Poor health cannot be changed directly, only the behaviors that cause poor health. One of those so identified may be smoking, thus changing smoking behaviors becomes a target behavior. In sum, one person might be able to be specific about the behavior to be changed—"I wish to stop smoking." Another person might not be able to be that specific, but can state a general condition to be changed. That person would have to be led to see that changing specific behaviors is necessary to changing the general condition.

Incidentally, we are talking here about behaviors a person wishes to change, not behaviors other persons wish him to change. The individual himself has to want a change in behavior, or a change in the condition, if there is to be self-management. If others wish his behavior to change, but he does not, that change can be produced, of course, but obviously this cannot be described as self-management.

Our attention throughout is directed to adolescents, but it might serve a learning purpose to note incidentally that children are capable not only of identifying behaviors they wish to change (Goshko, 1973), but in several researches have demonstrated self-management skills to the degree that they became "able to manage their own behavior . . . more effectively by self-reinforcement than is achieved through similar externally administered consequences" (Bandura, 1971, p. 267).

Acquiring Baseline Data

The next need is to determine how often and under what conditions there is an occurrence of an unwanted target behavior, or the frequency and conditions wherein a wanted target behavior does not occur. Collection of data around this need, which is called baseline data, is rather obvious and simple, such as in answer to the question of "How often and under what conditions do I smoke?" (or "fail tests," "disrupt classes," "fight with my parents," and so on). Smoking is an easily identified, precise behavior, and attendant circumstances are also identifiable. What, however, if the target behavior is a vague one like eliminating depression? As a nonprecise complex of behaviors, baseline collection will have to attend to the length of depressed states rather than simple counts of the number of times a person was in a depressed state. Study behaviors, as another example, will need number and length of times for proper baseline data collection; test anxiety requires measure of the duration of the episode. Whatever the behavior, the accompanying stimulus conditions also need to be recorded.

Setting up the Contingency Management Plan

Knowing when and under what conditions a behavior occurs permits the setting up of a plan whereby the individual rewards himself when he acts in the preferred way, and perhaps punishes himself for not acting in the desired way or for acting in an undesired way.

To set up this portion of the plan, the self-managing person identifies events or actions that are rewarding for him, and that can thus be used to reinforce desired behaviors. It is appropriate to write these out so that when a person contracts with himself to change a behavior and is setting up a plan to do so, he picks certain rewarding events as those that are to be used. Big rewards for big changes, small rewards for small changes.

Another first step, and one around which a self-management operation can succeed or fail, is to break down a target behavior into its smaller elements, a natural extension of the idea that a condition that needs changing requires first the identification of the behaviors that cause the condition. Smoking, for example, is not an elemental activity in behavioral terms; it is a pattern of behaviors, albeit, a tiny pattern. One first has to reach for a cigarette or other smoking device, then place it in the mouth, light it, and then draw the smoke into the mouth. Of those specific components of smoking, the crucial one for many persons is the reaching behavior, and, of course, recording "the conditions present in the environment at the time I reached for a smoke."

The importance of this identification of small portions of a named behavior relates to the principles of shaping and successive approximation presented in Chapter 5. Nothing magical here, just a lawful and more detailed explication of the old folk saying that a child has to learn to crawl before he learns to walk. No one learns to play basketball as such. The entry point is to learn to handle a basketball in a most elementary fashion, then to pass while standing still. Skills acquired later will be those of passing while moving and of aiming for and hitting the basket. After that there will be learning to dribble, followed by the behavior of dribbling and passing at the same time. After other specific learnings the desired outcome will have been reached: ability to play basketball. These illustrations, incidentally, accord with one dictum based on behavior principles: Think small.

For a person to attain the goal of satisfying relationships with others, for example, if the condition for which change is sought were summed up in a phrase like, "I have no friends and I wish I had," small behaviors comprising friendliness must be identified, as well as those small behaviors that comprise unfriendliness. The self-managing person begins with one small behavior and rewards himself when he shows that behavior, thus reinforcing that behavior. In the need-a-friend instance it might be so small a behavior as smiling at others. With smiling established in the behavior repertoire, the next step in the successive approximation of steps that will lead to having friends could be smiling and giving a simple greeting; then later a smile, a simple greeting, plus some complimentary comment.

The Think Small dictum applies in extinguishing behaviors too. In this illustration, the analysis into behavior elements may show the existence of one or more behaviors to be eliminated. Each will have to be separately attacked.

The emphasis in this section has been on rewarding small behaviors to establish or eliminate a behavior pattern or modify a condition. Punishing oneself might be part of the plan: emitting desired behaviors produces reward, thus reinforcement of the behavior; punishing undesired behaviors contributes to their extinction. One clever punishing procedure has been suggested in the self-management literature. This requires that there be set aside a sum of money and identification of an organization strongly disliked by the self-manager. An amount of money is designated as the worth of each instance of the undesired behavior. Every time the self-manager emits that behavior, he takes that designated amount and sends it to the hated organization! An illustration of a less unusual punishment is loss of a desired leisure time as the cost of emitting an undesired behavior.

Ending the Procedures

The fourth step in self-management is to determine that a certain portion or all of the contingency management program can be stopped—a decision based on an assessment of whether the target behavior has been established or extinguished and with sufficient thoroughness to warrant termination. Specifications in this step are beyond the scope of this presentation, but will be learned by persons who continue study in the guidance field.

A danger requires noting: this step is one of those wherein the success or failure of the self-management activity lies heavily. A decision to terminate may be made before a behavior is sufficiently extinguished or established. When the new behavior dies, or the old, unwanted behavior recurs, the individual applying self-management procedures may become discouraged and quit or, perhaps worse, conclude that "self-management procedures won't work for me."

The caution is further conveyed by comparison with a similar condition in medical practice. For a certain condition the physician may prescribe a course of medicine to be followed for a number of days. The patient, who felt miserable prior to the start of the treatment, rapidly recovers a feeling of good health after only a small portion of the medicine has been taken and decides on his own to stop the treatment. Within a few hours or a day he feels bad again, as effects of the uncured condition reemerge. Thus the usual medical dictum: take all of this medicine, in the dosage prescribed, for as long as you are supposed to. Self-managers will do well to overlearn rather than risk the discouragement of underlearning.

PRINCIPLES OF BEHAVIOR AS THE BASE

Some of the principles of behavior set out in Chapter 5 need review for this topic, but filtered for the specific purpose and added to as necessary. Because the essence of self-management is self-reinforcement, its nature requires further analysis. Bandura (1971) reports four elements of a self-reinforcing event.

1. *A Self-Imposed Standard*   A self-prescribed standard of the particular behavior being addressed that the person uses to judge how adequately he performs related to that behavior. It is not sufficient to just wish to lose weight, for example. The self-manager sets the standard that he shall weigh, say, 180 pounds. Or, "In order to cope with situation M I need to perform behavior A at X rate, although right now I perform behavior A at X minus," which is an insufficiency of that coping behavior, or perhaps he performs at X plus, an excess of that coping behavior.

2. *Standards Determined by Social Comparisons*   This element is not required for every behavior that is to be modified by self-management, but will be an element in some cases. If I choose to improve my performance on a musical instrument so that I can achieve a position in an orchestra, for example, the standard of performance I set must be determined partly by the standard appropriate for orchestra X, which might differ from that standard that would get me a position in orchestra Y. To self-manage academic attainments so as to enter a school of veterinary medicine, I have to know the typical academic attainments of persons who are admitted. These are not absolute standards, but socially determined ones. On the other hand, weight loss might be either. I can set a standard for weight loss with reference to no social comparisons, but solely because I find myself less able to move around, feeling uncomfortable in my clothes, or because of other entirely personal reasons. On the other hand, I might be contented with my weight, but in order to compete in a body-beautiful contest, a matter more potent than my satisfaction with my present weight, I move to alter my weight around the social standards set for winning that contest. In a different social context, one, for example, wherein chubby persons are prized, I might have to gain weight.

3. *Self-Control of the Rewards and Punishments*   Setting the standards a person wishes to achieve, with or without social reference, is

relatively easy in comparison with finding and using rewards that will reinforce his behavior changes. Material rewards come first to mind here, but research has established that what I say to myself when I show a desired behavior also has the reinforcing properties. "The verbal self-evaluation is an important defining component of a self-reinforcing event" (Bandura, 1971, p. 253).

Behavior principles rest predominantly on rewards, but punishments can be used to complement rewards, whether behavior management is carried out by others or by oneself, as illustrated earlier. In managing my own behavior I can deprive myself of a material reward or of a pleasant event (see Watson & Tharp, 1972, for numerous illustrations), or, as Bandura suggests, I can say punishing or rewarding things to myself. It can be understood that a person first coming across the idea that someone might deny himself goodies or might even punish himself so as to change his behavior could be skeptical that typical humans can behave this way. It will have to be sufficient for purposes here to say that perfectly normal persons who are trained in self-management do inflict unpleasant consequences upon themselves. The research support for this assertion is simple, although as usual its review here falls victim to space and other limitations. The position is that, if the motivation for change is of sufficient potency, and the self-manager of behavior understands a few of the principles, he will engage in self-administered denials or other punishments as well as in rewards.

4. *Oneself as Reinforcing Agent* This last element is stated for the record, although it is obviously inherent in the word "self-management." For persons doing advanced study and practice in this area, it can be a point of technical importance. In some instances this fourth element has been unintentionally violated, as when a trained person, after teaching self-management procedures to another, remains in contact with that person. The trained person, for this example, unconsciously continues to administer some reinforcers, and thus self-management is mixed with a contingency management program administered by another person.

TEACHING PRINCIPLES OF BEHAVIOR IN HIGH SCHOOL

Up to this point we have looked at behavior change and procedures that a person applies to himself after some instruction in principles and those procedures by a trained person. Because the concern of this book is guidance programs that cause all students to attain guidance objectives, we can move without delay to investigate the question of training all students in self-management. To train all means first to cause all to know principles of behavior.

Deliberate Psychological Education

Recently the idea that students can and ought to be educated psychologically has had special attention in two volumes directed to guidance workers.[2] This is not a new idea in the guidance movement, but new technologies and new social movements justify new emphasis under new titles. The idea of psychological education associated with the guidance movement was active in the 1950s, as exemplified by the books and displays of the National Forum series. Relative to today, however, the content and method of learning psychological matters by students in those days was most primitive, and that may account partially for the fall-off of such early efforts. Today there is a vast array of empirically supported substance for psychological education, and that same body of empirical evidence also provides a new and defensible learning methodology. There is also a greater readiness to have such programs among educators and the general public, I conjecture.

It is not sufficient to contrast what is meant here by educating students in psychology only with early efforts to do so. A contrast must also be made with yet another and even more recent effort that appears to mean the same thing: the formal teaching of psychology in high schools. In the 1960s there was a continuing increase in the number of courses in psychology in high schools, at first a duty casually assigned to a faculty member who had a smattering of psychology courses in his undergraduate training. Over a period of time the preparation of teachers was expected to cover more extensive study of psychology at the undergraduate level, but no states have teacher preparation programs in this area, as they do in English and History, for example. The more important point about high school psychology courses is that they often are academic, a secondary school version of the Introduction to Psychology course that the psychology teacher had in his own undergraduate study.

As used here, psychological education does indeed have an academic component, centering on the principles of behavior, but it moves well beyond that necessary academic component to applications of principles to individuals' behavioral experiences. The next section of this chapter, deal-

---

[2] This section's heading is the title of a 1971 monograph of *The Counseling Psychologist* series, with the major article written by Mosher and Sprinthall. In 1973 a special issue of the *Personnel and Guidance Journal* (1973, *51*, 9) was published under the title of Psychological Education: a Prime Function of the Counselor, and included thirteen articles.

ing with establishing social competency behaviors, is another example of psychological education as the term is used here and in guidance writing. Right now, however, we are considering self-management skills as one part of psychological education.

And that brings us back to the need for any form of behavioral competency to be grounded in a knowledge of principles of behavior, the starting point of psychological education. This learning will occur among *all* students, and in the same group setting wherein they will acquire the decision-making skills that they then apply to such needs as selecting an occupation, a proposition examined in Chapter 6.

For readers who may wish to start a group program for high school students in self-management there is available one program of ten instructional units with an instructor's manual (Kahn, Leibowitz, and Levin, 1974). It can be assumed that the ingenious materials prepared by Kahn and his colleagues presage a variety of such materials.

As those materials become available, their testing and refinement must occur. What is to be feared is that some schools are moving too quickly in setting up psychological education courses that all students must engage without the substance of those courses having been adequately prepared and tested. One high school is known to have recently set up a course titled Guidance in which all students were enrolled for a term and which met every day. The substance of that course is out-of-pocket (or off-the-seat-of-pants), with the danger that it may acquire a bad reputation with students. In fact, as a result of parental dissatisfaction because time from college-entrance studies was lost, the activity in that school was abandoned. Reestablishing a program of psychological education in that school will be enormously difficult. In setting up such programs it is better to observe behavior principles: think small, and engage in only those behaviors that can be done successfully. It may be better to start with a few students for a small bit of time and have so successful a program that those students become advertising agents for a good experience, which slowly can be expanded in time and number of students.

Training in Self-Management

Thinking of self-management skills only, the nature of deliberate psychological education becomes discernable by looking again at the four elements of self-management posited at the beginning of this chapter and applying them to an instructional program in self-management.

The first element, *identifying the target behaviors,* calls for several target behaviors to be set up, one being the demonstration of a general understanding of how humans acquire behaviors, and how behaviors are maintained or extinguished. After this it will be possible to explicate other target behaviors in self-management skills.

The second element, *acquiring base-line data,* will need first the skills of self-observation, and these skills will be acquired as a part of this learning. The "new" psychological education is partly academic, but in terms of time spent will be experiential to a large degree, and will result in the acquisition of skills typically not in a person's repertoire. Accurate self-observation is one of these. A fetching and appropriate phrase that summarizes the skill of self-observation is proposed by Mahoney and Thoreson (1972). They observe that the ancient maxim "Know myself" might be paraphrased as "Know thy controlling variables" (p. 5).

Setting up the contingency management plan, the third element, is also built on didactic learning and simple practices of principles of behavior. The fourth element, *ending the procedures,* also will be controlled by knowledge of behavior principles.

In guidance or psychological education groups, students will select small behavior change tasks and under supervision will practice self-management skills. This practice, joined with all other portions of the training, will result in the attainment of this guidance objective, which cannot be better summarized than by a portion of the title of the Mahoney and Thoreson article referenced above: Power to the People.

SOCIAL COMPETENCY BEHAVIORS

The optimally functioning adult, from a guidance perspective, makes studied decisions, manages his own behavior in the directions of choice, and behaves toward other humans in ways that not only are personally satisfying, but that serve the public good.

As with such fuzzy goals as independence and self-reliance, our society in general appears to value persons "getting along" with others, and without doubt this has been and remains an educational goal. One school system, for example, states as one of its goals (in excerpted form) that each of its student "must learn to live in a society . . . must gain knowledge of himself and the characteristics, needs, and desires he shares with others . . . must gain sensitivity to others . . . and gain the ability to function . . . as a member of a group" (Montgomery County, Md., Public Schools, 1973). In our society a goal of this kind is appropriate for education because the diversity of cultures and the conflicts among ethnic groups and between races exacerbate the need. In a more homogeneous society the goal would be equally tenable, but the need to specifically state this goal probably would not be as great.

Perusal of curriculum materials used for a long time in elementary schools will show that social competency goals have been stated in education for a long period and remain important for that level of schooling. The concern in this section is the contribution of guidance objectives and programs toward reaching this goal in secondary schools. Compared with other activities and programs in the school, the guidance objective in this area is limited in scope, but major in its contribution to the acquisition by all students of social competency behaviors.

THE GUIDANCE OBJECTIVES IN THIS DOMAIN

Two major guidance objectives, with additional subobjectives, are appropriate. One of these is to provide students with the capacity to identify the perceptions and feelings of other persons, and the second objective, which overlaps the first, is the acquisition of verbal behaviors of effective social interaction.

Identifying Perceptions and Feelings

In preparing to engage in the counseling functions of guidance, counselors have learned this skill in identification, or improved the skills they already had. Over thirty years ago the person who made clear the components of this skill in identifying and acknowledging others' perceptions and feelings, and who had great influence on counselor preparation for over a quarter of a century, Carl R. Rogers (1942), proposed that this pattern of skills could be learned in a few weeks' time. Although there are now many behavior mediation procedures beyond this skill, once considered the sole skill needed by counselors, it nonetheless remains essential. Indeed the several behaviors required within this skill can be acquired in a relatively short time. As with other behaviors not customarily in persons' repertoires, and typical of first efforts made to produce those behaviors, the first efforts to demonstrate the several subskills within this area cause some persons to believe that they cannot learn them. Persistence, however, rapidly pays off.

Analogously we can think of deliberate control of selected muscles. When asked to engage in frivolous muscle motion, such as ear wiggling, most persons who do not have the skill, and who make an effort to do it for the first time, say they cannot. Asked why others can, the customary reply has been the statement of an assumption that those who can wiggle their ears have some muscle abnormality that permits this peculiar behavior. In fact ear wiggling, or deliberate motion of other selected muscles, can be easily and quickly learned. Normal social interaction does not require that form of muscle control, or indeed may consider such behavior as bizarre, and because first efforts usually do not produce the end results, it is understandable why most persons believe that you have to be born that way in order to do it.

Normal social interaction does not produce among persons in general the level of skill of identifying other's perceptions and feelings referred to here, but research demonstrates that this skill can readily be acquired, along with the other package of verbal skills, all of which comprise the verbal behaviors needed for successful social interaction. Berenson, Carkhuff, and Myrus (1966) accomplished this with college students in sixteen hours, and Zunker and Brown (1966) prepared student counselors for a college setting with a forty-hour program and a ten-hour refresher course. Andrade (1972) prepared students in a high school as peer counselors with twenty-three hours of training, as did Leibowitz and Rhoads (1974) for the same population and purpose.

The stand was taken in Chapter 2 that a school's guidance team need not include peer counselors, and the justification for that stand is now more apparent: if a few students can acquire these behaviors that are so necessary for effective social interaction, then all students can and must be offered the opportunity to acquire them. If we can train any peer counselors, then train all students to be peer counselors.

Verbal Behaviors of Effective Social Interaction

Although social competency skills are discussed here in two modes—identifying others' feelings and perceptions and skill in the verbal behaviors of effective social interaction—actually training in one mode is not done without training in the other. The two skills constitute an inseparable training package.

Benjamin (1969) and Dulaney and Eisenberg (1972) have well analyzed these other social interaction behaviors, the former under the term "the helping interview," and the latter two under the term "the facilitating interview." Four specific verbal skills comprise the greatest portion of such skills used in the facilitating or helping interview and thus are of importance for counselors and students to learn. The first of these four was treated in Chapter 5, but merits review here.

ATTENTIVE LISTENER. Persons who enter a guidance worker preparation program are rarely attentive listeners, and there is no reason to expect youths to be. Prospective guidance workers learn to be attentive listeners, and they have more years of nonlistening behavior to overcome.

It is tenable to expect that youths can acquire this behavior more readily than adults because of their shorter behavior history of nonlistening.

A primary component of attentive listening is *silence,* a behavior that a person's social history has not tolerated. Said in converse fashion, persons are considered socially adept when they are ready conversationalists, that is, when they can be frequent and persistent talkers, with their talking punctuated by only brief periods of silence.

In addition to the skill of remaining silent, the "attentive" portion of attentive listening requires physical focus on a speaker, and the capacity to not be distracted by stimuli extraneous to the conversation. Attentiveness is not conveyed just by a physical focus and by silence per se, but by the use of brief oral utterances that reinforce the other person's talking. These utterances, we saw in Chapter 5, are represented by Um-hummmm, I see, Yes, or other nonintrusive vocalizations, but even if these are not used, there are effective physical reinforcers, such as head nods and certain facial expressions. Skillful attenders will use both oral and physical reinforcers.

RESTATEMENT. One of the easiest verbal behaviors to learn for effective social interaction, and one that demonstrates that attentive listening has been occurring, is to restate what the other person has said, or the essence of it.

REFLECTION. One step beyond restatement is the powerful device of reflection of feeling. In this skill we have the outward expression of the first modal skill addressed in this section: the capacity to know the perceptions and feelings of another person. There can be no reflection unless there is that more basic skill, and a capacity to sense another's feelings is of little use without the oral behavior of communicating that grasp. Restatement and reflections are both useful for that purpose, with reflection the more powerful skill.

CLARIFICATION. The last of the four skills offered here may include some reflection and restatement, but goes beyond them to join several conversational units together that the other speaker has not put together himself. The intended and often attained effect is a clarification of concepts, events, feelings, and relations among them.

Verbal skills of this kind, along with others, were once proposed and followed as the only form of counselor conference behaviors. Their continued usefulness will be demonstrated when their application by a neophyte counselor results sometimes in a counselee saying with awe and delight that his concerns are now cleared up. Moreover, when other behavior mediation procedures are to be used, to remind us of yet another point established earlier, the counselor employs these kinds of verbal behaviors at the outset and weaves them throughout the warp and woof of all interviews when the counselor judges the presence of a need for them. If they are the only counseling behaviors that high school students learn, they will have learned well. But they will not be the only kind, as this chapter's first section demonstrated. They will learn the more potent procedures of behavior modification, at least of self-application.

A HOMOGENOUS SOCIETY?

Are all youths to be good decision makers? To be self-managers? Are all to have uniform social interaction behaviors? If those questions seem to demand a "yes" in reply, and thus set off reactions of alarm that high school graduates will be carbon-copy, cookie-cutter replicas of each other, there has been an overreading of this chapter's substance, and a forgetting of the rationale for each objective. The competencies proposed in this and the prior chapter will not only not prevent individuality, they will abet it. Idiosyncrasies would be cultivated, as they should be. Those competencies will permit persons to engage more confidently and clearly in those behaviors that are distinctive to them and their emerging style. If their outcome could be any other than that, they would be completely outside the guidance movement, committed as that movement is to the maximization of individuals.

Instead of drifting into the several activities of adulthood, decision-making competencies will cause the individual to become more distinctive, through self-assessment, and to move committedly into areas of adult engagement. Self-management skills guarantee that the individuals will not be the victim of the leveling forces that might operate in society. The individual will have the skills that will permit him to eliminate many behaviors that gnaw away at his energies and that tug him from desired directions. Or, conversely, to establish behaviors needed to activate him toward desired directions when those behaviors are absent, or in too short supply. These two skills are bound to magnify a person's individuality.

For those still not sure that my demurrers are valid, reminder must be made that humans behaviors are shaped by a vastly varied array of psychosocial ecosystems mediated by widely varied neural and brain components. And, as previously noted, further diversity among humans is guaranteed by enrollments in nonpublic schools.

The social competency skills may be the one of the three sets of skills that have some leveling effect, yet there is no common acknowledgment in our society of a view that members of our society should not have common graces. Individuals who are not humanized through their concern for others and not marked by an eagerness for effective social intercourse will be defended by only a few in our society, and those few will not be educators, and particularly not guidance practitioners.

Those who know humans will see no loss of important traits of individuality in these proposals and do see important individual traits strengthened. They will also see the contribution of these traits to the goal of the pursuit of happiness.

REFERENCES

ANDRADE, B. M. *An Experimental Investigation of the Feasibility of Training High School Students to Conduct Facilitative Interviews with Their Peers.* Unpublished doctoral dissertation, University of Maryland, 1972.

ARBUCKLE, DUGALD S. "The School Counselor: Voice of Society?" *Personnel and Guidance Journal*, 1976, *54*, 8, 426–430.[3]

BANDURA, A. "Vicarious and Self-Reinforcement Processes. In R. Glasser (Ed.), *The Nature of Reinforcement*. New York: Academic Press, 1971.

BENJAMIN, A. *The Helping Interview.* Boston: Houghton Mifflin, 1969.

BERENSON, B., CARKHUFF, R., & MYRUS, P. "The Interpersonal Functioning and Training of College Students." *Journal of Counseling Psychology*, 1966, *13* (4), 441–446.

DULANEY, D. J., & EISENBERG, S. *The Counseling Process.* Chicago: Rand McNally, 1972.

GOSHKO, R. "Self-Determined Behavior Change." *Personnel and Guidance Journal*, 1973, *51* (9), 629–632.

KAHN, W. J. "Self-Management: Learning to be Our Own Counselor." *Personnel and Guidance Journal*, in press.

KAHN, W. J., LEIBOWITZ, Z., & LEVIN, L. *Individualized Instructional Program for Self-Management.* Washington, D.C.: Kahn, Leibowitz, and Levin Associates (2737 Devonshire Place, N.W., 20008), 1974.

LEIBOWITZ, Z., & RHOADS, D. "Adolescent Peer Counseling." *The School Counselor*, 1974, *21* (4), 280–284.

MAHONEY, M. J., & THORESON, C. E. "Behavior Self-Control: Power to the Person." *Educational Research*, 1972, *1* (10), 5–7.

MOSHER, R. L., & SPRINTHALL, N. A. "Psychological Education: A Means to Promote Personal Development during Adolescence." *The Counseling Psychologist*, 1971, *2* (4), 3–84.

NYE, L. S. "Client as Counselor: Self-Regulating Strategies." *Personnel and Guidance Journal*, 1973, *51* (10), 711–715.

[3] Arbuckle (1976) provides a look at the history of psychological education. It is an attention-keeping statement, not just for the history of the idea, but also for the personal history Arbuckle offers. To know psychological education is to know more than "best techniques," important as they are. This article by Arbuckle gives us the crucial ideas that are beyond technique.

Rogers, C. R. *Counseling and Psychotherapy.* Boston: Houghton Mifflin, 1942.

Watson, D. L., & Tharp, R. G. *Self-Directed Behavior: Self-Modification for Personal Adjustment.* Monterey, Calif.: Brooks/Cole, 1972.

Zunker, V. G., & Brown, W. "Comparative Effectiveness of Student and Professional Counselors." *Personnel and Guidance Journal,* 1966, *44* (7), 738–743.

12 The Counselor's Role in the Several Domains

THE COUNSELOR AND CAREER DEVELOPMENT

This chapter begins with restating a theme: the guidance movement is concerned with the maximization of individuals. A person's occupational career is a major source of his maximization, an occupation being one of the two axes around which the rest of life rotates, for most persons. A major dedication of guidance resources (persons and time), therefore, is to the domain of career development.

Another theme needs restatement: for all students to attain guidance objectives in this domain, all high school students are brought together in groups to acquire the needed behaviors. The groups' leaders are counselors, the pivotal practitioners on the guidance team, with this activity accounting for about three days of the counselor's weekly time. The other two school days are given over to conferences with individuals, in either the career development domain or in any other domain of concern to the individual for which the counselor has the appropriate strategies for giving assistance. Our attention is first called to the counselor's activities with groups, and in that topic, to consider the question, Why the counselor?

Why the Counselor as Group Leader?

In the cyclical way that certain activities carried on by institutions rise and fall as the favored procedures to attain goals, group procedures in guidance are on the ascendancy currently, having lost ground in prior years. In some cases, such waxing and waning can be accounted for by fadism. Other increases and decreases in popularity of procedures can be attributed to value changes or to new findings of science, among other reasons. The resurgence of group procedures in the career development domain, in my view, represents both a change in values and newer knowledge. The schools' publics now demand that schools do something about the career development of all students, the value change. In addition behavioral science now provides the new knowledge through an accounting of how behavior is acquired and through the technology that brings about the acquisition of needed career development behaviors.

In the past, group procedures within the guidance movement have been led by counselors. Use of group approaches has diminished in recent years, however. Those that have persisted seem to have been directed to the same purposes as individual counseling conferences: psychotherapy. It was natural, therefore, that those kinds of group activities would be under counselors' supervision. Moreover, although past use of group procedures was an economy resulting from a paucity of counselors, that reason no longer holds because of the massive increase in the proportion of counselors to students in the past fifteen years. That increase permitted the actualization of the view that came to be the ideal among many in guidance that guidance = counselors = individual interviews.

Arguments are read and heard, however, for having group activities in career development led by teachers instead of counselors. The position forwarded here is that at most it would be either an activity that counselors share with certain specifically trained teachers, or that only counselors lead such groups.

The argument to support counselor leadership of such groups is threefold. Counselors are trained to do so, whereas teachers are not and, more important, the counselor-student contact in groups brings to each student an occasion to know one counselor. This latter point is buttressed further through the fact that that contact in the group situation permits the counselor to identify students in need of individualized assistance, and to have that kind of assistance naturally flow out of the group setting. It is tenable to hold that a student who has come to know a counselor as a caring, helping (success-producing) person through his experience with the counselor in the group setting is more ready to engage the counselor in individual conferences than is the student to whom an assigned but unmet counselor is only a name over an office door.

The third reason does not readily submit to a brief statement. This reason lies within the nature of how the program of group activities must be run, and that is best understood through describing those activities. Attention to this third reason, then, is set aside until the end of the chapter.

The Content of the Group Experience

There is a scarcity of published programs, particularly programs that are explicitly based on behavior principles, to cause students to acquire behaviors appropriate to career success. One such empirically tested program continues to be used in Gaithersburg High School (Montgomery County, Maryland), however, and will be used here to illustrate.

Reverting to the theme of Chapter 2, we are reminded that in systematic guidance first there is an outcome, a goal, set up for the about-to-be graduated senior to achieve. This goal then is reworked into grade-level goals, and each set of those is further reworked into performance or behavior objectives.

TENTH-GRADE CAREER DEVELOPMENT OBJECTIVES. Repeated here in Table 6 are the objectives that tenth-grade students are to attain.

THE READYING ACTIVITIES. After goals and performance objectives have been set up, the next step in the guidance declension is to lay out the activities experienced by all students through which each will be readied to carry out the performances.

The array of activities below can be called a syllabus or an outline of the course content, if use of those more conventional terms is preferred. They were titled "readying activities" because that term fits the systems concept better. It takes the focus away from the activity as an important end in itself and places the focus on the objectives, which are the end. Readying activities, then, take their appropriate stance as means to the ends.

These readying activities fall into the modes shown in Table 7.

A detailed report about the first mode, the occupations game tasks, will bring together in operational fashion a number of principles. The game tasks' purpose is to build information-seeking behaviors and to provide students with knowledge of resources to be used throughout the program of readying activities and, more important, throughout their occupational careers.

These first game tasks are done by groups of a few students each, such as five groups of four students, and should be carried out either in a room that adjoins the Career Center or in the Center itself. The illustrations that follow represent use of an adjoining room setting. The importance of the setting's location will be made apparent.

The activities start in the Center, however. The counselor shows the locations of the copies of the Dictionary of Occupational Titles (DOT), Occupational Outlook Handbooks (OOH), and the file cabinets containing brief occupational descriptions. Even in this activity behavior principles are followed. The counselor draws attention to the discriminative stimuli that permit rapid identification of the resource. This is the appearance of

Table 6: Guidance goals and performance objectives, career development domain, 10th grade.

A. Students will begin to acquire occupational information-seeking behaviors
 1. Given a continuing rate of occupational stimulus, the student shall increase his rate of seeking occupational information
 2. Given the need for a type of occupational information, the student shall retrieve that information from the school's career information center with sureness and accuracy
B. Students will know the elements of the decision-making process, and how those elements are processed in making occupational decisions
 1. a. Given a hypothetical case, the student shall describe orally or in writing what information the decider needs, where the information can be found, and will name the elements of the process to be used in making an occupational decision.
    b. Given the need to choose a program of courses for the 11th grade, the student shall demonstrate decision-making skills by
       (1) choosing the 11th grade courses which accord best with her/his values and occupational objectives, and by
       (2) listing alternative courses if 1st choice courses are not available
    c. identify one hypothetical optimal occupation
    d. identify five other occupations justified by the decision-making process
C. Students will know such specific information about themselves as is required by the decision-making process
 1. Given a request for a written or oral report, the student shall
    a. identify in terms of stanines her/his level of
       (1) learning ability
       (2) achievement in
          (a) vocabulary
          (b) reading
          (c) language use
          (d) arithmetic concept use
       (3) achievement in class work as represented by her/his grade point average, and her/his
       (4) nonverbal IQ
    b. identify her/his aptitude code level in the vocational aptitudes measured by the GATB
    c. identify career-related personal characteristics other than those in b
    d. identify, through the GATB, occupations for which she/he has aptitudes
    e. identify the findings of a vocational interest inventory

(The goals are designated by capital letters, performance objectives by arabic numerals.)

Table 7: Readying activities, 10th-grade career development objectives

Sessions	Content
1, 2	Occupational information game tasks
3	Orientation to Career Information Center
4	Job-O administration
5	Job-O interpretation; practice occupational information-seeking behaviors related to findings
6, 7	Careers, life style development; actualization
8–10	Occupational information game tasks, cont'd: OOH, job briefs, based on Job-O findings
11–14	Administration of the General Aptitude Test Battery (GATB)
15–18	Decision making; life style versus values; "When I grow up" activity
19–25	Occupational information: clusters/families of occupations—A/V reports prepared by student teams
26–29	Postsecondary school information game tasks
30–35	GATB interpretations
36, 37	Other data about students from cumulative record
38–40	Occupational exploration based on data about self, and following decision-making process
40–45	Presentations by heads of academic departments about occupational relationships of interest and abilities manifested in their subject areas; choice of 11th-grade courses (by Fall group of 10th-grade students)

the books' spines, and any distinguishing feature of the briefs' file cabinet. Different students are asked to come up and touch each resource after all have been identified, while the seated students are asked to look at the resource as the student is moving up to touch it.

After this five-minute activity the students return to the room adjoining the Center and the first game task is ready to begin.

For this a large chart has been put on a wall giving the numerals and explanatory terms of the Data, People, Things code that is part of the description of every occupation in the DOT. That code is shown in Table 8.

On the table of each group is a card with three numerals on it, a decimal point preceding each set of numerals. It is announced that the student (or team of four) who first states the meaning of that set of three numerals will win first prize. No attention is called to the wall chart as students puzzle over the meaning. After approximately a minute of puzzling (and of facetious comments from students!), a cue is appropriate, such as "every one of you can know the meaning of that numeral; there is something in this room to tell you."

Table 8: The data, people, things code.

	Data	People	Things
0	Synthesizing	Mentoring	Setting-up
1	Coordinating	Negotiating	Precision working
2	Analyzing	Instructing	Operating, controlling
3	Compiling	Supervising	Driving, operating
4	Computing	Diverting	Manipulating
5	Copying	Persuading	Tending
6	Comparing	Speaking, signaling	Feeding, offbearing
7	No significant	Serving	Handling
8	relationship	No significant relationship	No significant relationship

In relatively short order one student says, in effect, "It's what's on that chart up there." Because that is not yet the answer, however, the counselor silently signs for further comment, reserving words for use as social reinforcers. Experience shows that one student will give the full meaning of the three numerals, that is, will give the descriptive terms for each of the three numerals. First prize is awarded, which in the instance of one group leader is simply a 3-by-5-inch card neatly labeled "First Prize."

Attention of all is now brought to the chart, and the words briefly explained, asking students to name any occupation they know that calls for the particular relationship to data, people, or things. My experience shows that tenth-graders can rarely name an occupation for any single code numeral, even as a guess, let alone with accuracy.

Next, 3-by-5-inch cards are distributed to each student. Each is asked to think of an occupation of interest—one about which each might wish to know more—and to then write three numerals representing each student's judgment about the data, people, things (DPT) code for that occupation.

After each has written his code, two students from each team are asked to go to the Career Center and return with a copy of DOT Vol. I. Because the first behavior related to acquiring information is to move toward a source of information when an occupational stimulus is offered, throughout the course and particularly during the occupational game task activities students go to the Career Center to get and return materials. This is carried even to the extreme of apparent inefficiency in asking students to bring a resource from the Center to the room, to return it after a brief use and bring another resource, then sending other students to return the second resource and to bring back the first one. Through repetition of this resource fetching and returning behavior, with social reinforcement frequently given, a behavior history in seeking out information is built. Proximity to the Career Center is necessary so that the frequent trips to the Center to bring and return resources are not aversive nor disruptive to school order. If the game climate is maintained and social reinforcers used, the jaunts to the Center are not only not aversive but pleasant. ("Each table send next its most intelligent person to the Center to bring back a copy of . . ." or "This time ask the person least likely to run away to bring . . .")

When copies of the DOT Vol. 1 are at each desk, pairs of students are told to look up the full occupation code for the occupation each named and write it underneath their guessed DPT code. Another first prize is awarded to the student whose guessed DPT code is closest to the actual DPT portion of the full code. Students whose guessed DPT code missed by a mile are not singled out or criticized. Behavior is acquired out of successful experiences, so only success is attended to, except that the group is told that those who were not close in their guesses will learn later how to be more accurate.

The counselor then asks students to look in their copies of DOT Vol. 1 at the place where the meaning of the first three numerals of the DOT code is explained. One student is asked to give full code for the occupation he named for this task. The other students are asked to give the meaning of the first three digits. The first to do so receives a first prize (only first prizes are distributed); these prizes can be droll, such as a paper clip, a hole reinforcer, or the customary primary one, a piece of candy). This activity continues with Vol. 2 being sent for, and discussion of the meaning of the DPT portion of the code, including examination of that section of DOT Vol. 2 wherein the descriptors of the DPT portion of the code are defined (p. 649), and by student examination of other features of Vol. 2 as the counselor points them out. Two other students from each table return the DOTs to the Center and are asked to bring copies of the Occupational Outlook Handbook (OOH).

On their return two new occupations from among those nominated by each student are selected at each table. Students are asked to find those occupations in the OOH and to find in the descriptions what outlook in numbers of workers needed in those occupations is given there. A first prize again is given to the team that first finds the data, but the activity continues until all have completed it. Then each table is asked to send one student to the briefs file in the Center to bring a copy of the brief for one of the two occupations, and another student to bring (again!) a copy of Vol. 1 of the DOT. The team examines the outlook section in the brief, compares the figure found there with the one found in the OOH, and compares the definition of the occupation in Vol. 1 of the DOT with the description given in both the brief and the OOH.

COMMENT. The activities so far and those that follow are planned to shape the students' behaviors into seeking information from varied sources and into a systematic analysis of information acquired, about which they made notes. The activities seek to put these behaviors into a chain, so that given an occupational stimulus a student goes for information, and follows a chain of other behaviors until his objective is reached.

The purpose of the gaming approach may be obvious, but had better be stated: dealing with occupational information can be nauseatingly dull. It carries with it no intrinsic reinforcers for tenth-grade youths (nor for students in counselor education programs), yet, if the needed behaviors are not acquired well before a student's senior year, they will not be there for the student when he does need them, and when seeking and analyzing information might have acquired reinforcing properties. The program of activities, therefore, has to depend on contrived reinforcers to cause students to acquire those behaviors each will need to be an independent, self-directing person in an area where each must perform, and wherein the manner of performance is of life-long significance.

The activities might have started from a different entry point instead of from the DOT. Two arguments favor using the DOT, however. For one thing, the data are precise and small. For another, students' early experience with the DPT portion of the DOT code establishes the fact that occupations differ as to "personal" characteristics required, and that that difference can be systematically, somewhat precisely, yet simply described. Later in Vol. 2 of the DOT they will learn about a more complex scheme for describing worker trait characteristics, and that will be explained later still by the aptitude patterns they will see about occupations appropriate for them as a result of their being measured by the General Aptitude Test Battery. For the outset, however, in accord with behavior principles, the knowledge called for is the most simple it can be, and the behavior called for revolves around that simple knowledge element.

ACTIVITIES CONTINUED. The next activity causes each student to repeat successfully essential behaviors acquired in prior activities. With all resources returned to the center, a sheet with the occupations on Table 9 is distributed.

As may be expected, student reaction to this list is a mixture of amusement and disbelief (adults are not far behind students in those reactions).[1] After each team of four has had time to read the list, each team is asked to nominate five occupations from the list. Each team then is asked to send

---

[1] I generated this list by reading all occupational titles in Vol. 1 of the DOT for use in the game-task described. The more obvious purpose of having this list is to arouse student interest in the occupations area, thus to increase motivation for the particular task. A not so obvious purpose is served by having a list of occupations of which most never heard, thus building the knowledge that there are many occupations in our society, but that they know about only a few. A defensible occupational decision for most youth requires knowledge of many occupations among which to choose. Other game-tasks cause the students to look over extensive lists of occupations, and this particular list is but an additional source of knowledge in this area.

Table 9: Occupations with unusual titles.

Back Washer	London Shrinking	Supercalendar Operator
Back Padder	Machine Operator	Take-off Man
Balcony Man	Mashing Hand	Tension Man
Ballyhoo Man	Milliskeener	Tin-whiz Machine
Bat-in Man	Monstrosity	Operator
Batter-out	Mooner	Toe Pounder
Bead Flipper	Mother Tester	Tooth Hobber
Belly Inspector	Mud Boss	Top & Bottom Man
Bessemer Bottom Maker	Odorization Man	Tromper
Bit-top-off Man	Pot Expediter	Tuscher
Blind Hooker	Profile Trimmer	Twin-Beam Clicker
Body Silencer	Puff Ironer	Upper-Doubler
Booking Prizer	Puritan Vamper	Upsetter
Bottom Duster	Sagger Soak	Vamper
Bottom Feller	Save-all Operator	Veil Dotter
Bowker	Shill	Viking Man
Cant Setter	Shop Cooper	Warm-in Boy
Can Turner	Shot Dropper	Wesand Piler
Car Chaser	Siderographer	Wet-char Beltman
Carney	Sinter Feeder	Wharfinger
Chef de Froid	Skoog Machine	Wigan Cutter
Crack-off Man	Operator	Wink Cutter Operator
Dinger	Slubber Doffer	Zanjero
Donkey Puncher	Slunk Skimmer	Zoogler
Dope Pourer	Smash Hand	Zye Mounter
End Frazer	Smutter	
Face Cutter	Snath Finisher	
Fettler	Soft Roll Try-Out Man	
Fine Hairer	Spare Boy	
Flenser	Spinning Bath	
Foreign Title Breaker	Patrolman	
Frickertron Checker	Spiral Runner	
Frothing Man	Spring-up Man	
Gambreler	Sprue Knocker	
Gandydancer	Squeak-Rattle &	
Grizzly Worker	Leak Man	
Hand Shaker	Starch Crab	
Heddles Tier	Steepman	
Hogshead Cooper	Sticker-Up	
Hop Strainer	Stitchdown-	
Irish Moss Operator	Threadlaster	
Jigger Crown Pouncer	Stogie Packer	
Kier Boiler	Strike Off Man	
Larryman	Stull Hewer	
Last Chalker	Sucker Machine	
Lay Down Boy	Operator	

one (or two) persons to the Center for the now-familiar DOT Vol. 1, and on return to look up by pairs the codes and descriptions of the five occupations nominated by the team. The full DOT codes of all five occupations are to be written on a 3-by-5-inch card. Each team selects the one most bizarre-sounding occupation from among the five it selected, gives its name to the group, describes it, and gives the DOT code.

COMMENT. No new behaviors are developed in this activity. The bizarre-sounding occupations are within the game ambience, and students' curiosity about them is motivation for learning more about them. The behaviors they follow are ones they have practiced before: emit (thus practice) the psychomotoric behavior pattern of going to get occupational information, and in an information resource, establish a basic classification of that occupation both as to its status in the organized work world (the first three DOT digits), and the worker requirements relative to data, people, and things called for by that occupation. The oral reports frequently called for (with first prizes and social reinforcers occasionally administered) establish the behaviors of talking about occupations. The outcome of acquiring reading-about behaviors was apparent in the activities, but it is hypothesized that it will be useful to acquire the behavior of talking about occupations. A lot of the table work both in pairs and the teams of four required students to talk about what they were reading in addition to writing.

ACTIVITIES CONTINUED. Only one more activity will be used for illustration of these information game tasks wherein they are not directed to student interests, but to establish behavior patterns to be used later around matters of student interest.

A delegation is sent to the center for copies of DOT Vol. 2. Each student is asked to look at the DPT code chart on the wall and to write on a 3-by-5-inch card the code each thinks best describes his level of performance, ability, or preference related to date, people, and things. Setting aside the cards, the counselor asks each team to follow in Vol. 2 while he leafs through it. Then students' attention is directed to pages 217–223 wherein can be found twenty-two major groups of occupations broken down into over one hundred more specific groups with the DPT code given for each. Students are asked to find any specific occupational groups that match the DPT code each wrote on his 3-by-5-inch card. Then each is shown how to go to the subsequent pages to find a full description of the worker traits required by occupations in those areas.

If, for example, a student placed on his card the DPT code .281, assessing that to be an accurate picture of his DPT preferences, consultation with pages 217–223 of Vol. 2 would show that one of the several groups of occupations that was coded with that DPT numeral was drafting and related work. Turning to the page given with that occupation, page 377, he would come to this entry.

In the earlier leaf-through of Vol. 2, students learned where the section was (Appendix B in Vol. 2) that explained the several codes under the Qualifications Profile found on these worker trait summaries. They are reminded of that place so each can translate the codes, now that he has before him an occupational group in which he is interested. After there has been sufficient time for students to translate the codes and study the full entry, and to talk among themselves about what they are finding, a few students are solicited to volunteer a description of the occupation each chose and their reactions to what they read.

COMMENT. In this activity students again practice information-seeking behaviors and also acquire an essential cognition: that a prior process, moving from occupation to person, can be run in reverse, that is, can move from a description of a person to find an occupation appropriate for that description. They also learn that there is a more complex way to describe the personal characteristics called out by an occupation than just the DPT manner of description.

From my experience in leading groups of tenth-grade students in these and other game tasks that ready them to perform the tenth-grade behavioral objectives, the activity reported above appears to be the one that marks a transition from students just playing games with contrived extrinsic reinforcers, and acquiring valuable behaviors thereby, to an activity that has its own reinforcers. It appears to be the moment through which some students learn that the organization of the world of work has meaning for them and their futures, and that seeking out information about that organized occupational world is of use to them and thus of importance.[2]

LATER USE OF GAME BEHAVIORS. One illustration is offered from among the other activities engaged in by the tenth-grade group to demonstrate the later applicability of these information-seeking behaviors; thus the reason for starting off this group program with occupational game tasks.

At session 4, the record presented earlier shows that students respond to a relatively new occupational selection device known as Job-O.[3] This instrument yields one or more occupations appropriate for the student, ac-

[2] A more complete array of information-seeking behavior-building game tasks will be issued by the U.S. Office of Education. The American Institutes for Research is preparing a number of training modules through a four-university consortium under a USOE contract. One of these modules is on the use of these game tasks.

[3] Job-O is published by CFKR Career Materials, PO Box 4, Belmont, California, 94002.

Table 10: Excerpt from *Dictionary of Occupational Titles*, vol. II

Drafting and Related Work
.181–.281

Work Performed

Work activities in this group primarily involve the translation of ideas, rough sketches, specifications, and calculations of engineers, architects, and designers into complete and accurate working plans for use in building or manufacturing.

Worker Requirements

An occupationally significant combination of: Ability and interest necessary to understand and apply technical knowledge and theoretical principles involved in drafting, engineering, mathematics, and related fields; ability to visualize spatial relationships, perceive slight differences in visual matter, and work with detail; and finger dexterity.

Clues for Relating Applicants and Requirements

Success in mechanical drawing and shop courses in high school.
Expressed preference for working around mechanical, architectural, or similar objects.
Demonstrated skill in drawing.

Training and Methods of Entry

Graduation from vocational or technical high school is frequently the minimum educational requirement for entry into the field. Many employers require additional training, such as that received in a technical institute, junior or community college, extension division of a university, correspondence school, or a college offering special 2-year programs. Training also may be obtained through 3- or 4-year apprenticeship programs or through on-the-job programs combined with part-time schooling. Courses include mathematics, physical sciences, mechanical drawing, standard methods of lettering, and tracing.

Related Classifications

Art Work (.081) p. 232
Engineering and Related Work (.187) p. 381
Engineering Research and Design (.081) p. 371
Technical Work, Engineering and Related Fields (.181:.281) p. 379

Qualifications Profile

GED: 4 5
SVP: 7
Apt.: GVN SPQ KFM EC
     2 3 2 1 2 3 2 2 3 5 4
              2   3 3

Int: 1 7 9
Temp: 0 Y
Phys. Dem: S

Table 10. (Continued)

00 } 01 } 001.	ARCHITECTURE AND ENGINEERING Architecture		DIE-DESIGNER APPRENTICE (mach. shop.) ENGINEERING ASSISTANT, MECHANICAL EQUIPMENT (profess. & kin.)		DRAFTSMAN, HYDRAULIC (ship & boat bldg. & rep.) DRAFTSMAN, SHEET METAL (ship & boat bldg. & rep.) DRAFTSMAN, SHIP ENGINEERING (profess. & kin.)
001.281	DRAFTSMAN, ARCHITECTURAL (profess. & kin.)	007.281	DRAFTSMAN, MECHANICAL (profess. & kin.)		
002.	Aeronautical Engineering		DRAFTSMAN, CASTINGS (profess. & kin.)		Drafting and Related Work
002.281	DESIGN DRAFTSMAN, RAM-JET ENGINE (profess. & kin.) DRAFTSMAN, AERONAUTICAL (profess. & kin.) ENGINEERING CHECKER (aircraft mfg.)		DRAFTSMAN, PATENT (profess. & kin.) DRAFTSMAN, TOOL DESIGN (profess. & kin.) LAY-OUT MAN AND CHECKER (profess. & kin.)	017. 017.281	AUTO-BODY DESIGNER (auto. mfg.) AUTO-BODY LAY-OUT DRAFTSMAN (auto. mfg.) CABLE-LAY-OUT MAN (tel. & tel.)
003.	Electrical Engineering	010. 010.281	Mining and Petroleum Engineering DRAFTSMAN, GEOLOGICAL (petrol. production) DRAFTSMAN, DIRECTIONAL SURVEY (petrol production) DRAFTSMAN, GEOPHYSICAL (petrol, production)		DESIGN DRAFTSMAN, ELECTROMECHANISMS (profess. & kin.) DETAILER (profess. & kin.) AUTO-BODY-DESIGN DETAILER (auto. mfg.) DETAIL MAN, FURNITURE (profess. & kin.) DRAFTSMAN, DETAIL (profess. & kin.) DRAFTSMAN, SHIP DETAIL (profess. & kin.) DRAFTSMAN APPRENTICE (profess. & kin.)
003.281	DRAFTSMAN, ELECTRICAL (profess. & kin.) DRAFTSMAN, RELAY (light, heat, & power) DRAFTSMAN, ELECTRONIC (profess. & kin.) ESTIMATOR AND DRAFTSMAN (light, heat, & power)				
005. 005.281	Civil Engineering DESIGNER, HIGHWAYS (gov. ser.) DRAFTSMAN, CIVIL (profess. & kin.) DRAFTSMAN, STRUCTURAL (profess. & kin.)	014. 014.281	DRAFTSMAN, MINE (mining & quarrying) Marine Engineering DRAFTSMAN, MARINE (profess. & kin.) DRAFTSMAN, HULL (profess. & kin.)		
007. 007.181	Mechanical Engineering DIE DESIGNER (mach. shop) DIE CHECKER (mach. shop) I				

300

017.281 Con.	DRAFTSMAN, BLACK AND WHITE (profess. & kin.)
	DRAFTSMAN, COMMERCIAL (profess. & kin.)
	DRAFTSMAN, HEATING AND VENTILATING (profess & kin.)
	DRAFTSMAN, MAP (profess. & kin.)
	DRAFTSMAN, OIL AND GAS (petrol. production; petrol. refin.)
	DRAFTSMAN, PLUMBING (profess. & kin.)
	DRAFTSMAN, REFRIGERATION (profess. & kin.)
	DRAFTSMAN, TOPOGRAPHICAL (profess. & kin.)
	MULTIPLEX-PROJECTION TOPOGRAPHER (profess. & kin.)
	TECHNICAL ILLUSTRATOR (profess & kin.)
	TRACER (any ind.)
018.	**Surveying and Related Work**
018.181	SURVEYOR, TOPOGRAPHICAL PHOTOGRAPHY (profess. & kin.)
018.281	EDITOR, MAP (profess. & kin.)
	MOSAICIST (profess. & kin.)
	PHOTOGRAMMETRIST (profess. & kin.)
019.	**Architecture and Engineering, n.e.c.**
019.181	AUTO-BODY-DESIGN CHECKER (auto. mfg.)
019.281	DRAFTSMAN, LANDSCAPE (profess. & kin.)
	OFFICE-LAY-OUT-SERVICE MAN (ret. tr.; whole, tr.)
24	**MISCELLANEOUS CLERICAL WORK**
249.	Miscellaneous Clerical Work, n.e.c.
249.281	DRAFTING CLERK (clerical)

301

companied by a caution from the counselor. They are urged to view the results as but a current indicator of what would be appropriate were they to have to decide on an occupation now, but these results may not be anywhere like those reached two, four, or more years hence. In short, they are cautioned to view occupations produced by this—or any—inventory given at their ages as one around which to practice decision making.

Attainment of the Job-O results leads each to go to the Career Center to seek information, starting with the DOT volumes, obtaining data from the OOH, and seeking an additional picture from an occupational brief.

OUTCOMES OF OTHER READYING ACTIVITIES

Other readying activities result in students acquiring an introductory level of decision-making skill, including a detailed analysis of self as related to occupational decisions (the GATB experience provides this) and behaviors related to postsecondary education information, for which game tasks are again used.

ARE TENTH-GRADE OBJECTIVES REACHED?

Yes. The program of readying activities was tested under experimental conditions and found to produce students who attained tenth-grade guidance objectives in the career development domain at a high statistically significant level in contrast to tenth-graders who did not experience the program.

IS THIS A COUNSELOR'S FUNCTION?

In addressing this question at the beginning of the chapter, note was made that there would be a third reason offered through descriptions of the activities as to why the counselor, from among all educators, is the appropriate person to conduct these group readying activities.

If the alternative to counselors' leading such groups is for teachers to do so, and, if that is to mean appending some portion of these activities to the teachers' subjects, that is, interrupting normal subjective treatment to engage some of these readying activities in the teacher's classrooms, then the difficulties can be apparent from the nature of the activities described previously. Training of teachers in behavior principles and coordinating their use of the Career Center and its resources would be a horrendous task, even if some teachers were willing to undertake this additional function at the price of subject-matter coverage.

But what of the student? The career guidance function would be disjointed. If a student were to wish a counseling interview, the counselor would not know the nature of the student's approach to occupational decision making, nor would he have any sense of how much of the needed information-seeking and decision-making behaviors would have been acquired.

A fourth reason for making this a counselor function needs to be added. The attainment of guidance objectives is more the responsibility of the school's full-time guidance practitioners than that of teachers. It is the guidance practitioners who are charged with the development of readying activities leading to the attainment of performance objectives. The responsible parties should be those who have an intimate relationship with the activities so as to evaluate their effectiveness and cause their modification. With their resources and training, counselors are prepared to develop, conduct, evaluate, and quickly modify readying activities of this sort.

But why not other members of the guidance team? The career development technician has multiple other functions, as Appendix A shows, and lacks the training needed to conduct activities of this kind. The behavior specialist is needed for practice at his level of expertise, a level desperately needed by a minority of students. Other technicians and specialists are not qualified in either time or training. Is it the counselor by default? No, by deliberation, because it is the counselor who is prepared to carry out strategies affecting the positive development of all youths, and there is no greater place to apply these strategies than in the career development domain.

Individual Interviews

Group activities do not obviate individual conferences between student and counselor in occupational or educational decision matters. In fact, they are imperative for most students. Being imperative, they will more likely be held because, as noted earlier, the group activity will bring student and counselor into frequent contact. It will be not only easier for the student to accept the offer of an individual conference, but the counselor can readily identify the student who could profit by a private conference.

A comparison brought up from an earlier chapter serves to sum up. There are two approaches to acquiring a suit of clothes: have a tailor custom-make one, or buy a ready-made one. For the former a man is measured by the tailor, the suit is made, and it fits perfectly. Cost: $300. Male body shapes have been extensively measured, and clothing manufacturers, in consequence, are able to make up suits that will fit in general the several different body sizes and shapes. To purchase a ready-made suit, a man puts on the suit that is closest to his size and shape. That suit may fit perfectly, but more than likely needs small adjustments, such as in sleeve or trouser length. To have these made, a tailor is called in to take the measurements. Once those adjustments are made, the suit fits almost like a tailor-made one. Cost: $100.

In the career development area, the common needs of students are known; thus the ready-made group approach. For some students, the outcomes of the group experience is a perfect fit. For many others, however, minor adjustments are needed, for which the counselor serves as the tailor.

If a school does not employ a group approach to the common needs, counselors must tailor-make each occupational suit. The ineffectiveness of this approach, which is the conventional one, has been recorded at numerous places in this book. It is ineffective partly because counselors commonly have not been trained to establish decision-making behaviors in youth. On the youths' side of this ineffectiveness, there has been no sharp awareness by them of their need for counseling in this domain. Thus they do not seek out the counselor's assistance. When the need is acknowledged and the motivation is strong enough to seek out counselor assistance, the minute proportion of students who do so approach such conferences ignorant of how best to use a counselor's help. As long as this conventional manner of delivery of occupational guidance persists, there will be dissatisfaction among students and parents as to the amount and quality of services received. Even if the new generation of counselors is knowledgeable of how to cause students to acquire information-seeking behaviors and other decision-making skills, and even if all students sought out conferences with counselors in the career domain, carrying out procedures common to the needs of all youths on a one-by-one basis is a staggering demonstration of inefficiency. It would be the same as stating to students, all of whom are required to take English: "You have an assigned English teacher who has an office in the English department; each of you make an appointment for a private conference to learn English."

Individual counseling conferences during or subsequent to the group activity are for refinements of what is covered in the group experience and thus do not differ in substance or procedures from those of the group activity. If a school does not employ group procedures in this domain, and the counselor is knowledgeable of the procedures that result in students' acquiring the knowledge and skill outcomes stipulated in performance objectives, then for each student who seeks counselor assistance, the counselor conducts a one-person course of the kind represented in Table 7.

THE COUNSELOR AND OTHER DOMAINS

The counselor's functions in the career development domain already reported demonstrated the primary characteristic of the counselor as differentiated from other practitioners on the guidance team. We saw there the counselor as a strategist, one who causes students to acquire those behaviors identified by both students and the adult population as needed by youth for successful coping with society.

As strategist the counselor serves a similar developmental function (as opposed to a corrective, remedial, or therapeutic function) in the two other domains that are given in this volume as modes of guidance concern: self-management and interpersonal or social competency. The setting for the application of counselor strategies is the same as in the career development area: group experiences for all, accompanied or followed by individual conferences for some.

SELF-MANAGEMENT. The counselor, assuming his knowledgeability of behavior principles, can generate materials for group experiences in this area, or he can use the materials prepared by others, such as those mentioned earlier prepared by Kahn, Leibowitz, and Levin (1974).

The essence of this activity is to teach students a few essential principles of behavior, how to pick out behaviors they wish to alter, how to observe and record their present level of behaviors, and, through application of behavior principles, how to modify any behavior chosen as target for this course. The general outcome of skill in this domain, to repeat, is to result in persons who can manage their own behaviors and thus not only be independent of the need to have the assistance of others but also, because they are knowledgeable about behavior control, be attentive in situations where others may seek to control their behavior deviously and harmfully. The latter is a secondary benefit; the primary one is a person who, in figurative terms, can take the reins of his destiny in his own hands and thus create for himself that kind of life he wishes to lead by doing the things he wishes to do and not doing the things he wishes to avoid.

SOCIAL COMPETENCY. Although defined in Chapter 2, this area can profit from a redefinition, starting with what it is not. It does not include social graces (how to set the table, write invitations, dress for the occasion, and the like) nor, and more emphatically not, is it training in how to manipulate and exploit others.

What it does cover comes from statements of youths' concerns repeated in surveys over the years. The two consistently pressing concerns of youth have been in the career area and in the matter of relationships with peers, and, to a lesser degree, with parents. Relationships are conveyed primarily through the oral-aural dimension, as we saw elsewhere, and the dominant characteristics of a good relationship, of good interpersonal experience, are found in the quality of communication. Communication skill, we also saw earlier, was subsumed in this text under the title "facilitative interview," and this, then, is exactly what is taught in this domain: how to be an attentive listener, how to identify and reflect feeling and otherwise convey empathy. Fortunately training materials are easier to generate in this area than in self-management and are also recorded in the several references relating to peer counseling given in Chapter 3.

THE COMPLETE GROUP PROGRAM

It will be assumed that guidance objectives in these latter two domains will be set up and defined in performance terms. The readying activities were roughly identified in the prior two sections. These, added to the career development activities to which greater exposition was accorded, constitute the semester's activities of each school year for the three high school years. The three topics are the same for each year, but there are more advanced objectives to attain in each year, and therefore more advanced readying activities. At the end of the senior year, students will meet the school system's educational goals, at least so far as the guidance program's responsibility for them. The program of guidance activities in groups will contribute most to their being independent decision makers who will be able to manage their own behaviors to their satisfaction, and who will have personally and socially satisfying interpersonal communication skills.

REFERENCES

Dictionary of Occupational Titles, Vols. I and II. Washington, D.C.: Government Printing Office, 1965.

KAHN, W. Jr., LEIBOWITZ, Z., & LEVIN, L. *An Individualized Instructional Program in Self-Management for High School Students.* Washington, D.C.: Kahn, Leibowitz, and Levin Associates (2737 Devonshire Place, N.W., 20008), 1974.

*Suggested Additional Reading,
Self-Management*

O'LEARY, K. D., and WILSON, G. T. *Behavior Therapy: Application and Outcome.* Englewood Cliffs, N.J.: Prentice-Hall, 1975.

MAHONEY, M. J., and THORESON, C. E., *Behavioral Self-Control.* New York: Holt, Rinehart and Winston, 1974.

THORESON, C. E., and MAHONEY, M. J., *Self-Control: Power to the Person.* San Francisco: Brooks-Cole, 1974.

13 Appraisal Principles and Procedures

PURPOSES

Whatever occurs is nomogenic; that is, its origins are scientifically lawful and its continued existence is lawful. Thus all behavior is lawful, including human behavior. Disorganized behavior is accounted for by the same precepts that explain the existence of its opposite, integrated or mentally healthful behavior. As with the behavior of individuals, the behaviors of collections of individuals, called societies, are lawful too. As a person's behaviors can disintegrate, so can societies'. Both healthy societies and disintegrated societies represent the functioning of laws of nature.

Because of the nomogenic nature of individual and social behaviors, civilizations and societies have developed some control over their lives, although mostly by accident. Individuals have exercised some of the same control over their lives too, although only a little. Now that principles controlling the behaviors of societies and the individual are known, however, knowledgeable persons can mediate societies' behaviors to some degree and their own and others' behaviors to a large degree. To do the former requires some detailed knowledge of the society in addition to knowing the principles by which societies form, develop, are maintained, are changed, and disintegrate. In parallel fashion, to mediate one's own or others' behaviors requires some descriptive knowledge about an individual's specific behaviors in addition to knowledge of behavior principles.

This knowledge of a behavior or pattern of behaviors, this effort to accurately describe, is what is meant by appraisal, for which the synonym "assessment" will also be used.

Assessment in schools is carried out to assist individual students and for research. Sometimes the use of appraisal data for assistance to individuals is bland and indirect, such as in measuring how well a student behaves in use of mathematical symbols and, in consequence of that assessment, placing him in section B of Math 101 instead of section A. At other times the assistance given is vital and direct, as in helping a youth plan an occupational career. These instances illustrate the two overlapping needs and uses of appraisal data and procedures: those for the general instructional outcomes of the school, and those used to enhance the development of each student, the latter being the guidance function of education.

The use of appraisal procedures for guidance purposes results in the greater use of student records and thus deserves greater specification. The appraisal procedure begins by first noting that every person accurately knows a portion of his own characteristics—is aware of behavior patterns described by such terms as abilities, achievements, likes, dislikes. Persons can also be mistaken about their own characteristics. A first way to define the function of appraisal procedures in guidance programs, then, is to say that they cause persons to increase their accurate knowledge of themselves and conversely to eliminate inaccurate knowledge.

Some persons see cause-and-effect or interactive relationships among certain of the characteristics they know about themselves such as "my hypersensitiveness to criticism, which I acquired from the way my parents treated me, causes me difficulties in keeping friends." At the same time those persons might not see relationships among other characteristics. The definition of the purpose of appraisal as equipping a person with accurate self-knowledge is now expanded to include causing persons to learn relationships among characteristics when they are ignorant of such relationships.

Many persons can see the significances of some of their characteristics, known individually or in relationship with other characteristics, for present behaviors and for the immediate and long-range future. Those same persons or others, however, may not be able to see those kinds of significances for other characteristics or patterns of them. The complete way to state the purpose of appraisal, then, is to say that it is intended to result in persons' being better able to cope with the present and to plan for the future because appraisal provides accurate knowledge of personal characteristics, the relationship between them, and the significance for the present and the future of these characteristics and interrelationships.

APPRAISAL BASED ON BEHAVIOR PRINCIPLES

In the approximately fifty years since appraisal procedures were introduced and became rooted in public education, there has been continuous growth in the content of assessment, but no clear direction for those changes because in all those years the guidance movement has had a variety of disciplinary roots, none of which were scientific. The recent availability of informing principles from the science of behavior now provides the single, scientific disciplinary base for the guidance movement and thus for appraisal. The future portends a great change in assessment content and procedures as guidance practices conform with scientific principles.

Chapter 4 reported that a theory is a systematic accounting for observed, natural phenomena. Thus a theory results in a series of procedures that accord with the theory and at the same time prohibit other operations or procedures. Historically guidance procedures have not been based on a theory of behavior science because until recently there were so few interrelated postulates established by the science of behavior. Guidance practices were based partly on the metaphorical, poetic, prescientific accountings of behavior, such as the psychoanalytic theory of behavior, and in some instances appraisal procedures were developed that congrued with such theory. Chapter 4 also informed us that proponents of the single most influential theory to dominate the guidance movement for a quarter-century, a theory compatible with psychoanalytic theory, either disclaimed that appraisal by standardized instruments was necessary, or at best was of minimal value, a view also in accord with psychoanalytic theory.

The major change in procedures of appraisal when applied to guidance purposes, which has emanated from behavior principles, is the subprinciple of limiting appraisal to assessment of a particular behavior or behavior pattern of a student, and primarily only when that student wishes to mediate that behavior. One exception to that restriction appears when school administrators are obligated to place students in class sections, an action for which students are not necessarily consulted, or when descriptive research must be carried out. The assessment principle of parsimony regarding studying students differs from the opposite practice in those schools wherein school officials and counselors take pride in the large amount of information collected about students. "We really know our students; look at the size of our cumulative records!"

Given the nondisciplinary base of guidance procedures in the past, there is nothing to be gained by faulting schools for the improper procedures they carried out in seeking to do well by their students. The non-standardized assessments that packed such cumulative records were appropriate to the psychoanalytic and other prescientific positions that diffused guidance practices up to the present. After all, the psychoanalytic accounting for behavior requires seeking out what is behind a behavior, any behavior being but an external (observable) symptom of a buried, hidden, or unconscious dynamic—this dynamic being the *real* matter to be sought out by appraisal. To truly know a high school youth, on those bases, we would need to know much about his childhood, and there can be found in the historical guidance literature proposals that the cumulative record data in elementary schools should show toilet training specifics, as one example.

Behaviors have origins in one's history, of that there is no question. Behavior principles now inform us, however, that a behavior or behavior pattern is changed by direct approach to that behavior as it exists now. Knowledge of the origin and history of that behavior may be useful but is rarely necessary for mediating the behavior. Conversely, the focus on insight, common to a number of prescientific accountings of behavior, is generally a false lead. An alcoholic might acquire insight as a result of much time spent in therapy and come to see and accept why he is an alcoholic. He thus becomes an insightful alcoholic. If being a nonalcoholic, or, more accurately, a nonpracticing alcoholic is the goal, then the alcoholic *behavior* must be changed. To that end knowing why one became alcoholic will not hurt, but it is not necessary.

PRINCIPLES OF APPRAISAL

The prior exposition can be summarized in the first of several principles that underlie school appraisal content and procedures.

1. *Only such data will be collected as are justified (a) for immediate use for a student's benefit, or (b) for planned research purposes that will improve school programs, thus having longer-range benefit to the student.*

Implicit in that principle is the corollary that all data sought will be around scientific principles of behavior, thus prohibiting collection of data on prescientific accountings of behavior. A further corollary of this principle is that a school will collect and maintain the least amount of data possible about each student, the opposite of past practices in many schools.

Principle 1 is vitiated, to some degree, by state laws that require the collection of certain kinds of data. In many instances present state laws were influenced by guidance practitioners operating on prescientific bases, reflected in the idea that knowing a person's past is necessary if something is to be done about a person's present. Laws about data collection vary among states, but it is not difficult to identify those states whose student records, mandated by law or state school board policy, were influenced by guidance officials toward the collection of many rather than few data. Principle 1, then, implies the demurrer that "Only such data *beyond that required by state law* . . ."

The second principle follows naturally from the first, conceptually picking up from the phrase "immediate use" in the first principle.

2. *Data will be recorded and retained for only as long as there is a demonstrable need that, beyond its immediate use, (a) such data will have a future use of benefit to the student, or (b) such data are needed for planned researches into school programs.*

In Hanna's second school year her reading ability was measured, and the information thus acquired was used to help Hanna read better. The immediate use of this datum is completed, yet the results were recorded in Hanna's cumulative record because it will be of help to Hanna later to have the results of a second measure of her reading ability compared with the results of the first measure. By the end of the fifth or sixth year, however, such information will have value no longer and thus will be expunged.

Standardized tests results are the type of data that most often will meet the criterion set by this principle. Indeed multiple measures by standardized tests in any one testing area are required before credence can be given to the results of a single test. More later about that point. As to the research element in these two principles, there is need to elaborate on the word "planned," because the substitute longer phrasing could have been, "research whose purposes and design have already been drawn up and approved," for that is the connotation of "planned." Without that implicit restriction of the word "planned," schools could use research as the justification for collecting and retaining the widest and wildest array of data about students. The rule: no research plan now, no data collected; or, if collected for another purpose, then not retained beyond that purpose's need merely on the basis that "someday we'll do some research about that."

The principles recorded here differ little from those of my analysis of over ten years ago (Byrne, 1963; see also Ch. 7), except that a speck on the horizon then has loomed now into a forbidding, dangerous cloud, necessitating an assessment principle that was not nearly so apparent then.

3. *No datum will be sought that is a demonstrable invasion of privacy unless the purpose of that datum is made known to the student; and, if such a datum is given, it may not be recorded in a central file. It will be recorded on temporary records maintained by the guidance practitioner, or other professional employee, and destroyed promptly when the need for which the datum was collected no longer is present.*

Public attention has been focused on the dangers to privacy now practiced both in educational institutions and by other community agencies as a result of the development of dossiers stored in computers. Citizens apparently have come to accept the fact of a computerized credit file, because citizens seek credit and can understand that a credit record must be maintained. Only recently, however, have citizens in general become aware of the possibility that erroneous derogatory data might show up in those credit files. And who of us knows what kind of record there is about us in the files of the Federal Bureau of Investigation? Some of the seamier uses of FBI records has been illuminated over the past ten or so years, including the presence in files of unevaluated information, which, nonetheless, is accessible to persons who have the right to demand access to such files.

If any community institution is to develop a social momentum against the dossier, it can be and must be public education, where data collection about the individual begins. Principal 3 will help with that momentum, and so will Principle 4.

4. *A student's complete cumulative record may be examined by him and, if the student is a minor, by his parents.*

This principle is paired with another to give weight to desired practice.

5. *No person other than a member of a school's professional staff may examine or be told any portion of information from a student's cumulative record without the explicit permission of the student or his parents.*

Even professional school system employees not members of that school's staff are restricted from examining a student's cumulative record without student or parent permission, let alone persons who are not professional employees of the educational enterprise.[1]

Although accuracy, including up-to-dateness, of a student's cumulative record is implied in prior principles, the fact of poor past and present practices requires the emphasis of a separate principle.

6. *Student cumulative records are a major supervisory responsibility of a school administrator, are monitored and culled by trained personnel, and are systematically examined to ascertain that they accord with all other principles, and that the data in them are accurate and current.*

Having set out these principles, let us turn our attention to procedures about and content of appraisal. Appraisal information, far from being an amorphous glob, is readily classified in several ways: immediate and long-term, parametric or nonparametric, mandated by law and optional, temporary or permanent, and so on. The choice here is to press a more detailed study around the classification of parametric and nonparametric data.

---

[1] Since the writing of this chapter federal law fortunately has pushed Principles 3, 4, and 5 out of the class of propositions and into the category of legal requirements. The history of the legislation, known as the Buckley Amendment to the Elementary and Secondary School Act of 1974, has its own irony. Senator Buckley (R-N.Y.) was moved to propose the amendment after viewing a television production around privacy invasion and other misuse of dossiers, including those associated with school records.

PARAMETRIC AND NONPARAMETRIC DATA

The word parametric as used in behavior measurement has a meaning that is an extrapolation from its primary use in mathematics, where it means a constant applied to several somewhat similar operations. As used in human appraisal, a use common to this technical area but not yet appearing in dictionaries, it has a meaning that is a literal translation from the Greek, "to measure beside," connoting that a person assessed by a parametric procedure is figuratively caused to stand beside other persons. Essential to parametrics is that parametric reports of similarities with or differences from other persons are given as arithmetical scores, which are further analyzed for an average score for the group tested and the degree to which an individual's scores are distant from that mean or average score.

Nonparametric data are those that do not have the characteristic of scores reported in arithmetical terms and likely are not reported in "score" terms at all. Nonparametric information is valuable because it describes a person as a unique being through data that have to be "collected by hand." An autobiography is an example of nonparametric data. Just to be clear, though, note that an autobiography makes reference to other persons, and indeed the writer of an autobiography gives his report its greatest dimension and meaning only by reference to other persons. But an autobiography is different from parametric reference to other persons because of the absence of mathematical scores, thus of norms, and, more important, the fact that it includes observations about the significance of those other persons to the autobiographer's life. In use of parametric data, on the other hand, the large number of individuals with whom a testee is compared are unknown and meaningless to him.

A most simple example of a parametric datum is height, and its consideration lets us further define the characteristics of parametrics. In measuring a person's height, so we can tell whether he is shorter, taller, or the same height as other persons, we figuratively measure him as he stands alongside other persons, although any of us also has been measured literally beside siblings or friends as children or adolescents to see who was taller. Or the child measured beside a parent—"Gee, Sidney's taller than you now, Sylvia, and he's only 12!"

Parametric or Nomothetic Assessment

The figurative "measuring beside" is done by comparing a person's score on a parametric assessment to the scores made by others, or to norms, to use a different term. In that the normative data of an instrument describes how a theoretical total population behaves relative to the matter tested, those norms are describing lawful behavior; thus the term "nomothetic" is used in appraisal literature as a synonym for parametric (*nomothetic* = giving or making laws). In still other terms, the normative data provide standards, thus giving us the familiar term "standardized test."

Group standardized tests of achievement and of intelligence began to be used in schools at the end of the first decade of the 1900s. The rate of growth of use of tests of these kinds was slow but steady in the ensuing four decades, given early impetus by the testing of military personnel during World War I.

The rate of growth in standardized test use spurted sharply upward when our social system competitors, the Soviet Union, flung Sputnik high in the sky in 1957 and scared the bejabbers out of our federal officials. The panicked reply to Sputnik by Congress in 1958 was the National Defense Education Act (NDEA), which contained lush provisions for standardized testing that was intended to identify gifted students who could then be guided into mathematics and sciences curriculums so that we too could bridge the space gap.

Reporting on that federal action requires the raising of a peripheral question: on the basis of guidance principles, can the guidance movement condone student appraisal activities for purposes other than assisting students to cope with current living and to plan futures? Was not the testing thrust of the NDEA a totalitarian or statist type of action not commensurate with guidance principles? "Totalitarian" or "satist" are too harsh; centrist action for the social good, yes. Despite the fact that this legislation was not for individual but for social purposes, individual students benefitted because many now had better knowledge about their interests and aptitudes than they would have had without the testing provisions of the NDEA. Moreover it is tenable to believe that many students for whom study in mathematics and sciences would have been appropriate did get to engage those studies as a result of their identification through NDEA-generated standardized testing and through NDEA support for higher education. The testing provisions of the NDEA, planned for abstract good, had outcomes for individuals consonant with guidance principles, and thus were in accord with the first principle above (appraisal must be for the good of individual students).

PRECISE NORMS. To make our earlier height illustration fit in with other standardized measurements, we will speak here of scores in centiles, rather than in the commonly used feet and inches. And we start by thinking of two children whose measured height was translated by the tables of normative data into scores at the 50th and 45th centiles, respectively. The child at the 50th centile is, by definition, exactly of average height, although as yet we know almost nothing about what that person's height really is.

Fiftieth centile? Compared with what persons? While we ponder that question, another bit of information about these two children is added: one is female, the other male. Was the same normative population used for both the attained scores? If so, a large error was introduced into the report of the results because females in general are shorter than males in general.

But we will assume that male and female tables were used; that is, normative data were collected separately for sexes. Not all potential errors in interpreting those scores are eliminated thereby; at least we cannot be sure of the elimination of error without having further data about the normative population. This point is illustrated by the additional datum that the boy is fourteen years old, and the girl sixteen. Any of us knows that sex is a major variable in height, and that age is too, until at least the mid-teens. Therefore we cannot know for sure the meaning of the reported centiles unless the norm tables are identified as to age as well as sex.

With that much now assumedly reported about the norm tables, error potential is reduced, but further error is possible, and unless information is given about these other matters in the norm tables, we cannot be certain of the scores' meanings. For example, if I used sex- and age-based norms to arrive at the centiles given, I would still err were I to believe those results if the norm table I used was acquired in 1921, which fact I might not know because my hypothetical norm table was not dated. Further interpretation error is committed because the norms were collected (I will hypothesize) by measuring children in the eastern part of the country. Heights might differ by regions as a result of diet, for example; thus for me to have measured the two children, one raised in Nevada and the other in Mississippi and to have applied my eastern states' norms may well be another source of error.

This relatively unimportant characteristic of height has provided occasion to set out some of the desiderata of parametric instruments by looking at potential errors when identifying the normative population of a standardized instrument. We continue with the topic of norms, but leave the specific illustration of measuring height.

MULTIPLE NORMS. Any norm tables must be precisely defined and used. But to use a single set of norms is to not know as much about a person's results on a standardized test as if multiple norms were used.

For example, Brad is raised in a maximum experience family in a college town in New England; Doris in a minimum experience family in a rural area of the South. In the fourth year of school the reading ability of both is measured by the same test. The results of both children are recorded as being at the 50th centile on sex-based, fourth-grade national norms acquired two years prior to the test. That is not sufficient information for understanding the reading skill of these two persons, however. Use of local and regional norms is necessary. Local norms show Brad to be at the 27th centile, and Doris at the 83rd. Regional norms place Brad at the 44th centile, and Doris at the 67th. These three norm results tell us more about each of these children than a national norm only does.

Local norms are particularly important. The population on which those norms are based is comprised, by definition, of children with whom a tested child is living and compared day by day, and with whom he may eventually be competing for local jobs or entrance into local postsecondary educational institutions.

Recently a superintendent of an urban school system was interviewed by a number of newspaper reporters. Part of her report treated standardized testing and included the statement that she was unwilling to use any standardized test results unless there were local norms for that test, a statement fully consonant with best assessment practice. However, there was an error demonstrated in the same report in understanding the nature of national norms when the superintendent went on to say that she did not wish the population of her schools (poor and black) to be compared with the school population of a certain city in a distant state, which was predominantly rich and white. Her statement implies the error that national norms can be based on one city or on one class of persons. By definition, national norms are a blend of scores of all classes of persons in all regions of the nation: urban, suburban, and rural; black, native American, white, Oriental; rich, middle class, and poor. There could be no way the achievement of the superintendent's charges could be compared with those of the distant city unless she asked that school system for its local norms.[2] As valid as is the need for local norms, a superintendent's or anyone's understanding of students would be gravely incomplete without knowing their standing on national and regional norms.

More basic to an understanding of parametrics than the topic of norms is the matter of the truthfulness or accuracy of the instrument used. In customary testing parlance this topic is labeled "validity."

TEST VALIDITY. The validity of a test cannot be directly measured, but can be inferred from statistical data. In concept and technique the topic of validity is of a complexity warranting only a brief treatment here. Data for estimating a test's validity are collected around three modes that let us infer a test's *construct validity, content validity,* and *criterion validity.*[3]

[2] This material is from the report of a lengthly interview entitled "Changing Our Schools," which appeared in *The Washington Post,* July 7, 1974.

[3] These three forms of validity are those agreed upon by a committee composed of members of the American Psychological Association and the American Education Research Association and are found in *Standards for Educational and Psychological Tests* (APA, 1974). Other forms of validity are sometimes referred to, but this statement of standards generally is held as definitive.

Content validity refers to the degree to which a test samples all facets of the measured area. A standardized test of a foreign language must touch on all aspects of language to have content validity. Were a test of Russian composed only of verb declensions, the test would seriously violate content validity.

Criterion validity is the term that shows the commonality of two subtypes of validity, *concurrent* and *predictive*. Assessments of a test's concurrent validity give knowledge about how truthfully the test simultaneously describes persons in their relationship to a criterion. Predictive validity requires the seeking out of the relationships of scores earned on the test with a criterion attained at some future time. For example, assuming that a panel of mathematics teachers can make valid judgments about the algebra aptitude of a group of prospective algebra students who also take an algebra aptitude test, the teachers' judgment is the concurrent criterion, with which the results of the algebra aptitude test are correlated. The coefficient (the numerical expression of the degree of correlation) gives us one basis for inferring the test's criterion validity through a concurrent approach to the question.

The results of the algebra aptitude test are retained, we will suppose, and are later correlated with the algebra course mark or grade earned by those who took the test. That coefficient lets an inference be made about the test's predictive validity, the other form of criterion validity.

Construct validity is the fundamental, most important criterion. It inquires about the area to be measured, demanding that that area be accurately defined. A test's construct validity is easy to attain when the area to be assessed is simple to define, as a foreign language or the history of ancient Egypt, or even more precisely defineable, such as geometry and chemistry. It was not in an area of clear definition that testing began, interestingly enough, but in a highly abstract area, for which the term "intelligence" was used. Because this construct, and its measurement, have been a millstone around the guidance movement's neck, the topic of construct validity will be examined by using intelligence as the focus.

This construct and its measurement were introduced earlier in these pages, at one place by asking for the definition of intelligence, and replying there with the oft-used cynical answer, it is what an intelligence test tests. The other introduction of this topic was around the issue of measuring the intelligence of blacks and other racial and ethnic groups outside the white, predominantly Anglo-Saxon culture of the United States. These issues about intelligence and its measurement have been with us from the start of the century and have been exacerbated recently by the publications of Shockley, Jencks, Herrnstein, and others.

Any who observes others' behavior notices that among the numerous ways persons differ in behavior are (a) in the quantity of symbols they use;

(b) the speed with which symbols are learned; (c) the quality of symbols used, such as the degree of abstractness with which individuals can effectively deal; and (d) the speed of seeing relationships between things and between abstractions. Because these four modal behaviors vary together (much of one, much of all others, and vice versa), it is tenable for some to say that these four behaviors represent the operation of a single "something," and that something has been called intelligence, which is, thus, a hypothetical construct. Some hold that it is intelligence that correlates positively with school achievement and occupational success and causes that success. Thus would it not be helpful to measure intelligence? Then we could predict how persons would cope, at least with the scholastic demands of school. Measurement of those four behaviors indeed is appropriate and can be done, but not around the construct intelligence.

At one time use of the construct intelligence was appropriate, or at least understandable. When the construct surfaced, there was no scientific knowledge of how humans behaved, and the psychoanalytic accounting of behavior was waxing. This point of view looked for "what is in back of" whatever behavior is focused on, behavior being but symptomatic of the true and important underlying reason for its occurrence. How easy it was, then, to look for "something in back of" the differing quality of persons' behaviors, and that something was found in the construct of intelligence.

Today we know the function of the brain and nervous system, and we know much about how behaviors are formed and maintained. Today there is no need for the construct intelligence. Those elements that are important in studying human behavior are the differences in the pattern of behaviors that persons demonstrate in their acquisition and use of symbols. These behaviors can be measured without claiming that something which is called intelligence lies between these behaviors and the functioning of the brain and the central nervous system. These behaviors do not have intelligence in back of them. What is in back of them are "things," a genetically influenced brain and nervous system, and the opportunity to acquire those behaviors. The proportion of contribution of either of these cannot be known at this time and thus cannot be measured. When it is said that opportunity to acquire these behaviors partly accounts for the differences among persons in the degree to which they demonstrate such behaviors, we are saying that a test claiming to measure intelligence is better labeled an achievement test, and I and many others see so-called intelligence tests as just that.

One feature of measures labeled as testing intelligence is the portion dealing with vocabulary. Indeed some short intelligence tests measure vocabulary only. There is nothing to wonder about in that, for such tests permit an assessment of differences in the quantity and abstractness of a person's verbal symbols and the relationship he makes among abstractions (the Miller Analogies Test, for example). A person learns or achieves a vocabulary, so a vocabulary test is an achievement test. The other variable affecting the test result is, of course, the neural functioning of the individual. It not only serves no purpose, but creates opportunity for dangerous misuse of data to say that some abstraction called intelligence accounts for differences in results.

Incidentally, the two errors—that there is a thing called intelligence and that it can be measured—are compounded by the apparently common assumption among persons-in-the-street that it is of an unchanging amount and that therefore there only needs to be but one measure of it in a lifetime. In fact, an intelligence test score reflects a number of variables occurring at the moment of testing, many of which produce erroneous scores, as will be shown in more detail in the next section. Moles (1967) has interesting words for this point. He tells of experiments that show that IQ scores of poor children were raised by changing the topic of questions, reading the test questions aloud, and providing practice sessions. Moles concludes by reporting Haggard's experiment, noting that *"the reward of a theater ticket for a good score produced the most marked improvement in I.Q. scores"* (p. 35, italics added).

So it is that major errors in standardized testing can be committed because of construct error, and in no area more so than in that labeled intelligence. And an *obiter dictum* about that area, which is better labeled something other than intelligence, such as wide-range achievement, or the more popular term, scholastic aptitude, is brought forward from an earlier chapter and restated for emphasis. No matter whether or not the quality of behavior shown by a person in this measurement area has a large heredity factor in addition to being influenced by achievement opportunities, the guidance practitioner is concerned with the behaviors that occur right now, and with helping the student to increase desired behaviors and to remove undesired behaviors.

TESTING ERRORS. The correct administration and use of standardized tests require technical considerations mostly outside the scope of this presentation. What is germane for thought here are some of the testing errors practiced. To state them is to negatively define good practice, thus their instructional value.

Errors in standardized test administration and use stem from ignorance, not lack of care, with this condition of error resulting partly from the general availability of such tests for use by persons not trained in the technical knowledge needed for their proper administration and interpretation. In analogy this question is posed: should there not be a well-stocked medicine chest in every teacher's classroom? Although an argument could be made that teachers, wishing good health for individual students, could then rectify health deficiencies, no one could favor that availability of medicines because teachers lack the training needed for their appropriate use.

What, then, of standardized test results? Not so vital a question as the hypothetical one about teachers' use of medicines, yet it is one that rests on the same issue of the needed technical training. The pro argument is similar: teachers, wishing the best outcomes for each student, would be in better position to assist students. The hypothetical question about teachers' having a supply of medicine cannot alarm us, because it does not occur and by law may not occur. However, teachers, and other school personnel who also may not be trained in testing, do have access to standardized testing information.

Are teachers really untrained? Some states' teacher certification requirements do not demand training in testing, and many of us know of teacher preparation programs that do not include training in measurement. That is at least a puzzling state of affairs in view of this set of equations: the goal of teaching = learning; knowing whether learning has been attained = measurement; useful measurement = standardized testing and teacher-made measures of achievement; thus a fundamental knowledge needed by teachers is that of standardized testing and teacher-made tests. The lack of measurement and other assessment knowledges on the part of teachers is the basis for one of the counselor's activities related to the school: in-service instruction of teachers in appraisal matters.

Ignorance about parametrics results in the commission of errors and in not being aware that errors might be happening by chance. The interview with the city superintendent of schools referenced earlier shows how test knowledge lets you seek out testing errors. In that report the superintendent described a phenomonon she found in a school of which she was then principal. The children appeared to be alert, but scored very low on IQ tests. She told of her rooting out one cause of low scores when she found by accident that children did not know the meaning of such directions as "draw a line around the word 'boy,'" "drawn a line under . . . ," "Place an X beside . . ." Once the children were taught how to work a test, results of testing were much improved.

That inability to understand directions illustrates one of numerous possible test administration errors. Other examples: inaccurate timing of tests by teachers, teachers thinking that a test's directions are not clear and thus elaborating on them, the numerous opportunities for errors when standardized tests are hand scored and added, and the errors demonstrated in the copying of scores onto student records.

Most of these once-prevalent administrative errors are now eliminated through the use of computer scoring and issuance of computer printed results for the students' records. The one error that may be the worst, and that is undetected because it is not apparent to any observer, is a student's placing answers in wrong response areas on answer sheets deliberately or accidentally. Similar errors are made by students in taking a test.

The lack of technical knowledge has its worst effects in errors of use of standardized test results. No matter how much construct and other validities a test has, and how faultless its administration, the good that can come from standardized tests stands or falls on how results are used. Any one test is interpreted around the norm tables for that test, and its standard error of measurement (SE_{meas}).

Except for computerized print-outs of test scores, the results of standardized tests on a student's cumulative record typically do not state the nature of the population that constitutes the norm population of the test. Persons ignorant of the technical issues related to standardized testing, on seeing a test result given as a centile, may accept that result as if the test were reporting some proportion of an absolute instead of some relative position on a scale developed from a certain population. The test result is not interpretable unless the norming population is identified, and unless several interpretations for each test are given through use of differing norming populations.

Not only is a test score not reporting possession of some proportion of an absolute, but the test score reported is actually only an index for an area within which the true score might lie. The width of this area is shown by the SE_{meas}. Old villages and cities have center squares, marking, as the name states, the hub of the community. To report a person as being in Oldburg leaves no doubt about his not being in Newville. But where is he in Oldburg? To say he is there might mean that he is in its Center Square. And just as accurately it might mean a block away, two blocks away, and any of all blocks away right to the city limits. So too with a reported test score; it is the "center square" of an area, and a person might be standing (have a true score) right on "center square," and with equal accuracy might be any distance from that midpoint, right out to the stated limits of that band of scores identified by the SE_{meas}. The reported score might be 112, but with a SE_{meas} of 10, you cannot know where he actually stands between 102 and 122. Some errors of test result use which are practiced stem from ignorance of this technical characteristic of measurement.

The last use error we consider lies in the truth that a high score on a test is a valid score, but a low score must be viewed at first only as a low score. If told that Bunny threw a ball 200 feet, we know that a powerful thrower has been identified (it is a valid score). Marcie is reported as throwing the same ball 20 feet. That is an unusually short distance, and, without knowing any other data about Marcie, we are obliged to accept that throw just for what it is—a low score—but we do not view it as a valid score until other data are available to corroborate it. It was found that students who attained low scores on an IQ test in the previous anecdote had a low score partly because they could not follow the directions for responding to questions, a good illustration of why a low score at first must not be viewed as a valid score, merely as a low score. A trained person never acts on the basis of a single low score. There must be other testings and other data collected.

Even these comments, when forced up against the wall, are not quite accurate. "The more deviant the score [from the average score] the larger the error of measurement it probably contains," say two research and measurement authorities (Campbell and Stanley, 1963) in their treatment of the topic of regression toward the mean on any measurement. Knowledge of regression is another of the technical needs of those who deal with standardized test results.

What conclusions from this discussion are to be drawn by the guidance practitioner? There may be numerous ones, but one stands out as of paramount significance: if the only information available about a student in an area is a single group standardized test score, particularly if scored and recorded by hand, putting credence on that score and acting on it is an exercise in folly. It is also an unethical display of ignorance about parametrics.

Considerable space was given to parametric assessment instruments because ours is a test-happy society. Thus some of the problems related to use of standardized tests have to be known by anyone concerned with schooling, but particularly by guidance practitioners. Such instruments are sometimes down-valued, but their great contribution to individuals is acknowledged here, as long as errors such as those detailed above are not practiced, and as long as appropriate nonparametric assessment procedures are also carried out when germane.

Standardized Testing Anyone?

These concerns about and problems with standardized testing, accompanied by the public's discontent with testing, leads one to ask rhetorically if *anyone,* other than test publishers, favors standardized testing now. If the question merited a reply, mine would be, "Of course; I do." A respondent, however, would have to acknowledge that standardized testing has been taking its lumps in increasing quantity and stridency and around no test area more so than in measurements of intelligence.

Whatever may have been the public and professional concern about standardized tests twenty years and more ago, the past fifteen years have been marked by a heightened worry about IQ tests, a result of society's efforts to redress racial wrongs, particularly in schooling. Although there was some racially integrated schooling prior to the Supreme Court decision that found legislated segregated schooling to be unconstitutional, the question of disparity between blacks' IQ test scores and whites' received only scattered, scholarly attention. Whether or not blacks were less intelligent than whites, as white folklore would have it, was of little practical matter decades ago. Few blacks completed high school, and fewer still sought to enter higher education; those who did went in greatest majority to black institutions. Whether or not blacks finished a college education, as adults they became invisible in a socioeconomic class below the majority of whites or at least because they lived in enclaves away from whites.

The Supreme Court decision changed blacks' schooling circumstances, but of equal or greater importance for the theme of the moment is that other social forces erupted, chiefly among blacks, that changed forever their acceptance of the inferior status thrust upon them. As black leaders asserted their claims to constitutional rights and protections and found a suddenly increased and sympathetic white audience, all the strategies that were used to keep blacks in their place, even if benignly used, were nominated for challenge by blacks.

One of the prominent strategies among educators for alloting students and applying programs has been the IQ test; thus it inevitably attracted the lightning of challenge. The dispute has been going on for a decade and is building rather than diminishing. It is the concern of an increasingly larger number of the public as well as of professionals and spills over into an increased doubt about all kinds of standardized tests. Although mostly a product of exceptions taken by blacks, the challenge of standardized testing has been applied to by other subpopulations such as Chicanos.

Readers of this text will likely find the volume of criticism increasing for a number of years. They may observe an increase in the number of school systems that choose to give up standardized testing and also may see much change in the content of tests. A concerned profession remains concerned, ready to clean its own house. Ebel (1975) acknowledges that "tests . . . are imperfect. Indeed, some are seriously flawed. They are sometimes used unwisely, misinterpreted, or handled as weapons rather than as tools" (p. 83). Who could disagree? But imperfect as they are, use of standardized tests, acknowledging their imperfections, is justified, in my view. Only, however, if there is "constant vigilance against test abuse and insistence upon elimination of discrimination based on test results" (Green, 1975, p. 92).[4]

Nonparametric and Idiographic Assessment

The two terms in this heading are not used uniformly in measurement literature. "Nonparametric" provides little difficulty. Data that are nonparametric are those items of information about a person that do not require a numerical score and norm table interpretation in order for those

---

[4] There is a large and increasing amount of literature reflecting the challenges to and defenses of standardized testing. I suggest one volume that considers the controversy about IQ, edited by Bridger and Schwebel (1975).

data to give useful information about the individual. An autobiography was used earlier as an illustration of nonparametric information.

There is more difficulty in defining the term "idiographic." Sometimes that term is equated with "nonparametric." From its Greek origins, however, the word can mean any material that describes a person, including, therefore, parametric data. Indeed a clearly idiographic document like an autobiography can include parametric data like test scores. We settle here on using the term "nonparametric" to define any datum about a person that does not require a numerical comparison with other persons in order to extract its major meaning, and "idiographic" will refer to an organized collection of related data about a person, assembled in thematic sequence. Because parametric information by itself cannot be organized into a life history, idiographic data has to include nonparametric data and is indeed mostly characterized by nonparametric data. This may account for the fact that some persons use those terms interchangeably.

By these refined definitions, then, it is better to refer to an autobiography as idiographic, comprised primarily of nonparametric data. More often than not some portions of the nonparametric data that are found in an autobiography are collected separately, rather than as part of an autobiography, illustrated by a record of likes and dislikes, activities and hobbies, favorite travel, books most influential in the person's life, and so on. These have been listed for illustration, not with any force of recommendation. To the contrary, collection of these kinds of data will be rare, when the appraisal principles above are applied.

Three kinds of idiographic material that fall within the appraisal principles and the larger requirements and restraints of guidance programs are (1) behavior histories, (2) the more comprehensive behavior analyses, and (3) the even more extensive case write-ups.

Why are nonparametric data acquired? Under what conditions is a case developed? A behavior analysis made? A behavior history acquired? To answer all those questions is a big order, one that can be only partially fulfilled here.

Consonant with the appraisal principles given at the beginning of the chapter, an answer common to all questions is offered: nonparametric data are acquired, cases developed, and behavioral histories and analyses written when the good of the student requires that any of these be done. Parametric data, on the other hand, may be acquired in the absence of an immediate need for them because the administration of standardized tests is complex and must be fitted into time and fiscal budgets. Moreover, the value of parametric data for individual student benefit is clearly established, as used both directly with the individual and through research that ultimately benefits the individual. In addition the results of standardized tests have value over time, assuming that none of the numerous errors that can militate against good results has occured. In sum, then, collection of parametric information about a student might occur without there being an immediate need, despite the strictures of the first appraisal principle, for the reasons given. Nonparametric data, however, is collected only as immediately needed.

Each of us has experienced standardized testing, and we know of its use in selection and placement (administrative use of results) and advisement (guidance use of results). Some, perhaps, are unfamiliar with the acquisition of nonparametric information. Its use is demonstrated in any decision making and has been well illustrated by the career decision-making activities described in several prior chapters.

The decision-making paradigm, applied to occupational choice, requires each student to explicate and examine (a) his values; (b) histories of enjoyed and disliked activities, with the occupational significance of those arrays; (c) inventoried occupational interests (which may be either parametric or nonparametric); (d) abilities and aptitudes (also likely obtained from parametric instruments); and (e) achievement histories (a record of school marks over the years is one form of an achievement history).

Two characteristics of assessment procedures related to the collection and use of these kinds of appraisal data must be highlighted: (1) these data were collected only when the decision-making need emerged, and (2) they were not only generated by the student, but they are retained only by him. Two additional procedural characteristics fall from those first two: (1) the student retains each datum as long as he wishes, and (2) the nonparametric data collected for this need are not placed into the student's cumulative record. Appraisal principles 1 (data collected only for student benefit), 2 (data retained only for a demonstrated need), and 6 (records must be current) exercise a somewhat mild restraint against putting these nonparametric data in the cumulative record. Principle 3, however (records may not invade student's privacy), emphatically speaks against retaining these data in the cumulative record. The cumulative record contains all usable (current) parametric data about the student, of course, and some nonparametric data that has counseling value, the student's course mark record, for example. But an explicit and forceful "No" must be pronounced about placing in the cumulative record these other data assembled about himself by a student for the occupational decision-making need.

ISSUES IN ADMINISTERING AN APPRAISAL PROGRAM

Are a school's appraisal activities an aspect of the guidance program, or do they lie within the administrative functions? Or are both portions of the question to be answered affirmatively? If so, then who is in charge?

Who says what shall be appraised, and who administers the cumulative record file? Examining school practices will not illuminate these questions with firm answers and may indeed result in a confusion of conclusions.

The prime source of confusion lies in the fact that there are two general purposes for collecting data about students, the guidance purpose and the school-management purpose, which includes the legal requirement for certain records about students to be maintained.

At the start of the century there were no records collected and used for guidance purposes, and school management was simple. Records about students then appear to have been little more than "name, rank, and serial number."

Changes occurred slowly over the years. The value placed on individuals increased as the purposes of the Declaration of Independence worked their way through society. Schools became more complex in their course offerings, and society became more complex in the matter of occupational decisions to be made. Ideas and technologies related to appraisal increased, and all these changes were accompanied by the start and spread of the guidance movement and of guidance practitioners.

Guidance specialists and appraisal practices feed on each other. The greater the appraisal need, the more need for specialists who know something about appraisal, and the more there are knowledgeable specialists, the more appraisal is carried out.

By the 1950s appraisal for school administrator use and appraisal for guidance purposes had become intertwined. In some schools the permanent (legal) record was maintained separately from the cumulative (guidance) appraisal record. In other places the guidance-generated data were incorporated by law into the permanent record, which became a cumulative record. The variations in practices is still prevalent.

That guidance practitioners would commonly become charged with all student record keeping is understandable, even if not tenable. As a class, guidance functionaries had a greater interest in the substance of records than did other classes of school professionals, and they were typically the only class of school employees that had training in the area. Requirements for the certification of counselors, who were the only kind of in-school guidance specialists for many years, moved from no preparation, through one or a few "guidance courses," to the common requirement today of a master's degree. In the post–World War II years guidance was commonly defined throughout the country as being comprised of six services, and for each of four of these there was a course in approved counselor training programs.[5]

---

[5] The period of the late 1930s through the mid-1950s is a time of history in the guidance movement that many find fascinating. During this period, up to 1952, state guidance activities were supported by federal funds administered for most years under provisions of the George-Barden Act of 1946. The unit in the Office of Educa-

One course was commonly titled Analysis of the Individual and contained study of both parametric and nonparametric appraisal procedures. In some counselor preparation departments today, however, the master's degree program contains two and even three courses dealing with appraisal. Graduates of these programs, then, are the appraisal experts in the school.

Guidance institutes and other activities emanating from the provisions of the NDEA of 1958 had a consciousness-raising effect on guidance specialists, and concerted grumbles against nonguidance duties were heard about the land. Record keeping was fingered as a major culprit, an activity that counselors easily identified as an administration responsibility (appraisal principle 6). It can be safely conjectured that any effect of this disclaimer about record keeping would have been slow in coming, but NDEA provisions came to the rescue—not by reversing the trend that had been moving record management from administrators to guidance specialists, but by providing the guidance specialists with clerks, paid by NDEA monies, who could keep the records. Clerks abound today in guidance suites, long after the passing of the provisions of the NDEA, and the record-keeping function came to be formalized in the position of registrar. Clerk and registrar support from local funds is now taken for granted.

Providing Teachers with Appraisal Assistance

Guidance and instruction have been stated as two school programs with sufficient discretion to be identified by name. It has not been proposed that they are fully discrete programs, however; they are modes. As such, therefore, there are areas wherein both programs overlap. Teachers, for example, even though meeting with students in groups, as do counselors, are typically concerned about individual student success in mastery of subjects. This is an instructional expression of the guidance movement, and it is not only appropriate but incumbent upon counselors, those practitioners on the guidance team who have responsibility for strategies and for communications with teachers, to assist teachers in knowing their students' individual learning behaviors.

There are numerous ways counselors can carry out that duty. The one obvious way is consultation with a teacher about an individual student, helping the teacher to acquire needed supplemental data, as well as to know the student through interpretation of his cumulative record. Another is

---

tion that administered those funds required state plans, and these were approved when they matched a model. Preparation of counselors was also supported and also had to conform to a model. Thus the enormous growth of guidance programs and practitioners, particularly after World War II, is due mostly to federal support, and the commonness among many states of training certification and school programs could thereby be expected. I have given this topic a more extended treatment elsewhere (Byrne, 1963).

through helping the school's administrators prepare and send to teachers certain summaries of data for groups of their students, particularly standardized test data, when this procedure has been adopted by teachers and administrators. If the latter were done, it should be preceded by another activity wherein the counselor has a major part: in-service instruction of teachers in the interpretation of cumulative record data, particularly of standardized tests.

In summing counselor time use per week appropriate to the stipulations of this text, we find the counselor with groups of students three days per week (which, of course, could be more or less), and conferring with students, parents, and teachers individually, or the latter two classes in groups at times, for the other 2 days. As with any guidance practitioner, the counselor uses his trained skills with any kinds of persons, individually or in groups, who will bring benefit to individual students. As to whether or not there should be two school records—the administrative and guidance records—the matter seems to be too petty to take an exclusive stand on. I opt for a single official record. If one wishes to view it in the following way, it can be said also that there are and likely will continue to be multiple-record systems because certain guidance practitioners and teachers maintain their own temporary records about students. The issue perhaps is resolved for those who hold as I do that the school's chief guidance officer is the principal, and that the school's records are under his supervision or that of a delegated administrator.

Within the extensive guidance literature there are volumes that address the question of administration of appraisal programs in appropriate depth (e.g., Hatch & Stefflre, 1965), and there is no need for further exploration here.

APPRAISAL AND MEMBERS OF THE GUIDANCE TEAM

The CDT and the CET

The career development and continuing education technicians are program strategy and information specialists within the areas defined by their titles. Their duties do not call for them to appraise students; therefore they routinely neither study nor contribute to students' cumulative records.

Counselors

These, the traditional guidance specialists, are wide-range program strategists whose skills are applied to individuals in groups. They also assist individuals as individuals to make future plans and to acquire skills to cope with current problems of a minor nature. Counselors' functions often require study of cumulative records and sometimes to make a contribution of information about a student to them. Mostly, however, counselors' work with students does not result in data being placed in their cumulative records. When counselors learn about a student while assisting individually or in groups in occupational decision-making matters or in solving minor coping problems, that information is not placed in the cumulative record. Moreover, the counselor typically destroys any notes he might have made when the need for his assistance with the immediate problem is ended.

When assisting students in decision making in group or individual settings, counselors cause students to learn about themselves, and that is one occasion for causing students to see their cumulative records. The counselor's function in this instance is that of teaching each student how to interpret cumulative record data in conjunction with other data that the student provides for the current purpose. The primary cumulative record data for most instances will be standardized test results. The data collected and retained by the student will be a variety of nonparametric information, and, in addition to these two kinds of information, some inventorying of interests might be specially done.

The counselor's teaching students how to interpret standardized tests is parallel to the counselor's teaching students social competency skills, such as attentive listening and reflection, and teaching them self-management skills, which necessitates student learning of some behavior principles. In each of these areas the counselor is causing students to acquire some of the counselor's skills, in the same way that a competent athlete hired as a physical education teacher and coach seeks to have his charges learn as much as possible of his own athletic skill.

The competence the counselor needs for his varied functions is not just technical knowledge and skills in parametrics, but in drawing out significances for decision making or noncomplex coping problems from all interrelated data. He has, in short, the case development competency necessary for these two general purposes and the competency to teach these skills to students. The counselor's goal in appraisal, as in student self-management of behavior, is to cause students to acquire knowledge and skills so as to act independently for their own benefit in as wide a sweep of concerns as possible, while retaining the confidence that, when independent action is not producing results, the guidance team is available and eager to help.

Behavior Specialists

Counselors assist students' on-goingness; behavior specialists' principal function is the restoration of good development of those students who have been extruded from it. Behavior specialists have different functions from counselors and have special training for these advanced functions. In consequence their daily technical practices, including the area of appraisal, differ somewhat from those of counselors.

A behavior specialist, when assisting a student, is attending to a behavior or pattern of behavior that is to be lessened or increased, or some parts lessened and some increased. Facilitative interview techniques have brought the student and specialist to the point where behavior outcomes of the specialist's intervention are set, as well as a time span for attaining those outcomes. The specialist proceeds to a behavior analysis, as it is sometimes called, but for our purposes it can also be described as a patterned study of the student which addresses certain topics. Osipow and Walsh (1970) propose that the behavioral analysis will focus on these topics: problem behavior, problem situation, work (school) environment, family environment, interpersonal (social) environment, thinking process, and biological and physical attributes.

Should information about those areas be in the student's cumulative record? No, partly because it would be a clerical impossibility, but far more importantly because routine collection of such information is a violation of a number of appraisal principles. Such data are collected when there is a clear and present need to know. They take a relatively short time to acquire when the need is there, and they are destroyed when their current usefulness is ended.

Teacher-Advisors

One prime function of these guidance team members is ascertaining that a student is on course by engaging and adequately coping with needed courses. These practitioners have no need for appraisal information for this function and rarely need it for their other functions. The making of the larger decision, which is the controlling variable as to which courses to study, has been and continues to be the responsibility of the counselor in both group and individual settings. The teacher-advisor is serving only a technical function related to the outcome of those decisions and as a first-line identifier of student difficulties.

The physician-nurse relationship to a patient rises as a comparison. The nurse, let's say in a hospital setting, ascertains that the patient takes the prescribed course of medicine and does so in the proportions and at the times set by the physician. Should a pharmaceutical prescribed by the physician appear to be having no effect, it likely would be the nurse who would first notice it, but it is the physician's responsibility to reconsider the treatment. In like manner, if a check-up by a teacher-advisor of a student's effectiveness in his current program of studies shows that certain courses are not "taking," the teacher-advisor can seek out and mediate relatively surface causes. For reconsideration of the decision that led to the selection of the troublesome courses, however, the teacher-advisor causes the student to confer with his counselor. Teacher-advisors have neither the trained competencies nor the time to carry out other functions. Were they to have, they should be called teacher-counselors, but, of course, to have such practitioners would be an eminent illustration of poor staffing.

Other Guidance Team Members

Because a guidance team is composed of those occupations needed so as to result in all students' reaching guidance objectives, some occupations on the team vary around student, school, and community characteristics. They also vary as to when each is started, and for how long each occupation is needed. These varying occupations are satellites to the three fixed occupations on each high school's guidance team: behavior specialists, counselors, and career development technicians.

One varying practitioner noted in Chapter 2 is the field or outreach counselor. This person's functions may be defined by one school as being the same as those of an in-school counselor, with a certified counselor used as field counselor. In that case the field counselor's use of appraisal data may be generally the same as that of the in-school counselor. If a person is employed as field counselor because of personal characteristics rather than his training, the field counselor will have different needs for appraisal skills.

Case Worker

A school may add a case worker instead of or in addition to a field counselor. The need for a field counselor may be for just a year or two, but a school might employ a case worker indefinitely for persistent needs. The case worker's functions are supplemental to the assistance provided by in-school guidance team members and focus on family and community agency contact. The case worker receives assignments from the behavior specialist and will collect appraisal data for a behavior analysis, particularly about the student's family.

THE CASE OF FRANCINE

A school's experience with Francine, and vice versa, permits the refiltering of general points made above, but around an individual, the way appraisal data are used typically.

This factual case has additional fictional material added to it for illustrative purposes and considerably disguises the real facts. What is real and what fictional is not important to know as long as the credibility of the person is supported by the data used, resulting in an opportunity to validly test concepts and procedures.

Francine appeared at Pineville High School in August to enroll. She reported that she had just moved to Pineville and had finished the ninth grade in a school in a distant state. She had no documents, stating that her report card for the ninth grade was "somewhere in the boxes of stuff at home, I guess." The registrar later that day sent off to the former school for a transcript.

One of the counselors (C) on duty then conferred with Francine (F). He asked her about courses she had taken, liked and disliked, grades earned, and discussed tenth-grade courses with her so she could choose them. The counselor's notes stated that Francine was not an easy talker, "seemed evasive," and answered questions with little affect shown.

When C asked F about her family, she replied that she "told that lady over there (the registrar)," but C persisted, saying that he wanted to know F better so he could help her get a good start in PHS. F said that her father was a plumber (later it became known that he was her stepfather and was not a licensed plumber), that her mother wasn't working yet, but always had worked. The mother had no paid occupation, but apparently took whatever jobs were available to her at little other than a laborer's level. In their former community her mother had worked in a "chicken factory" (a chicken-raising, slaughtering, and processing establishment). She didn't know what her mother did there. No, she didn't work in the office; she worked "where they fixed up the chickens—got 'em ready to sell." Her family moved here because "my Daddy's gonna work with my uncle who lives here." C asked about the uncle, but did not recognize the name, nor could F state her uncle's occupation or what her father would be doing with him. The home address placed the family in a deteriorated neighborhood where housing costs were low, confirming for C his earlier classification of F's family as at a middle-lower socioeconomic level.

C asked F about any test results that she might have known about herself. She recalled taking tests, but claimed no knowledge of the results. For better course decision and placement, C decided to assess F's present level of achievement in several areas by a standardized achievement test used by the school system. The results of group administrations of the test were normally computer scored by the publisher, but F's test answer sheet was to be machine scored through arrangements made with a nearby university's student services office. Results would be available in about three days. F agreed to return the next morning to take the test. She did not appear, and, because the family had no telephone, she was not immediately pursued.

The following day C decided to go by F's house. A woman was on the porch looking through one of several cartons. C identified himself, asking if she was Mrs. G., F's mother. The response was a noncommittal assent. C cheerily stated that he was pleased that F had "joined our family of students at Pineville High School," said that he was eager to help F start off well the next month, and went on to tell about the planned test taking for which F did not turn up. "We was off to a church meeting," Mrs. G. informed him. "Fran knowed we was going so she shouldn't a told you she would come to school yesterday." C passed off the matter casually and asked if F were home so he might set up another test day. "No, she's gone off with her Daddy today; he needs her over at the shop. He might need her tomorrow too. Why do you need her at school?"

C explained again, pointing out that because they did not have any records about F from her old school as yet, the results of this test would help her plan the courses to take for the tenth grade. A conversation developed between C and Mrs. G about F's schooling up to now and produced the observation that in Mr. and Mrs. G's view, Francine should get out of school in November when she will be sixteen (the legal withdrawal age) and take a job, that marriage and family raising were what a "woman is cut out for," and she should be helping with the house now (contributing to family finances) and save money so when she marries she will be better off. (This conversation took place with the mother standing on the porch holding some cloth she had taken out of the box, and C standing at the base of the three steps leading to the porch.) Mrs. G. appeared to say as little as she could, with little affect, very much matter of factly. Despite Mrs. G's general noncommunicative manner, C was told the following: Francine resents her stepfather, but does as he says or he will make her stay in her room. Otherwise "she don't cause no trouble, much; she don't like to go to church as much as she should, but we just don't put up with that. She knows she is to honor her father and mother, and she does." C learned that the Gs were members of a fundamentalist Christian sect and learned later that elders in the church they belonged to in the other state were snake handlers. Mrs. G expressed doubt about F's going to PHS because "high schools put wrong ideas into children's heads," and her church friends told her that PHS was filled with "lots of the wrong kinds of kids." Her husband knew some plumbing from having helped a plumber in their other location. His brother-in-law, for whom he is now working, has an air-conditioning installation and repair business he started several months ago. Mr. G moved here to work for his brother-in-law for more money, but "it sure don't go as far here. We're no better off than we was back home. Worse. I ain't working yet."

As a further bit of information we now add that Francine's academic record for the ninth grade, received a short time later, was slightly above average. Yet the valid meaning of her grades could not be grasped because the standards of her junior high school were not known. To have the best knowledge of Francine as a learner, standardized test results will have to be consulted; thus the counselor was carrying out an appropriate procedure in seeking to have Francine measured by a standardized achievement test.

DISCUSSION. Of all that was learned so far about Francine, what do you think should be put into the cumulative record? Answers to questions required by law is one uncontestable answer—that is, answers to the questions asked by the registrar. What of the information that fell out of the porch-step interview with Mrs. G? That question is answered by reference to the appraisal principles, which in turn provide other questions to be asked. One question: is there a clear and present need for these data (Principle 1)? No. If there were overly solicitous persons on the PHS staff, they would want to know everything about all students and would treasure that information by turning the cumulative records into tabernacle of titillating trivia. "No" is Principle 1's answer, but even more emphatically Principle 3's command (no invasion of privacy). Much can be learned about students from gossip, parental reports, observation, and self-reports. What is possible to record and retain is one matter; what is ethically permissible is another.

But surely the counselor's observations about the family as a psychosocial ecosystem should be placed in the cumulative record? Ought not teachers and other school practitioners know who is reared in maximum and minimum experience families, or in families placed between these extremes? It is my view that pleaders for such recording must justify the need. Any datum that is to be used to assist a student in development is a good datum, so it is incumbent on those who urge the recording of a datum to show how it is needed for the student's benefit. Will teacher X of subject Y cause Francine to learn more about subject Y knowing that information? If that can be established, then teacher X should receive the datum, but that is still no argument for invading Francine's privacy in general by making a notation in her cumulative record. Conversely it is a simple fact that if knowing Francine's family as an ecosystem does become important for a later need to help her it is information easy to acquire. For the nonce, Principles 1 and 3 prevail.

To help Francine get off to a good start in PHS her knowledge to date must be assessed, and that is just what the counselor planned as part of her course selection. In addition, a standardized achievement measure that assesses more subtle learnings, called a scholastic aptitude test (or an intelligence test by some), will be needed, and the counselor will use that measure too. This pair of tests will give some temporary knowledge of Francine's potential for school-type learning and will show what she has actually learned to date. If the counselor finds high aptitude but low achievement, there will be need for further appraisal. If he finds the results of both measures to be below average, he will remember the dictum that a high score is a valid score, but a low score is a low score and will realize that the "true" facts of the case will still have to be ferreted out.

The results of these two standardized measures applied to Francine showed that she was pronouncedly above average in scholastic aptitude and above average in standardized achievement test results (ninth grade, national norms), this latter fact not snugly fitting Francine's reported course mark record, which averaged out to only a bit above average.

FURTHER APPRAISAL ACTIVITIES

Additional appraisal activities carried out about Francine will be reported from here on in general terms. A conference with C elicited first the information that she was unhappy in her former school, but on further inquiry it turned out to mean that she had ill-defined discomforts with her general life, mostly with her home life. C surmised that this state was reflected in her general school behaviors, and particularly in her less-than-appropriate course grades. Courses and their levels were selected, with F and C both feeling comfortable about the specifics, and the school year began.

In F's tenth-grade guidance class the decision-making training called for F to identify values, interests, and aptitudes and to connect small portions of each of these personal data, as they became identified, with occupational information. In setting up the members of these group sections, C asked to remain as F's counselor and to have her be in one of his group sections. He was thus able to capitalize on his earlier synthesis of data about F and to keep a close check on her success with the program she and he had worked out. (A teacher-advisor typically does this, but there were no teacher-advisors in PHS.)

DISCUSSION. Because the class activities were carried out by individuals or small groups, and rarely by the twenty-six students uniformly, there was much individual conference time during class sessions. C was able to discuss a number of matters with F, particularly the data about herself that she was compiling. These data she kept, for they were data for her to use for her own benefit. Conversely, they were not placed in the cumulative record, and to have placed them there would have suggested that someone would study them so as to do something *to* F.

The occupational decision-making activities showed F's ambition for nursing, and she accumulated considerable information about that occupation for her career folder. She was led by the programmed activities to examine all occupations in the health field, supported by C's efforts to expand female students' considerations beyond sex-stereotyped occupations, but she was fixed on nursing and said she wanted to earn a bachelor's degree in the area.

Jumping over intervening periods of data collection and conferences, the following summary is offered. F is a bright student, a fact that C eventually came to appreciate, he later confessed, having at first guessed her to be typical of students from lower socioeconomic strata, an idea cued off by her sluggish, unresponsive manner at their first interview, and his turning-off experience with F's mother at the front porch conversation. That C could be led to such hypotheses is illustrative of the kind of person-in-the-street behaviors that counselors typically have before entering a guidance preparation program and that can persist even after training and experience.

So Francine is not only bright, but she is in conflict with her family on major issues. She does not accept her parents' religious convictions ("I don't know what I believe, but not *that!*"), and certainly not their position about "woman's place," which is in the home as wife and homemaker. It was never clear how her mother could hold that view and have worked so many years; perhaps she felt that her income was the greatest contribution she could make to "homemaking." Francine became known to her counselor, acquired decision-making competencies, quickly matured socially in PHS, and had nothing put into her cumulative record after her first interview with the registrar except her eventually received transcript, the results of standardized tests, and her course record, all required by law in the state. All the assessment information turned up in the first year was used by the counselor for Francine's benefit, but was not placed in her record, except as noted. Over time the counselor learned about Francine's standing among other students, her dating problems because dating was barely tolerated by her parents, and then only with certain boys, early homecoming, no drinking, no X, no Y, no Z, and so on.

Francine was doing well enough in PHS, but each week brought her closer to crisis moments. After her sixteenth birthday her parents, mainly her stepfather, told her that, if she didn't withdraw "now," she had to at the end of the school year. Appraisal potentials about Francine were plentiful during that year, and indeed her counselor did learn much about her. The lesson to be learned by thinking about Francine is that much is learned about students, but little recorded. What is learned about a student is often acquired by casual contacts and sometimes by deliberate effort. No matter how acquired, the use of appraisal data is controlled by the appraisal principles above.

EPILOGUE

In April of her sophomore year in PHS Francine left the community without her parents' permission and has not yet been found. It is assumed that she left with an eleventh-grade dropout (male), also missing, who became her best friend in Pineville. What went wrong? Should the school have carried out a psychological appraisal at greater depth than was done and recorded more information about her?

Some employees of school systems are devastated by any skirmish lost, and I suppose it is better that way than if school personnel were to be hardened professionals. No member of a school staff, no member of a school's guidance team, is justified in self-flagellation because one student did not work out by short-run measures.

In Francine's case, appraisal was all that it should be, and the cumulative record contained all that it should. Francine's withdrawal from school is no event of serious implications. There is still much opportunity for her to be educated and trained as she might wish. What of her devastated, worried-to-death mother (her stepfather is bitter and vengeful, just waiting until "she is caught")? The guidance worker's loyalty is tested by questions of this kind. Does he side with the past, with the idea that children shall be cultural carbon copies of their parents, or does he hold the view that each person must march to his own drumbeat, must account for himself to society on his own terms, must be authentic no matter what the heartbreak such authenticity causes elders? The difficulty in answering such questions is apparent. They touch value questions at the core of a guidance practitioner's professional behaviors. For concerns here, dealing with appraisal, such questions may seem to be somewhat peripheral. The fact is that topics can be addressed separately for instructional purposes, but in real life, as in the case of Francine, appraisal procedures and outcomes, counselor case treatment, and matters of values cannot be separated.

SUMMARY

Appraisal of individuals' behaviors is a technical area of importance to a school's guidance program. Appraisal in schools has occurred for about fifty years, but its basis until recently has had to be on prescientific theories. Appraisal or assessment content and procedures described in this chapter are based on the principles of behavior that emanate from the scientific study of behavior. Six principles were identified, stating (1) that only data for which there is a clear and present need are obtained; (2) that data are retained only as long as their continuing value is demonstrable; (3) no invasion of privacy will be forced on a student, as part of appraisal, and, if private data are acquired, they will not become part of the cumulative record; (4) students and parents (if the student is a minor) may examine the school's cumulative record about the student; while at the same time (5) persons who are not professional employees of that school may not examine or be told data in the cumulative record; and (6) the management of the cumulative record is an administrator's responsibility, and it will be culled, updated, and validated systematically.

The substance of an appraisal program is the collection of parametric information about all students through standardized tests and such non-parametric information as called for either by law or as needed to assist the student to cope with a present behavior. Parametric assessment is a highly technical area, and many errors in administration and use of standardized testing data growing out of ignorance of this technical knowledge were examined. Three forms of validity were explored, but most attention was paid to construct validity by focusing on an area of assessment, called intelligence, whose construct validity was questioned.

Note was made of the differences in appraisal practices associated with different members of the guidance team, showing that counselors and behavior specialists have most to do with assessment procedures and content and other fixed and varying team members, such as the career development and continuing education technicians, have no need to collect or use appraisal information. A number of these ideas were tested and illustrated by a brief report of the case of Francine.

REFERENCES

BRIDGES, W. H., & SCHWEBEL, M. "The Impact of Ideology on the IQ Controversy." *Journal of Mental Health*, 1975, *3,* 4.

BYRNE, R. H. *The School Counselor.* Boston: Houghton Mifflin, 1963.

CAMPBELL, D. T., and STANLEY, J. C. *Experimental and Quasi-Experimental Designs for Research.* Chicago: Rand McNally, 1963.

EBEL, R. L. "Educational Tests: Valid? Biased? Useful?" *Phi Delta Kappan,* 1975, *57,* (2), 83–88.

GREEN, R. L. "Tips on Educational Testing: What Teachers and Parents Know." *Phi Delta Kappan,* 1975, *57,* (2), 89–93.

HATCH, R. N., & STEFFLRE, B. *Administration of Guidance Services* (2nd ed.). Englewood Cliffs, N.J.: Prentice-Hall, 1965.

MOLES, O. C. "Educational Training in Low Income Families." In L. M. Irelan (Ed.), *Low-Income Life Styles.* Washington, D.C.: Government Printing Office, 1967.

OSIPOW, S. H., & WALSH, W. B. *Strategies in Counseling for Behavior Change.* Englewood Cliffs, N.J.: Prentice-Hall, 1970.

Standards for Educational and Psychological Tests. Washington, D.C.: The American Psychological Association, 1974.

14 Professional Issues

INTRODUCTION

The members of any occupation in the public's notice, when linked in an organization, will come up against issues, problems, or concerns. Some of these are persistent, while others may be ephemeral. A few of these issues are considered as major, some as trivial, others in between. No organized occupation is exempt: any labor union, each professional association, guild, or interest group. All organized facets of public education are always at some major or minor crossroads, or even facing a road block. The guidance movement faces its share of fresh and continuing issues, which are the topics of this chapter.

It would not have been incorrect to have titled a number of prior chapters with the additional phrase, "The Professional Issues of . . . ," for, indeed, a number of topics treated earlier merit pro and con elaboration, rather than simple exposition, because those topics are active professional issues. This chapter raises other concerns expressed in the organized voices of the occupation, its journals, or assemblies, although some topics presented in earlier chapters are treated afresh here.

The chapter title can be used to introduce the first issue. There is no question about the world "issues," but what of "professional"? In its day-to-day usage the word has two meanings. One is for general conversation or writing and is used in a variety of forms and applied to almost any occupation in the sense when one speaks of "the oldest profession," or a "professional carpenter," meaning one who earns his living by that trade as opposed to someone who engages in carpentering behaviors for reasons other than income. "That's a professional job" might be said, in this loose use of the term, in reference to the way a homeowner has cut and trimmed his lawn, meaning that it is an effort that produced superior results. Guidance practitioners are urged to join their professional association, another example of the loose use of the term. That association, the American Personnel and Guidance Association (APGA), if the word "professional" was used precisely, would be termed an interest or occupational association rather than a professional organization.

The other meaning is the narrower one for identifying those few occupations among the twenty thousand in this country that occupational sociologists have determined are qualified for that label to contrast them with other classes of occupations. Psychologists, many health practitioners, and lawyers illustrate this use of the term. The American Bar Association is correctly termed a professional association, an organization of professionals. Within this chapter the word will be used both ways, with the particular usage being identified by the context.

ARE GUIDANCE OCCUPATIONS PROFESSIONS?

In the 1950s and for part of the 1960s the issue about school counseling being a profession seemed to be important to some of the APGA membership, but it now appears to be far less so, as evidenced by the disappearance of journal articles treating the topic. Even if dormant, it merits a bit of attention. The question can be addressed by reference solely to counselors. Those occupations of the guidance team that require less preparation are surely not professions. The behavior specialist may merit that classification some of the time, but that occupation need not be of concern at this moment.

Whether or not an occupation is classed as a profession is legally determined in some states, but not at all at the federal level. Yet federal departments have a practical bearing on the question through the development of occupational classification schemes. The most pervasively influential of these schemes is that of the Department of Labor as exerted in its occupational classification on which the Dictionary of Occupational Titles (DOT) is built. The DOT, however, avoids a position as to whether or not counseling is a profession; indeed it fails to say whether any occupation is a profession. This avoidance is achieved by the DOT's classification scheme, which bunches professions with managerial and some other types of occupations that require advanced preparation and require functions of higher reponsibility or skill. However counseling might be classified by the DOT in the occupational hierarchy, it is useful to measure it against the criteria of professions generated within occupational sociology.

Greenwood (Nosow & Form, 1962) posits five characteristics of professions, and these can serve as criteria for judging whether or not an occupation is a profession. To Greenwood's five I have added a sixth (Byrne, 1963).

1. *There is a systematic theory on which the practices of the occupation are based.* It is in this area that I have faulted the past of the guidance movement, but now counseling can be based on principles of behavior. Currently, however, counseling does not meet this criterion.

2. *The occupation is granted authority by society.* The best way to see the thrust of this criterion is to mull over the standing of physicians. In general their directives are accepted and followed. Some physicians still do not let patients know the name or type of prescribed medicine, a secrecy abetted by pharmaceutical houses that package their products so that labels can be readily removed before turning them over to patients. This is a course of secrecy designed to enchance the authority of the physician. Physicians learn authoritative behaviors toward patients as part of their training. But the authority of physicians is no more boldly exampled than in their legislated right, which is theirs alone, to declare persons to be dead or to commit persons to psychiatric institutions without the person's approval.

Parents and students do ask counselors for opinions, but evidence is lacking about the degree to which such advice is followed. Some counselors appear to have authority in schools, in such areas as determining courses for students and in matters relating to student suspension. Such authority, however, is delegated by the principal and is not inherent in the occupation. In fact, counselors have complained about receiving this kind of assignment from principals, seeing such actions about youth as being contrary to proper counselor functioning. A factor that furthers the nonauthority stance of the counselor is that the counselor's training, in diametric opposition to the training of the physician, seeks to prepare persons to behave professionally in an unauthoritarian way.

In another important way counselors are shown to have little authority. This is in the frequency with which counselors are required to respond to the directions of noncounselors, be they principals, the U.S. Congress, the local school board, or a group of parents. This is not merely an outcome of being in a socialized occupation, either. Consider, for example, the school nurse. That person occupies an identically socialized occupation yet engages in no activities during the day that are not self-determined or assessed by a medical supervisor. Counselors, on the other hand, are directed to do scheduling, carry out orientation, and do other administrative chores partly because theirs is a nonauthoritative, disciplineless occupation.

In sum, up to now counseling has had no more authority than teaching, a nonprofessional occupation. Because there is now a theory on which productive practices can be based, accompanied by statements of guidance objectives to be attained by all students, counseling might acquire community acknowledgment as an authoritative occupation in the coming years.

3. *There are sanctions granted to the occupation by the community.* This is the other side of the authority coin. School counselors have gained one sanction in some states: privileged communication, which provides them legal exemption from divulging what students tell them. This exemption is general in some states and specific in others, such as in Maryland where the exemption applies only to any communication with the counselor about drug use. The matter of sanctions is a fuzzy area in which to make judgment, requiring the unsatisfactory summation that counseling has partially acquired some community sanctions in some states.

4. *There is an ethical code under which the occupation polices its members.* Yes, there is an ethical code set up by members of the APGA (see Appendix B). No, there are no provisions for the occupation to police itself; there is no process for peer review of practices, let alone provisions for disbarment from the occupation of counseling. The occupation on this score alone is placed outside the classification of a profession.

5. *There is an occupational culture.* There is a society of counselors within which there is a thin culture. Physicians and lawyers, to use again two clear illustrations of professionals, enter their profession and generally stay for life. Their occupation is selective, and the training long and difficult, a period during which the weaker aspirants are sloughed away. The occupation of counselor has only just now arrived at the expectancy of a year's preparation as a common standard, and only after a slow journey during which resistance was great. In the 1950s a half-year's preparation was considered a great amount, but through the 1960s a year's preparation gradually emerged as the mode.

Even though a clear length and substance for the preparation of counselors has emerged, persons continue to enter and leave counseling, a condition of noncommitment to the occupation clearly shown by the number for whom counseling is but a way-station on the high road to school administration. Persons who enter counseling do so mostly from the occupation of teaching, a fact that again points out the nonprofessional status of counseling. Counseling is so sufficiently akin to teaching that a teaching credential was once a universal requirement among those states that certified counselors for schools. This state certification stipulation is no longer universal, but the question is still argued with vigor. Regardless of the merits of the arguments on either side, relative to the issue of professions the resolution of the issue is clear: professions, as a committed way of life, do not require their members to first enter and practice in another occupation before readying for and practicing in the profession. The way to accurately picture the culture of counseling is to move under it and say that, if there is any educational profession in the years of common schooling, it is that of teaching. Counseling, then, would have to be viewed as a specialized form of the occupation of teaching as it is clearly viewed in other countries.

If an occupation has a culture, its members will. To be identified as having a culture a group will have members identify themselves in those terms that define that occupation as a way of life, a term that connotes prideful commitment to an order of behavior and loyalty to the group. The group that has a culture, whether it is a nation or an occupation, is selective and restrictive about its membership. On that score the occupations of steam fitting and plastering have more attributes of a culture than counseling does. The words of another time are still valid:

> There is no guarded door leading into the inner sanctum of counseling. It is a wide-open door, with no initiation rites and with only the threshold of state certification to step over. There are ways to enter without even crossing that threshold. Because it is not a culture difficult to enter or leave, there is constant coming and going. The culture is so sparse that it exerts little gravity pull on those who do become school counselors. [Byrne, 1963, p. 281]

Those observations lead to this summing statement: counseling is insufficient in the quantity and quality of occupational culture to merit being classed as a profession. The future, now that there is an empirically validated theoretical base on which the professional behaviors of counselors can rest, may provide a professional level of culture for counselors, and particularly for behavior specialists. The result will more likely be that persons will prepare for the occupation without first preparing for another and will stay in it for life.

6. *The practitioners have occupational autonomy.* They hang out a shingle and announce their readiness to accept clients or patients. Professionals are in independent practice marked by a community view of them as authoritative persons, skilled practitioners of the comprehensive theory underlying their occupation, living by an ethical code that is policed by their fellow professionals as one of the sanctions granted the occupation by the community, and earning their income by charging each person a fee for services.

Despite this private practice characteristic, considered by many to be a major, if not the major, attribute of a profession, I retain the view that this is not a truly essential characteristic, merely a common one. Illustrations of this counterpoint abound. Business X employs a full-time physician and four full-time nurses. Are they no longer professionals because they are now salaried? Are counselors-at-law who are similarly employed no longer professionals? The veterinarians employed by the Department of Agriculture? "The criterion of occupational autonomy reflects historical accident rather than an essential characteristic" (Byrne, 1963, p. 282), the accident of history permitting certain occupations to emerge wherein the practitioner of that occupation had no choice but to set up shop and engage in private practice. This applied not just to accountants (theirs being actually the oldest profession in the precise sense of the term), lawyers, and barber/physicians, but eventually to plumbers, trashmen, and practitioners of countless other occupations. Teachers were autonomous two centuries ago. The fact that counseling was generated by a socialized institution is an accident of time, and not a reason why it should not be classified as a profession.

The sum of the application of the first five criteria is that counseling is not yet a profession. It is a worthy occupation of potentially great value, one with which I am pridefully associated, and which perhaps someday will be truly a profession.

SHIFTING SANDS: A POOR BASE FOR GUIDANCE PRACTICES

Is it possible for the guidance movement to have a scientific base, and if so, when? This topic has been before us in other chapters, but earns a retreatment in this chapter because issues falling within it are of concern to the persons who constitute a profession, the word being used in both its precise and loose senses. If any of us were physicians, we would be concerned about the quality of thought underpinning our practices and would be attentive to the ripple effect of those thoughts (the theory) of our occupation's authority and sanctions. We would use the arena of professional associations to identify the issues and act remedially as such need was identified.

The statements of concern in prior chapters about the lack of a theoretical base for guidance practices up to recent years were selected to meet the instructional needs of those chapters. Here they are restated relative to the needs of the profession.

The absence of a disciplinary base for guidance practices in the past has resulted in a condition that would be undesirable for any occupation: the occupational behaviors of its practitioners are subject to the whims, fancies, and directives generated outside the occupation.

Counseling and counselors for years could make claim only to good intentions. Lacking a bedrock disciplinary base, and building only on theoretical soft sands, the structure of counseling practices had an ill-defined character of that kind that astute principals could identify as not of great importance relative to the whole territory of the school on which they gazed from their pinnacles. School needs coupled with vague practices inevitably resulted in principals' assigning a variety of duties to counselors which eased the administrative burden. Is it correct that counselors work for individuals? Fine, here then are individuals with all kinds of needs: course changes, difficulties with teachers, attendance delinquencies, and so on, and these will be handled by counselors. They are clearly administrative concerns, of course, but in the inadequate logic behind counseling, puzzled counselors had no basis for resisting these administrative assignments despite ill-defined thoughts that there were other, more important fish that they were supposed to fry.

Other outside demands pushed the guidance structure into skewed positions. The NDEA of 1958 said that testing and the identification of the gifted must be done. Counselors liked that sense of direction and readily accorded. If the drop-out rate must be attacked, then we will set up extensive summer programs of counseling drop-outs. Such a situation occurred in 1957, incidentally, with interesting results. Drop-outs were stimulated to come to school, and school-attending behaviors were reinforced for awhile, but the greater aversive conditions of schooling which forced the students to drop out in the first place became more potent, and the reentered drop-outs redropped out.[1]

The shifting sands that gave so poor a base to the guidance structure were mostly those of the phenomenological view of man and the counseling practices that emanated from it. There were several results of note. For one, that view gave sanction to a nonnomogenic stance about behavior. It also gave sanction to the synecdoche that one array of procedures was sufficient for mediating all forms of behavior. In addition, it drew guidance practices away from programmatic interventions of profit to all youth and moved them toward practices based on the indefensible equation, guidance = counseling.

The translation of that equation into practice is found in the insistence by supervisors and others within the guidance field that counselors are to counsel, that is, to engage in one-to-one interviews, although assisting an individual in a group setting (group counseling) was also acceptable as a guidance practice. One crushing effect of this counseling-only characteristic of guidance practice was the limitation of assistance to a minority of those students who had coping concerns and the strength to seek help with them. The fallacy of that practice can be rationalized away because, when a phenomenological view of man undergirds counseling technology, there is also required a phenomenological teleology: there are not nor can there be

---

[1] Extensive coverage of this topic was given in a popular magazine a few years ago. Arguments there as well as in the recent professional literature bear essentially the same message as presented about two decades ago (Byrne, 1958).

common, specific guidance objectives, only the general objective of assisting each person who seeks assistance. The phenomenological position, contrary to clear evidence, is that each person has a unique pattern of concerns, therefore guidance objectives have to be drawn up uniquely by and for each person. This teleology foreordains, therefore, the need to serve individuals only as individuals in one-to-one counseling.

Bedrock at Last?

Yes, as a possibility, as so often stated, but not in practice. Holding with the metaphor, new sand dunes keep being built up between guidance practices and bedrock. New techniques are spawned and promotional appeals for followers sent out by the new schools of technology. The confusion is abetted in counselor preparation programs and by the chief interest association of counselors, as shown by the popularity of a film issued by the APGA that allegedly demonstrates three kinds of counseling founded by three practitioners. One person is interviewed by each of the three founders, and in the end votes for which one she preferred! I ask you to imagine a medical school showing a film that demonstrates three different views of the cause and cures of illness, in which a patient is treated by the founder of each of the three technologies. The final imaginary scene shows the patient voting for the technology she likes best, with the film being shown so as to educate future physicians about biological science and the practice of medicine based on that science. Did I lose you somewhere? Has an impossible condition been proposed in that analogy? Impossible within medicine and other professions, yes. The issuance by the APGA and the common use of that film in counselor preparation programs were offered to illustrate the present sorry state of guidance practitioner preparation vis-à-vis the existent science of behavior. The science—the bedrock—is there, but a struggle of unpredictable outcome roils as to whether guidance practices, particularly the mediation of behavior, can be fixed to a disciplinary bedrock before being torn and shredded by multiplying adisciplinary and even antidisciplinary technologies. No issue can be more fundamental to a profession.

PROFESSIONAL ISSUES REGARDING GUIDANCE OCCUPATIONS

What about new guidance team occupations? Will there be a professional or interest association home for them? The incorrect equation, guidance = counseling, will pass away as the guidance movement is freed from the equally incorrect equation, counseling = therapy. Another change that will occur when the latter equation is no longer in force will be the freedom to adopt guidance objectives for all youth.

Once guidance objectives have been adopted, the logic shown in Chapter 2 will follow. There is a step in that logic that calls for establishment of the occupations that will be needed to conduct the guidance program and to thereby attain the objectives. This collection of guidance occupations has been referred to here as the guidance team. Some difficulties related to these multiple occupations is foreseeable, so let's look at one.

The thrust toward converting public education to career education has had a ripple effect in the guidance area. The documented claim that school guidance programs have abrogated their historical commitment of assistance to youth in career development and decision making has produced a small but growing movement to add to schools a new type of guidance practitioner who would be independent of other guidance practitioners. This new occupation is titled "vocational" or "career counselor." I am among the chorus that holds that the outcomes assigned to this new occupation must be reached by every school; to do it with a supposedly new occupation is a spurious way to reach the goal. It is as if a new superintendent in a school system discovered that high school principals were not doing their job and established an additional occupation, called school manager, to get the job done. The expense and confusion resulting from adding a new occupation is a poor way to resolve a problem that could easily be resolved by having principals in that hypothetical school system do their assigned functions.

But vocational or career counselors are now a growing reality, and what this is going to mean for school guidance teams cannot be precisely foretold; what can generally be predicted for high schools is confusion, jockeying for grazing rights on professional pasture lands, envy, dissipation of resources, and a no-less-confused high school student body. Which says nothing of the confusion among students readying for guidance occupations.

Team Identifications

The standard guidance team proposed in Chapter 3 is comprised of three occupations: the behavior specialist, the counselor, and the career development technician. What accommodations must be made for them; what professional groups will speak for them?

THE BEHAVIOR SPECIALIST. This new practitioner, reconstructed out of the old two-year counselor idea that never could make ground against certification realities, might in some states be eligible for affiliation with a group of professional psychology practitioners, particularly local associations of school psychologists. As envisioned here the behavior specialist would have more graduate preparation than many school psychologists currently have. Yet professional identity with psychologists might be a divisive factor within the guidance team. In that this practitioner is not prepared for some of the functions carried out by school psychologists and has his strongest practice identity with school counselors, it seems appropriate to have them lie in the same interest-association bed. The APGA can readily accommodate this new practitioner.

OTHER TEAM MEMBERS. Counselors, the traditional members of guidance teams, long since have had a professional association, nationally, at the state level, and locally. Career development technicians and the workers of optional occupations on the guidance team can also be accommodated within the APGA.

Team Building

Giving guidance team members an identification is important. Certain prospective occupations, not evolving within a society but aritficially created on the basis of reasoning, have failed to be accepted by employers. Persons prepared for such rational occupations, such as Ph.D.-holding psychiatrists, were not accepted by professional associations and thus could not get the license and other legal sanctions necessary for employment. Having no professional association, they were voiceless. Being voiceless, they were powerless. Rational processes are hastening the emergence of guidance occupations that are naturally evolving, and the APGA can readily absorb new guidance occupations. The concern, therefore, is not whether new occupations will have an associational home, but whether the professional issues of the employment of new types of practitioners in schools at a faster rate than their natural evolution would permit, the establishment of their unique functions, the meshing of the functions of all guidance occupations into an effective team, and matters related to preparation of practitioners can be dealt with.

The career development technician (CDT) is one guidance team occupation that, if established widely and quickly enough, may serve to counterthrust the divisive other new occupation mentioned earlier, the vocational or career counselor. If the single occupation guidance team is modified by any one school to include the CDT, that functionary's roles can be established, while at the same time counselor functions are being modified. With one year's experience behind these two occupations, the school will be ready to employ a behavior specialist (and figure out an acceptable title for that practitioner). In that first year with the CDT as a member of the team, the school begins its group activities designed to have all students attain guidance objectives. In the second year, with the behavior specialist added, schemes for identifying those youths who evidence severe behavior imbalances will have been developed and procedures established for referral to that specialist. The essential team would then be operating: counselors, the mediation strategists, who work mostly with groups, and whose individual conferences deal with additional assistance youths need with normal development; the CDT, who rounds out the career decision strategies that counselors cause groups of students to acquire; and the behavior specialist, who acts to restore to normal development that small percentage of youths who have been extruded from it.

Prior to the boiling over of the pot of discontent about guidance programs' lack of attainments in the occupational decision area, a pervasive discontent about the lack of a disciplinary base and the inefficiencies of "services," as they were then known, resulted in the establishment in 1962 of the Interprofessional Research Commission on Pupil Personnel Services (IRCOPPS) with over $1 million of funding. Sufficient information about IRCOPPS was given in Chapter 3. All that needs recording here is that even though there were great quantities of publications emanating from the IRCOPPS centers and central office, no resolution of the difficulties, for which purpose IRCOPPS was set up, was reached. It is reasonable to conjecture two causes among others for that outcome: first, the five-year funding was too short—good directions were set up, but could not be followed through—second, the findings of behavioral science, now so readily available, were not then available in sufficient quantity to permit IRCOPPS research to take off from an empirically supported disciplinary base.

PREPARATION OF TEAM MEMBERS

What is the significance for training programs of the new directions recorded or proposed here? For all but the most recent history of the guidance movement preparation of guidance practitioners meant counselors. Organized sequences of courses for preparation of counselors did not become the usual practice until after World War II, although single courses were no longer unusual in the 1930s. Two weighty influences in the history of the preparation of counselors had origins in the providing of federal funds, one in the implementation of the provisions of the George-Dean and George-Barden Acts and the other in portions of the NDEA. The influence of both these thrusts has been examined in other places, and only one effect merits additional comment. The U.S. Office of Education (USOE) managers of these programs used a portion of the funds for at least annual conferences of counselor educators, and these conferences, followed by other regional and national meetings under the successor act of the NDEA, brought a uniformity and sense of national cohesion to programs to prepare counselors. Federal funds, readily accessible for 20 years, dried up in the early 1970s, and I predict one result will be greater diversity among counselor preparation programs in the absence of such federally funded meetings.

Coupled with this change are others. The realist versus idealist philosophical division is being met squarely in a number of counselor preparation departments. The results are sometimes an astonishing accommodation: in effect two counselor preparation programs within one department, one of them based on principles of behavior, the other on the phenomenological-perceptive basis that undergirded most programs 20 years ago. Other changes that have fallen on the guidance movement, each of which has had sufficient exposition in other places here, can be nothing other than forces for further diversification among counselor preparation programs. Other forces not yet focused upon are recent variables. For one, a few states have changed, or are about to change, counselor certification requirements to performance statements, rather than course completion statements, a movement that is likely to spread. For another, the great fall-off in demand for counselors, with the likelihood that the smaller counselor preparation programs, those mostly in private institutions, will either retrench or fold, unless the team idea becomes well established in public education, and such preparation programs are committed to readying team members in addition to counselors.

Giving away the Profession

Under this catchy title Division 17 of the American Psychological Association (APA), the Division of Counseling Psychology, to which many counselor educators and doctoral level practitioners belong, is studying the question of how much, if at all, the clients of counseling psychologists shall be taught counseling. Prior chapters have stated the case for this giving away, centering the argument on the idea that within education each teacher hopes that his students will know not only as much as he knows, but will even stand on the teacher's shoulders, metaphorically speaking. Job security cannot be the issue, because teachers persist, even after giving away their knowledge. Relative to this section's topic of guidance program practices, the issue to be faced is whether guidance practices are done to students or give students the capacity to do for themselves. Having come down on the side of the latter, this text favors causing students to acquire decision-making skills, self-management skills, including those acquired through biofeedback instrumentation, and the communication skills represented by the helping or facilitating interview procedures. This is favoring, in more colorful phrasing, giving the profession away, to some degree.

FEDERAL GOVERNMENT RECOGNITION OF THE GUIDANCE MOVEMENT

Has the federal government helped the guidance movement up to now, and is it going to in the future? Adding to items already recorded earlier about the federal government's role in guidance is the degree of acknowledgment of the guidance movement made through staff positions in the USOE.

When the Occupational Information and Guidance Service section of the Division of Vocational Education in the USOE was abolished in 1952 because of internal disagreements, there were no persons in the USOE to represent the guidance interests of schools. The APGA had recently been formed and joined with the APA in a vigorous lobbying effort for the restoration of some form of guidance consultation and coordinating office in the USOE. A new unit was established, and its staff and influence grew over the years under the leadership of Dr. Frank L. Sievers. Passage of the NDEA resulted in an excess of riches: there now were two units in the USOE concerned with guidance. Because power follows money, the additional unit under the leadership of Drs. Ralph C. Bedell and C. Harold McCully, even though its scope of guidance interests was limited by law to counselor preparation, became an office of considerable influence on the direction of guidance practices throughout the country because that office funded guidance institutes.

NDEA funds for institutes passed, other NDEA support for guidance was absorbed in new federal legislation, and eventually this also was reduced severely. Before the mid-1970s not only had federal funds for support of guidance in the states been curtailed, but again the unit in the USOE responsible for guidance support and coordination was abolished. Although the office was done away with less dramatically than in 1952, its loss is regretted. Yet only token effort was mounted this time to bring about its reestablishment.

Incidentally, one contribution of the guidance branch in the USOE to the profession was the compiling and publishing of data about guidance preparation and practices. The abolition of that branch resulted in the loss of this central data collection and publication, a sorely missed service that, strangely enough, has not been picked up by any unit in the APGA.

Meanwhile in the early 1970s the National Institute of Education (NIE), a unit intended to be for education what the National Institutes of Health are for that area, was created by Congress. One of the NIE's major efforts has been in support of career education and thus of career development. The influence of this NIE thrust is only now starting to be noticeable, but, it can be reasonably predicted, will be rapidly increasing. Another example of the apothegm, power follows money.

Influence of Other Federal Agencies

Although not as pronounced in influence and as comprehensive in scope, other units in the federal establishment have been sources of influence in the school guidance movement.

Support for the preparation of counselors in rehabilitation agencies has had a long history and continues. Counselors for rehabilitation functions in a variety of agencies are also employed in schools and are often prepared in programs that also prepare counselors for other settings and functions. The studies of mediation procedures sponsored by the now-titled Rehabilitation Services Administration can apply to behavior intervention no matter in which setting it is practiced.

The U.S. Employment Service for an extended period employed counselors who typically were prepared in the same programs that prepared school counselors. The contributions of the USES, now Training and Employment Services, to mediation practices are numerous, but perhaps that unit is most widely known for its development and issuance of the General Aptitude Test Battery (GATB), which has been and is used with benefit for youth in high schools.

The presidency of L. B. Johnson produced a quantity and quality of legislation bearing on human resources called, in sum, the War on Poverty. Each unit established to carry out that war had a guidance component: Job Corps, Neighborhood Youth Corps, and Manpower Development and Training Act facilities among them. These and guidance elements of other new or altered agencies of the War on Poverty, along with the guidance functions in well-established federal units, such as the Veterans Administration, let alone the firmly rooted guidance component of public education, were potentials for erratic diversification and overlapping of services. Into this messy condition, which contained the likelihood of increased messiness, a federal unit moved hoping to bring order. The actions of this unit permitted hope of stabilizing the erratic developments in guidance, of giving some commonality of purpose and substance, and of eliminating wasteful, cross-purpose actions among all types of agencies that provide guidance services in the United States. This unit was the Counseling and Manpower Utilization branch of the Department of Labor under the leadership of David H. Pritchard.

Pritchard was instrumental in the establishment of a nationwide panel on counseling, testing, and selection, and later he instigated the formation of an Interagency Task Force on Counseling. The task force had on it representatives of all federal agencies that had interest in counseling, as well as representatives from those professional associations that represented the same concerns. Through the published findings of that task force, which studied counseling services for a year, coupled with the conclusions of an earlier national conference (McGowan, 1965) whose convening also originated with Pritchard, legislation was proposed that, had it passed, would have permanently and parametrically altered counselor preparation and functions in all sectors represented by task force members, throughout the country (Gregory, 1967).

The results of the activities of that branch had great potential for influencing the direction of guidance everywhere. Why that influence never passed beyond the astute findings and proposed legislation resulting from the massive amount of personpower given to those studies is open to some conjecture, but doubtless the reasons include the distractions from worthwhile purposes accruing to the executive department's increasing involvements in the Vietnam war. Additionally the abrogation of the War on Poverty by the Nixon administration, along with Pritchard's departure from the Department of Labor are tenable as reasons.[2] He is now education research specialist (guidance), USOE.

The quarter-century of influence of the federal government on the guidance movement has greatly lessened, in contrast to the pervasive influences of the past. Such influence as there is today is focused on the career area, but in the long run may turn out to influence the direction of guidance in the years to come far more than any past federal actions have.

PROFESSIONAL ASSOCIATIONS

Is the guidance movement well represented by its main interest association, the APGA? A professional association, through its publications, meetings, and lobbyings, furthers the purposes of the practitioners it represents. The National Vocational Guidance Association (NVGA) was established in 1913 and has remained a significant voice for school counselors and guidance practitioners in other settings. Associations of human

[2] A profession's culture has its villains and its heroes, as has any culture. Villainy often is well publicized. Heroes, on the other hand, in the manner of the cliché, are often unsung. Pritchard is one of those whose contributions to the guidance movement have had some public notice, but others of his efforts that could have had potentially profound significance for the guidance movement have been unacknowledged. There might have been that kind of public acknowledgement some years back had not the internal politics of the APGA at that time required that its annual award for merit go to a person from a certain other classification. As one with extensive first-hand knowledge of Pritchard's vigorous, imaginative, and indeed daring efforts for the benefit of the guidance movement, it is a pleasure to acknowledge in these pages his valuable contributions, although a poor substitute for the acknowledgement owed him by the profession.

resources practitioners in other settings were established over the years, and because the NVGA membership and that of the other associations knew that a collective voice was better than each unit's speaking by itself, a number of associations with similar interests set up a Council of Guidance and Personnel Associations. Each association retained full autonomy, a condition analogous to that in America prior to 1789. Just as sages saw in the post–Revolutionary War period that a confederation of states would not be as useful as a federation, so too did the leaders and members of the majority of associations comprising the council view their structure, and the decision by those units was for federation. In 1951 the NVGA joined four related associations in creating the American Personnel and Guidance Association (APGA).

To represent the constituency in the APGA with the largest population, school counselors, a division for them was set up in 1953, the American School Counselor Association (ASCA). State guidance supervisors whose salaries and activities were supported by federal George-Barden funds administered by the USOE's Occupational Information and Guidance Section (OIGS), were represented by an association called the National Association of Guidance Supervisors (NAGS), which had been set up after World War II. In 1950 NAGS admitted those counselor trainers, as they were called, who also were supported by OIGS-administered funds, and the group's name was changed to NAGSCT. That organization was one that joined the others to form the APGA and in the early 1950s was again restructured to admit guidance supervisors from local administrative levels. At the same time it was renamed the Association of Counselor Educators and Supervisors (ACES). The new title reflects history. No more "guidance." The new name reflected a shift from interest in program to an interest in the single type of guidance practitioner of those days. It furthered the entrenchment of the equation guidance = counselors = individual counseling conferences.

Of the now eleven APGA divisions, NVGA, ASCA, and ACES are those with most significance for school guidance practitioners. There are state and local branches of those divisions in most states, and each division publishes a journal and other literature, all in addition to the journal and extensive publications of the APGA, which also has a growing tape and film productivity.

This placid recital does not convey the tugs and turmoils that have marked the APGA from its outset, that continue to do so, and that are quite normal in any viable association. Just as the APA has been racked with talk about secession by some of its units, so has the APGA. The division titled the American College Personnel Association, one of the founding units of APGA, considered for a number of years the appropriateness of withdrawing from the APGA and federating with other non-APGA college guidance associations to form a new organization. The ACPA membership voted to remain a division of the APGA in 1974.

The APGA has had a code of ethics for many years, restudied and revised as deemed necessary at intervals. Every guidance practitioner must be apprised of its provisions, and the code will be found in Appendix B. Although there are no policing provisions within APGA related to that code, a lack that does not indicate an associational deficiency but does reflect the lack of legal standing of counselors and other guidance practitioners, the APGA is responsible for one form of protection of the public. In the 1950s the number of agencies that offered guidance services to the public increased greatly. Building on prior activities of the NVGA, the ruling body of the APGA set up an independent board, now titled the International Association of Counseling Services, to evaluate agencies that offer guidance services to the public. Those agencies that meet criteria applied by the association's evaluating board are permitted to include a statement of that approval in their professional announcements. The directory is available in public libraries; thus the public could be more certain of the quality of help available if it knew such evaluation was carried out.

As in any professional group, within the APGA there has been need to face concerns about sexism and racism. In response to those issues, not only has the APGA taken clear affirmative action within its structure, but through its journals and conventions has provided an appropriate arena for examination of such undesirable practices in schools and other agencies within the association's concerns and has led in proposals for changed practices, as recorded elsewhere here. The association's national headquarters staff in Washington for years has been active in educating the federal establishment about guidance matters and has lobbied effectively for the passage of guidance-oriented legislation. It has thus fulfilled one of the major functions of an occupational or interest association.

This history of selected highlights sums, in my view, to a portrayal of an association that is flexible, vigorous, reflective of membership wishes, and productive. It has a high degree of democracy and social awareness. It is a fine voice for guidance practitioners.

GUIDANCE PROGRAMS IN OTHER SETTINGS

How much commonality and how much distinctiveness should there be in guidance activities and practitioners in various kinds of settings? Perhaps this issue has professional significance only for programs that prepare guidance practitioners. If there is more commonality than diversity, then a single preparation program suffices, as at the University of Maryland. In other institutions there are two or more preparation programs, each setting-specific, thus giving testimony that others find the diversity greater than the commonality.

The starting point in addressing the question is not kind of programs or practitioners, but the characteristics of humans served by the agencies that provide guidance services. The issue will be examined by consideration of the two educational settings between which secondary schools are sandwiched, elementary and postsecondary schools.

Elementary schools deal with children, secondary schools with adolescents, and postsecondary schools with young adults. That is not just stating the obvious; those three different words convey great differences in the clientele served and thus in the differences called for in program and kinds of practitioners.

Before focusing on the two settings, which bracket the high school setting, we entertain a reminder about characteristics of adolescents so as to permit a better comparison among the three settings. Adolescents have recently had the second of two births to which all humans are subjected. The first of these, the biological, is a relatively abrupt emergence in contrast to that of the second, in which we leave the comfortable womb of childhood in a time span measured in months, not minutes or hours. But we humans are born again, and somewhat suddenly we are conscious of self, eager to be independent of adults, interested in the opposite sex, aware of and concerned about our future, with these and other characteristics giving a sense of urgency to life. The needs of humans at this developmental level in this culture are unique relative to children, but far less so relative to young adults.

Elementary Schools

Because only psychologically independent, future-oriented, choice-facing persons need counsel, and elementary school children are not marked by such characteristics, why are there counselors in elementary schools? Response to that question must include such variables as professional politics; good will; "whatever they have in X school system we must have in ours," an educational keeping-up-with-the-Joneses; more good will; skill in selling ideas, even not very rational ideas; federal and other outside funds; and still more good will. The good will is important. It shows a pervasive caring about children that lets officials of a school system say that if guidance activities in secondary schools are good for students, accepting that on faith, and because guidance = counselors, then, it could be believed, "we must have counselors in our elementary schools." Further impetus was given for employing elementary school counselors, I am certain, by the shift in high school counselor function a quarter-century ago from the historic forms of assistance to youth by means of general programs to a one-to-one therapeutic activity. In this function counselors closeted themselves with individual youths who had problems, and through the Rogerian procedures that almost all counselors-to-be learned then as the sole behavior intervention procedure, they provided psychotherapy. This approach inevitably was followed by the view that instead of waiting to help youth with big problems, schools should help children with the small problems before they become the big ones. The need was seen, therefore, for counselors (therapists) in elementary schools. The counselor-as-psychotherapist aberration has almost died out now, but the detritus of that movement remains in elementary schools: counselors.

The message here is not to do away with a guidance specialist in elementary schools, but to not use counselors, simply because children do not need counseling. There is need for a guidance practitioner who has the training to attend to the school as a psychosocial ecosystem, as a social system that can nurture development around accepted mental health criteria, or that, at the other extreme, can impede development. They will be system interventionists, experts in child development, teachers of teachers and parents, knowledgeable of how behavior is formed, maintained, and can be changed. If tradition, politics, or other forces require that these practitioners be titled counselors instead of child development specialists, then at least let their functions acknowledge the facts of child psychology through their behaving professionally as child development specialists.

Postsecondary Institutions

Humans do not move as abruptly in nature from childhood into adolescense, or from adolescence into young adulthood, but institutions do move them abruptly between those periods. The junior high or middle school appeared over a half-century ago as a bridge between the first two developmental epochs, but for long there was no transitional educational institution available to most youth to bridge the sharp jump from an institution serving adolescents to the one serving young adults. More and more that transitional function is being served by community or junior colleges, however, with the prediction that public bachelor degree–granting institutions may soon take in only juniors, thus forcing many youths to first enroll in community or junior colleges.

The differences between the late adolescent in high school and the freshman in college are not great, but the differences between the two institutions are. The high school graduate who views himself on Commencement Day as grown up and sophisticated, as he contrasts himself with his not-too-distant childhood, suddenly finds himself in an environment that at times makes him feel childish all over again.

The guidance activities of the college or university, which will in great probability be labeled "student personnel services," serve to assist students in that difficult transition by helping them exploit the assets of the institution for maximum individual benefit, and by making the transition to the real world after graduation. Guidance practitioners at the college or university level are likely to have titles similar to those in high schools who carry out similar functions, now that high schools are moving to the multiple-occupation guidance team idea that has been always the situation in higher education. There are basic differences in program, however. A case can be made, and has been attempted throughout this text, that high schools will have to offer activities for all students, through groups, of course, so that youth will attain common guidance objectives. That case is difficult to make for young adults who, by definition, should be managing their own lives. Thus the tradition in higher education student services has been to give guidance assistance only to those who seek it, with the exception of orientation activities that freshmen are urged, if not required, to attend.

Humans are divided into children and all others, thus there is least in common between objectives, programs, and personnel provided for children and those provided to the others, whether they are the adolescents and adults in educational institutions or are those served in rehabilitation and other community agencies. For adolescents and adults, the weight is on the side of similarities rather than diversities. For that clientele, therefore, common preparation programs and a common national association is justified.

THE FUTURE

Have the directions guidance is to take in the future been charted? This is an area of judgment, and mine is that the newer directions have been charted: an emphasis again on career development, the use of guidance teams, the stating of guidance objectives in performance terms, and the use of behavior intervention strategies based on behavior principles are some of these. Some of these are rare, others more advanced. Some directions have been recently set that will receive increased attention. These are focusing on subpopulations.

Racial and Ethnic Minorities

The signs I see say that attention to blacks, Hispanics, and native Americans not only has not peaked among guidance practitioners but is scarcely under way. One of the bigger issues within this area is whether you have to be one to counsel one. The claims made so far in either direction have not been supported by convincing evidence, although the principle has long been recognized in the practice of ascertaining that high schools have both male and female counselors.

Because poverty is the one shared characteristic between the three groups named, it may be as correct or even better to state that in the future the guidance movement will attend more to poor youth. If so, it will mark a return to the original population for which guidance activities were set up. Fiscally the rich get richer, thus the poor poorer, and that maxim holds for guidance assistance too. Graff and his colleagues (1971) studied the question of differences in quantity and quality of guidance assistance received by youth when broken down into several classifications. They found no difference in guidance assistance received between the sexes or among the races, but did find that lower class students received significantly less assistance than upper class students relative to (1) choosing a post-high school educational institution, (2) making career decisions, and (3), resolving interpersonal problems. That list, in fact, covers all the concerns guidance traditionally has had except high school academic problems. The future will bring change here, I foretell. The poor, the disadvantaged, will be served by those who will reach out to help them (Amos & Grambs, 1968).

Adults

The thought that the great amount of concern about occupations and careers in them is specific to adolescents and young adults, and that once well into adulthood persons' lives, including the occupational career aspect, are stable is a myth. Schlossberg (1975) posits that "it is more realistic to view life—and adulthood especially—as consisting of a number of role transformations or role changes in four basic areas: work, family, intimacy, and community" (p. 681). The guidance functions in these role changes is apparent when one examines just the data about adults continuing with or returning to education, for example. Schlossberg suggests that one way to deliver the guidance assistance needed by adults is through community-based centers. Although she believes that such centers should be free from the control of "nearby educational institutions," such institutions may in fact provide the genesis of such centers, particularly in such budget-tight times as now. A few high school guidance centers have long served as community centers, but the current professional discourse suggests that such centers will become less rare than they are now.

Other Groups

Effort will continue to reduce bias against females, such as in the appraisal area (Birk, 1974) and in occupational choice, and we will see further study about and procedures particular to subpopulations that at one time were not tolerated in schools: married couples, unmarried mothers, and homosexuals.

THE LAST WORD

I end as I began, by noting that all portions of this text in fact deal with professional matters. In this chapter some of them were brought together and run through a different filter. Then there was a sample of other professional concerns not treated elsewhere in this text. Still other issues have been left untouched.

Some of the issues to be confronted today by any person concerned with school guidance differ from those of 10 years ago; others have been around for decades, still unresolved. One can be certain that 10 years hence there will be issues that cannot be imagined today, thus setting out the prospect that the guidance movement will be as fascinating in the future as it is today.[3]

REFERENCES

AMOS, W., & GRAMBS, J. *Counseling the Disadvantaged Youth.* Englewood Cliffs, N.J.: Prentice-Hall, 1968.

BIRK, JANICE M. "Interest Inventories: A Mixed Blessing." *Vocational Guidance Quarterly,* 1974, 22, 4, 280–286.

BYRNE, R. H. "Beware the Stay-in-School Bandwagon." *Personnel and Guidance Journal,* 1958, 36, 493–496.

BYRNE, R. H. *The School Counselor.* Boston: Houghton Mifflin, 1963.

GRAFF, R. W., GORREL, W. T., MACLEAN, G. D., & AUSTIN, B. A. "Socioeconomic Status and Students' Reactions toward School Guidance." *The High School Journal,* 1971, 54, 484–492.

GREGORY, F. A. *Report of the Interagency Task Force on Counseling.* Washington, D.C.: U.S. Department of Labor, 1967.

MCGOWAN, J. F. (Ed.). *Counselor Development in American Society.* Washington, D.C.: Government Printing Office, 1965 (Dec. #1966).

NOSOW, S., & FORM, W. H. *Man, Work, and Society.* New York: Basic Books, 1962.

POPPEN, W. A., & THOMPSON, C. L. *School Counseling Theories and Concepts.* Lincoln, Neb.: Professional Educators Publications, 1974.

SCHLOSSBERG, NANCY K. "Programs for Adults." *Personnel and Guidance Journal,* 1975, 53, 9, 681–685.

[3] Poppen and Thompson (1974, Ch. 6) present an array of professional issues of a perceptive quality that merits study.

Appendix A
Job Description
The Career Development Technician in Secondary Schools

Department of Counseling and Personnel Services
Secondary Schools Specialty Area
University of Maryland, College Park

I. Coordinates all functions with other members of school's guidance team.
   A. Receives general supervision from chairman, guidance team.
   B. Submits regular reports, oral and written, to other members of guidance team.
II. Is responsible for school's Career Information Center.
   A. Relative to career information materials:
      1. Acquires.
      2. Evaluates.
      3. Stores.
   B. Relative to disseminating information:
      1. Assists teachers in using information in classes.
      2. Maintains random-access system of information finding in Career Information Center.
      3. Maintains open hours of Center beyond school hours and days.
   C. Relative to administration of Center:
      1. Trains and supervises student, parent, and other assistants in Center.
      2. Manages funds provided for information purchase and dissemination program and for computer terminal rental.

D. Relative to information service to students:
1. Assists students who have questions or problems related to finding information.
2. Assists students in use of computer terminal for problem solving or information retrieval.
3. Organizes and conducts group information activities in coordination with teachers and other members of the guidance team.
4. Brings into contact with other guidance team members those students who demonstrate needs beyond information acquisition.

III. Is responsible for job placement services.
A. Coordinates placement functions of diversified occupations teachers.
B. Provides placement services for students not in diversified occupations programs.
1. Part-time employment.
2. References to state and other employment services for full-time employment.

IV. Develops survey of the local occupation community relative to employment opportunities:
A. Post–high school.
B. Work study.
C. Part-time.
D. Volunteer jobs.

V. Develops, conducts, disseminates, and interprets follow-up of student's postschool occupational experiences.

VI. Develops survey of post–high school nondegree occupational training settings.

VII. Develops cadres of occupational specialists willing to provide exploration or experiential opportunities for students.

VIII. Builds relationships with agency resources:
A. Uses—occupational outlook and local resources.
B. Personnel administration.
C. Businessmen's organizations.
D. Labor organizations—apprentice programs.
E. Private employment agencies.
F. Junior Achievement, clubs, Golden Age resource groups.

IX. Establishes a parent resource group for dissemination and participation.

Appendix B
Ethical Standards of the American Personnel and Guidance Association

PREAMBLE

The American Personnel and Guidance Association is an educational, scientific, and professional organization whose members are dedicated to the enhancement of the worth, dignity, potential, and uniqueness of each individual and thus to the service of society.

The Association recognizes that the role definitions and work settings of its members include a wide variety of academic disciplines, levels of academic preparation, and agency services. This diversity reflects the breadth of the Association's interest and influence. It also poses challenging complexities in efforts to set standards for the performance of members, desired requisite preparation or practice, and supporting social, legal, and ethical controls.

The specification of ethical standards enables the Association to clarify to present and future members and to those served by members the nature of ethical responsibilities held in common by its members.

The existence of such standards serves to stimulate greater concern by members for their own professional functioning and for the conduct of fellow professionals such as counselors, guidance and student personnel workers, and others in the helping professions. As the ethical code of the Association, this document establishes principles which define the ethical behavior of Association members.

SECTION A: GENERAL

1. The member influences the development of the profession by continuous efforts to improve professional practices, teaching, services, and research. Professional growth is continuous throughout the member's career

and is exemplified by the development of a philosophy that explains why and how a member functions in the helping relationship. Members are expected to gather data on their effectiveness and to be guided by the findings.

2. The member has a responsibility both to the individual who is served and to the institution within which the service is performed. The acceptance of employment in an institution implies that the member is in substantial agreement with the general policies and principles of the institution. Therefore the professional activities of the member are also in accord with the objectives of the institution. If, despite concerted efforts, the member cannot reach agreement with the employer as to acceptable standards of conduct that allow for changes in institutional policy conducive to the positive growth and development of counselees, then terminating the affiliation should be seriously considered.

3. Ethical behavior among professional associates, members and nonmembers, is expected at all times. When information is possessed which raises serious doubt as to the ethical behavior of professional colleagues, whether Association members or not, the member is obligated to take action to attempt to rectify such a condition. Such action shall utilize the institution's channels first and then utilize procedures established by the state, division, or Association.

The member can take action in a variety of ways: conferring with the individual in question, gathering further information as to the allegation, conferring with local or national ethics committees, and so forth.

4. The member must not seek self-enhancement through expressing evaluations or comparisons that are damaging to others.

5. The member neither claims nor implies professional qualifications exceeding those possessed and is responsible for correcting any misrepresentations of these qualifications by others.

6. In establishing fees for professional services, members should take into consideration the fees charged by other professions delivering comparable services, as well as the ability of the counselee to pay. Members are willing to provide some services for which they receive little or no financial remuneration, or remuneration in food, lodging, and materials. When fees include charges for items other than professional services, that portion of the total which is for the professional services should be clearly indicated.

7. When members provide information to the public or to subordinates, peers, or supervisors, they have a clear responsibility to ensure that the content is accurate, unbiased, and consists of objective, factual data.

8. The member shall make a careful distinction between the offering of counseling services as opposed to public information services. Counseling may be offered only in the context of a reciprocal or face-to-face relationship. Information services may be offered through the media.

9. With regard to professional employment, members are expected to

accept only positions that they are prepared to assume and then to comply with established practices of the particular type of employment setting in which they are employed in order to ensure the continuity of services.

SECTION B: COUNSELOR-COUNSELEE RELATIONSHIP

This section refers to practices involving individual and/or group counseling relationships, and it is not intended to be applicable to practices involving administrative relationships.

To the extent that the counselee's choice of action is not imminently self- or other-destructive, the counselee must retain freedom of choice. When the counselee does not have full autonomy for reasons of age, mental incompetency, criminal incarceration, or similar legal restrictions, the member may have to work with others who exercise significant control and direction over the counselee. Under these circumstances the member must apprise counselees of restrictions that may limit their freedom of choice.

1. The member's *primary* obligation is to respect the integrity and promote the welfare of the counselee(s), whether the counselee(s) is (are) assisted individually or in a group relationship. In a group setting, the member-leader is also responsible for protecting individuals from physical and/or psychological trauma resulting from interaction within the group.

2. The counseling relationship and information resulting therefrom must be kept confidential, consistent with the obligations of the member as a professional person. In a group counseling setting the member is expected to set a norm of confidentiality regarding all group participants' disclosures.

3. If an individual is already in a counseling/therapy relationship with another professional person, the member does not begin a counseling relationship without first contacting and receiving the approval of that other professional. If the member discovers that the counselee is in another counseling/therapy relationship after the counseling relationship begins, the member is obligated to gain the consent of the other professional or terminate the relationship, unless the counselee elects to terminate the other relationship.

4. When the counselee's condition indicates that there is clear and imminent danger to the counselee or others, the member is expected to take direct personal action or to inform responsible authorities. Consultation with other professionals should be utilized where possible. Direct interventions, especially the assumption of responsibility for the counselee, should be taken only after careful deliberation. The counselee should be involved in the resumption of responsibility for his actions as quickly as possible.

5. Records of the counseling relationship including interview notes, test data, correspondence, tape recordings, and other documents are to be considered professional information for use in counseling, and they are not part of the public or official records of the institution or agency in which the counselor is employed. Revelation to others of counseling material should occur only upon the express consent of the counselee.

6. Use of data derived from a counseling relationship for purposes of counselor training or research shall be confined to content that can be sufficiently disguised to ensure full protection of the identify of the counselee involved.

7. Counselees shall be informed of the conditions under which they may receive counseling assistance at or before the time when the counseling relationship is entered. This is particularly so when conditions exist of which the counselee would be unaware. In individual and group situations, particularly those oriented to self-understanding or growth, the member-leader is obligated to make clear the purposes, goals, techniques, rules of procedure, and limitations that may affect the continuance of the relationship.

8. The member has the responsibility to screen prospective group participants, especially when the emphasis is on self-understanding and growth through self-disclosure. The member should maintain an awareness of the group participants' compatibility throughout the life of the group.

9. The member reserves the right to consult with any other professionally competent person about a counselee. In choosing a consultant, the member avoids placing the consultant in a conflict of interest situation that would preclude the consultant's being a proper party to the member's efforts to help the counselee.

10. If the member is unable to be of professional assistance to the counselee, the member avoids initiating the counseling relationship or the member terminates it. In either event, the member is obligated to refer the counselee to an appropriate specialist. (It is incumbent upon the member to be knowledgeable about referral resources so that a satisfactory referral can be initiated.) In the event the counselee declines the suggested referral, the member is not obligated to continue the relationship.

11. When the member learns from counseling relationships of conditions that are likely to harm others, the member should report *the condition* to the responsible authority. This should be done in such a manner as to conceal the identity of the counselee.

12. When the member has other relationships, particularly of an administrative, supervisory, and/or evaluative nature, with an individual seeking counseling services, the member should not serve as the counselor but should refer the individual to another professional. Only in instances where such an alternative is unavailable and where the individual's condi-

tion definitely warrants counseling intervention should the member enter into and/or maintain a counseling relationship.

13. All experimental methods of treatment must be clearly indicated to prospective recipients, and safety precautions are to be adhered to by the member.

14. When the member is engaged in short-term group treatment/training programs, e.g., marathons and other encounter-type or growth groups, the membership ensures that there is professional assistance available during and following the group experience.

15. Should the member be engaged in a work setting that calls for any variation from the above statements, the member is obligated to consult with other professionals whenever possible to consider justifiable alternatives. The variations that may be necessary should be clearly communicated to other professionals and prospective counselees.

SECTION C: MEASUREMENT AND EVALUATION

The primary purpose of educational and psychological testing is to provide descriptive measures that are objective and interpretable in either comparative or absolute terms. The member must recognize the need to interpret the statements that follow as applying to the whole range of appraisal techniques including test and nontest data. Test results constitute only one of a variety of pertinent sources of information for personnel, guidance, and counseling decisions.

1. It is the member's responsibility to provide adequate orientation or information to the examinee(s) prior to and following the test administration so that the results of testing may be placed in proper perspective with other relevant factors. In so doing, the member must recognize the effects of socioeconomic, ethnic, and cultural factors on test scores. It is the member's professional responsibility to use additional unvalidated information cautiously in modifying interpretation of the test results.

2. In selecting tests for use in a given situation or with a particular counselee, the member must consider carefully the specific validity, reliability, and appropriateness of the test(s). "General" validity, reliability, and the like may be questioned legally as well as ethically when tests are used for vocational and educational selection, placement, or counseling.

3. When making any statements to the public about tests and testing, the member is expected to give accurate information and to avoid false claims or misconceptions. Special efforts are often required to avoid unwarranted connotations of such terms as IQ and grade equivalent scores.

4. Different tests demand different levels of competence for admin-

istration, scoring, and interpretation. Members have a responsibility to recognize the limits of their competence and to perform only those functions for which they are prepared.

5. Tests should be administered under the same conditions that were established in their standardization. When tests are not administered under standard conditions or when unusual behavior or irregularities occur during the testing session, those conditions should be noted and the results designated as invalid or of questionable validity. Unsupervised or inadequately supervised test-taking, such as the use of tests through the mails, is considered unethical. On the other hand, the use of instruments that are so designed or standardized to be self-administered and self-scored, such as interest inventories, is to be encouraged.

6. The meaningfulness of test results used in personnel, guidance, and counseling functions generally depends on the examinee's unfamiliarity with the specific items on the test. Any prior coaching or dissemination of the test materials can invalidate test results. Therefore, test security is one of the professional obligations of the member. Conditions that produce most favorable test results should be made known to the examinee.

7. The purpose of testing and the explicit use of the results should be made known to the examinee prior to testing. The counselor has a responsibility to ensure that periodic review and/or retesting are made to prevent counselee stereotyping.

8. The examinee's welfare and explicit prior understanding should be the criteria for determining the recipients of the test results. The member is obligated to see that adequate interpretation accompanies any release of individual or group test data. The interpretation of test data should be related to the examinee's particular concerns.

9. The member is expected to be cautious when interpreting the results of research instruments possessing insufficient technical data. The specific purposes for the use of such instruments must be stated explicitly to examinees.

10. The member must proceed with extreme caution when attempting to evaluate and interpret the performance of minority group members or other persons who are not represented in the norm group on which the instrument was standardized.

11. The member is obligated to guard against the appropriation, reproduction, or modifications of published tests or parts thereof without the express permission and adequate recognition of the original author or publisher.

12. Regarding the preparation, publication, and distribution of tests, reference should be made to:

a. *Standards for Educational and Psychological Tests and Manuals,* revised edition, 1973, published by the American Psychological Association on behalf of itself, the American Educational Research Association, and the National Council on Measurement in Education.

b. "The Responsible Use of Tests: A Position Paper of AMEG, APGA, and NCME," published in *Measurement and Evaluation in Guidance* Vol. 5, No. 2, July 1972, pp. 385–388.

SECTION D: RESEARCH
AND PUBLICATION

1. Current American Psychological Association guidelines on research with human subjects shall be adhered to (*Ethical Principles in the Conduct of Research with Human Participants*. Washington, D.C.: American Psychological Association, Inc., 1973).

2. In planning any research activity dealing with human subjects, the member is expected to be aware of and responsive to all pertinent ethical principles and to ensure that the research problem, design, and execution are in full compliance with them.

3. Responsibility for ethical research practice lies with the principal researcher, while others involved in the research activities share ethical obligation and full responsibility for their own actions.

4. In research with human subjects, researchers are responsible for their subjects' welfare throughout the experiment, and they must take all reasonable precautions to avoid causing injurious psychological, physical, or social effects on their subjects.

5. It is expected that all research subjects be informed of the purpose of the study except when withholding information or providing misinformation to them is essential to the investigation. In such research, the member is responsible for corrective action as soon as possible following the research.

6. Participation in research is expected to be voluntary. Involuntary participation is appropriate only when it can be demonstrated that participation will have no harmful effects on subjects.

7. When reporting research results, explicit mention must be made of all variables and conditions known to the investigator that might affect the outcome of the investigation or the interpretation of the data.

8. The member is responsible for conducting and reporting investigations in a manner that minimizes the possibility that results will be misleading.

9. The member has an obligation to make available sufficient original research data to qualified others who may wish to replicate the study.

10. When supplying data, aiding in the research of another person,

reporting research results, or in making original data available, due care must be taken to disguise the identity of the subjects in the absence of specific authorization from such subjects to do otherwise.

11. When conducting and reporting research, the member is expected to be familiar with and to give recognition to previous work on the topic, as well as to observe all copyright laws and follow the principle of giving full credit to all to whom credit is due.

12. The member has the obligation to give due credit through joint authorship, acknowledgement, footnote statements, or other appropriate means to those who have contributed significantly to the research, in accordance with such contributions.

13. The member is expected to communicate to other members the results of any research judged to be of professional or scientific value. Results reflecting unfavorably on institutions, programs, services, or vested interests should not be withheld for such reasons.

14. If members agree to cooperate with another individual in research and/or publication, they incur an obligation to cooperate as promised in terms of punctuality of performance and with full regard to the completeness and accuracy of the information provided.

SECTION E: CONSULTING AND PRIVATE PRACTICE

Consulting refers to a voluntary relationship between a professional helper and help-needing social unit (industry, business, school, college, etc.) in which the consultant is attempting to give help to the client in the solution of some current or potential problem. When "client" is used in this section it refers to an individual, group, or organization served by the consultant. (This definition of "consulting" is adapted from "Dimensions of the Consultant's Job" by Ronald Lippitt, *Journal of Social Issues,* Vol. 15, No. 2, 1959.)

1. Members who act as consultants must have a high degree of self-awareness of their own values and needs in entering helping relationships that involve change in social units.

2. There should be understanding and agreement between consultant and client as to the task, the directions or goals, and the function of the consultant.

3. Members are expected to accept only those consulting roles for which they possess or have access to the necessary skills and resources for giving the kind of help that is needed.

4. The consulting relationship is defined as being one in which the client's adaptability and growth toward self-direction are encouraged and

cultivated. For this reason, the consultant is obligated to maintain consistently the role of a consultant and to avoid becoming a decision maker for the client.

5. In announcing one's availability for professional services as a consultant, the member follows professional rather than commercial standards in describing services with accuracy, dignity, and caution.

6. For private practice in testing, counseling, or consulting, all ethical principles defined in this document are pertinent. In addition, any individual, agency, or institution offering educational, personal, or vocational counseling should meet the standards of the International Association of Counseling Services, Inc.

7. The member is expected to refuse a private fee or other remuneration for consultation with persons who are entitled to these services through the member's employing institution or agency. The policies of a particular agency may make explicit provisions for private practice with agency counselees by members of its staff. In such instances, the counselees must be apprised of other options open to them should they seek private counseling services.

8. It is unethical to use one's institutional affiliation to recruit counselees for one's private practice.

SECTION F: PERSONNEL ADMINISTRATION

It is recognized that most members are employed in public or quasi-public institutions. The functioning of a member within an institution must contribute to the goals of the institution and vice versa if either is to accomplish their respective goals or objectives. It is therefore essential that the member and the institution function in ways to: (a) make the institution's goals explicit and public; (b) make the member's contribution to institutional goals specific; and (c) foster mutual accountability for goal achievement.

To accomplish these objectives it is recognized that the member and the employer must share responsibilities in the formulation and implementation of personnel policies.

1. Members should define and describe the parameters and levels of their professional competency.

2. Members should establish interpersonal relations and working agreements with supervisors and subordinates regarding counseling or clinical relationships, confidentiality, distinction between public and private material, maintenance and dissemination of recorded information, work load, and accountability. Working agreements in each instance should be specified and made known to those concerned.

3. Members are responsible for alerting their employers to conditions that may be potentially disruptive or damaging.

4. Members are responsible for informing employers of conditions that may limit their effectiveness.

5. Members are expected to submit regularly to review and evaluation.

6. Members are responsible for inservice development of self and/or staff.

7. Members are responsible for informing their staff of goals and programs.

8. Members are responsible for providing personnel practices that guarantee and enhance the rights and welfare of each recipient of their service.

9. Members are expected to select competent persons and assign responsibilities compatible with their skills and experiences.

SECTION G: PREPARATION STANDARDS

Members who are responsible for training others should be guided by the preparation standards of the Association and relevant division(s). The member who functions in the capacity of trainer assumes unique ethical responsibilities that frequently go beyond that of the member who does not function in a training capacity. These ethical responsibilities are outlined as follows:

1. Members are expected to orient trainees to program expectations, basic skills development, and employment prospects prior to admission to the program.

2. Members in charge of training are expected to establish programs that integrate academic study and supervised practice.

3. Members are expected to establish a program directed toward developing the trainees' skills, knowledge, and self-understanding, stated whenever possible in competency or performance terms.

4. Members are expected to identify the level of competency of their trainees. These levels of competency should accommodate the paraprofessional as well as the professional.

5. Members, through continual trainee evaluation and appraisal, are expected to be aware of the personal limitations of the trainee that might impede future performance. The trainer has the responsibility of not only assisting the trainee in securing remedial assistance, but also screening from the program those trainees who are unable to provide competent services.

6. Members are expected to provide a program that includes training in research commensurate with levels of role functioning. Paraprofessional

and technician-level personnel should be trained as consumers of research. In addition, these personnel should learn how to evaluate their own and their program effectiveness. Advanced graduate training, especially at the doctoral level, should include preparation for original research by the member.

7. Members are expected to make trainees aware of the ethical responsibilities and standards of the profession.

8. Training programs are expected to encourage trainees to value the ideals of service to individuals and to society. In this regard, direct financial remuneration or lack thereof should not influence the quality of service rendered. Monetary considerations should be allowed to overshadow professional and humanitarian needs.

9. Members responsible for training are expected to be skilled as teachers and practitioners.

10. Members are expected to present thoroughly varied theoretical positions so that trainees may make comparisons and have the opportunity to select a position.

11. Members are obligated to develop clear policies within their training institution regarding field placement and the roles of the trainee and the trainer in such placements.

12. Members are expected to ensure that forms of training focusing on self-understanding or growth are voluntary, or if required as part of the training program, are made known to prospective trainees prior to entering the program. When the training program offers a growth experience with an emphasis on self-disclosure or other relatively intimate or personal involvement, the member should have no administrative, supervisory, or evaluative authority regarding the participant.

13. Members are obligated to conduct a training program in keeping with the most current guidelines of the American Personnel and Guidance Association and its various divisions.

Index

Academic achievement of delinquent youths, 213
  in CASE project, 215–16
Academic skills, development of, as educational goal, 32
Accurate empathy, caring and, 189–90
ACES (Association of Counselor Educators and Supervisors), 354
Achievement, see Academic achievement
ACPA (American College Personnel Association), 354–55
Activity, stimulation and, in behavior development, 117–23
Adolescent development, 181–84
Adults, programs for, 266–67
  future, 359
Advertising, operant conditioning in, 155–56
Aesthetic expression, as educational goal, 33
American College Personnel Association (ACPA), 354–55
American College Testing Program, 19, 239, 248n
American Personnel and Guidance Association (APGA), 76, 204, 340, 342, 348, 351, 353–55
  ethical standards of, 363–73
American Psychological Association (APA), 350, 351
American School Counselor Association (ASCA), 354
Amos, W., 359
Analogy, theory and, 92–94
Andrade, B. M., 70, 283
Ann Arundel County (Md.), 21n, 72n–73n

Annapolis High School (Md.), 72
Ansell, E. M., 229
Anxiety, coping behavior and, 197–98
APA (American Psychological Association), 350, 351
Apathy, 122–23
APGA, see American Personnel and Guidance Association
Appraisal (assessment), 307–38
  based on behavior principles, 309–10
  case study of, 331–37
  data used for, see Data
  issues in administration of appraisal programs, 325–28
  members of guidance team and, 328–31
  purpose of, 307–8
Arbuckle, Dugald S., 266n
Armor, D. J., 8, 16
Armstrong, J. C., 70
ASCA (American School Counselor Association), 354
Assessment, see Appraisal
Assessment of Career Development (American College Testing Program), 239
Association of Counselor Education and Supervisors (ACES), 354
Attentiveness, caring and, 189–90; see also Listening
Authority
  of groups, as source of knowing, 102
  of individuals, as source of knowing, 101–2
Autonomy, professionalism and occupational, 342–43

375

Index

Bachrach, P., 233
Baker, R. D., 252
Baker, S. B., 190
Baltimore (Md.) school system, 262
Bandura, A., 189, 274, 277, 278
Barker, R. G., 161n, 162
Barton, A., 259
Baseline data, acquisition of, for self-management, 274, 281
Bedell, Ralph C., 351
Behavior development
  body-mind dichotomy and, 141–42
  operant conditioning and, 127–36
    contingency management and, 134–35
    reinforcers in, 127–31
    reinforcing contexts for, 131–34
    significance for guidance practices, 135–36
  respondent conditioning and, 123–27
  stimulation, activity and, 117–23
  symbol system and, 136–41
Behavior specialists, 53, 58
  appraisal and, 329–30
  nurturing functions of, 59
  professional issues regarding, 347–48
  as remediators, 54–55, 61–62
Behavior theory
  applied to occupational decision making, 234–36
  appraisal based on, 309–10
  philosophical bases of, 99–103
    epistemological issues in, 101–3
    taking measure of, 110–13
    theological bases of, 103–4
Behaviorism, 144–57
  operant conditioning and, 149–57
    humanism vs. science and, 151–52
    as secretive and manipulative, 154–57
    as technique of unlimited applicability, 152–54
    pleasure-seeking, pain-avoiding principle in, 146–49, 212, 230–31
Behaviors
  chief instrument of changes in, 110
  defined, 188
  entry, defined, 235
  fixed, 119
  intellectualized, as dehumanized, 182n
  regularities of, defined, 43
  target, 273–74, 281
  See also Coping behavior; Mediating behavior
Belkin, G. S., 3
Benjamin, A., 198n, 283
Benjamin, Harold, 227n
Berdie, R., 76
Berenson, B. G., 70, 283
Bernstein, A., 110
Beyond Freedom and Dignity (Skinner), 150
Biggers, J. L., 252, 254

Biological ecosystems, 161, 163
Blacks, *see* Minorities
Blocher, D. H., 13
Body-mind dichotomy, 141–42
Bordin, E. S., 13n
Boredom, what is, 122
Brainwashing, defined, 94
Bridger, W. H., 323n
Brown, W., 283
Brown, W. F., 70
Buckley, James, 312
Buckley Amendment to Elementary and Secondary School Act, 312n
Burger, H. G., 131n
Byrne's test, 30, 34

California State College (Los Angeles), 71n
Campbell, D. T., 322
Career, defined, 222
Career Center, 260, 263
  occupational/educational component of, 249–53
  readying activities conducted in, 290, 293, 297, 302
Career Days, 254–55
Career decision-making (CDM), 16–17; *see also* Occupational decision making
Career development, 194, 221–38
  behavioral theory applied to CDM and, 234–36
  counselors and, *see* Counselors—group activities of
  definitions used in, 221–23
  as goal, 29, 30, 33
  objectives of, readying activities to achieve, 290–98, 302
  occupational decision making and, 229–37
    behavior theory applied to, 234–36
    description of adequate decisions, 236–37
    first, 229–31
    substance of, 231–34
  as uppermost concern of students, 30
  programs in, 239–69
    computer-assisted, 255–57
    factors to consider in setting up, 239–47
    guidance team and, 248–49; *see also specific members of guidance team; for example:* Career development technicians
    to help students acquire decision making competence, 247–48
    interest inventories and, 262–64
    job development technicians and outreach counselors in, 261
    occupational/educational component of Career Center and, 249–53
    placement officers in, 261–62
    registrars in, 260–61

Career development, programs in (*cont.*)
   under special conditions, 264–67
   social competency and, 41; *see also* Social competency
Career development technicians (CDT), 53, 249
   appraisal and, 328
   CETS compared with, 260
   functions of, 55–57, 62–65, 251–55
   job description of, 361–62
   mediating behavior of, 194, 195
   professional issues regarding, 348–49
Career education, 21–23
   defined, 223
   work ethic and, 21, 22
Career entry, difference between job placement and, 224
Career guidance, defined, 223
Career Maturity Index (Crites), 239
Caring, 189–90
   defined, 189
Carkhuff, R., 70, 76, 189, 283
Carline, E. T., Jr., 258
CASE project, 213–15
Case workers (outreach counselors), 66–67, 261, 331
CDM (career decision making), 16–17; *see also* Occupational decision making
CDT, *see* Career development technicians
Census, Bureau of, 9
Centrifugal guidance, defined, 264
Centripetal guidance, defined, 264
Certification requirements, 13–14
CET, *see* Continuing education technicians
Child development specialists, function of, 76*n*
Childhood development, 181–84
Clarification, as verbal behavior of effective social interactions, 284–85
Closed system, guidance as, 27
Cognitive system (symbol system), 136–41
Cohen, H. L., 213, 216
Coleman, J. S., 184*n*
College counselors, training of, 15
College Entrance Examination Board, 247*n*
College information, 258–59; *see also* Continuing education technicians
College Night, 258
Colleges (postsecondary institutions)
   early 19th-century, 5–6
   guidance in, 71*n*
   future, 357–58
Common Sense (Paine), 3
Communication, guidance objectives and, 27–28
Competency, *see* Social competency
Competition

Competition (*cont.*)
   cooperation vs., 169
   as reinforcer, 131
Computer-assisted career development programs, 255–57
Computer-Based Vocational Guidance Systems (U.S. Office of Education), 257
Conditioned stimuli (CS), 123, 125
Conditioning
   counterconditioning, 205
   defined, 197*n*
   deconditioning, defined, 197*n*
   respondent, 123–27
   See also Operant conditioning
Congress (U.S.), 21
Construct validity of tests, 316–17
Content validity of tests, 316–17
Contingency management, 209–16
   illustrated, 210–16
   operant conditioning and, 134–35
Contingency management plan, setting up, for purposes of self-management, 275–76
Continuing education technicians (CET), 65–66, 258–60
   appraisal and, 328
   mediating behavior of, 195
Cook, David C., 12*n*
Cooperation, competition vs., 169
Copernicus, 89, 101, 108, 145–46, 155
Coping behavior, 175–76
   fear, anxiety and, 197–98
Council of Guidance and Personnel Associations, 354
Counseling, *see* Mediating behavior
Counseling Psychologist, The (magazine), 41
Counseling and the Social Revolution, 265
Counseling Technology (report), 257
Counselor-centered guidance
   curriculum-centered vs., 19
   program-centered vs., 15
Counselors, 53–58
   appraisal by, 328–29
   life style and developmental, 13
   functions of
      developmental functions, 55–57
      nurturing functions, 62–65
      in self-management, 305
      in social competency development, 305–6
   group activities of
      complete group programs, 306
      as group leaders, 288
      group readying activities, 290–302
      individual interviews and, 303–4
   meaning of term, 12–13
   number of (1916), 8
   outreach, 66–67, 261, 331
   peer, 70–71
   as professional functionaries, 64*n*

Counselors (cont.)
  psychological, 13
  structure of counseling practices as professional issue, 344–46
  training of, 73–77, 349–50
    beginning and expansion of, 14–18
    college counselors, 15
    inadequacy of, 20
    See also Mediating behavior and specific types of counselors; for example: Career development technicians
Counterconditioning, 205
  defined, 197n
Cox, W. H., 68
Cramer, S. H., 190, 223, 242, 251, 266
Crawford High School (San Diego, Calif.), 250, 255
Criterion validity of tests, 316–17
Crites, J. O., 21n, 222, 234, 239
CS (conditioned stimuli), 123, 125
Culture, professionalism and occupational, 342–43
Culture as a Reason for Being, 265
Cunningham, G., Jr., 62n
Curriculum-centered guidance, counselor-centered guidance vs., 19

Data
  acquiring baseline, for self-management, 274, 281
  collection of, 310–12
  nonparametric and idiographic, 323–25
  parametric (nomothetic), 313–23
    multiple norms in, 315–16
    precise norms in, 314–15
    test validity and, 316–19
    testing errors in, 319–22
Data, people, things code (DPT code), 293–95, 297, 298
Daubner, E., 99
Decision making
  acquiring skills necessary for, 217, 235–36
  career development program and, 247–48
  training in, 193, 194
  See also Career decision making; Occupational decision making; Vocational decision making
Declaration of Independence (1776), 66, 183, 193, 236, 265, 326
  guidance movement rooted in, 2–7, 11, 22
Deconditioning, defined, 197n
Defense, Department of, 9
Dehumanized behaviors, overly intellectualized behaviors as, 182n
Delaney, D. J., 198, 218
Delgiorno, J. E., 68n
Delinquent youths

Delinquent youths (cont.)
  academic achievement of, 213
  in CASE project, 215–16
  career development for rehabilitated, 265
Democritus, 91
Desensitization
  defined, 197n, 205–6
  facilitative interviews used as, 197–98
  need for, 202–4
  purposes and procedures of, 204–9
Development, *see* Behavior development; Career development; Human development; Intellectual development; Physical development; Vocational development
Developmental counselors, 13
Dewey, John, 60, 247
Dickens, Charles, 212
Dictionary of Occupational Titles (DOT), 222, 251, 340
  used in readying activities, 290, 292, 294, 295, 297, 302
Direct verbal mediating behavior, 193–201
  excitation as, 195–96
  facilitative interviews as, 197–202
  reasoning as, 193–95
  supportive counseling as, 197–98
  See also Densensitization
Disruptive students, as threat to teachers, 163
DOT, *see*: Dictionary of Occupational Titles
DPT code (data, people, things code), 293–95, 297, 298
Drop-outs, 184
Dulaney, D. J., 283
Dworkin, A. L., 190
Dworkin, E. P., 190

Ebel, R. L., 323
Eclecticism, 107–9
Ecological psychology, defined, 162
Ecosystems
  defined, 117n
  schools as, 161–65, 226–29
Education
  changes in (1800–1900), 8–9
  as end in itself, criticized, 20
  of guidance practitioners, 13–14
  psychological, 41
    self-management and, 279–80
  pursuit of happiness in, 5–7
  right to full, 8–9
  of scientists, 106
  See also Career education; Schools; Training
Educational goals
  guidance objectives and, 31–33
  social value statements as, 29–30
Educational Technology Magazine (magazine), 257

Effect, law of, 150
Eisenberg, S., 198, 218, 283
Elementary schools
   early 19th-century, 5
   guidance programs in, 58n, 356-57
Elementary and Secondary School Act (1974), Buckley Amendment to, 312n
Elkes, C., 76
Ellis, A., 195, 218
Emotions, 188
Empathy, caring and, 189-90
End-of-schooling educational goal, defined, 30
Entropy in guidance movement, 27
Entry behaviors, defined, 235
Environment, the individual and his, 159-61
Epistemological issues in behavior theories, 101-3
Erickson, E. H., 184n
Esposito, D., 161
Established behaviors (fixed behaviors), 119
Ethical code
   of APGA, 363-73
   professionalism and existence of, 342
Ethnic minorities, see Minorities
Evans, J. R., 248n
Excitation, as direct verbal mediating behavior, 195-96
Excitement, defined, 122
Experiences
   occupational decision making and learning, 234
   as source of knowing, 101

Facilitative interviews
   skilled use of words in, 198-202
   used as limited desensitization, 197-98
Family
   as ecosystem, 166
   as subculture, 169
   See also Maximum experience families; Minimum experience families
Fantasy City, 46-47
FBI (Federal Bureau of Investigation), 312
Fear
   coping behavior and, 197-98
   desensitizing, 205-7
Federal Bureau of Investigation (FBI), 312
Federal government, need for recognition by, 351-53
Feelings
   defined, 208n
   identifying, 282-83
Feibelman, J. K., 103
Females, career development programs for, 266, 357
Filipczak, J., 213, 216

Firestone Park Elementary School (Akron, Ohio), 21n
Fixed behaviors (established behaviors), 119
Flanagan, John C., 252, 253
Flint, A., 76
Florida State University, Counselor Education Department of, 65
Folk psychology, aphorisms of, 138, 149, 184
Fondling, as stimulation, 119-20
Foods, as reinforcers, 128, 130-31
Form, W. H., 341
Franklin school system (N.H.), 21n
Freaks, 170-72
Freedman, M. B., 259
Freud, Sigmund, 111, 112
Friedenberg, E. Z., 184n
Fuller, F. F., 163n

Gaithersburg High School (GHS: Montgomery County; Md.), 36-40, 290
Galileo, 104, 145, 152-53, 155
Game approach to career development objectives, 290-98
GATB (General Aptitude Test Battery), 295, 352
Gelatt, H. B., 248n
General Aptitude Test Battery (GATB), 295, 352
General Subcommittee on Education (House), 18
General systems theory (GST), principles of, 28n
Genetics, growth and, 174-75
Genuineness in caring, 189-90
George-Barden Act (1946), 326n, 349, 354
George-Dean Act, 349
Goals
   school, 166-73
   self-management as, 270-73; see also Self-management
   See also Educational goals; Guidance goals
Golan, S. E., 76
Gold, B. K., 70
Goldman, C., 63
Goshko, R., 274
Gottlieb, D., 176n
Graff, R. W., 359
Grambs, J., 359
Grant, C. W., 11, 70
Greasers (rednecks), 170
Green, R. L., 323
Greenspoon, J., 137
Greenwood, 341
Gregory, F. A., 353
Gross National Product (GNP), percentage of, going to public education, 20
Group activities of counselors
   complete group programs, 306

Group activities of counselors (*cont.*)
 as group leaders, 288
 group readying activities, 290–302
 individual interviews and, 303–4
Groups, principles of mediating behavior applied to, 217–18
Growth, genetics and, 174–75
Guidance
 dropping or retaining term, 11–12
 future of, 358–59
Guidance goals
 establishing, 28–33
 unique, 42
 See also Objectives
Guidance movement, 1–25
 beginnings of, 7–17
 current characteristics of, and need for changes in, 18–23
 forces shaping growth of, 17–18
 political roots of, 2–7, 11, 22
Guidance objectives, *see* Objectives
Guidance-oriented schools, described, 248
Guidance teams
 building, 348–49
 in colleges, 71*n*
 members of, 51, 53
  appraisal and, 328–31
  career development programs and, 248–49; *see also* Career development
  characteristics of, 189–90
  parents as, 73
  professional issues affecting, 346–49; *see also* Professional issues
 See also Behavior specialists; Career development technicians; Continuing education technicians; Counselors; Job development technicians; Outreach counselors; Placement officers; Registrars; Specialists; Teacher-advisors
Guidance technology, scientific base of, 84–88
Guidelines for Preparing and Evaluating Occupational Materials (National Vocational Association), 251
Gysbers, N., 223

Haggard's experiment, 319
Hamilton, J. A., 253
Hansen, J. C., 229
Happiness, pursuit of, in education and occupation, 6–7
Hatch, R. N., 328
Hedrich, V., 254*n*
Heinsohm, A. L., 176*n*
Henle, Peter, 233
Herr, E. L., 223, 242, 251, 266
Herrnstein (author), 317
High schools
 early 19th-century, 5–6
 as ecosystems encouraging occupational decisions, 226–29

Hispanics (Spanish-speaking Americans), 182*n*; *see also* Minorities
Hitt, W. D., 100*n*
Holland, John L., 232, 263
Hollingshead, A. B., 184*n*
Homme, L., 150
Homology, theory and, 92–94
Homosexuals, guidance for, 359
Hoppock, R., 64
Hoyt, Kenneth B., 12, 18, 20
Human development, 158–86
 course of, 173–85
  in childhood and adolescence, 181–84
  emergence and maintenance of behaviors and, 175–76
  genetic resources and growth and, 174–75
  human as robots and, 176–81
 schools' goals, program regularities, behavior regularities and, 166–73
 social systems and, 159–65
Humanism, science vs., 151–52
Hypothetical constructs of theory, 94–96

Idealism, 100–101
Idiosyncrasy, cultivation of, 226–27
Idiographic data, 323–25
Imitative behavior, 126
Indian Affairs, Bureau of, 169
Individual, the, society and
 individual's place in, 33
 social competency and, 41
Individual interviews, 303–4
Infant activity, behavior development and, 118–22
Information
 college, 258–59; *see also* Continuing education technicians
 impact of technology on availability of, 9
 See also Data
Infrastructure, guidance as compact, 27–28
Inglis, C., 4
Inhibition, reciprocal, defined, 197*n*
Instrumental conditioning, *see* Operant conditioning
Intellectual development, as educational goal, 32
Intellectualized behaviors, as dehumanized behaviors, 182*n*
Interagency Task Force on Counseling, 352–53
Interest inventories, 262–64
Interior, Department of the, 169
Interprofessional Research Commission on Pupil Personnel Services (IRCOPPS), 349
Interviews
 facilitative, 192–202
 skilled use of words in, 198–202

Interviews, facilitative (cont.)
  used as limited desensitization, 197–98
  individual, 303–4
Inventories, interest, 263–64
IQ (intelligence quotient), 175, 319–23
IRCOPPS (Interprofessional Research Commission on Pupil Personnel Services), 349
Irelan, Lolo M., 176n
Isaacson, L. E., 251
Iscoe, I., 62n
Ivey, A. E., 189

Jacobson, T. J., 249n
Jefferies, John, 72n
Jencks (author), 317
Job, defined, 222
Job Corps, 352
Job decisions, occupational decision making vs., 233
Job descriptions of CDTs, 361–62
Job development technicians, 261
Job placement, difference between career entry and, 224
Job-O (device), 298–302
Johnson, Lyndon B., 352
Johnson, R. G., 252
Juvenile delinquents, see Delinquent youths

Kahn, W. J., Jr., 129n, 272, 280, 305
Kant, Immanuel, 101n
Katz, M., 248n, 259
Katzell, R. A., 56n
Kinesthetic stimulation in infancy, 119–20
Kirsh, S. P., 18
Knowing, sources of, 101–3
Koehler, Anne, 73n
Korman, A. K., 56n
Kornhauser, A., 233
Krumboltz, J. D., 202, 234–36, 252
Kuhn, T. S., 112

Labor, Department of, 251, 340
  Counseling and Manpower Utilization branch of, 352
Labor movement, job dissatisfaction and growth of, 6–7
Lang, P. J., 205, 206
Laramore, D. D., 249
Learned behaviors, 175–76
Learning experiences, occupational decision making and, 234
Leibowitz, Z., 70, 280, 283, 305
Leighton, J. A., 101n
Leisure, impact of technology on, 10
Levin, Louis, 72n, 280, 305
Levine (author), 119–20
Levine, E. L., 56n
Levine, L. S. 58n
Life expectancy, 9–10

Life style, occupational decision making and, 232
Life style counselors, 13
Limited desensitization, supportive counseling and facilitative procedures used as, 197–98
Lincoln School (Dayton, Ohio), 21n, 252n
Listening, 200
  attentive, 283–84
  in facilitative interviews, 207, 209
Lister, J. B., 70
Lloyd-Jones, E., 264
Lobitz, W. C., 70
Long Island University, 71n

McCully, C. Harold, 12n, 351
McGowan, J. F., 353
Mach, Ernst, 101n
MacMichael, David C., 20n
Mager, R. F., 30
Mager's test, 34, 35
Magoon, T. M., 76
Mahoney, M. J., 281
Management, see Contingency management; Self-management
Manipulation in operant conditioning, 154–57
Manpower Development and Training Act, 66, 352
Marland, S. P., Jr., 21, 66
Married couples, guidance for, 359
Marx, George L., 72n
Marx, M. H., 95
Maryland, University of, 355
Maryland school systems, 21n, 64, 72n–73n, 262, 281
Matheny, K., 190
Maximum experience families
  adolescence in, 183
  childhood development in, 182
  first occupational decisions and influence of, 229–30
Mayer, G. R., 189
Mediating behavior (counseling), 187–220
  characteristics of guidance practitioners and, 189–90
  complexity of, 191–92
  consultation in, 216–17
  contingency management as, 209–16
    illustrated, 210–16
    operating conditioning and, 134–35
  direct verbal, 193–210
    excitation as, 195–96
    facilitative interviews as, 197–202
    reasoning as, 193–95
    supportive counseling as, 197–98
    See also Counselors; Desensitization
  modes of, 193
  principles of, applied to groups, 217–18
Mental health movement, 17

Mental measurement movement, *see* Standardized tests
Mentally-retarded children, selection of reinforcers for, 129*n*
Metaphors, theory and, 91–94
Mezzano, J., 225*n*
Miller, C. H., 4, 18
Miller, Gordon P., 247*n*
Miller Analogies Test, 319
Mind-body dichotomy, 141–42
Minimum experience families
  adolescence in, 183–84
  childhood development in, 182
  computer-assisted career development programs for youths of, 255
  first occupational decisions and influence of, 229–30
Minor, Frank J., 256–57, 262
Minorities
  career development program for, 265–66
  future guidance programs for, 358–59
  standardized tests for, 322–23
Mirenzi, Joseph, 72*n*
Mitchell, J. V., Jr., 164*n*
Moles, O. C., 319
Money, as reinforcer, 212, 214–15
Mosher, R. L., 279*n*
Montgomery County Public Schools (Md.) 281
Myers, Roger A., 256
Myrus, P., 283

National Advisory Council on Vocational Education, sixth report of (1972), 20
National Association of Guidance Supervisors (NAGS), 354
National Defense Education Act (1958; NDEA), 19, 69, 314, 327, 345, 349–51
National Education Association, 18
National Institute of Education (NIE), 351–52
National Training School for Boys, 213, 216
National Vocational Guidance Association (NVGA), 8, 13, 223, 251, 257, 353–54
Native Americans, Pueblo Indians, 169; *see also* Minorities
Natural stimuli, 123, 124
NDEA (National Defense Education Act; 1958), 19, 69, 314, 327, 345, 349–51
Negative conditioning, 125–26
Neighborhood Youth Corps, 352
Neutral stimuli, 123, 124
New Yorker (magazine), 258
NIE (National Institute of Education), 351–52
Nixon, Richard M., 353
Nobel, Alfred, 146

Noeth, R. J., 194*n*
Nonparametric data, 323–25
Nonpossessive warmth, caring and, 189–90
Norms, parametric assessment of, 313–16
Nosow, S., 341
Novick, B., 64*n*
Nurturing function, 43–44
  of behavior specialists, 59
  of counselors, 62–65
  parental, 175
NVGA (National Vocational Guidance Association), 8, 13, 223, 251, 257, 353–54
NVGA Bibliography of Current Occupational Literature (National Vocational Guidance Association), 251
Nye, L., 272

Objectives, 26–44
  differences between goals and, 28; *see also* Guidance goals
  establishing, 28–33
    educational goals and, 31–33
    origins of objectives and, 29–31
  nurturing and restorative, 43–44
  pervasive, 40–43
  as related to self-management, 282–84
  specifying, 33–40
    in Gaithersburg High School, 36–40
    performances and, 35–36
  systems theory and, 26–28
Occupation
  defined, 222
  pursuit of happiness in, 6–7
Occupational autonomy, professionalism and, 343–44
Occupational culture, professionalism and, 342–43
Occupational decision-making, 229–37
  behavioral theory applied to, 234–36
  description of adequate decisions, 236–37
  first, 229–31
  substance of, 231–34
  as uppermost concern of students, 30
Occupational/educational component of Career Center, 249–53
Occupational Information and Guidance Service section (OIGS; U.S. Office of Education), 351, 354
Occupational Outlook Handbook (OOH), 290, 294
Ohio school system, 21*n*
OIGS (Occupational Information and Guidance Service section; U.S. Office of Education), 351, 354
OOH (Occupational Outlook Handbook), 290, 294
Open system, guidance as, 27
Operant (instrumental) conditioning, 119, 123

Operant (instrumental) conditioning (*cont.*)
  behavior development and, 127–36
    contingency management and, 134–35
    reinforcers in, 127–31
    reinforcing contexts for, 131–34
    significance for guidance practices, 135–36
  behaviorism and, 149–57
    humanism vs. science and, 151–52
    as secretive and manipulative, 154–57
    as technique of unlimited applicability, 152–54
Osipow, S. H., 198, 202, 330
Outcomes, objectives and, 42–43
Outreach counselors (case workers), 66–67, 261, 331
Overly intellectualized behaviors, as dehumanized behaviors, 182*n*
Overstreet, P., 224*n*

Pain, defined, 148
Pain-avoiding, pleasure-seeking principle, 146–49, 212, 230–31
Paine, Tom, 3–4
Palo Alto Unified School District (Calif.), 58*n*
Parametric data (nomothetic data), 313–23
  multiple norms in, 315–16
  precise norms in, 314–15
  test validity and, 316–19
  testing errors in, 319–22
Parent Effectiveness Training (PET), 73
Parental nurturing, school readiness and, 175
Parents
  as manipulators, 156–57
  in maximum and minimum experience families, 229–30; *see also* Maximum experience families; Minimum experience families
  as members of guidance team, 73
Passow, A. H., 185
Patouillet, Raymond, 58*n*
Pavlov, Ivan, 123, 146
Pearson, Karl, 101*n*
Peer counselors, 70–71
Perceptions, identifying, 282–83
Personal guidance counselors, *see* Counselors
Personality, 117–18
Personnel and Guidance Journal, 257
Personnel and Guidance Journal: What Guidance for Blacks, 265
Pervasive objectives, 40–43
PET (Parent Effectiveness Training), 73
Philosophical bases of behavior theory, 99–103
PHO (public health officers), 59–60
Phobias, 126

Physical development, as educational goal, 32
Placement officers, 261–62
Plato, 101
Pierce-Jones, J., 62*n*
Pierson, G. A., 11
Pleasure-seeking, pain-avoiding principle, 146–49, 212, 230–31
Political roots of guidance movement, 2–7, 11, 22
Position, defined, 222
Positive conditioning, 125
Postsecondary institutions, *see* Colleges
Prediger, D. J., 194*n*, 231*n*
Premack, D., 212, 215
Principals, school, 163, 165
Pritchard, David H., 353–54
Privacy, data collection and, 311–12
Professional associations, 348, 353–55
Professional issues, 338–53
  determining professionalism of guidance practitioners as, 340–44
  need for federal government recognition as, 351–53
  preparation of guidance team members as, 349–50
  regarding guidance programs in settings other than high schools, 355–58
  regarding guidance team members, 346–49
  structure of counseling practices as, 344–46
Professionalism, 340–44
Program-centered guidance, counselor-centered guidance vs., 15
Psychological counselors, 13
Psychological education, 41
  self-management and, 279–80
Psychologists, training of, 74–75
Psychology
  ecological, 162
  emergence of, 7
  folk, 138, 149, 184
Psychotherapy movement, 14–15, 17, 18
Public education, *see* Education
Public health functions
  of behavior specialists, 54, 59, 61
  of counselors, 56
Public health officers (PHO), 59–60
Public higher education, *see* Colleges
Public primary education, *see* Elementary schools
Public secondary education, *see* High schools
Pucinski, R. C., 18
Punishment
  rewards replacing, 150
  self-control of, 277–78
Pupil services (pupil personnel services; student personnel services), 12, 355–56
Pyle, R. R., 70

Querengo, Monsignor, 145
Questioning behavior in facilitative interviews, 200

Race
  first occupational decisions and, 231
  school integration and, 322–23
  as subcultural variable, 172
Racial minorities, see Minorities
Readying activities to achieve career development objectives, 290–302
Real City, 47–52
Realism, 100–101
Reasoning, as direct verbal mediating procedure, 193–95
Reciprocal inhibition, defined, 197n
Rector, W. H., 62n, 73
Rednecks (greasers), 170
Reflection, as verbal behavior of effective social interactions, 284
Regional minorities, see Minorities
Registrars, 68–70, 260–61
Rehabilitatees, career development for, 265
Rehabilitation Services Administration, 352
Reinforcers
  in contingency management, 210–14
  oneself as, 278
  in operant conditioning, 127–31
  symbols as, 137–38
  types of, 212, 214–15
  See also Rewards
Reinforcing contexts, 131–34
Relaxation procedures, 206–7
  in facilitative interviews, 201
Remediators, behavior specialists as, 54–55, 61–62; see also Behavior specialists
Respondent conditioning, 123–27
Restatements, as verbal behavior of effective social interaction, 284
Restorative objectives, 43–44
Rewards
  punishment replaced by, 150
  self-control of, 277–78
  See also Reinforcers
Reynolds, G. S., 189
Rhoads, David J., 70, 72n, 283
Rhodes, J. A., 19
Rioch, M. J., 76
Robots, humans as, 176–81
Rodin, Auguste, 139
Rogers, Carl R., 85, 111, 198, 201, 282
Roth, J. D., 194n
Russell, Bertrand, 102

Samler, Joseph, 266
Sandman, Peter M., 255n
Santilliana, G. de, 145
Sarason, S. B., 43
Schell, E., 99
Schlossberg, Nancy K., 267, 359

School readiness, 175
Schools, 161–73
  career development in, 224–29
  as ecosystems, 161–65, 226–29
  goals of, 166–73
  guidance-oriented, described, 248
  integration of, standardized tests and, 322–23
  need for desensitization in, 202–4
  See also Colleges; Elementary schools; High schools; Students; Teachers; and specific schools; for example: Gaithersburg High School
Schwebel, M., 323n
Science
  humanism vs., 151–52
  as source of knowing, 102
  theory and characteristics of, 107–9
Scientific base of guidance technology, see Theory
Scientific theory, 88–105
  proof and evolution of, 89–99
  scientists and, 105–7
Scientific understanding, as educational goal, 33
Scientists, theory and characteristics of, 105–7
S-DS (Self-Directed Search), 263–64
Seattle public school system, 21n, 254n
Secrecy in operant conditioning, 154–57
Seidman, E., 58n
Self-control of punishment, 277–78
Self-Directed Search (S-DS), 263–64
Self-imposed standards of behavior, self-management and, 277
Self-management, 270–87
  basis of, 277–78
  counselors' role in, 305
  as goal, 270–73
  guidance objectives as related to, 282–84
  as pervasive objective, 41–42
  procedures of, 273–77
  setting up contingency management plan for purposes of, 275–76, 281
  social competency behaviors and, 281–82, 285–86
  teaching principles of behavior and, 278–81
Self-observation generalizations, 234–35
Self-reference statements, altering deficient, 194–95
Sexual behavior, adolescent, 183
Shaw, M. C., 62n, 73, 75
Shaping of behaviors, 211
Shertzer, B., 184n
Shockley, William, 317
Sievers, Frank L., 351
Silence, 284; see also Listening
Sizi (author), 145
Skinner, B. F., 150
Slocum, W. L., 233
Smith, R. D., 248n

Smith, R. L., 161
Snyder, D. U., 165n
Snyder, F. A., 70
Social class, first occupational decisions and, 231
Social competency, 281–82, 285–86
   as pervasive objective, 40–41
   role of counselors in, 305–6
   See also Self-management
Social ecosystems, occupational decision making and, 232, 233
Social interactions, verbal behaviors of effective, 283–85
Social systems, human development and, 159–65
Social value statements, as educational goals, 29–30
Society, the individual and
   individual's place in, 33
   social competency and, 41
Sonoma County schools (Calif.), 64
Sound stimulation, 120, 121
Spang, A. T., Jr., 131n
Spanish-speaking Americans (Hispanics), 182n; see also Minorities
Specialists, 45–81
   basis for determining functions of, 53–57
   complete team of, 71–73; see also Guidance teams
   in Fantasy City, 46–47
   guidance needs and, 59–62
   in Real City, 47–52
   titles of, 57–59
   training of, 73–77
   See also specific types of specialists
Speech, connotative meanings of, 136–37
Spencer, Herbert, 101n
Sprinthall, N. A., 279n
Squares (student subculture terminology), 170
Staats, A., 125
Staats, C., 125
Standardized tests, 17–18, 314
   errors in administration of, 319–22
   school integration and, 322–23
   validity of, 316–19
   See also specific tests; for example: Miller Analogies Test
Stanley, J. C., 322
Statements
   restatements, 284
   self-reference, 194–95
   social value, 29–30
Stefflre, B., 328
Stern, Herbert J., 9, 72n
Stevens, S. S., 106
Stewart, N. R., 253
Stimulation, activity, behavior development and, 117–23
Stimuli
   conditioned, 123, 125

Stimuli (cont.)
   neutral and natural, 123, 124
   unconditioned, 124, 125
Stockdale, Jane A., 70, 72n
Stone, S. C., 184n
Student personnel services (pupil services), 12, 355–56
Students
   career development programs and assessment of, 239, 242
   guidance needs of, 59–62; see also specific aspects of guidance
   occupational decision making as uppermost concern of, 30; see also Occupational decision making
   schools as ecosystems and, 163–65
   subcultures of, 168–73
Subcultures, student, 168–73
Sulzer, B., 62n, 189
Summerskill, J., 259
Super, Donald E., 224n, 233, 256
Support personnel, as defined by American Personnel and Guidance Association, 64n
Supportive counseling used as limited desensitization, 197–98
Symbol (cognitive) system, 136–41
Symbolic behavior, 120
Symbols
   patterns of behavior controlled by, 138–40
   as reinforcers, 137–38
Synecdoche, 96–99
System, behavior as, 191–92
Systematic guidance, defined, 28
Systems theory, 26–28

T-A (teacher-advisors), 67–68, 330–31
Tactile stimulation, 119–20
TALENT, Project, 252
Target behaviors, self-management and identifying, 273–74, 281
Task approach skills, 234–35
Teacher-advisors (T-A), 67–68, 330–31
Teachers
   disruptive students as threat to, 163
   providing, with appraisal assistance, 327–28
   schools as ecosystems and, 163–65
Technological change, impact of (1800–1900), 8–9
Technology, theory and, 84–88
Technology in Guidance (special magazine issue), 257
Tennyson, W. W., 262
Tested Practices: Computer Assisted Guidance Systems (NVGA), 257
Tests, see Standardized tests
Tharp, R. G., 189, 212n, 273, 278
Theological bases of behavior theory, 103–4
Theory
   and characteristics of science, 107–9

Theory (*cont.*)
 need for, 84–85
 systems, 26–28
 technology and, 84–88
 See also Behavior theory; Behaviorism; Scientific theory
Thoreson, C. E., 151, 202, 281
Thorndike, E. L., 150
Titles in guidance counseling, 10–13
T. K. Young Laboratory Schools, 21*n*
Training
 counselor, 73–77, 349–50
 beginning and expansion of, 14–18
 college counselors, 15
 inadequacy of, 20
 in decision making, 193, 194; *see also* Decision making
 Parent Effectiveness Training, 73
 in self-management, 280–81; *see also* Self-management
Truax, C. G., 70, 189, 202
Tucker, I. F., 112, 119–20

UCS (unconditioned stimuli), 124, 125
Ullman, L. P., 152*n*
Unconditioned stimuli (UCS), 124, 125
Understanding, scientific, as educational goal, 33
United Nations Charter, 4
United States Employment Service (USES; now U.S. Training and Employment Services), 262, 352
United States Office of Education, 14, 16, 21, 57, 257, 349, 351
United States Training and Employment Services (*formerly* U.S. Employment Service; U.S.E.S.), 262, 352
Unmarried mothers, guidance for, 359

Varenhorst, B. B., 70
Verbal skills in facilitative interviews, 198–202
Vernon, W. M., 189
Verplanck, W., 138
Veterans Administration, 352
Vocation, defined, 222

Vocational Counselor and Social Action, The (Samler), 266
Vocational decision making, as primary thrust of guidance movement, 18–19; *see also* Career decision making; Occupational decision making
Vocational development, defined, 223
Vocational education, career education vs., 223
Vocational and educational guidance counselors, *see* Counselors
Vocational Guidance Quarterly, The (VGQ; journal), 251, 266
Vocationalization, defined, 222–23
Von Bertalanffy, L., 28*n*, 93
Vreind, T. J., 71

Walsh, W. B., 198, 202, 330
War on Poverty, 352, 353
Ware, C., 70
Watson, D. L., 273, 278
Webster, W. J., 253
Wetzel, R. J., 189, 212*n*
Whitley, A. D., 62*n*
Williamson, E. G., 194
Wolpe, Joseph, 197*n*
Work ethic, career education and, 21, **22**
Work-sample materials in Career Center library, 252
Work satisfaction, 7
 in assembly-line jobs, 233
 factors in, 230–31
World community, scientists as members of, 106–7
Wrenn, C. Gilbert, 11, 13*n*, 248

Youth
 development of, as basis for determining functions of specialists, 53–57
 guidance needs of, 59–62; *see also specific aspects of guidance*
 See also Delinquent youths; Students

Zerface, J. P., 68
Zetts, A., 70
Zunker, V. G., 70, 283
Zytowski, D. G., 8*n*